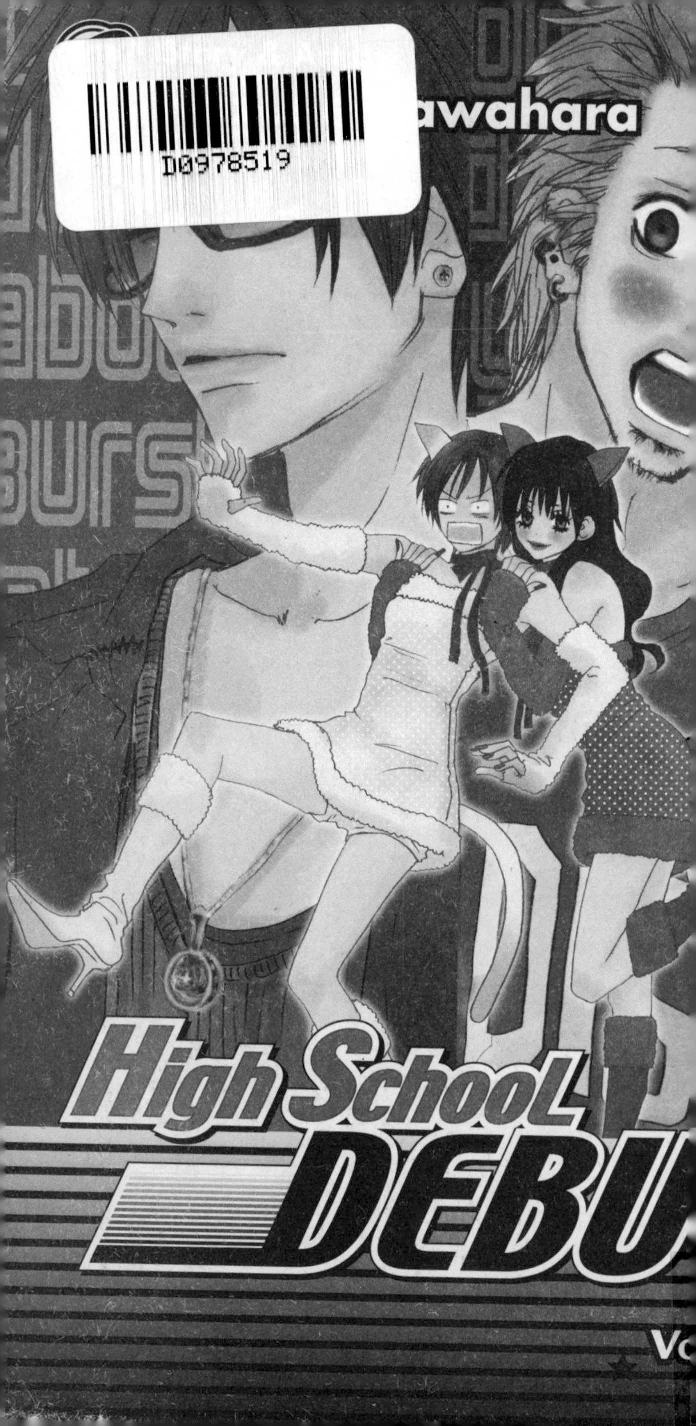
awahara
High School
DEBU
Vo

High School DEBUT

★★ Contents

Thus Far... ★★

freshman Haruna used to spend all her time playing softball in
but now she wants to give her all to finding true love instead! While
ach" Yoh is training her on how to be popular with guys, the two
dating. Their relationship has its fair share of drama, but it only
heir bond. ♥

aruna rescues a girl named Makoto from a pervert on a train and
r. She starts helping Makoto with her relationship troubles and
her to try to win back her ex-boyfriend. What Haruna doesn't know
to is actually Yoh's ex-girlfriend! When Haruna finally figures this
kind to abandon Makoto and even asks Yoh to see his ex. Yoh
k with Makoto, but afterwards, he returns to a worried Haruna and
oves her...

Tell us what y about Shojo Beat Manga!

Our
avai

shojobeat.com/mangasurvey

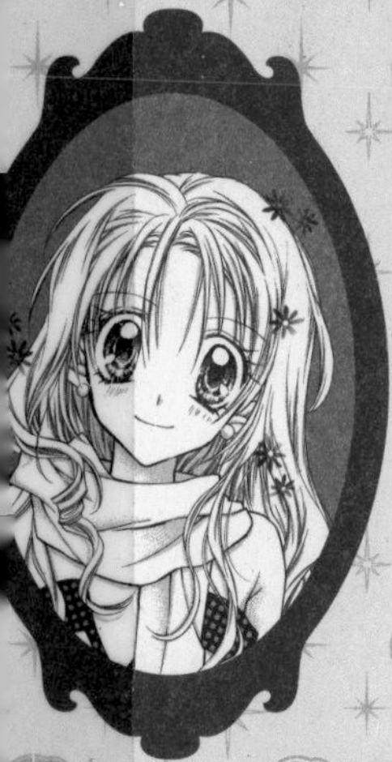

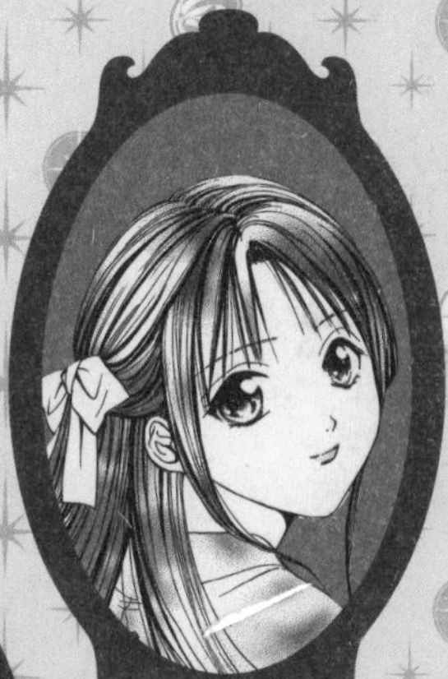

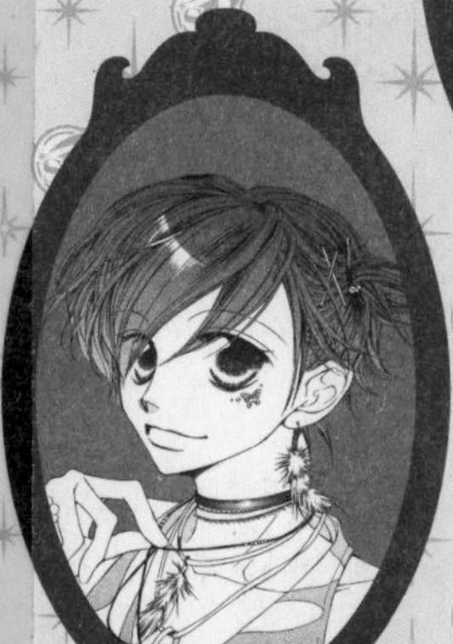

Help us make our product offerings better!

viz media

Shojo Beat MANGA from the HEART

THE REAL DRAMA BEGINS IN...

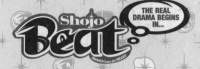

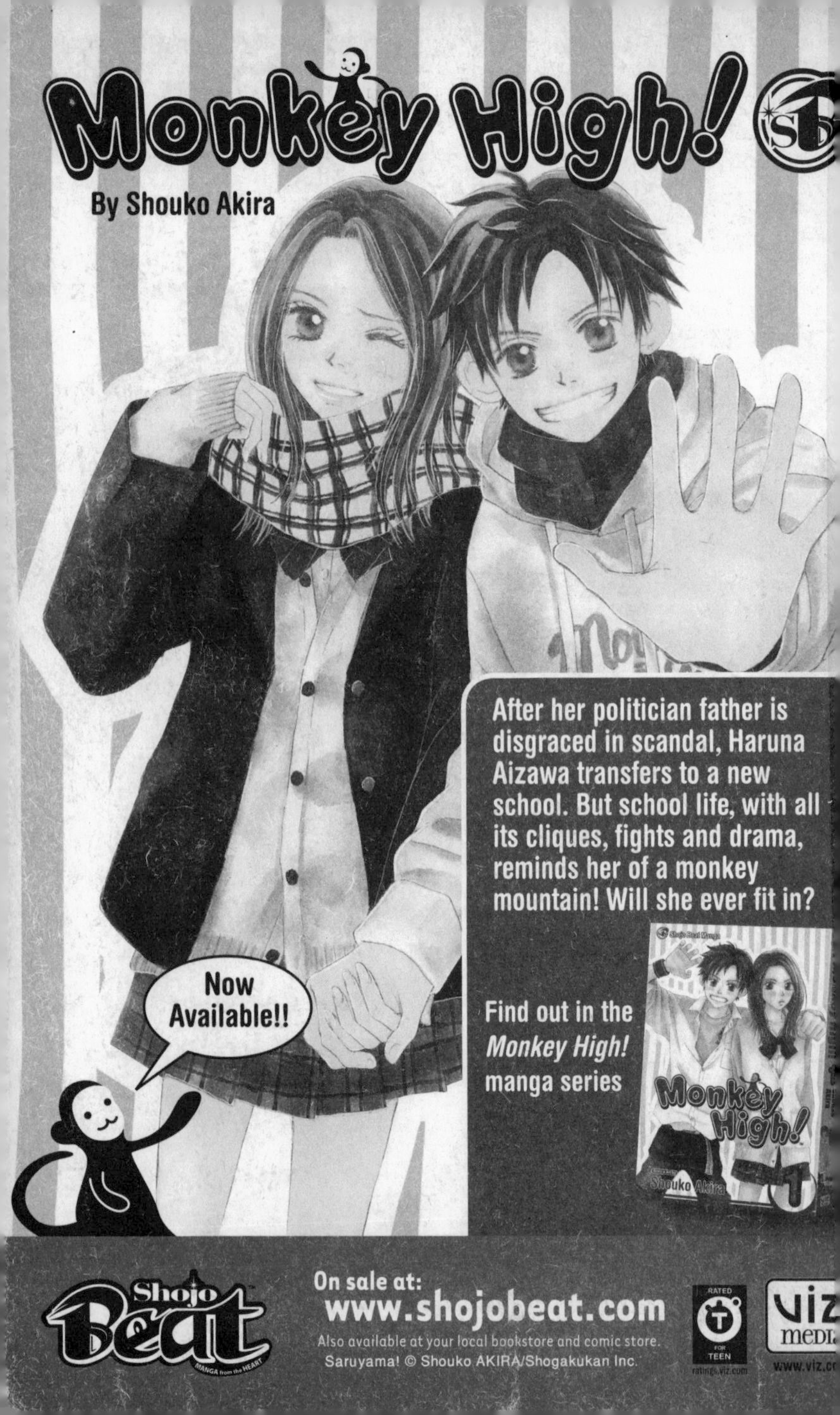
Monkey High!
By Shouko Akira
After her politician father is disgraced in scandal, Haruna Aizawa transfers to a new school. But school life, with all its cliques, fights and drama, reminds her of a monkey mountain! Will she ever fit in?
Find out in the *Monkey High!* manga series
Now Available!!
Shojo Beat Manga
Monkey High!
Shouko Akira
1
Shojo Beat
MANGA from the HEART
On sale at:
www.shojobeat.com
Also available at your local bookstore and comic store.
Saruyama! © Shouko AKIRA/Shogakukan Inc.
RATED
T
FOR TEEN
ratings.viz.com

HIGH SCHOOL DEBUT
VOL. 7
The Shojo Beat Manga Edition

STORY & ART BY
KAZUNE KAWAHARA

Translation & Adaptation/Gemma Collinge
Touch-up Art & Lettering/HudsonYards
Cover Design/Izumi Hirayama
Interior Design/Carolina Ugalde
Editor/Amy Yu

Editor in Chief, Books/Alvin Lu
Editor in Chief, Magazines/Marc Weidenbaum
VP, Publishing Licensing/Rika Inouye
VP, Sales & Product Marketing/Gonzalo Ferreyra
VP, Creative/Linda Espinosa
Publisher/Hyoe Narita

KOKO DEBUT © 2003 by Kazune Kawahara
All rights reserved.
First published in Japan in 2003 by SHUEISHA Inc., Tokyo.
English translation rights arranged by SHUEISHA Inc.
The stories, characters and incidents mentioned in this publication are
entirely fictional.

Printed in Canada

Published by VIZ Media, LLC
P.O. Box 77010
San Francisco, CA 94107

Shojo Beat Manga Edition
10 9 8 7 6 5 4 3 2 1
First printing, January 2009

www.viz.com

store.viz.com

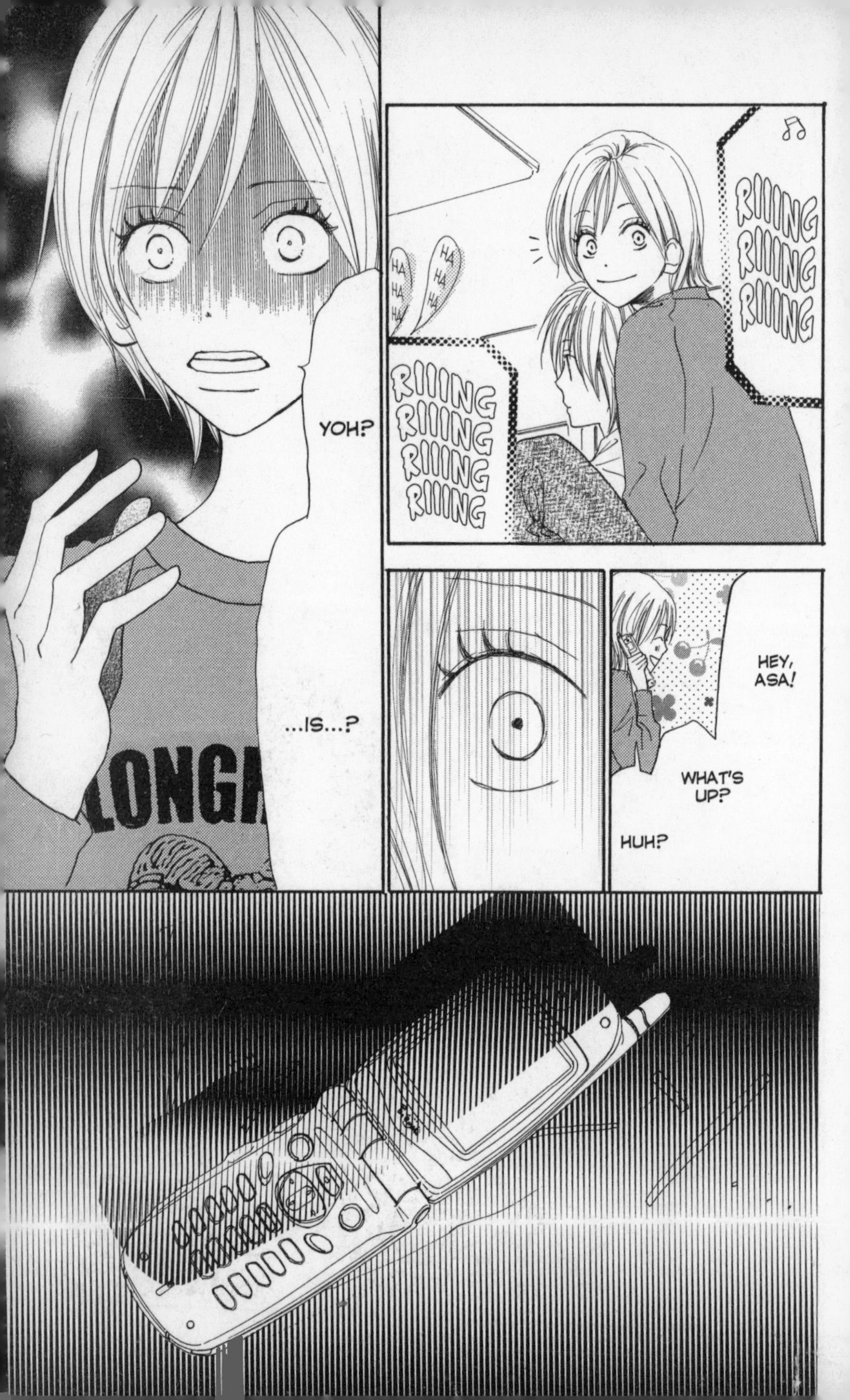
♪
RIIING RIIING RIIING
HA HA HA
HA HA HA HA
RIIING RIIING RIIING RIIING
HEY, ASA!
WHAT'S UP?
HUH?
YOH?
...IS...?

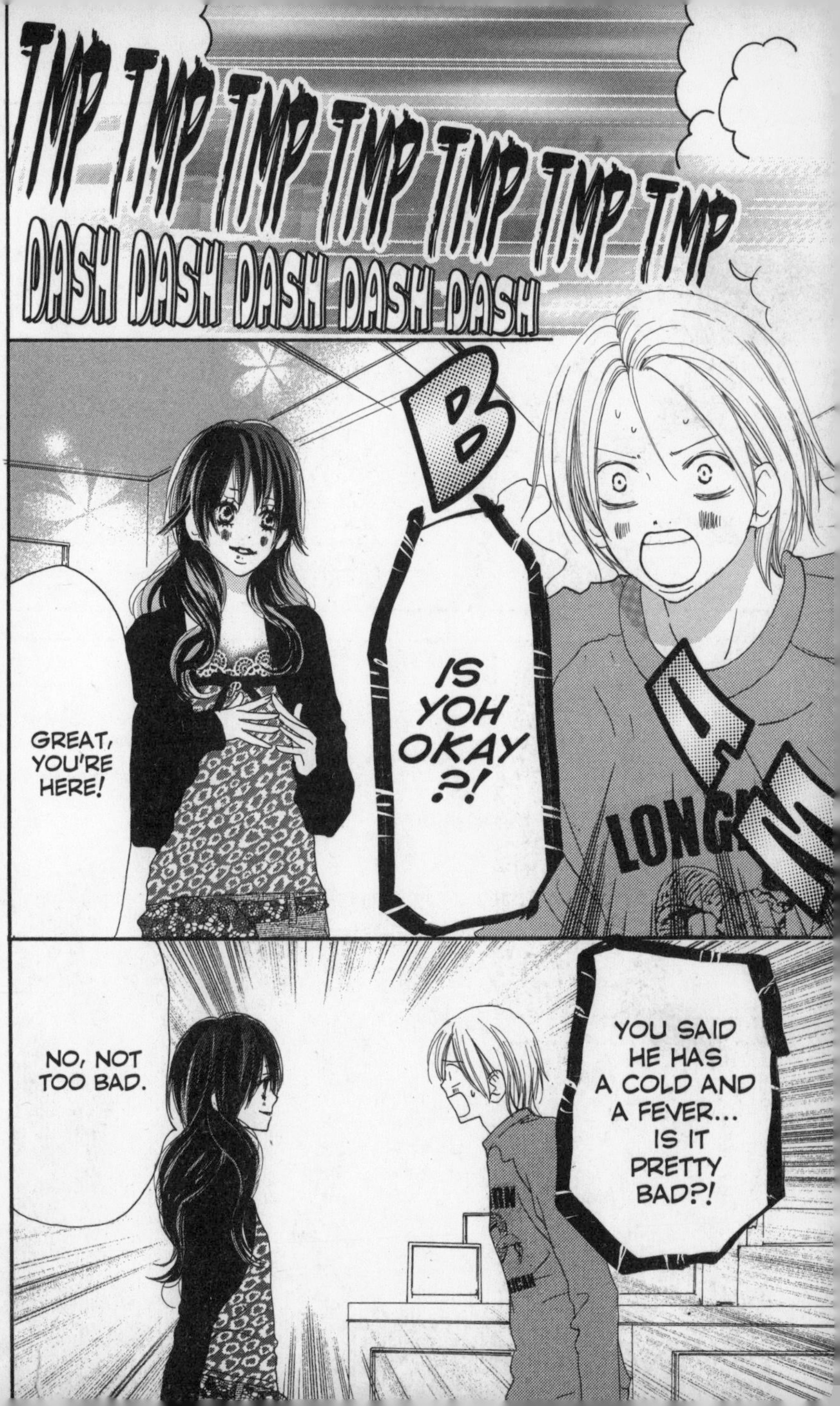
TMP TMP TMP TMP TMP TMP TMP
DASH DASH DASH DASH DASH
B
IS YOH OKAY?!
GREAT, YOU'RE HERE!
YOU SAID HE HAS A COLD AND A FEVER... IS IT PRETTY BAD?!
NO, NOT TOO BAD.

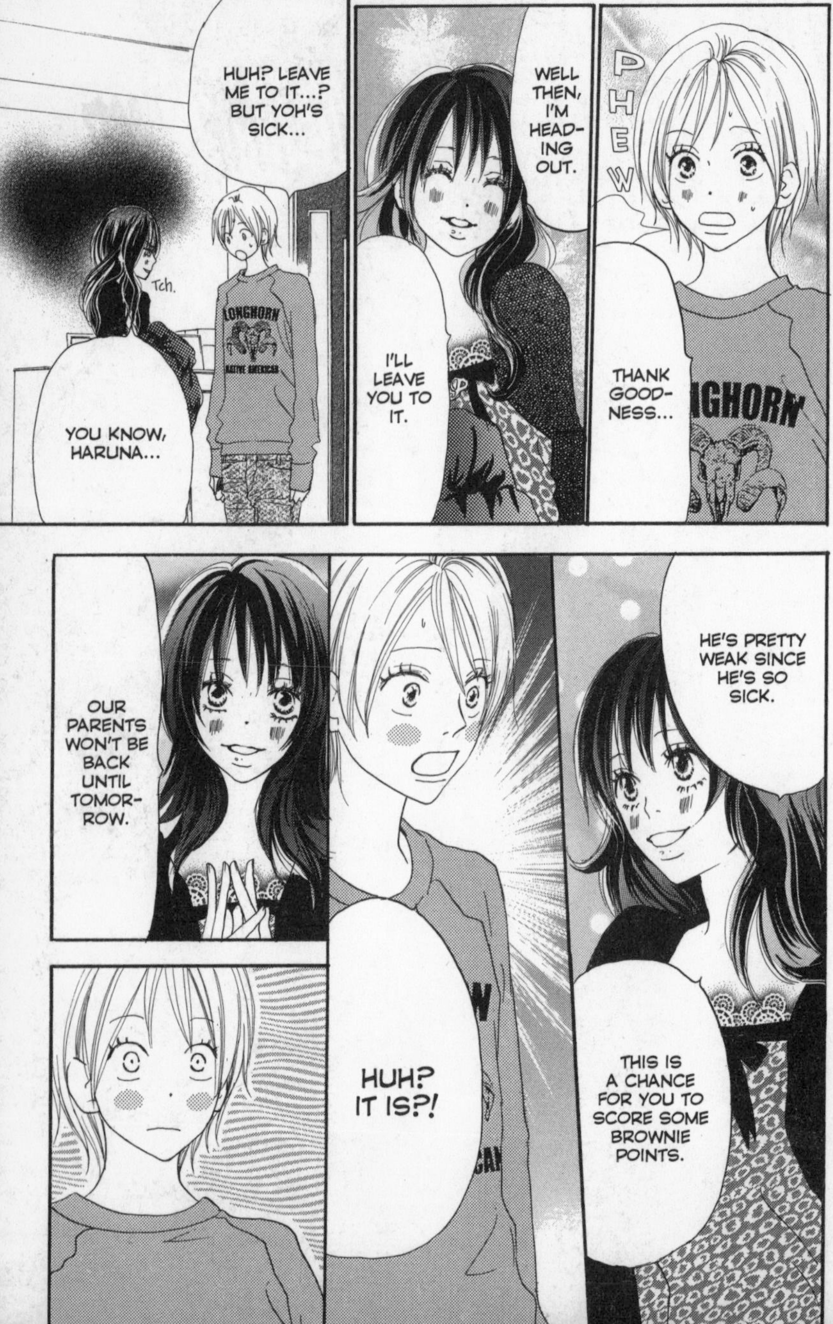
PHEW
THANK GOOD-NESS...
LONGHORN
WELL THEN, I'M HEAD-ING OUT.
I'LL LEAVE YOU TO IT.
HUH? LEAVE ME TO IT...? BUT YOH'S SICK...
Tch.
LONGHORN
YOU KNOW, HARUNA...
HE'S PRETTY WEAK SINCE HE'S SO SICK.
THIS IS A CHANCE FOR YOU TO SCORE SOME BROWNIE POINTS.
HUH? IT IS?!
OUR PARENTS WON'T BE BACK UNTIL TOMOR-ROW.

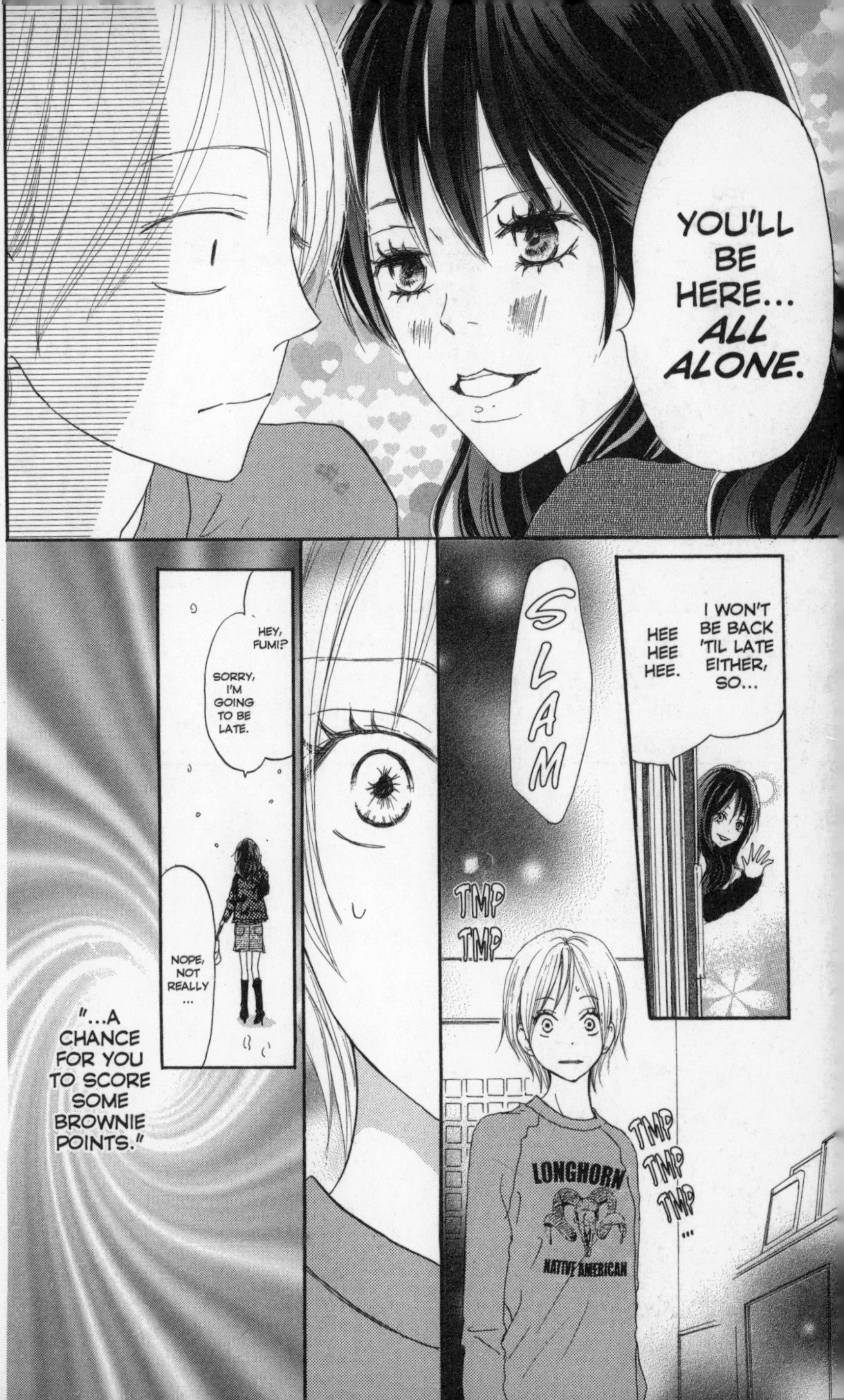
YOU'LL BE HERE... ALL ALONE.
I WON'T BE BACK 'TIL LATE EITHER, SO...
HEE HEE HEE.
SLAM
TMP TMP
LONGHORN
NATIVE AMERICAN
TMP TMP TMP...
HEY, FUMI?
SORRY, I'M GOING TO BE LATE.
NOPE, NOT REALLY...
"...A CHANCE FOR YOU TO SCORE SOME BROWNIE POINTS."

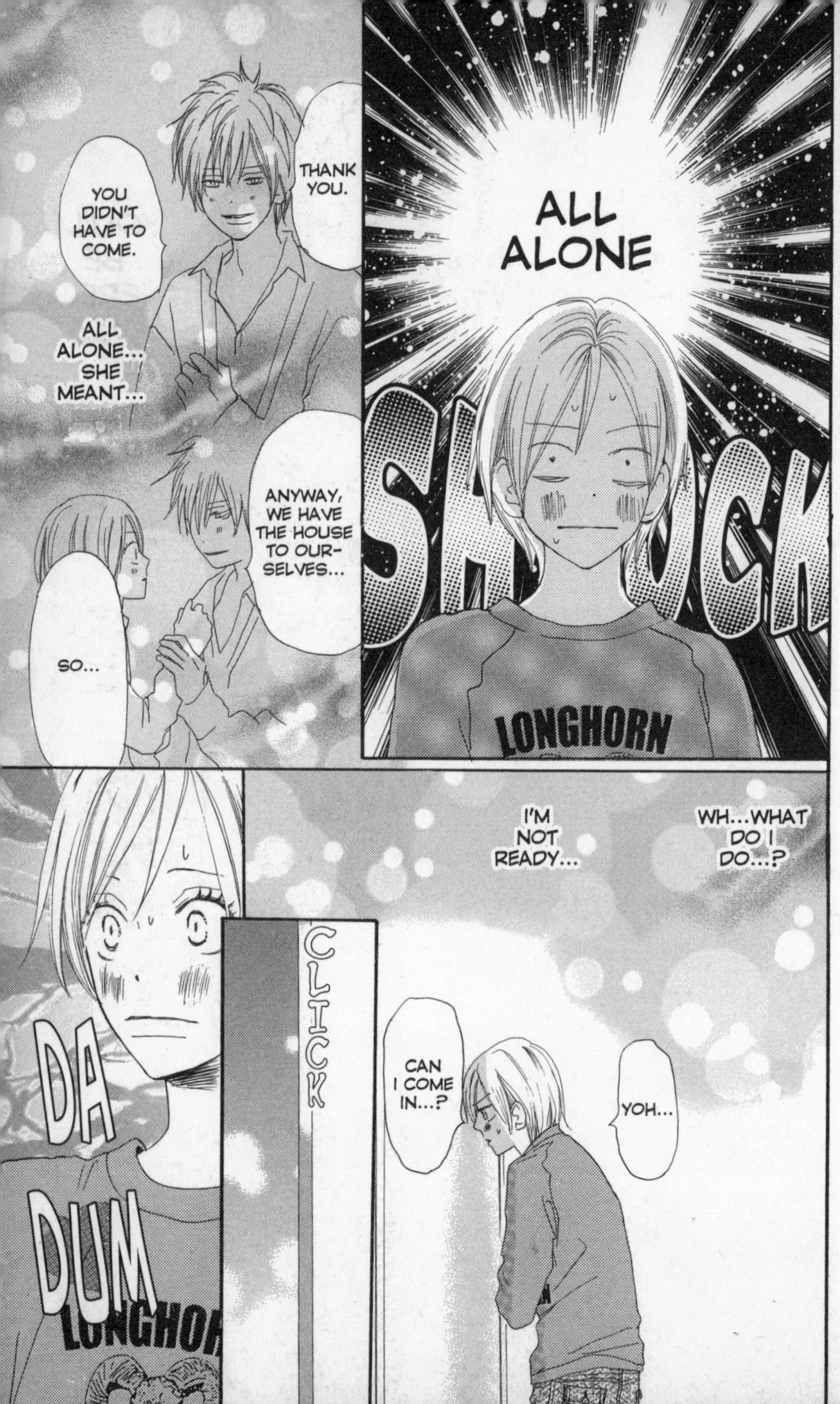
ALL ALONE
SHOCK
LONGHORN
THANK YOU.
YOU DIDN'T HAVE TO COME.
ALL ALONE... SHE MEANT...
ANYWAY, WE HAVE THE HOUSE TO OURSELVES...
SO...
WH...WHAT DO I DO...?
I'M NOT READY...
YOH...
CAN I COME IN...?
CLICK
DA DUM
LONGHOR

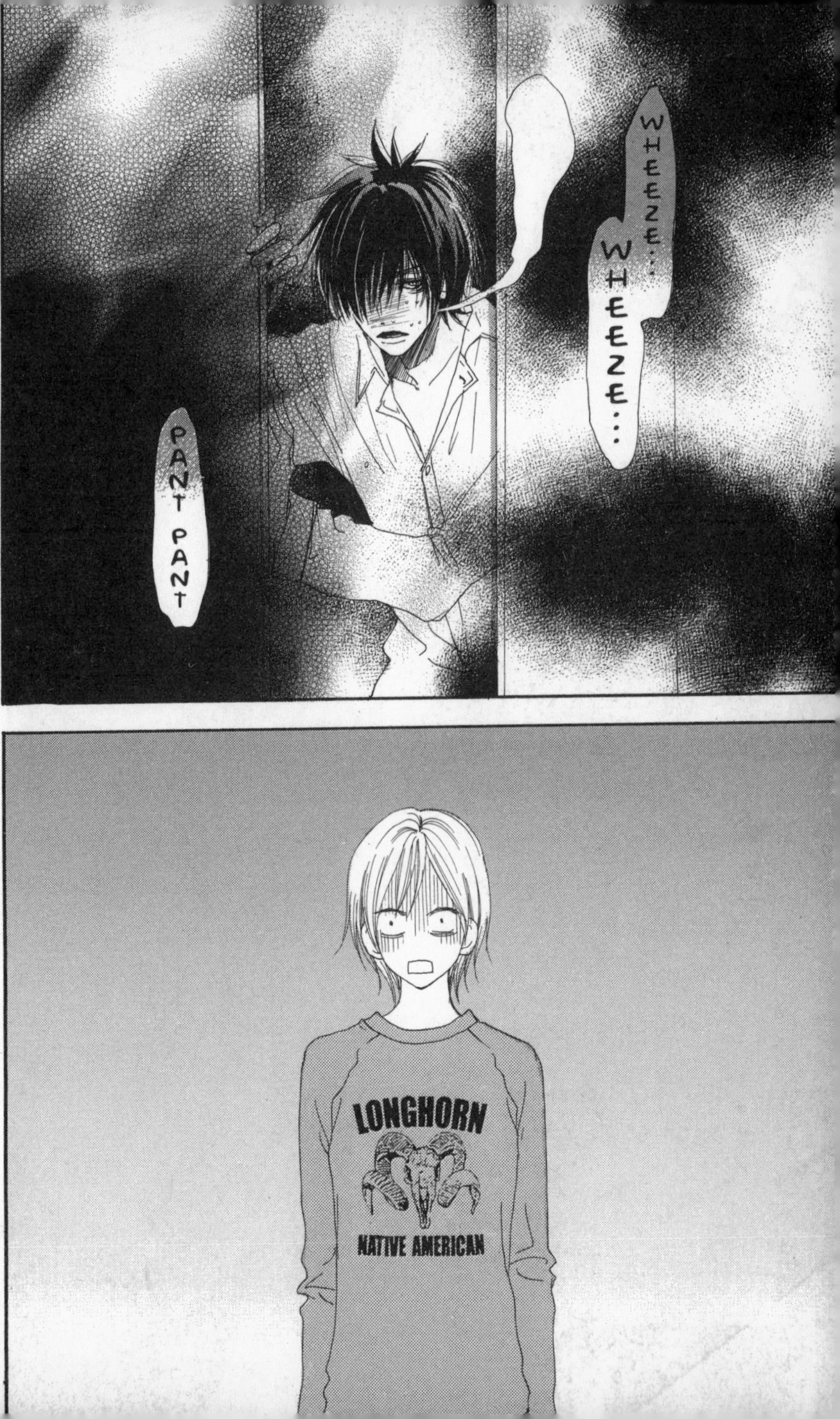
WHEEZE...
WHEEZE...
PANT PANT PANT
LONGHORN
NATIVE AMERICAN

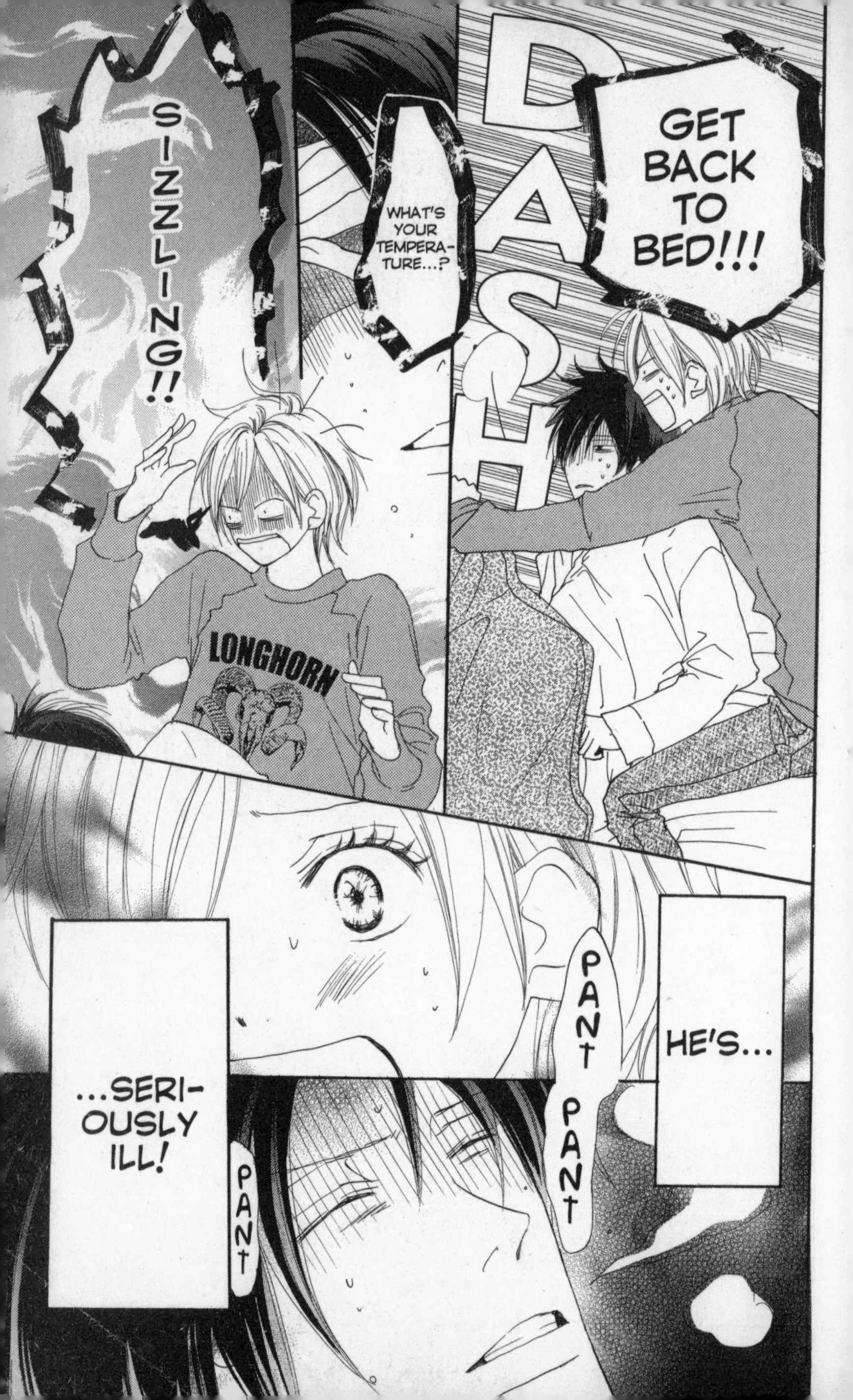
GET BACK TO BED!!!
DASH
WHAT'S YOUR TEMPERA-TURE...?
SIZZLING!!
LONGHORN
HE'S...
PANT PANT
PANT PANT
...SERI-OUSLY ILL!
PANT

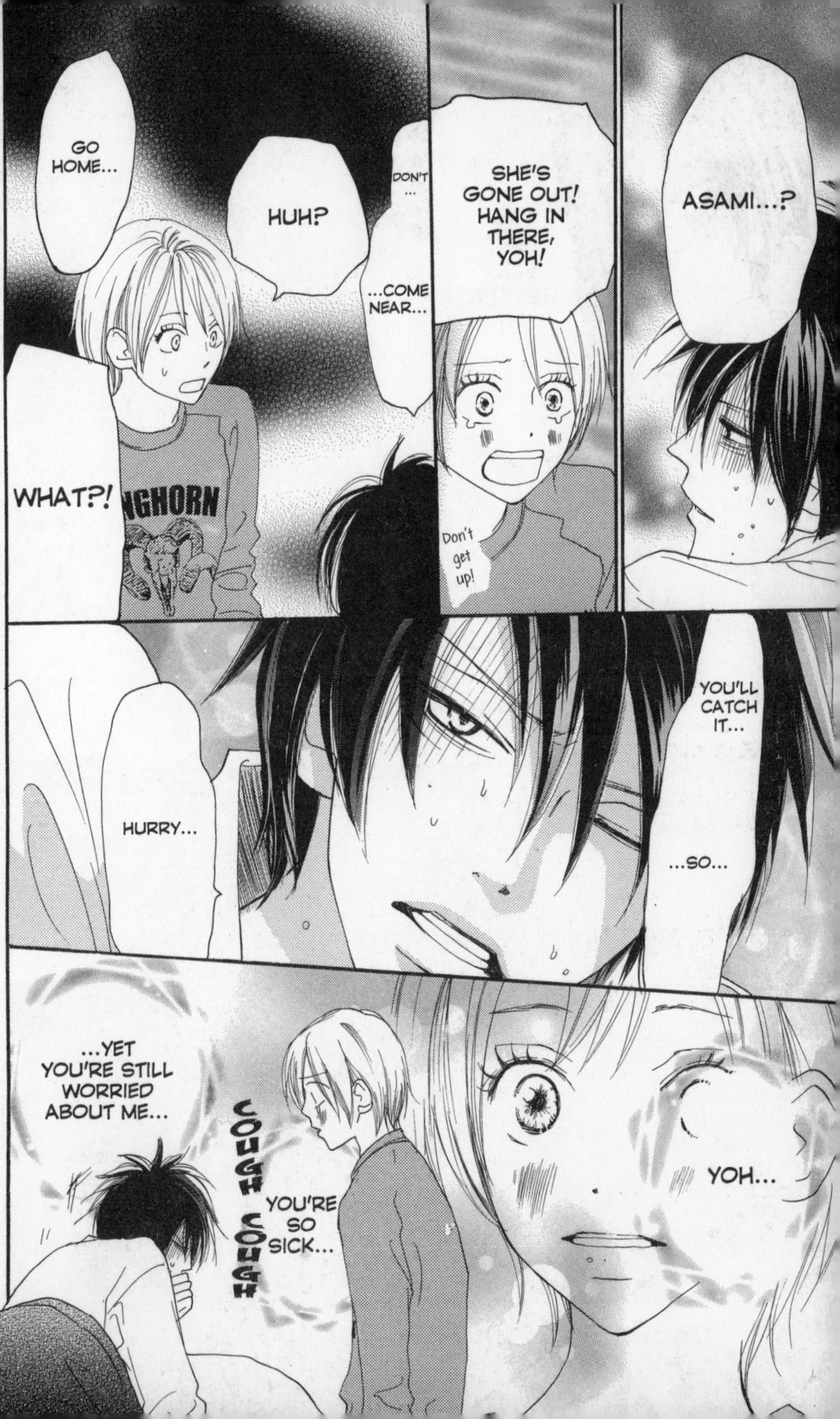
ASAMI...?
SHE'S GONE OUT! HANG IN THERE, YOH!
Don't get up!
DON'T ... ...COME NEAR...
HUH?
GO HOME...
WHAT?!
YOU'LL CATCH IT...
...SO...
HURRY...
YOH...
YOU'RE SO SICK...
COUGH COUGH
...YET YOU'RE STILL WORRIED ABOUT ME...

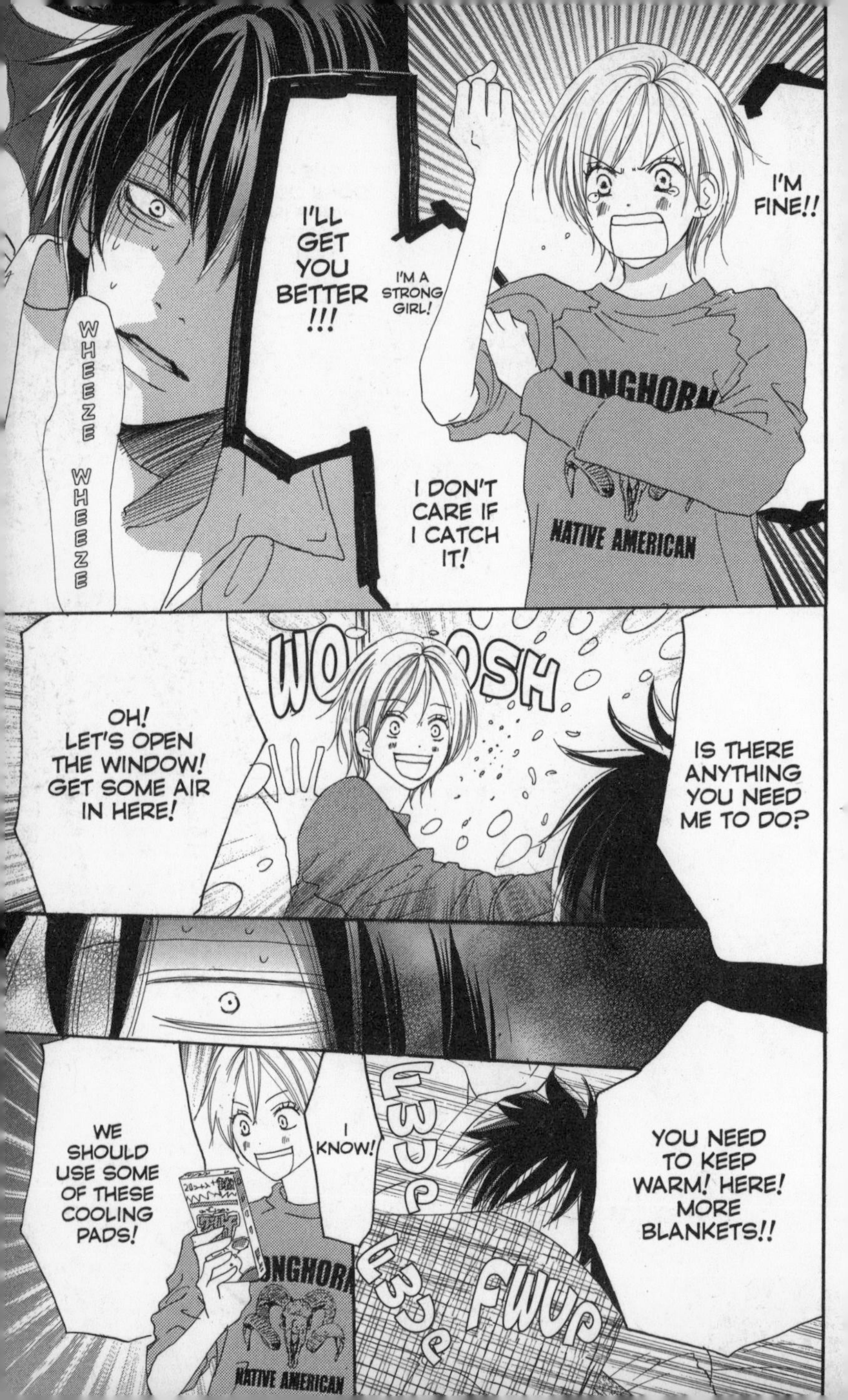
I'M FINE!!
I DON'T CARE IF I CATCH IT!
I'M A STRONG GIRL!
I'LL GET YOU BETTER!!!
WHEEZE WHEEZE
NATIVE AMERICAN
IS THERE ANYTHING YOU NEED ME TO DO?
OH! LET'S OPEN THE WINDOW! GET SOME AIR IN HERE!
YOU NEED TO KEEP WARM! HERE! MORE BLANKETS!!
FWUP
FWUP
FWUP
I KNOW!
WE SHOULD USE SOME OF THESE COOLING PADS!
NATIVE AMERICAN

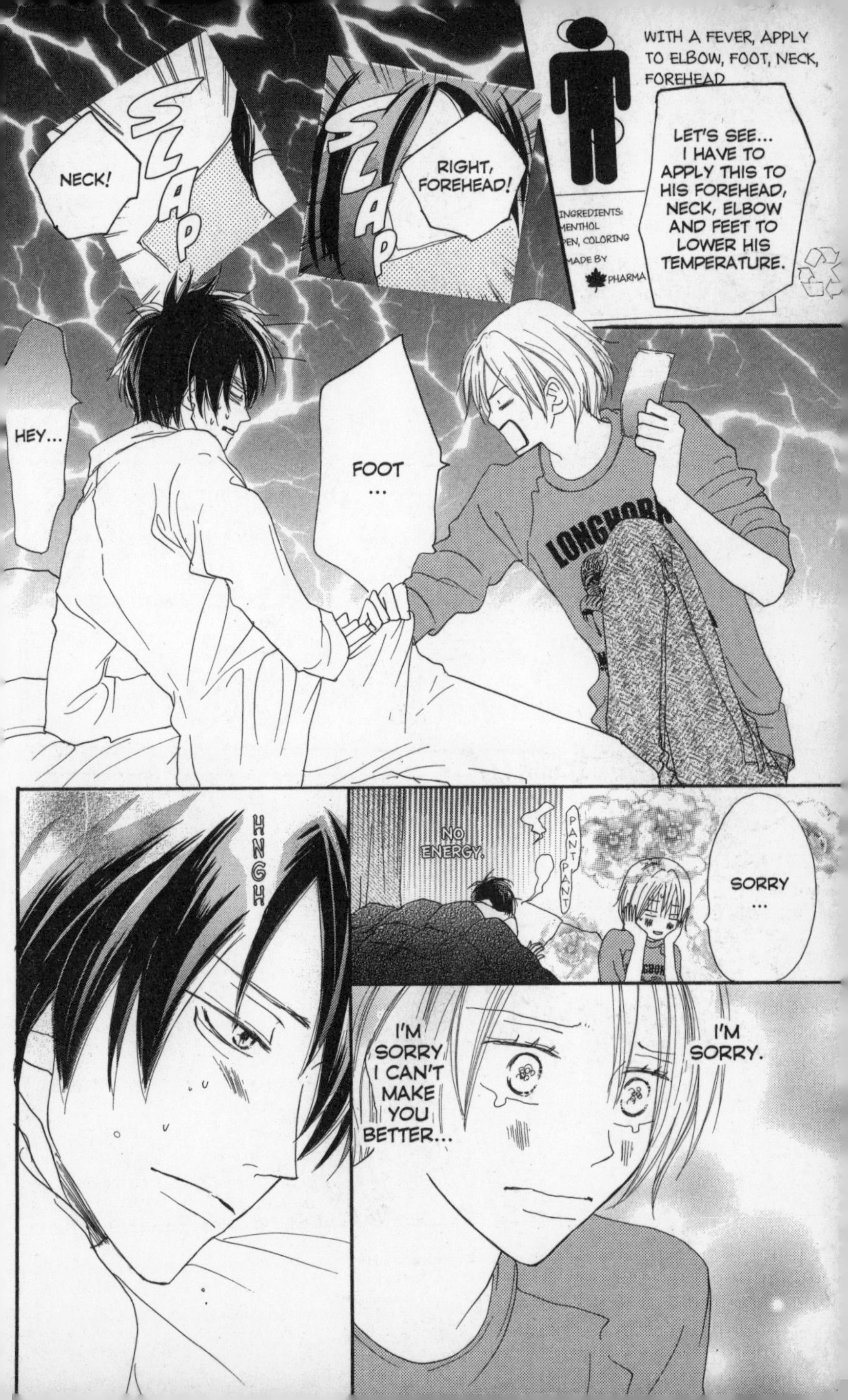
WITH A FEVER, APPLY TO ELBOW, FOOT, NECK, FOREHEAD
INGREDIENTS: MENTHOL
PEN, COLORING
MADE BY PHARMA
LET'S SEE... I HAVE TO APPLY THIS TO HIS FOREHEAD, NECK, ELBOW AND FEET TO LOWER HIS TEMPERATURE.
RIGHT, FOREHEAD!
SLAP
NECK!
SLAP
FOOT ...
HEY...
SORRY ...
PANT PANT
NO ENERGY.
I'M SORRY.
I'M SORRY I CAN'T MAKE YOU BETTER...
HNGH

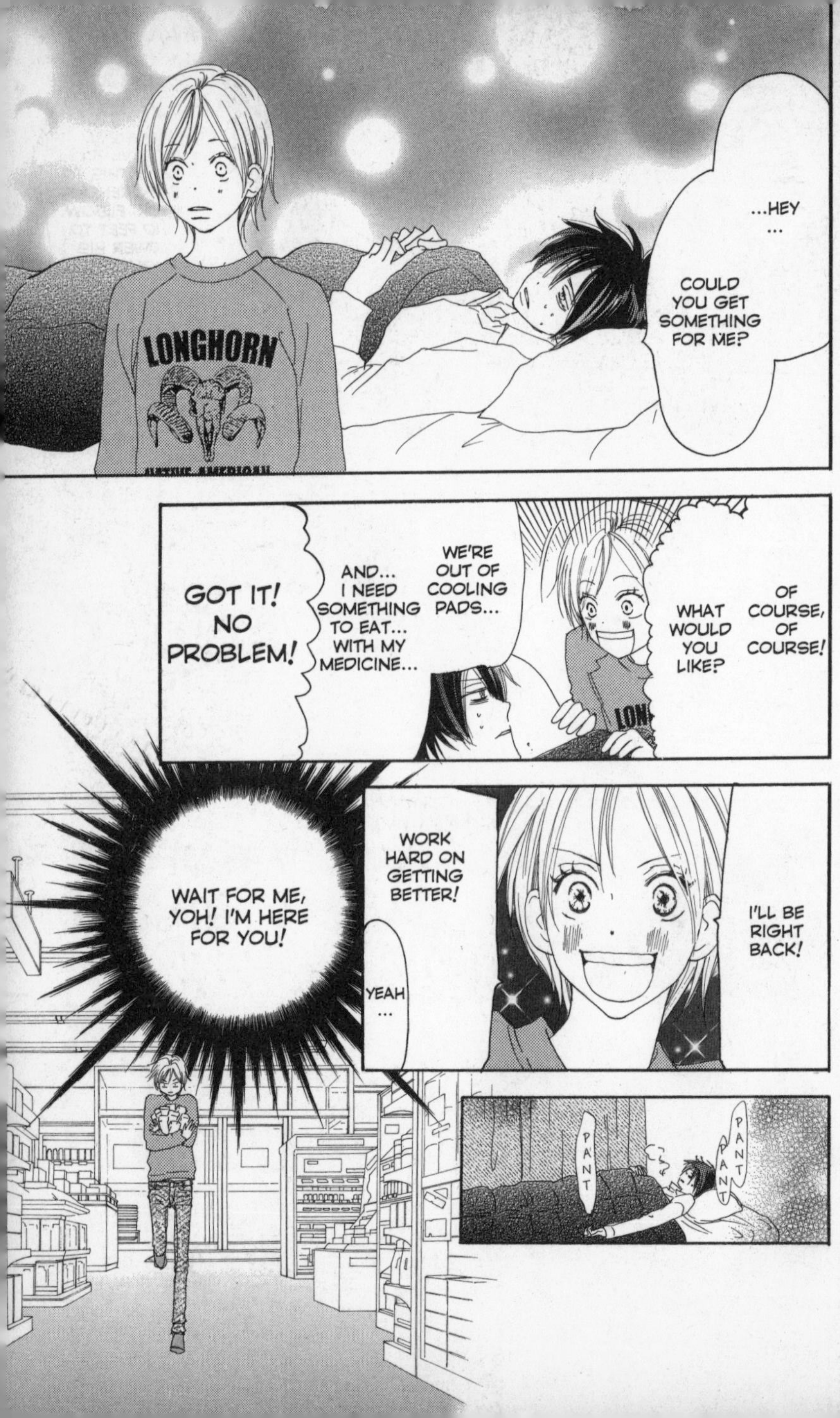
...HEY ...
COULD YOU GET SOMETHING FOR ME?
OF COURSE, OF COURSE!
WHAT WOULD YOU LIKE?
WE'RE OUT OF COOLING PADS...
AND... I NEED SOMETHING TO EAT... WITH MY MEDICINE...
GOT IT! NO PROBLEM!
I'LL BE RIGHT BACK!
WORK HARD ON GETTING BETTER!
YEAH ...
PANT
PANT
PANT
WAIT FOR ME, YOH! I'M HERE FOR YOU!
LONGHORN

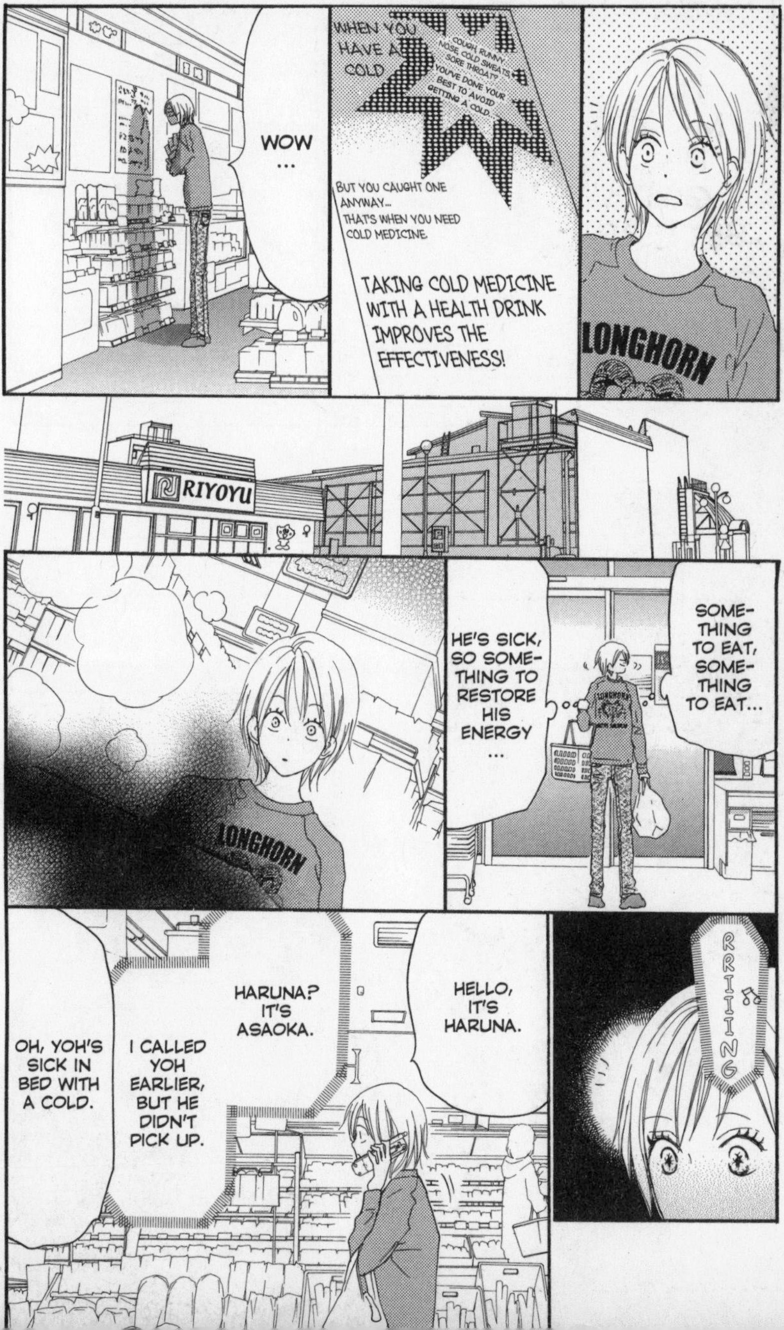
WHEN YOU HAVE A COLD
COUGH, RUNNY NOSE, COLD SWEATS, SORE THROAT? YOU'VE DONE YOUR BEST TO AVOID GETTING A COLD.
BUT YOU CAUGHT ONE ANYWAY... THAT'S WHEN YOU NEED COLD MEDICINE.
TAKING COLD MEDICINE WITH A HEALTH DRINK IMPROVES THE EFFECTIVENESS!
LONGHORN
WOW ...
RIYOYU
SOME-THING TO EAT, SOME-THING TO EAT...
HE'S SICK, SO SOME-THING TO RESTORE HIS ENERGY ...
LONGHORN
RRIIING
HELLO, IT'S HARUNA.
HARUNA? IT'S ASAOKA.
I CALLED YOH EARLIER, BUT HE DIDN'T PICK UP.
OH, YOH'S SICK IN BED WITH A COLD.

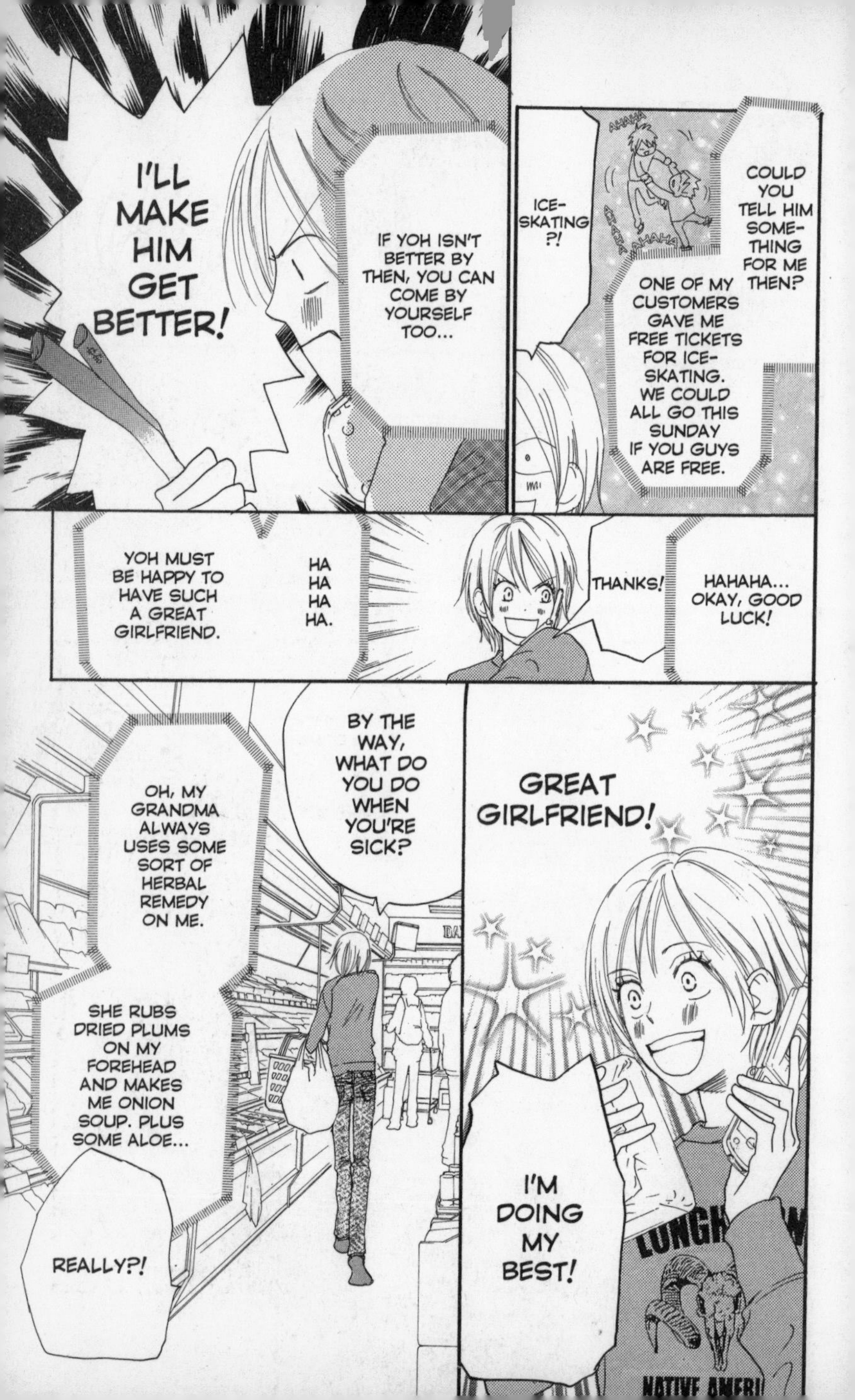
COULD YOU TELL HIM SOMETHING FOR ME THEN?
ONE OF MY CUSTOMERS GAVE ME FREE TICKETS FOR ICE-SKATING. WE COULD ALL GO THIS SUNDAY IF YOU GUYS ARE FREE.
ICE-SKATING?!
IF YOH ISN'T BETTER BY THEN, YOU CAN COME BY YOURSELF TOO...
I'LL MAKE HIM GET BETTER!
HAHAHA... OKAY, GOOD LUCK!
THANKS!
HA HA HA HA.
YOH MUST BE HAPPY TO HAVE SUCH A GREAT GIRLFRIEND.
GREAT GIRLFRIEND!
I'M DOING MY BEST!
BY THE WAY, WHAT DO YOU DO WHEN YOU'RE SICK?
OH, MY GRANDMA ALWAYS USES SOME SORT OF HERBAL REMEDY ON ME.
SHE RUBS DRIED PLUMS ON MY FOREHEAD AND MAKES ME ONION SOUP. PLUS SOME ALOE...
REALLY?!

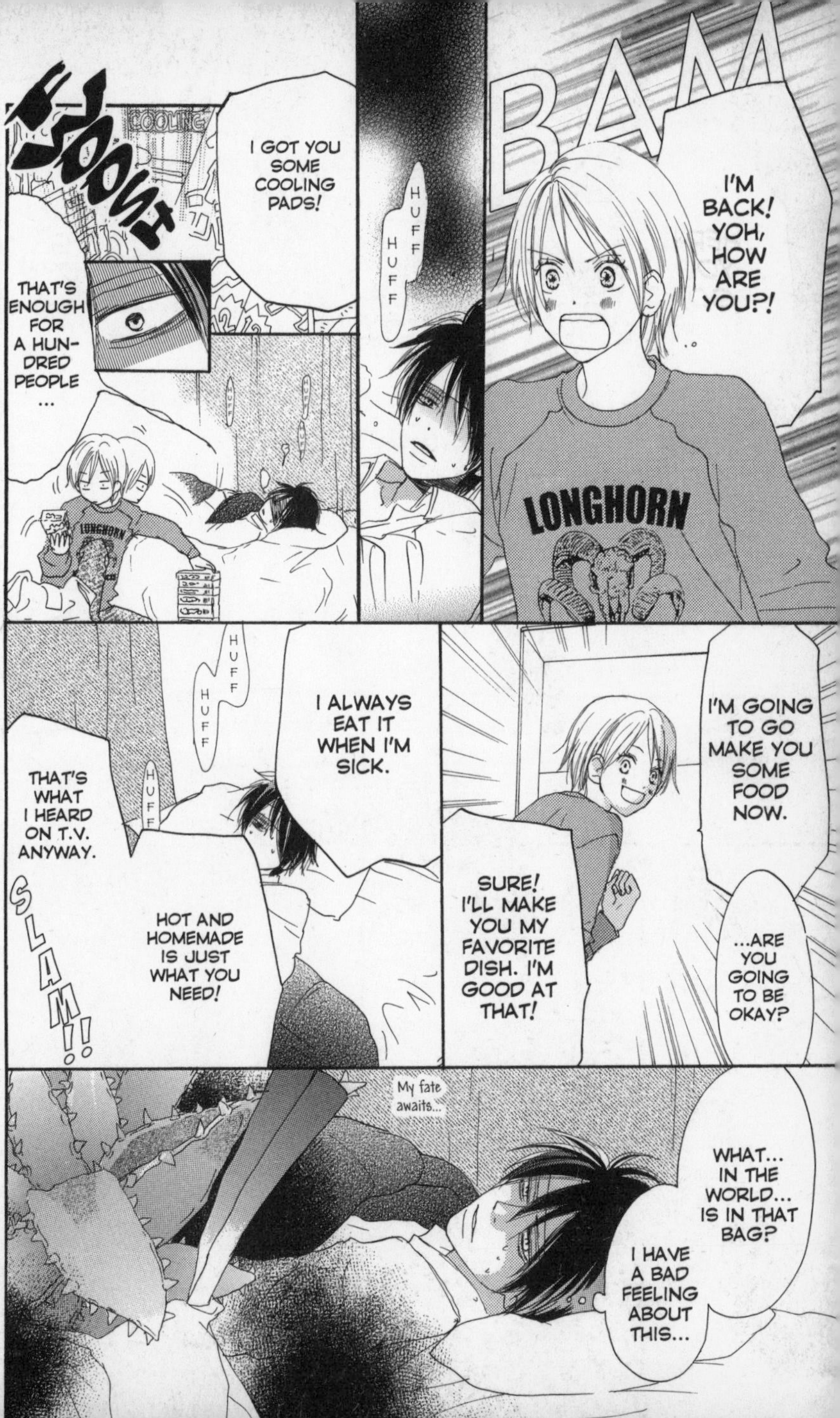
BAAM
I'M BACK! YOH, HOW ARE YOU?!
HUFF HUFF
I GOT YOU SOME COOLING PADS!
COOLING
THAT'S ENOUGH FOR A HUNDRED PEOPLE...
I'M GOING TO GO MAKE YOU SOME FOOD NOW.
...ARE YOU GOING TO BE OKAY?
SURE! I'LL MAKE YOU MY FAVORITE DISH. I'M GOOD AT THAT!
I ALWAYS EAT IT WHEN I'M SICK.
HUFF HUFF
HUFF
THAT'S WHAT I HEARD ON T.V. ANYWAY.
HOT AND HOMEMADE IS JUST WHAT YOU NEED!
SLAM!!
WHAT... IN THE WORLD... IS IN THAT BAG?
I HAVE A BAD FEELING ABOUT THIS...
My fate awaits...

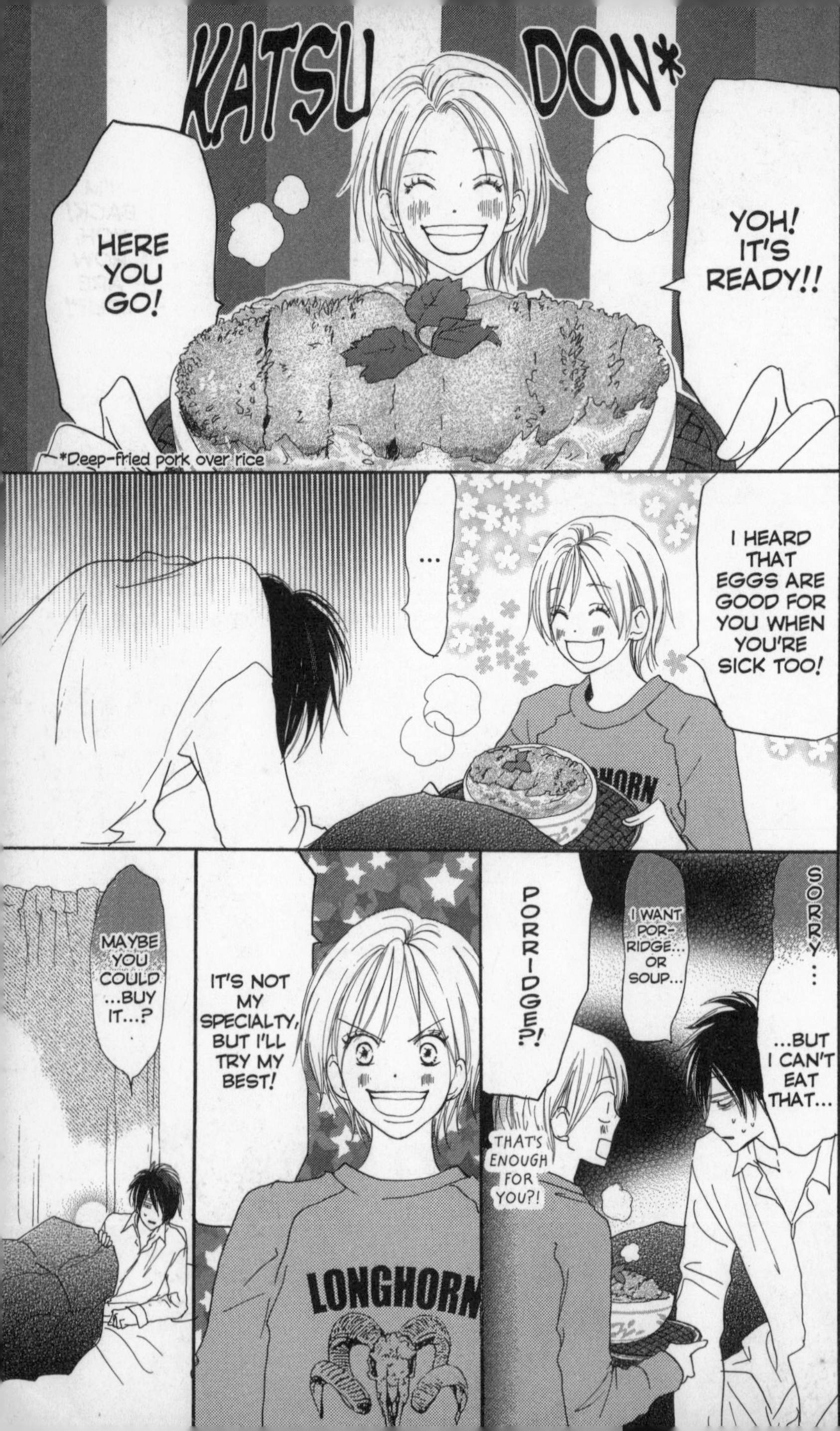
KATSU DON*
YOH! IT'S READY!!
HERE YOU GO!
*Deep-fried pork over rice
I HEARD THAT EGGS ARE GOOD FOR YOU WHEN YOU'RE SICK TOO!
...
SORRY...
...BUT I CAN'T EAT THAT...
I WANT POR-RIDGE... OR SOUP...
PORRIDGE?!
THAT'S ENOUGH FOR YOU?!
IT'S NOT MY SPECIALTY, BUT I'LL TRY MY BEST!
LONGHORN
MAYBE YOU COULD ...BUY IT...?

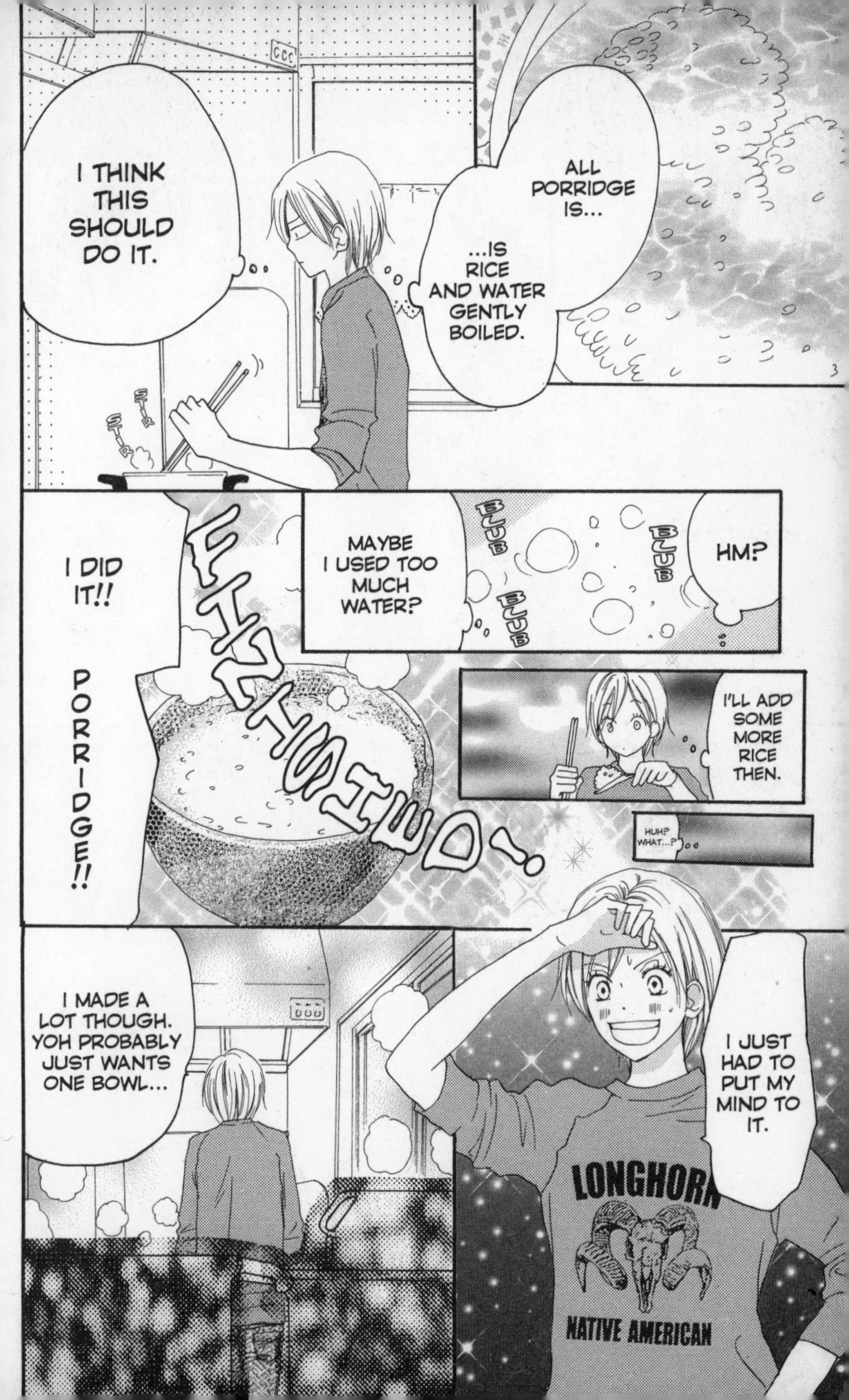
ALL PORRIDGE IS...
...IS RICE AND WATER GENTLY BOILED.
I THINK THIS SHOULD DO IT.
STIR STIR
HM?
BLUB BLUB BLUB
MAYBE I USED TOO MUCH WATER?
I'LL ADD SOME MORE RICE THEN.
HUH? WHAT...?
FINISHED!!
I DID IT!!
PORRIDGE!!
I JUST HAD TO PUT MY MIND TO IT.
LONGHORN
NATIVE AMERICAN
I MADE A LOT THOUGH. YOH PROBABLY JUST WANTS ONE BOWL...

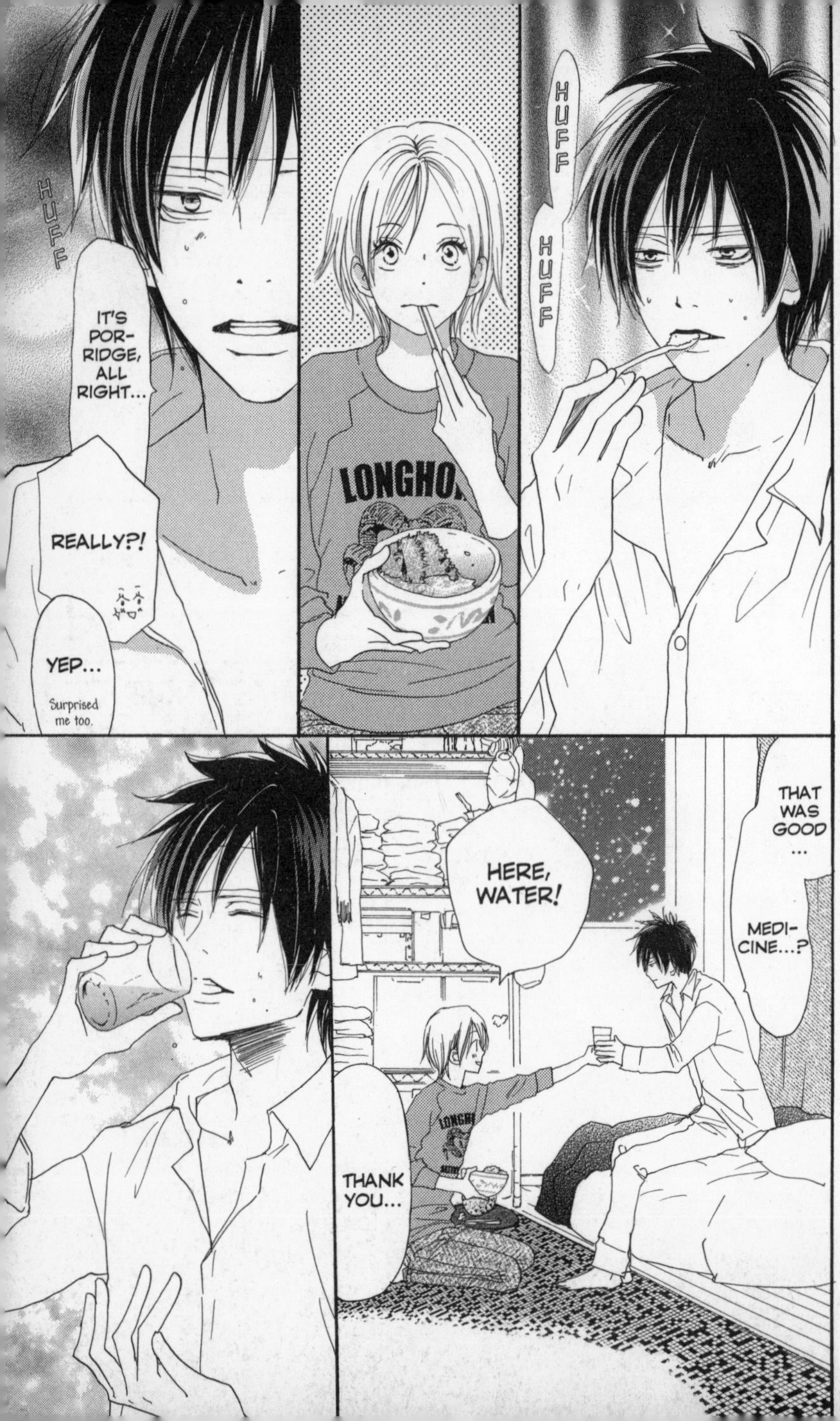
HUFF
HUFF
HUFF
IT'S PORRIDGE, ALL RIGHT...
REALLY?!
YEP...
Surprised me too.
THAT WAS GOOD ...
MEDICINE...?
HERE, WATER!
THANK YOU...

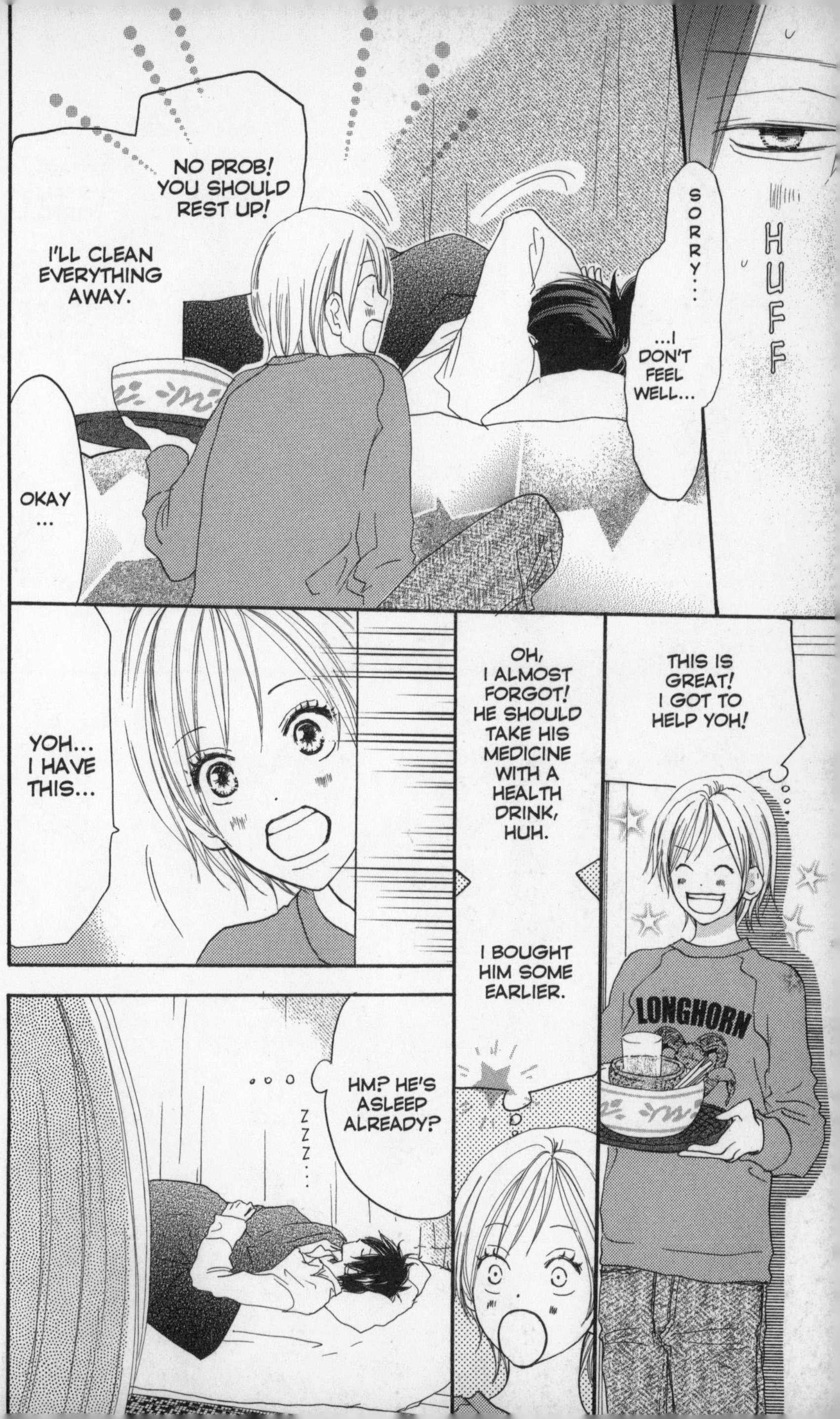
SORRY...
HUFF
...I DON'T FEEL WELL...
NO PROB! YOU SHOULD REST UP!
I'LL CLEAN EVERYTHING AWAY.
OKAY...
THIS IS GREAT! I GOT TO HELP YOH!
LONGHORN
OH, I ALMOST FORGOT! HE SHOULD TAKE HIS MEDICINE WITH A HEALTH DRINK, HUH.
I BOUGHT HIM SOME EARLIER.
YOH... I HAVE THIS...
HM? HE'S ASLEEP ALREADY?
ZZZ...

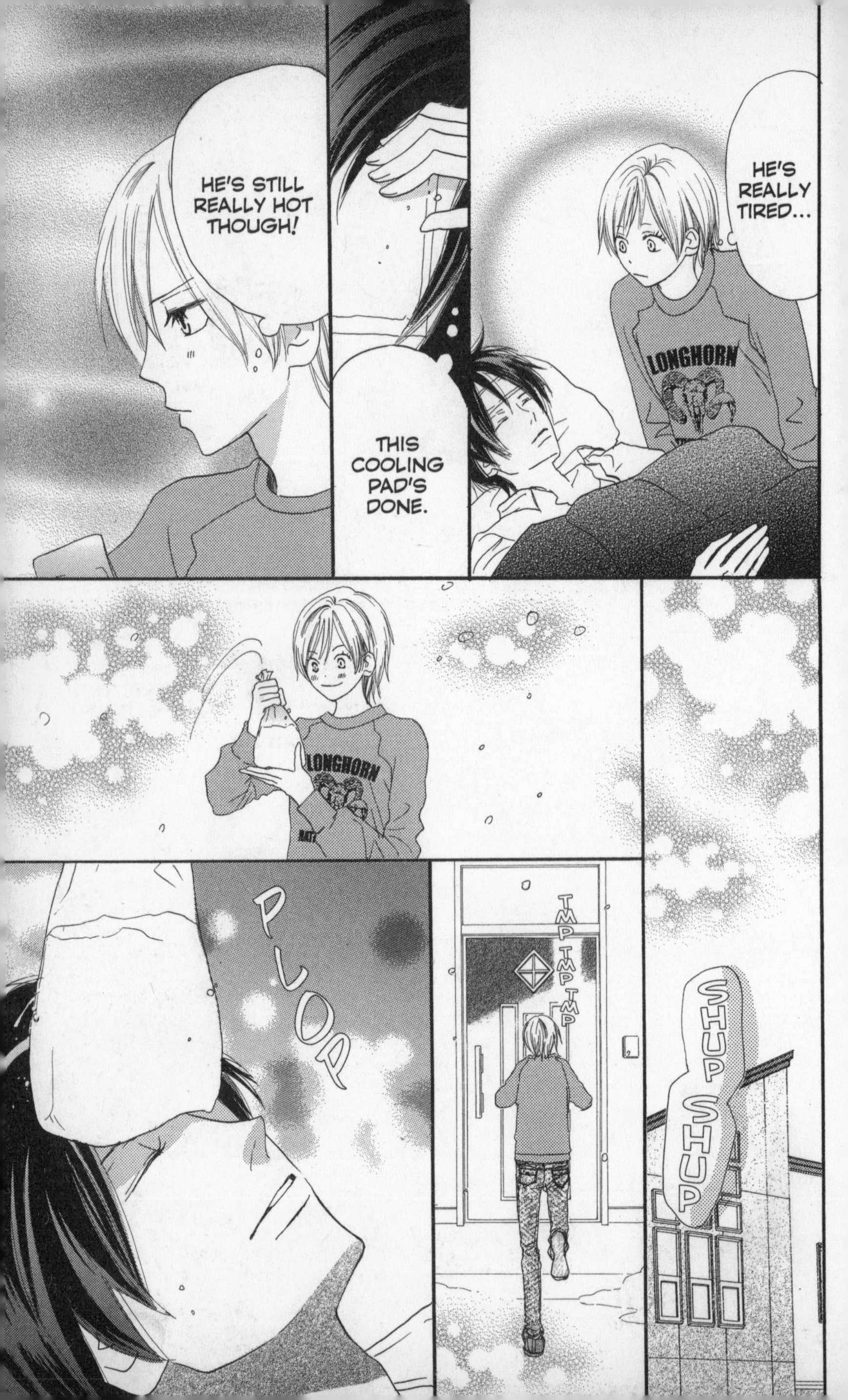
HE'S REALLY TIRED...
THIS COOLING PAD'S DONE.
HE'S STILL REALLY HOT THOUGH!
SHUP SHUP
TMP TMP TMP TMP
PLOP

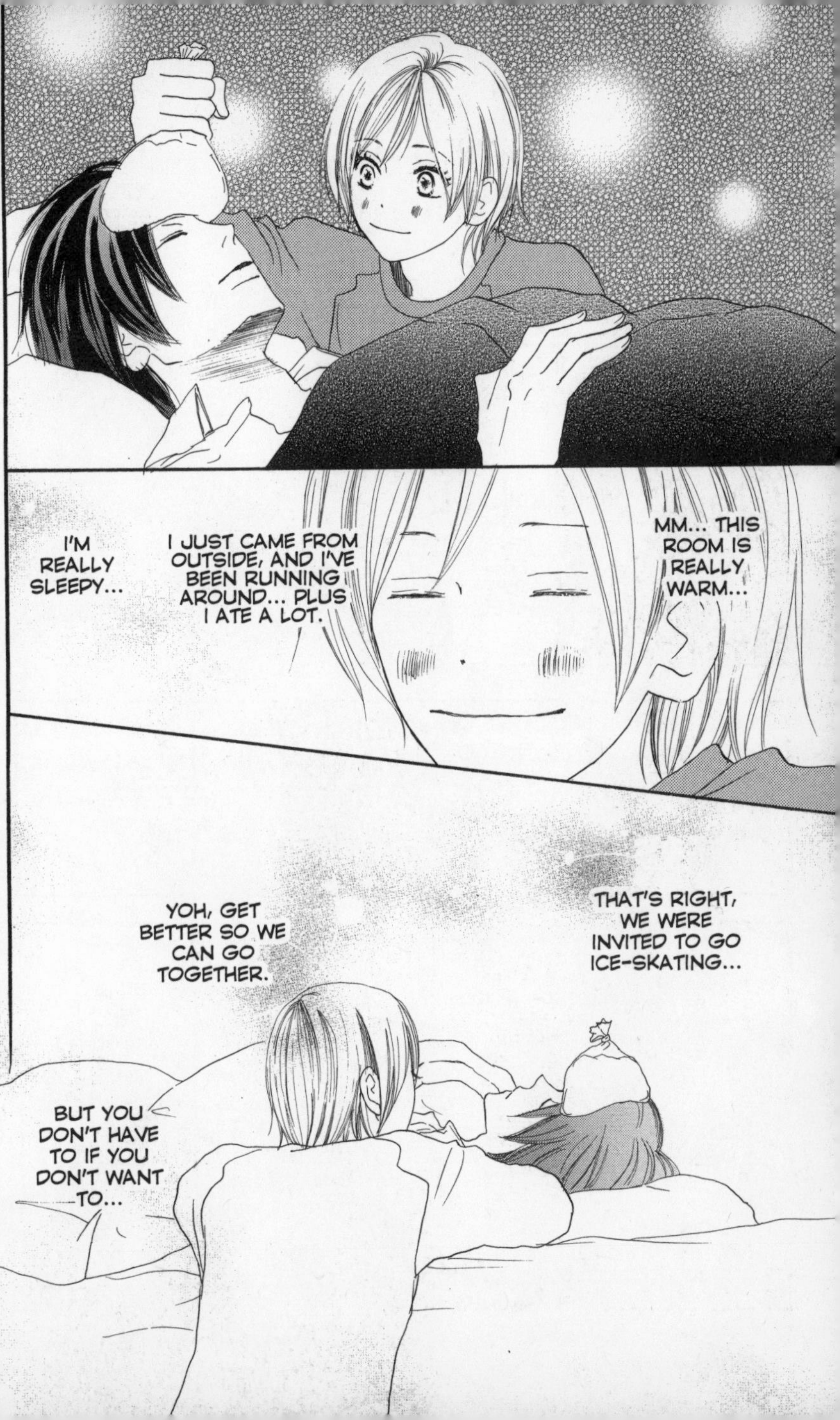
MM... THIS ROOM IS REALLY WARM...
I JUST CAME FROM OUTSIDE, AND I'VE BEEN RUNNING AROUND... PLUS I ATE A LOT.
I'M REALLY SLEEPY...
THAT'S RIGHT, WE WERE INVITED TO GO ICE-SKATING...
YOH, GET BETTER SO WE CAN GO TOGETHER.
BUT YOU DON'T HAVE TO IF YOU DON'T WANT TO...

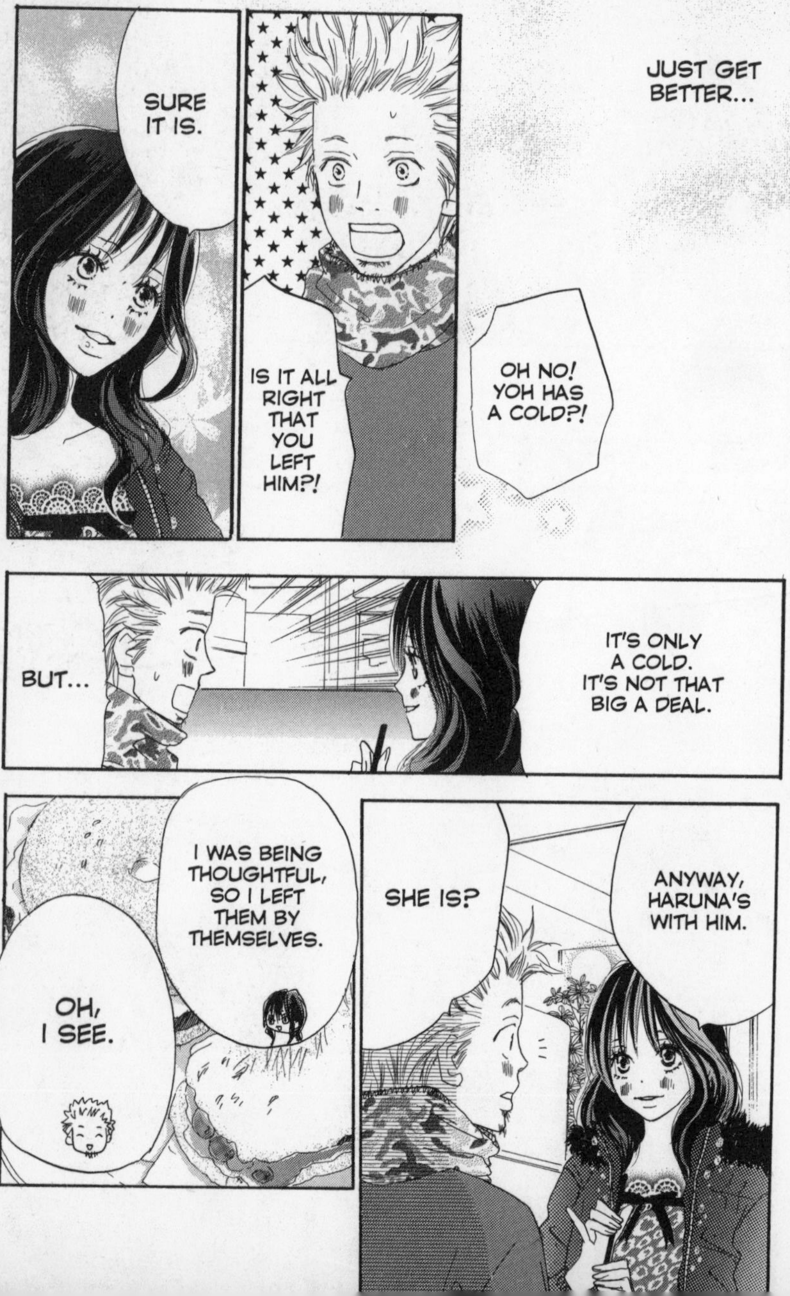

JUST GET BETTER...
OH NO! YOH HAS A COLD?!
IS IT ALL RIGHT THAT YOU LEFT HIM?!
SURE IT IS.
IT'S ONLY A COLD. IT'S NOT THAT BIG A DEAL.
BUT...
ANYWAY, HARUNA'S WITH HIM.
SHE IS?
I WAS BEING THOUGHTFUL, SO I LEFT THEM BY THEMSELVES.
OH, I SEE.

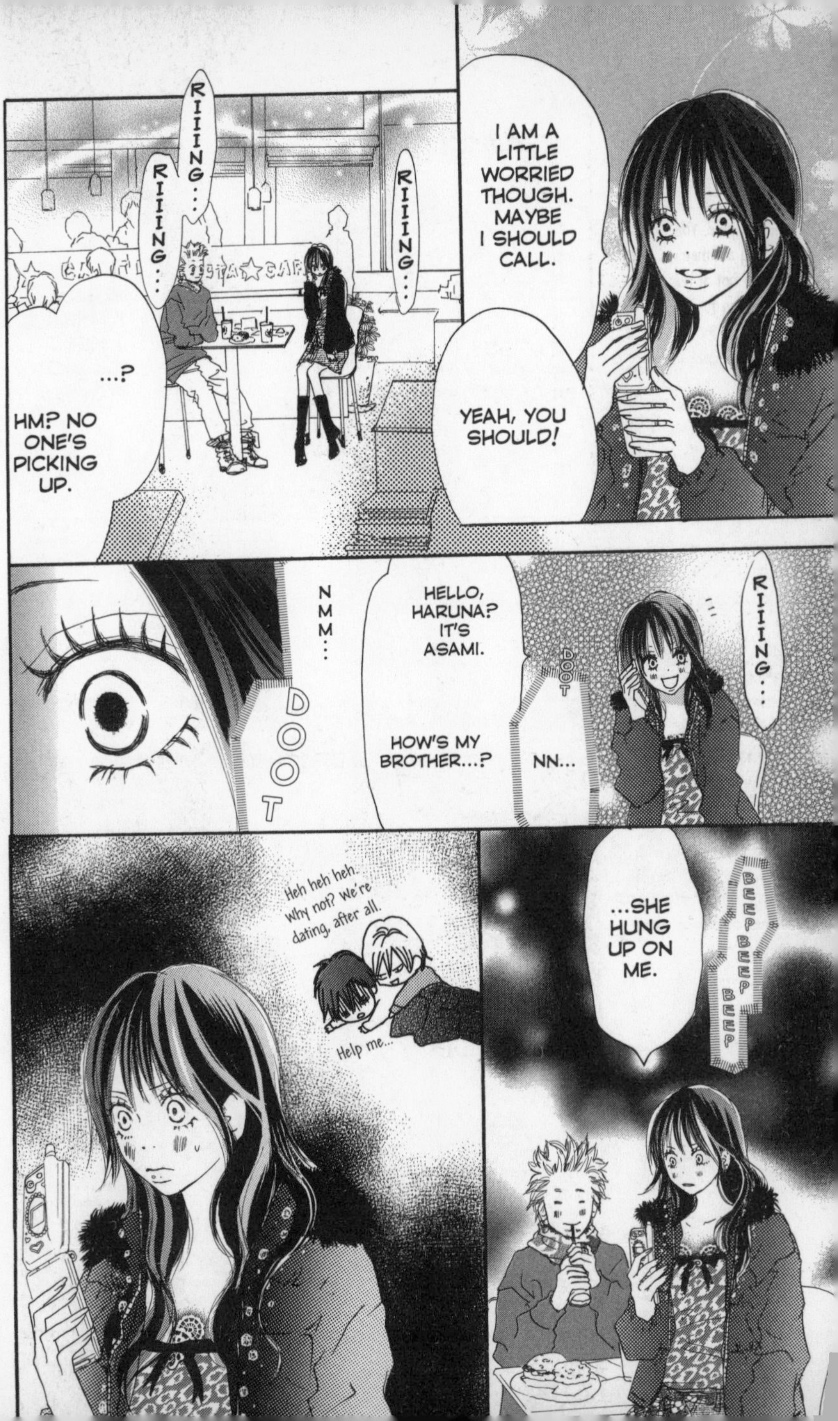
I AM A LITTLE WORRIED THOUGH. MAYBE I SHOULD CALL.
YEAH, YOU SHOULD!
RIIING...
RIIING...
RIIING...
...?
HM? NO ONE'S PICKING UP.
RIIING...
DOOT
NN...
HELLO, HARUNA? IT'S ASAMI.
HOW'S MY BROTHER...?
NMM...
DOOT
...SHE HUNG UP ON ME.
BEEP BEEP BEEP BEEP
Heh heh heh. Why not? We're dating, after all.
Help me...

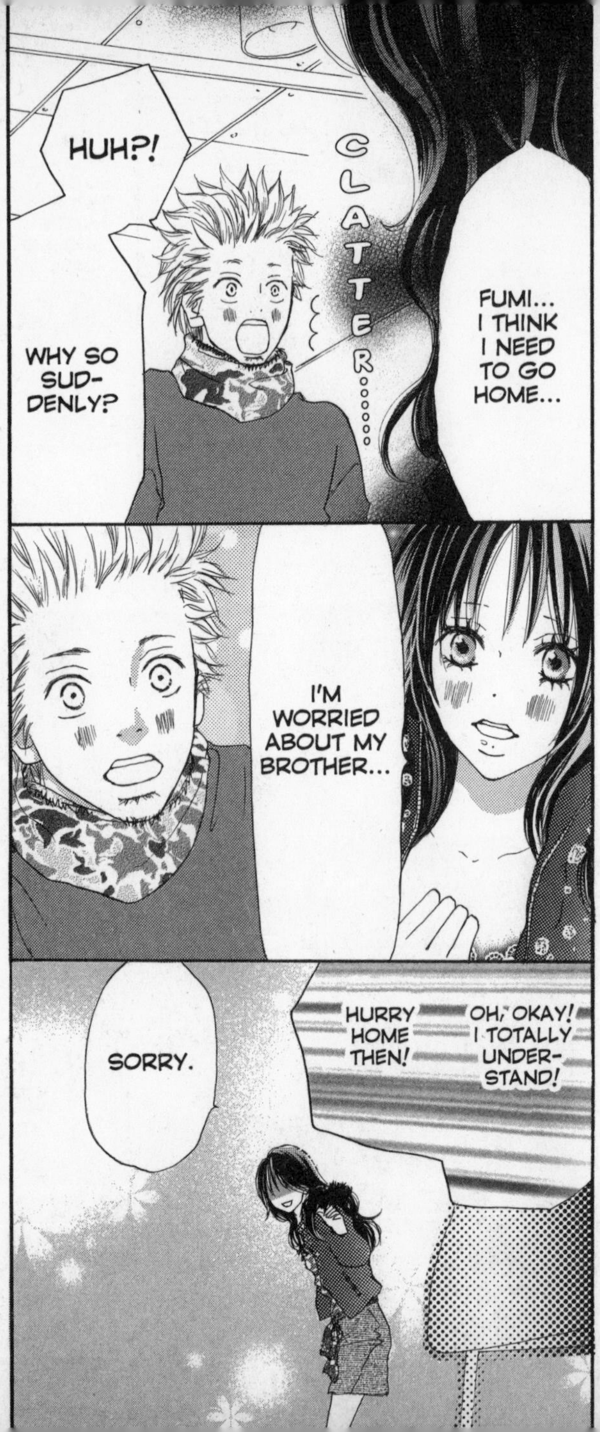
FUMI... I THINK I NEED TO GO HOME...
CLATTER......
HUH?!
WHY SO SUD-DENLY?
I'M WORRIED ABOUT MY BROTHER...
OH, OKAY! I TOTALLY UNDER-STAND!
HURRY HOME THEN!
SORRY.

1

Hi everyone. Thanks for buying another volume! I'm so hot at home I think I'm going to die. But I've been working hard, so I hope you enjoy it.

I fell over and scraped my knees today. There was so much blood. But I've been working hard, so I hope you enjoy it.

Last night, some bug bit me over ten times. But I've been working hard, so I hope you enjoy it.

I've been wanting to do some gardening this year. I failed miserably. But I've been working hard, so I hope you enjoy it.

Is that enough for you?

Seriously, thanks to everyone for reading this! Thanks to you, we're at volume 7!

But what am I going to do about my garden...?

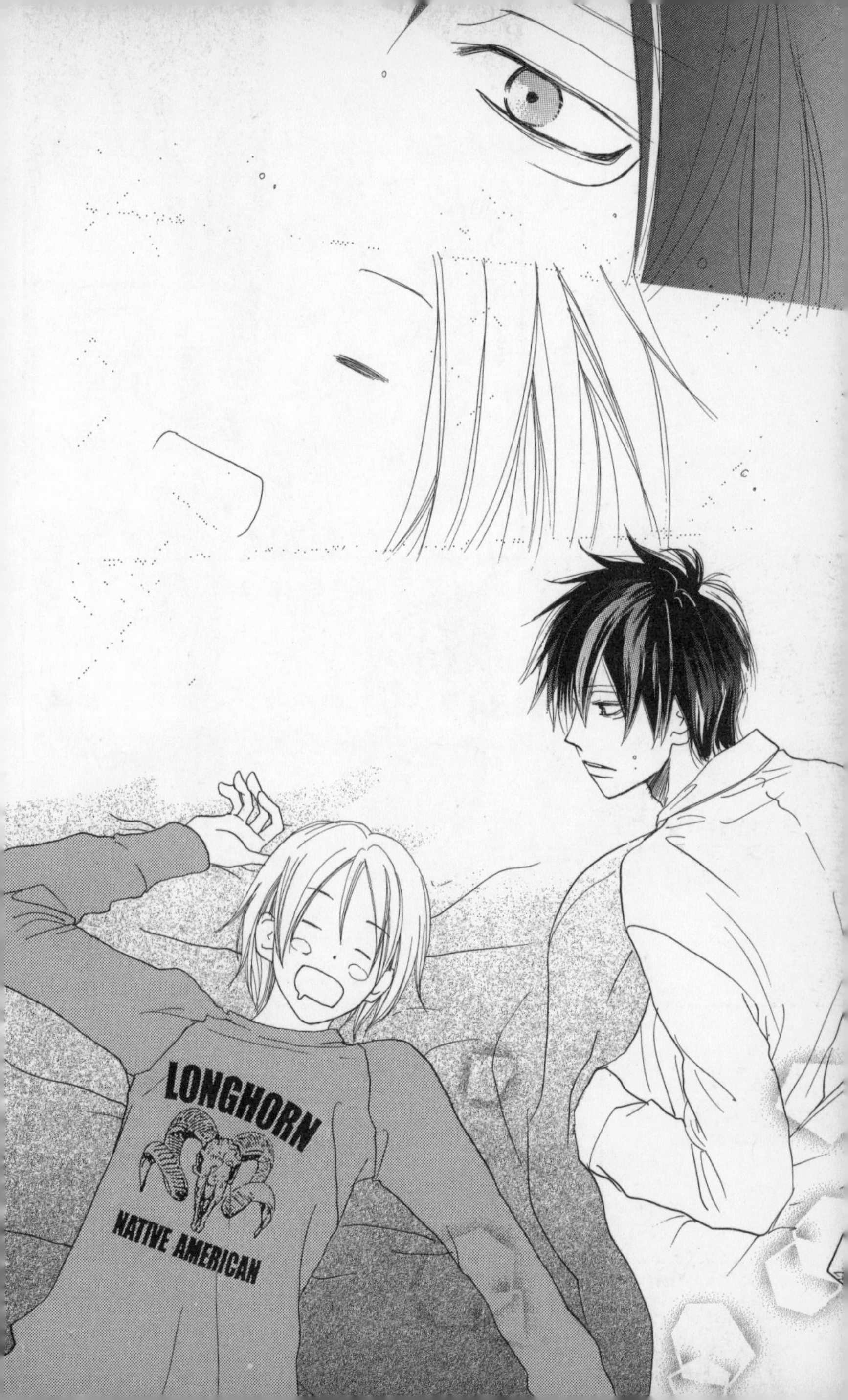
LONGHORN
NATIVE AMERICAN

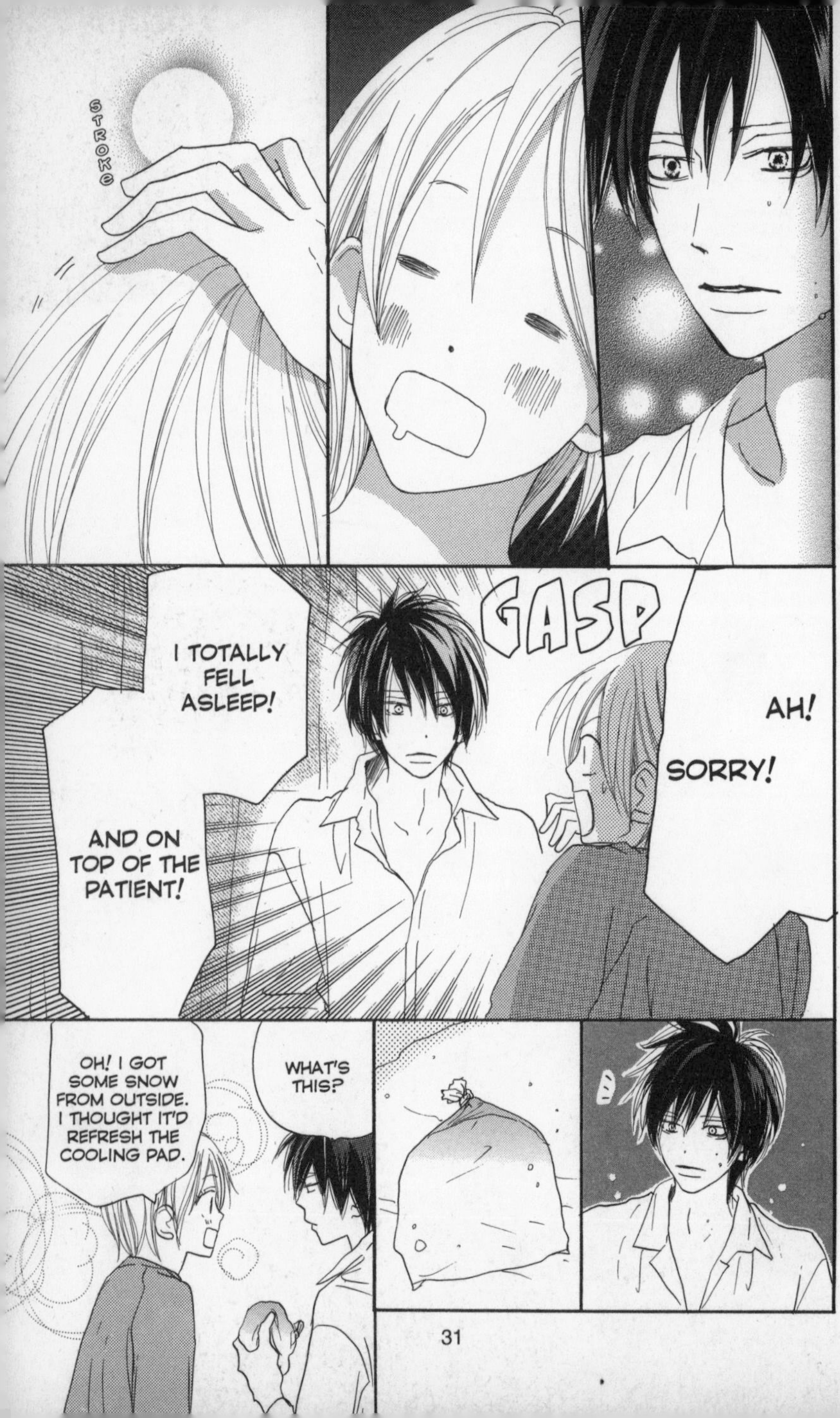
STROKE
AH!
SORRY!
GASP
I TOTALLY FELL ASLEEP!
AND ON TOP OF THE PATIENT!
WHAT'S THIS?
OH! I GOT SOME SNOW FROM OUTSIDE. I THOUGHT IT'D REFRESH THE COOLING PAD.

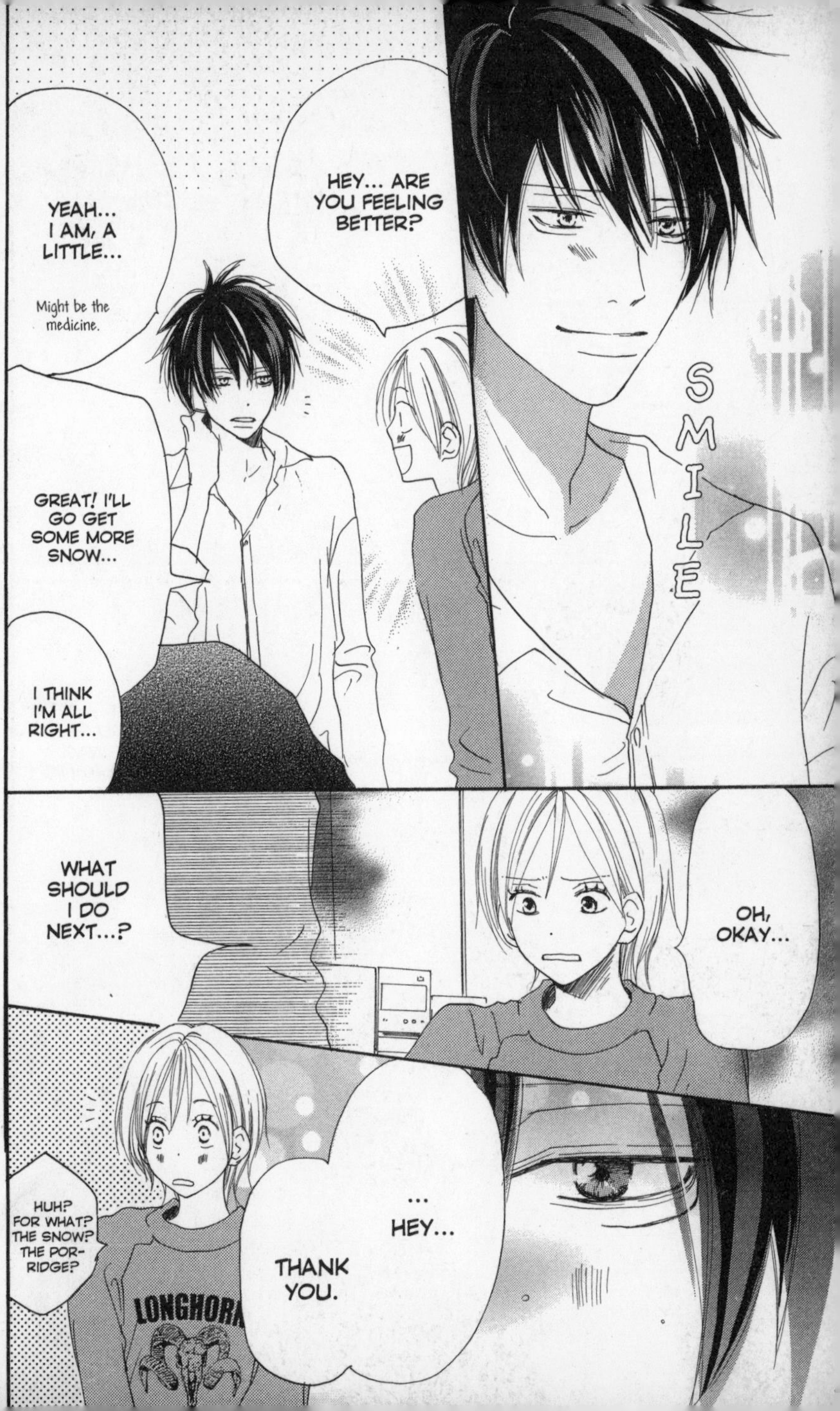
SMILE
HEY... ARE YOU FEELING BETTER?
YEAH... I AM, A LITTLE...
Might be the medicine.
GREAT! I'LL GO GET SOME MORE SNOW...
I THINK I'M ALL RIGHT...
OH, OKAY...
WHAT SHOULD I DO NEXT...?
... HEY...
THANK YOU.
HUH? FOR WHAT? THE SNOW? THE POR-RIDGE?

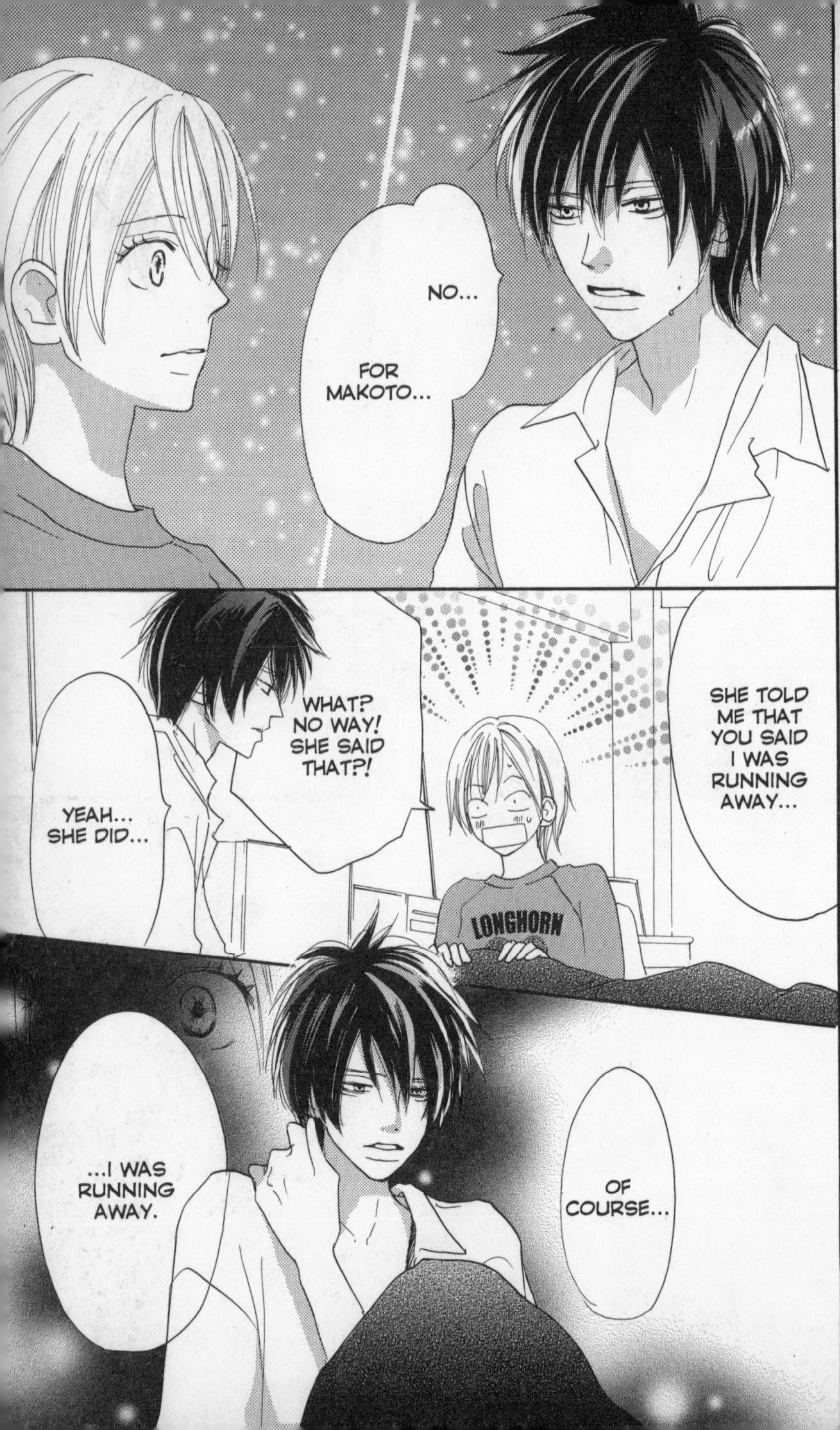
NO... FOR MAKOTO...
SHE TOLD ME THAT YOU SAID I WAS RUNNING AWAY...
WHAT? NO WAY! SHE SAID THAT?!
LONGHORN
YEAH... SHE DID...
OF COURSE...
...I WAS RUNNING AWAY.

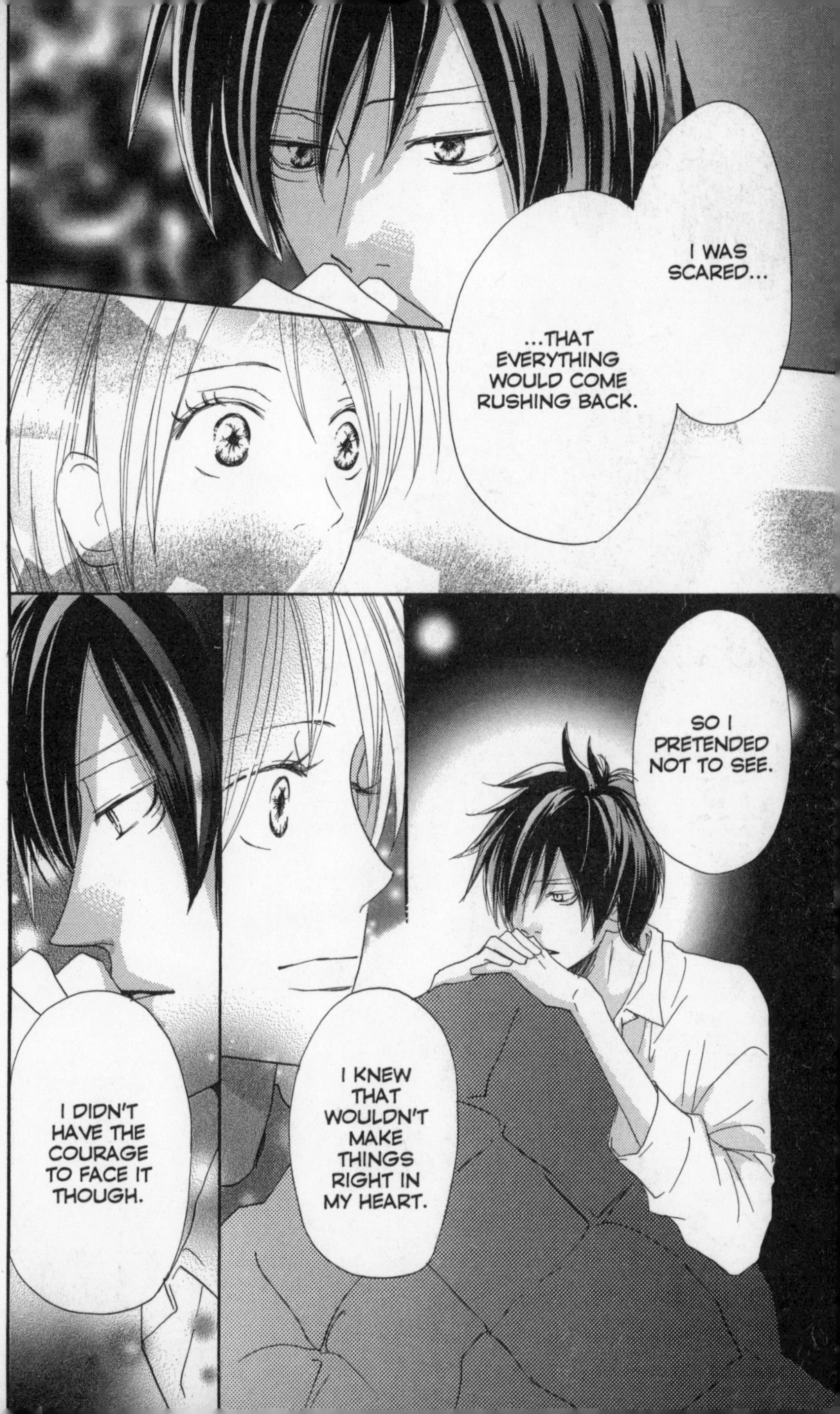
I WAS SCARED...
...THAT EVERYTHING WOULD COME RUSHING BACK.
SO I PRETENDED NOT TO SEE.
I KNEW THAT WOULDN'T MAKE THINGS RIGHT IN MY HEART.
I DIDN'T HAVE THE COURAGE TO FACE IT THOUGH.

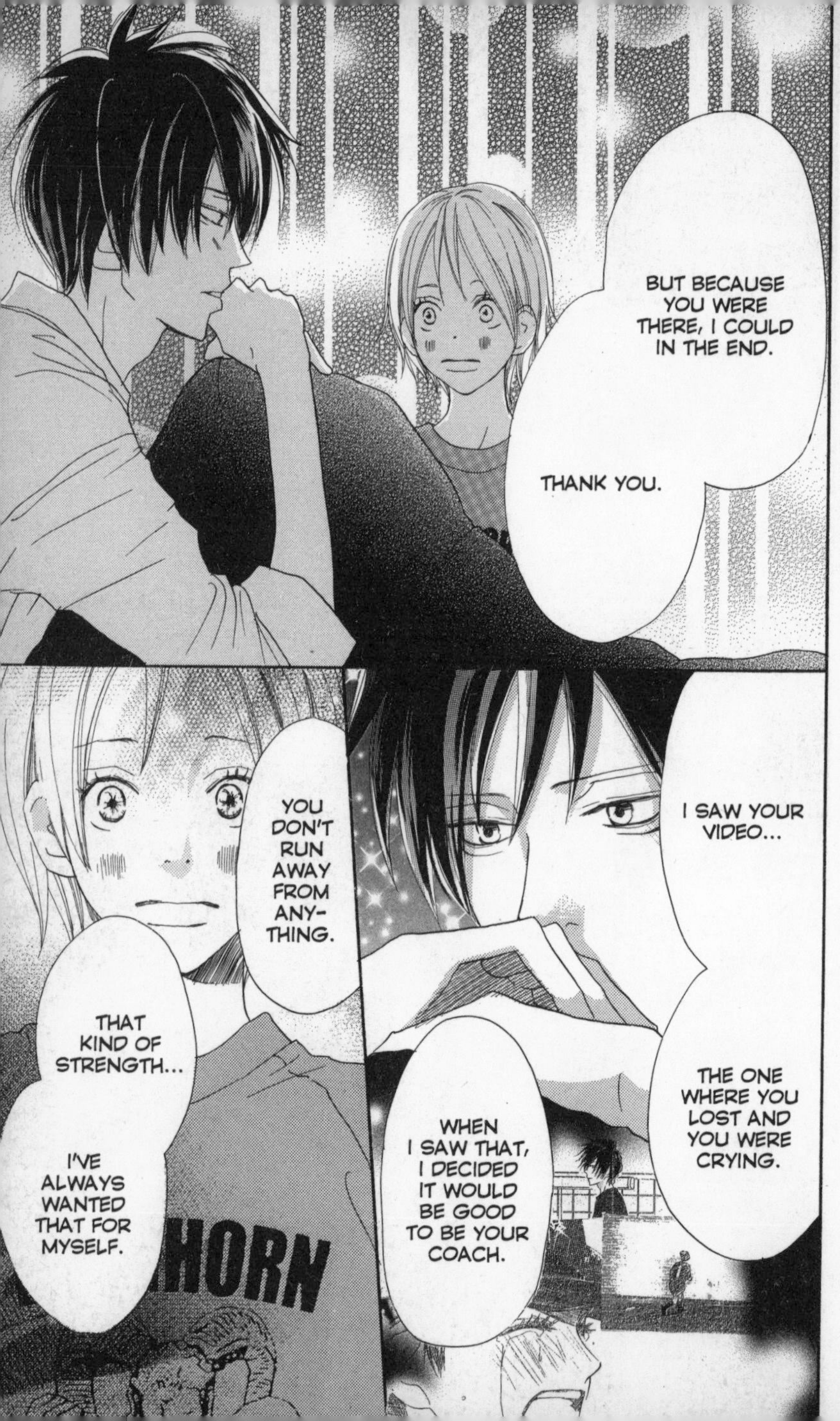
BUT BECAUSE YOU WERE THERE, I COULD IN THE END.
THANK YOU.
I SAW YOUR VIDEO...
THE ONE WHERE YOU LOST AND YOU WERE CRYING.
WHEN I SAW THAT, I DECIDED IT WOULD BE GOOD TO BE YOUR COACH.
YOU DON'T RUN AWAY FROM ANY-THING.
THAT KIND OF STRENGTH...
I'VE ALWAYS WANTED THAT FOR MYSELF.

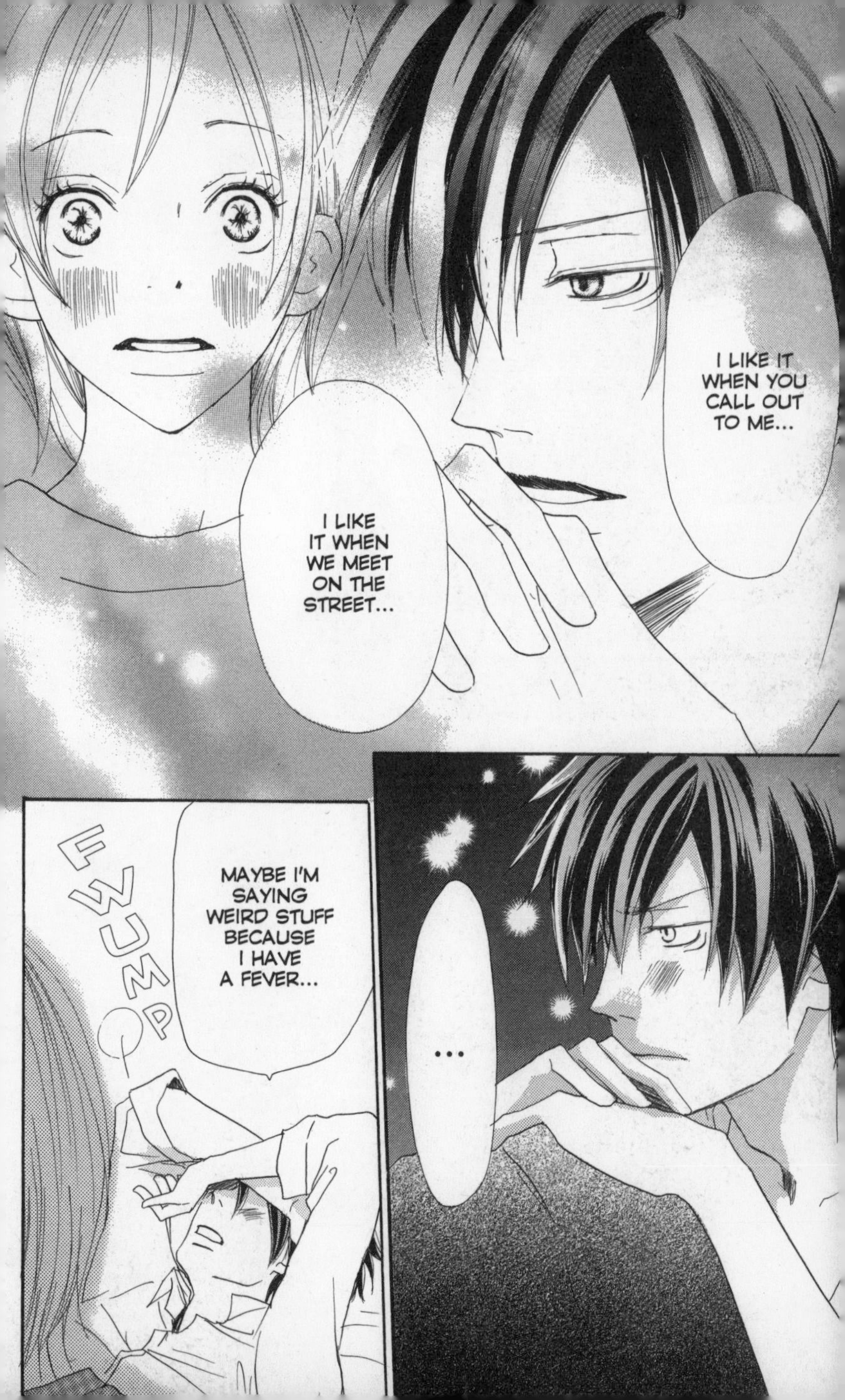
I LIKE IT WHEN YOU CALL OUT TO ME...
I LIKE IT WHEN WE MEET ON THE STREET...
...
MAYBE I'M SAYING WEIRD STUFF BECAUSE I HAVE A FEVER...
FWUMP

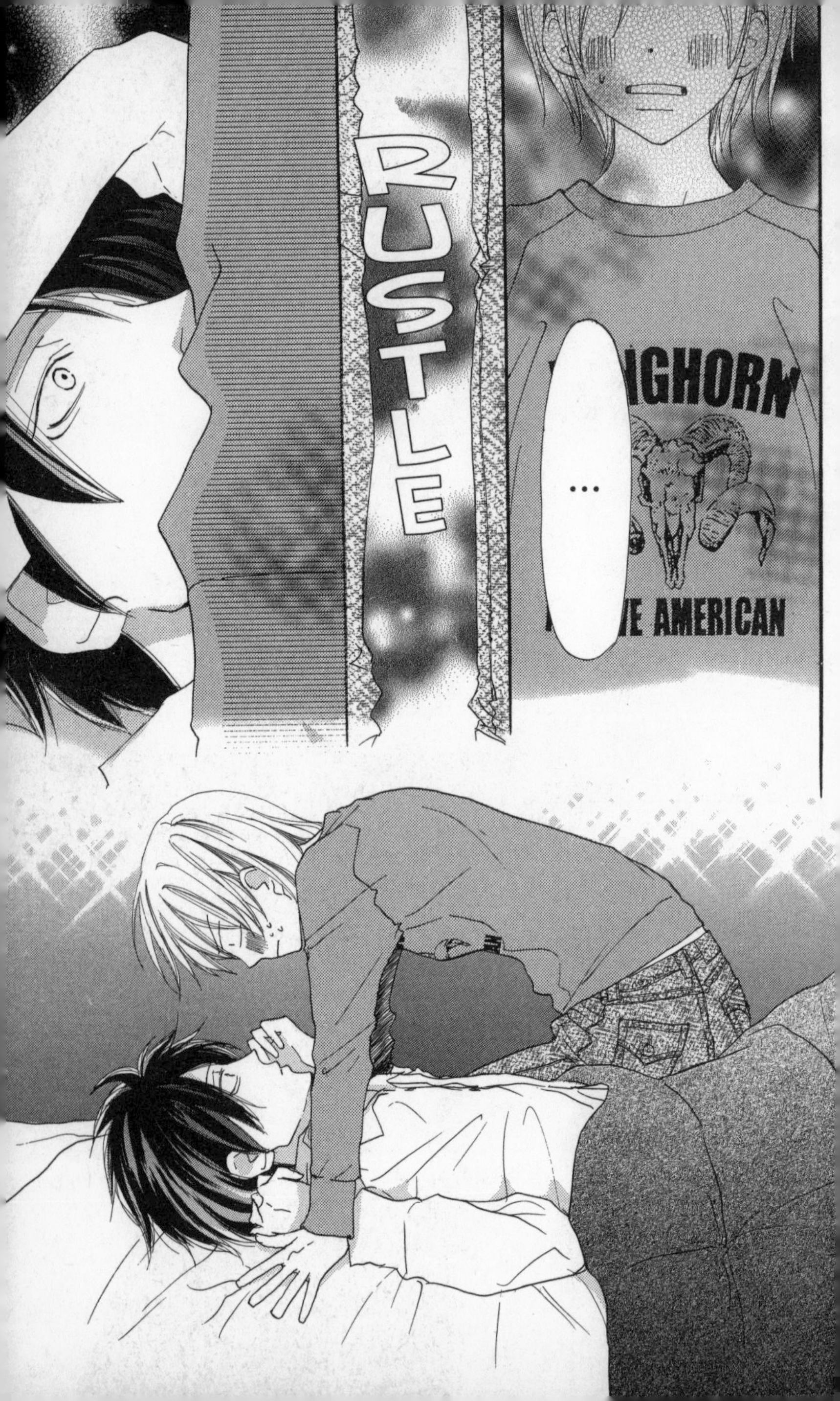
...
IGHORN
VE AMERICAN
RUSTLE

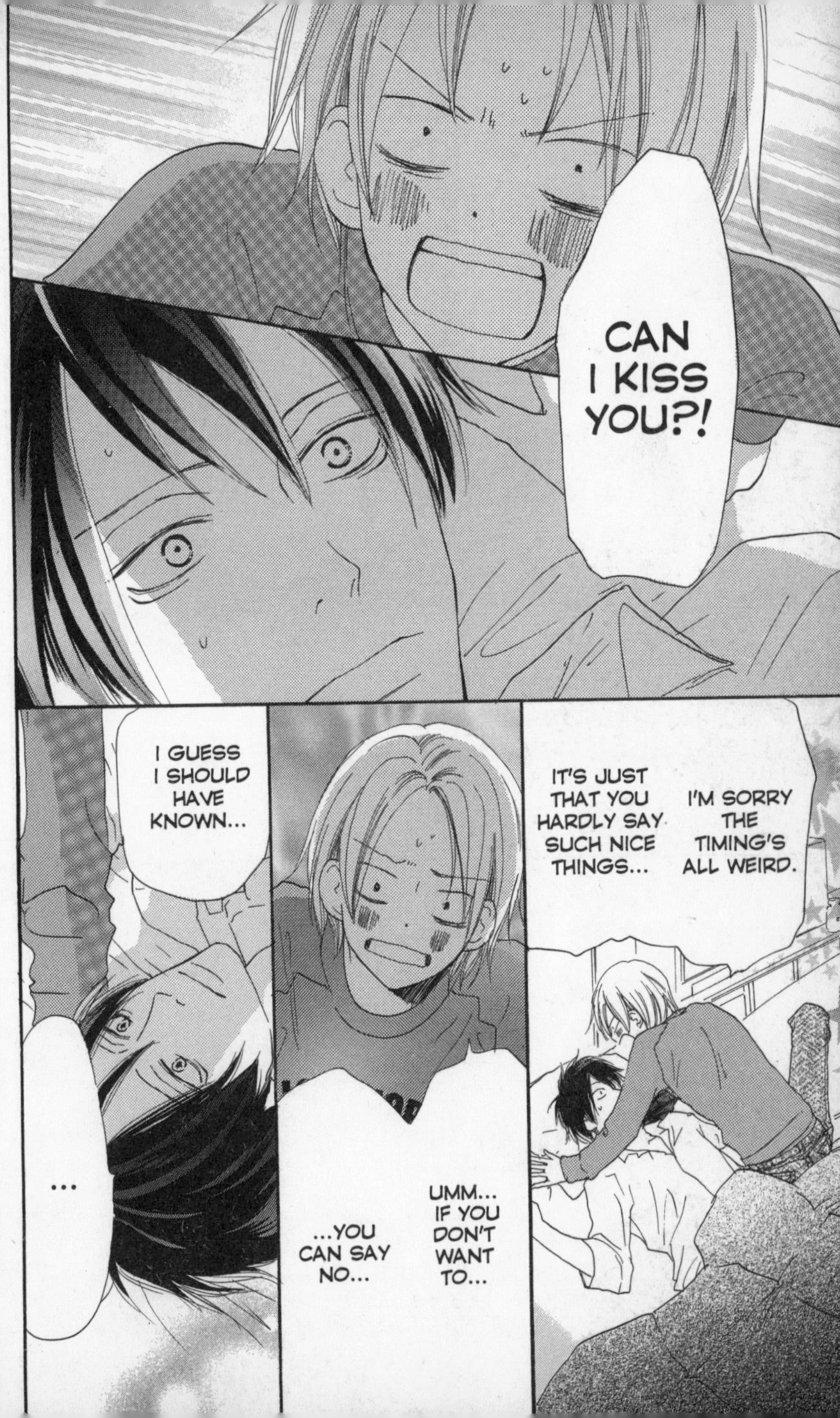
CAN I KISS YOU?!
I'M SORRY THE TIMING'S ALL WEIRD.
IT'S JUST THAT YOU HARDLY SAY SUCH NICE THINGS...
UMM... IF YOU DON'T WANT TO...
...YOU CAN SAY NO...
I GUESS I SHOULD HAVE KNOWN...
...

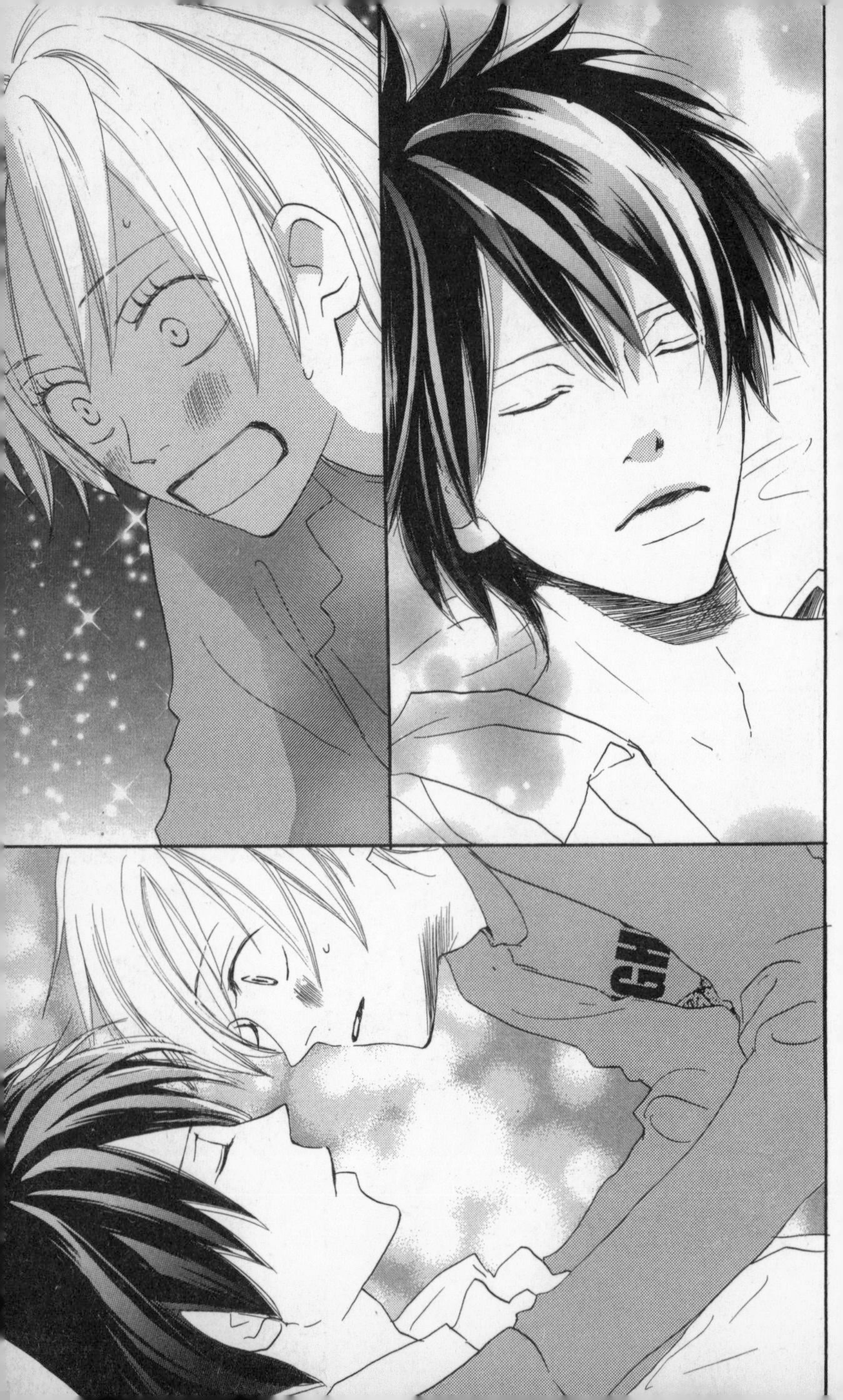

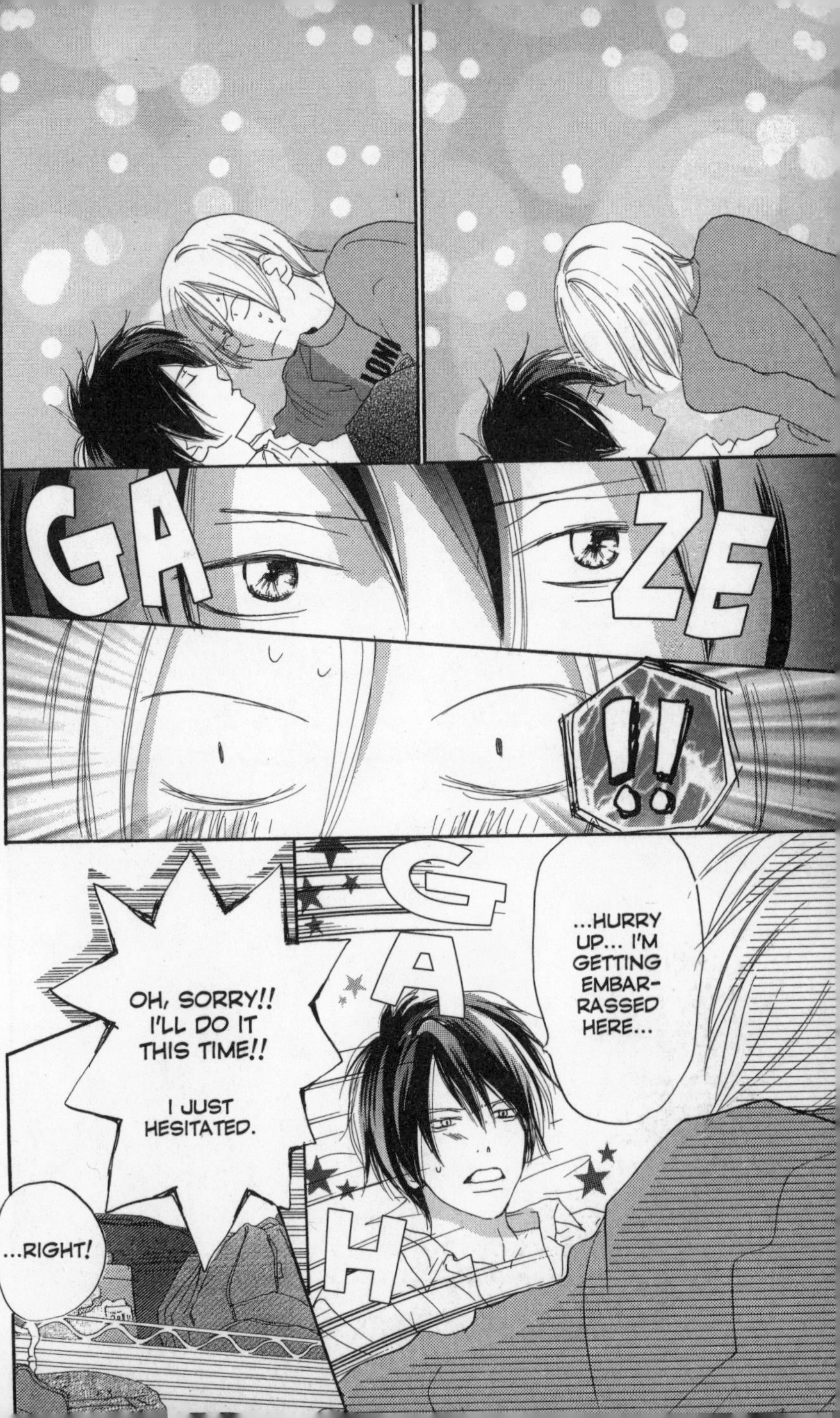
GAZE
!!
...HURRY UP... I'M GETTING EMBARRASSED HERE...
GAGH
OH, SORRY!! I'LL DO IT THIS TIME!!
I JUST HESITATED.
...RIGHT!

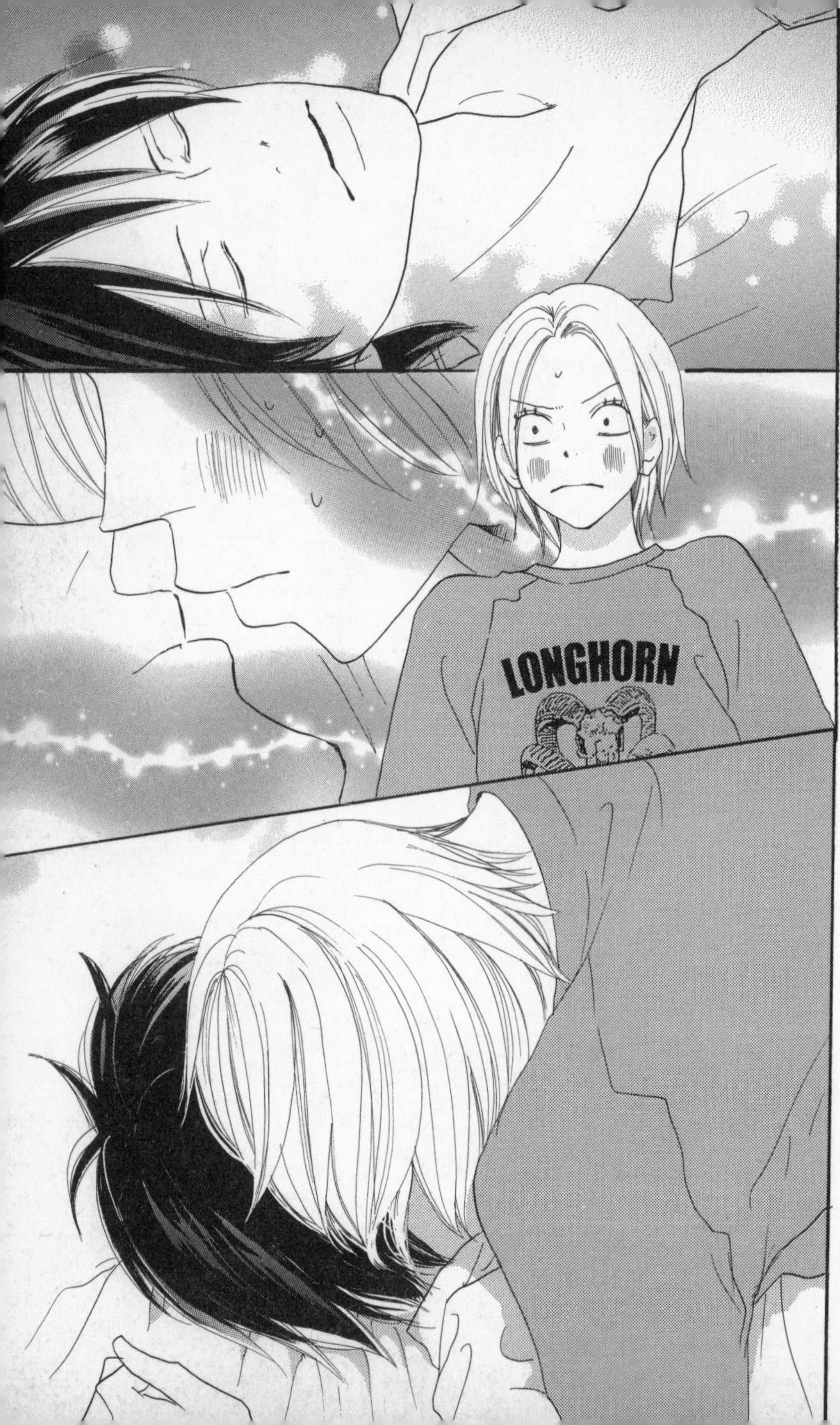
LONGHORN

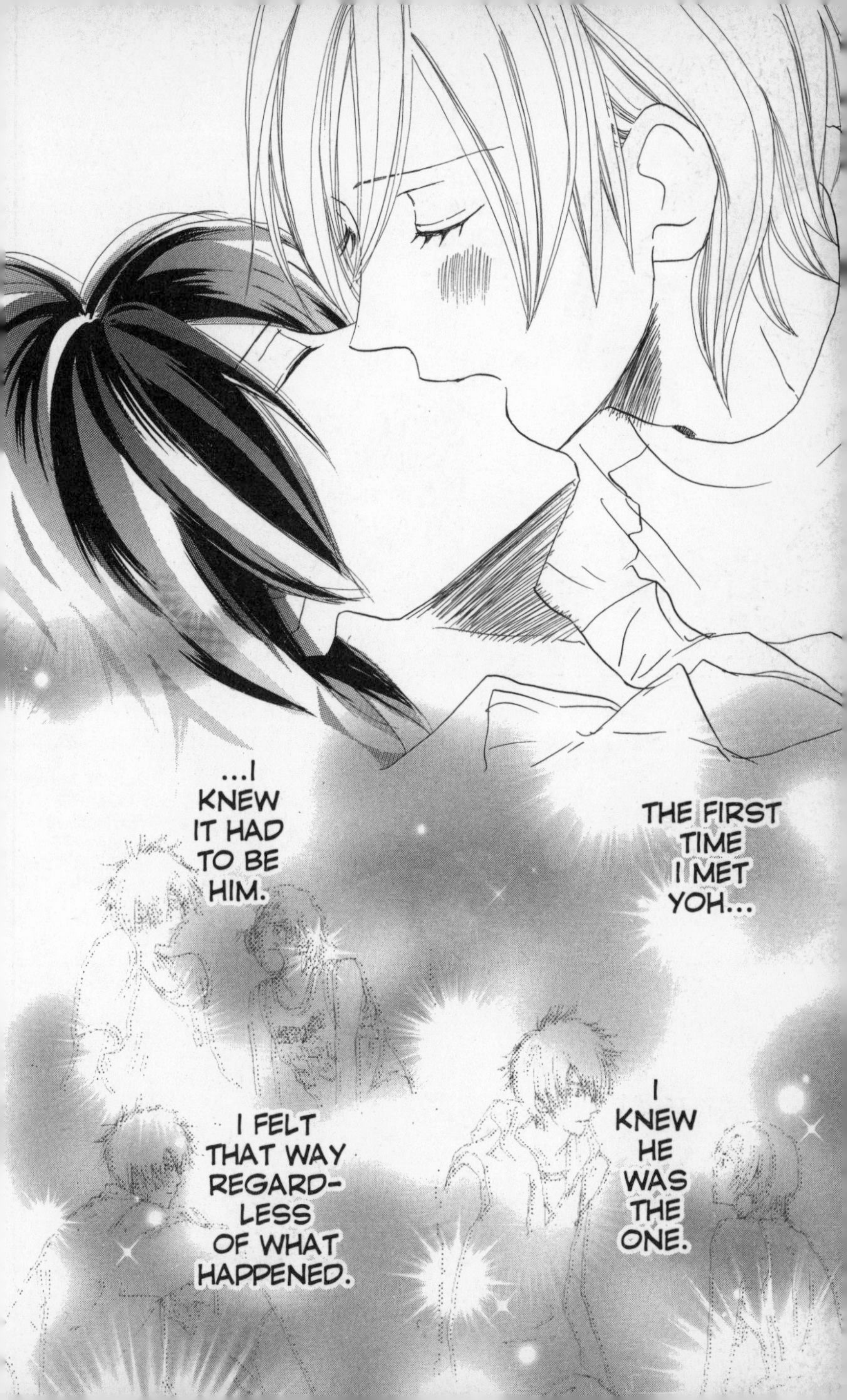
THE FIRST TIME I MET YOH...
...I KNEW IT HAD TO BE HIM.
I KNEW HE WAS THE ONE.
I FELT THAT WAY REGARDLESS OF WHAT HAPPENED.

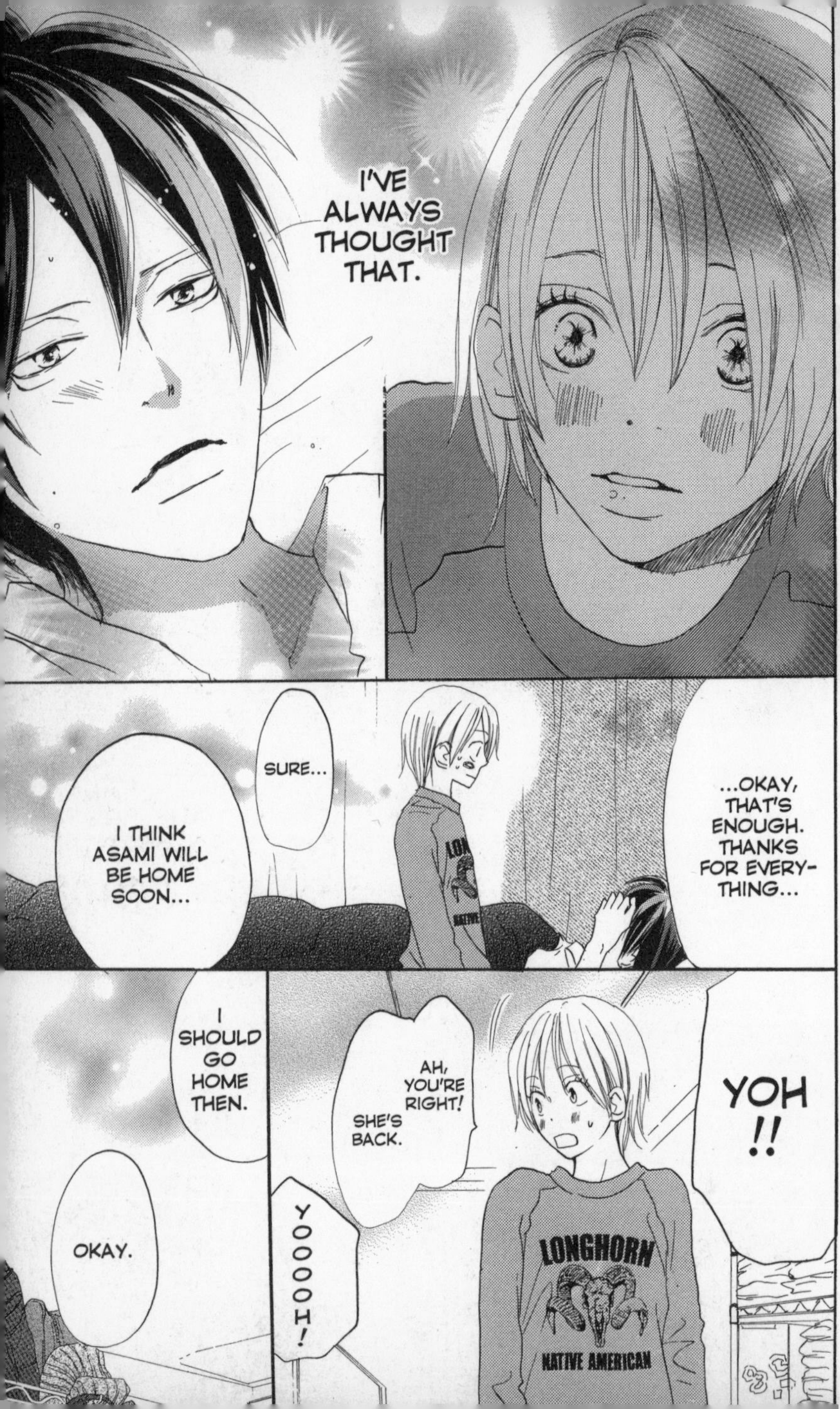
I'VE ALWAYS THOUGHT THAT.
...OKAY, THAT'S ENOUGH. THANKS FOR EVERY-THING...
SURE...
I THINK ASAMI WILL BE HOME SOON...
YOH !!
AH, YOU'RE RIGHT! SHE'S BACK.
YOOOOOH!
LONGHORN
NATIVE AMERICAN
I SHOULD GO HOME THEN.
OKAY.

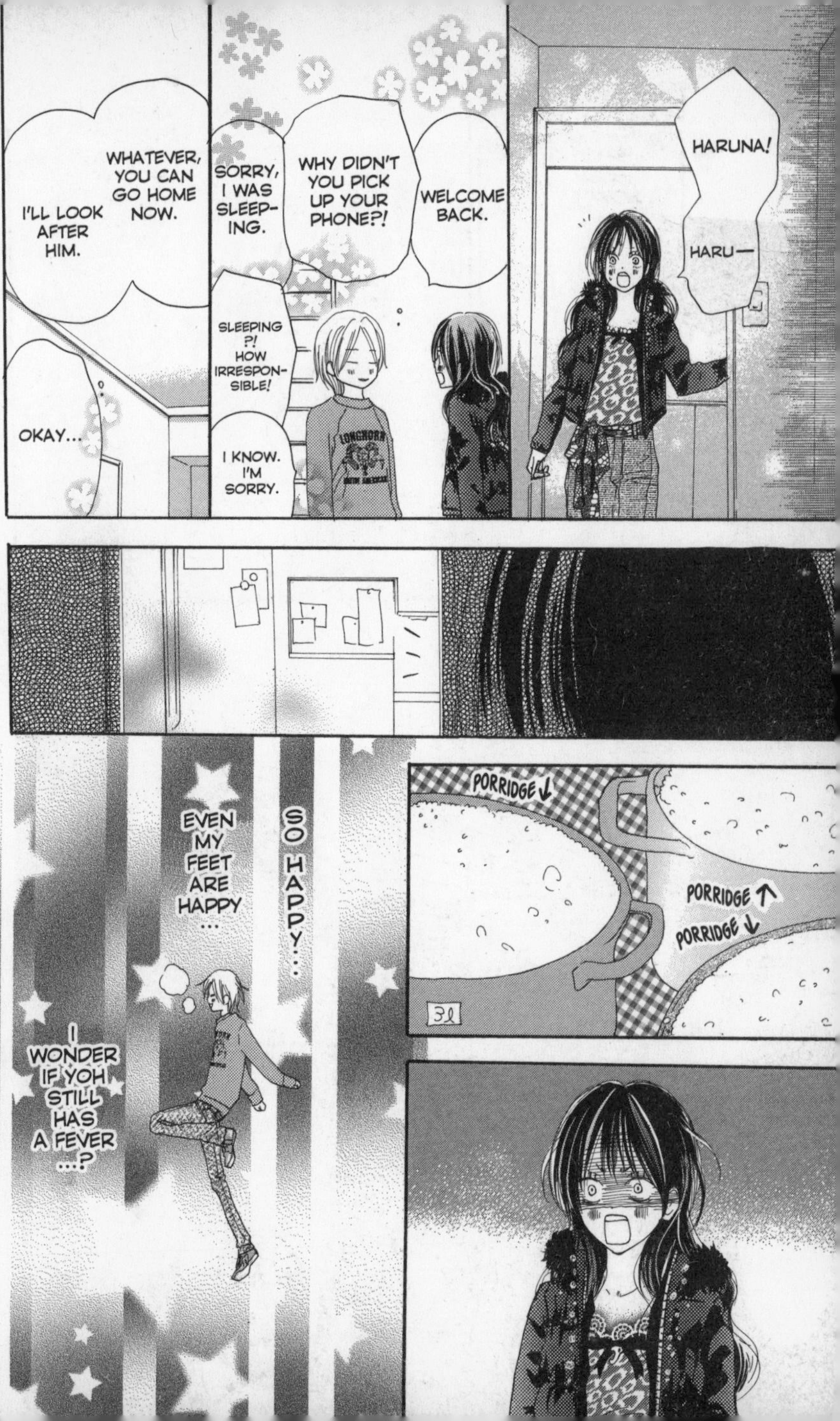
HARUNA!
HARU—
WELCOME BACK.
WHY DIDN'T YOU PICK UP YOUR PHONE?!
SORRY, I WAS SLEEPING.
SLEEPING?! HOW IRRESPONSIBLE!
I KNOW. I'M SORRY.
WHATEVER, YOU CAN GO HOME NOW.
I'LL LOOK AFTER HIM.
OKAY...
PORRIDGE ↓
PORRIDGE ↑
PORRIDGE ↓
31
SO HAPPY...
EVEN MY FEET ARE HAPPY...
I WONDER IF YOH STILL HAS A FEVER...?

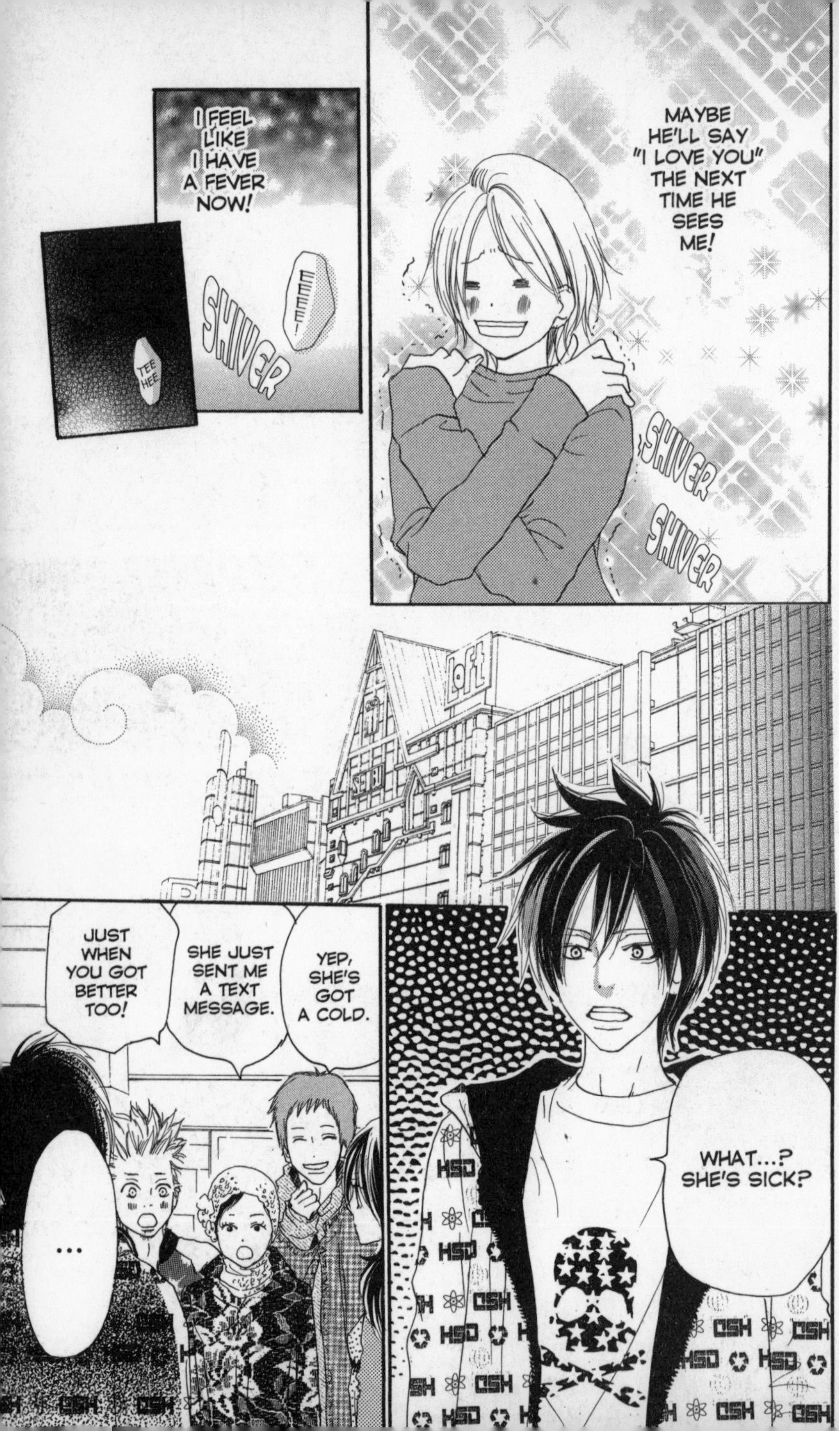
MAYBE HE'LL SAY "I LOVE YOU" THE NEXT TIME HE SEES ME!
SHIVER
SHIVER
I FEEL LIKE I HAVE A FEVER NOW!
EEEE!
SHIVER
TEE HEE
WHAT...? SHE'S SICK?
YEP, SHE'S GOT A COLD.
SHE JUST SENT ME A TEXT MESSAGE.
JUST WHEN YOU GOT BETTER TOO!
...

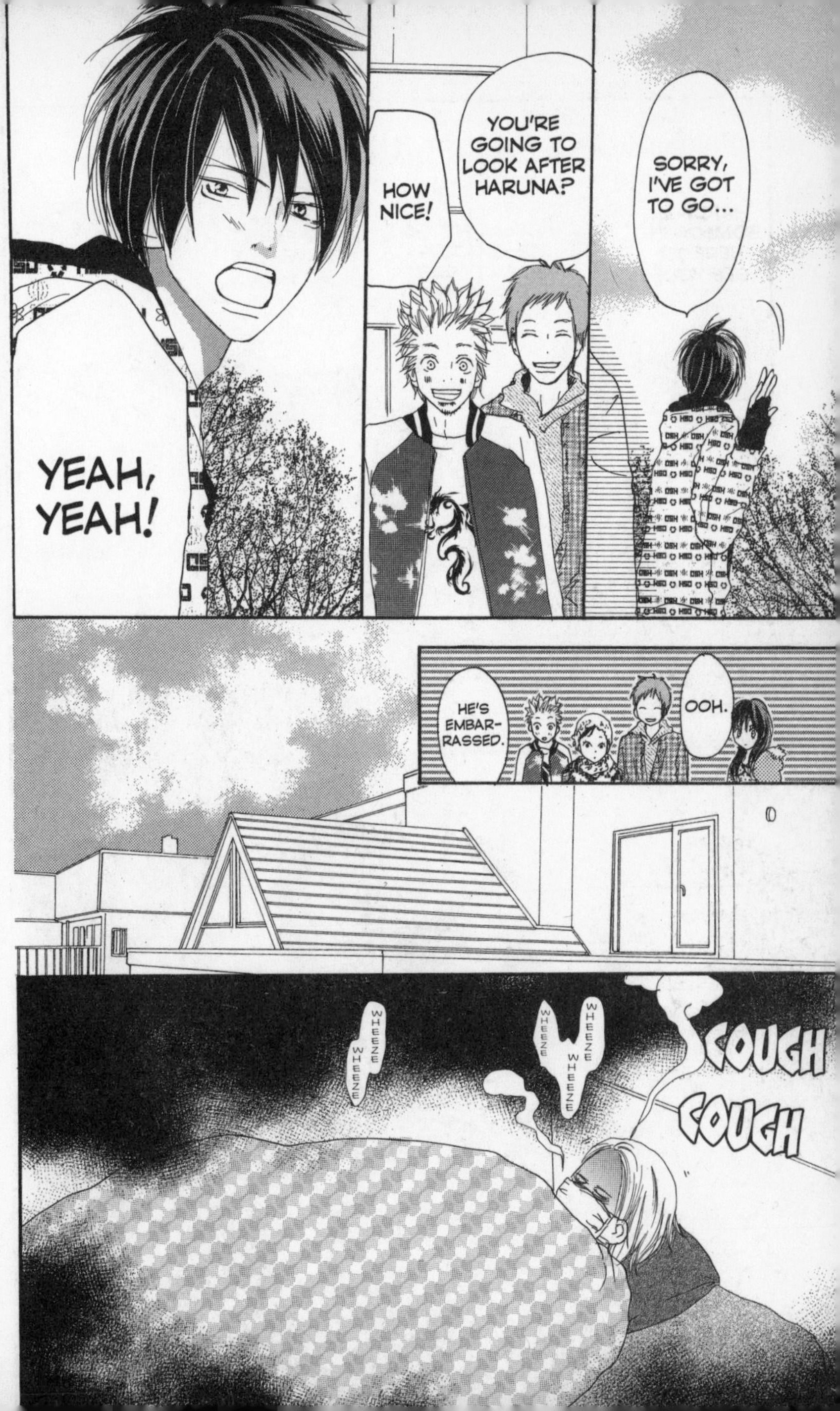
SORRY, I'VE GOT TO GO...
YOU'RE GOING TO LOOK AFTER HARUNA?
HOW NICE!
YEAH, YEAH!
OOH.
HE'S EMBARRASSED.
COUGH
COUGH
WHEEZE WHEEZE
WHEEZE WHEEZE
WHEEZE WHEEZE

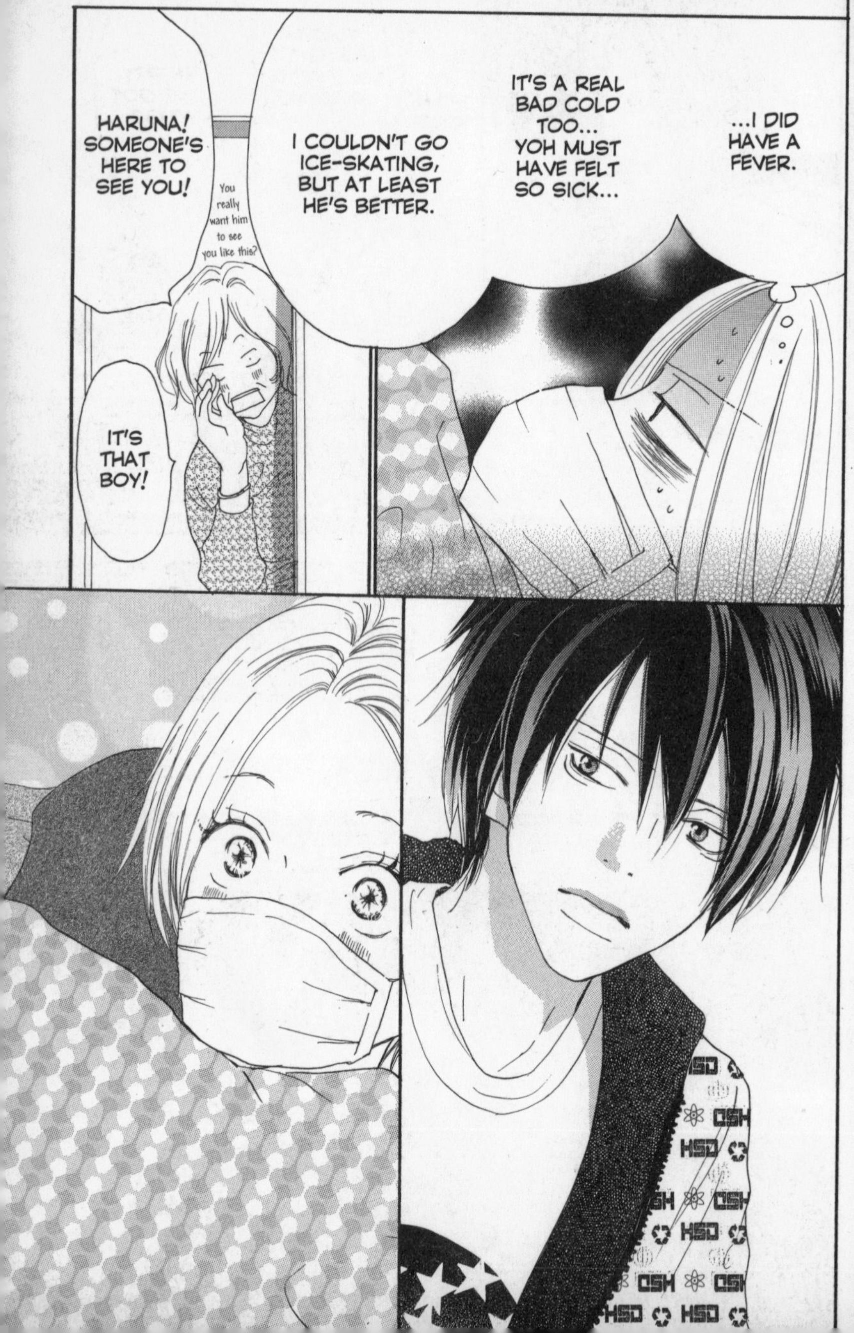
...I DID HAVE A FEVER.
IT'S A REAL BAD COLD TOO... YOH MUST HAVE FELT SO SICK...
I COULDN'T GO ICE-SKATING, BUT AT LEAST HE'S BETTER.
HARUNA! SOMEONE'S HERE TO SEE YOU!
You really want him to see you like this?
IT'S THAT BOY!

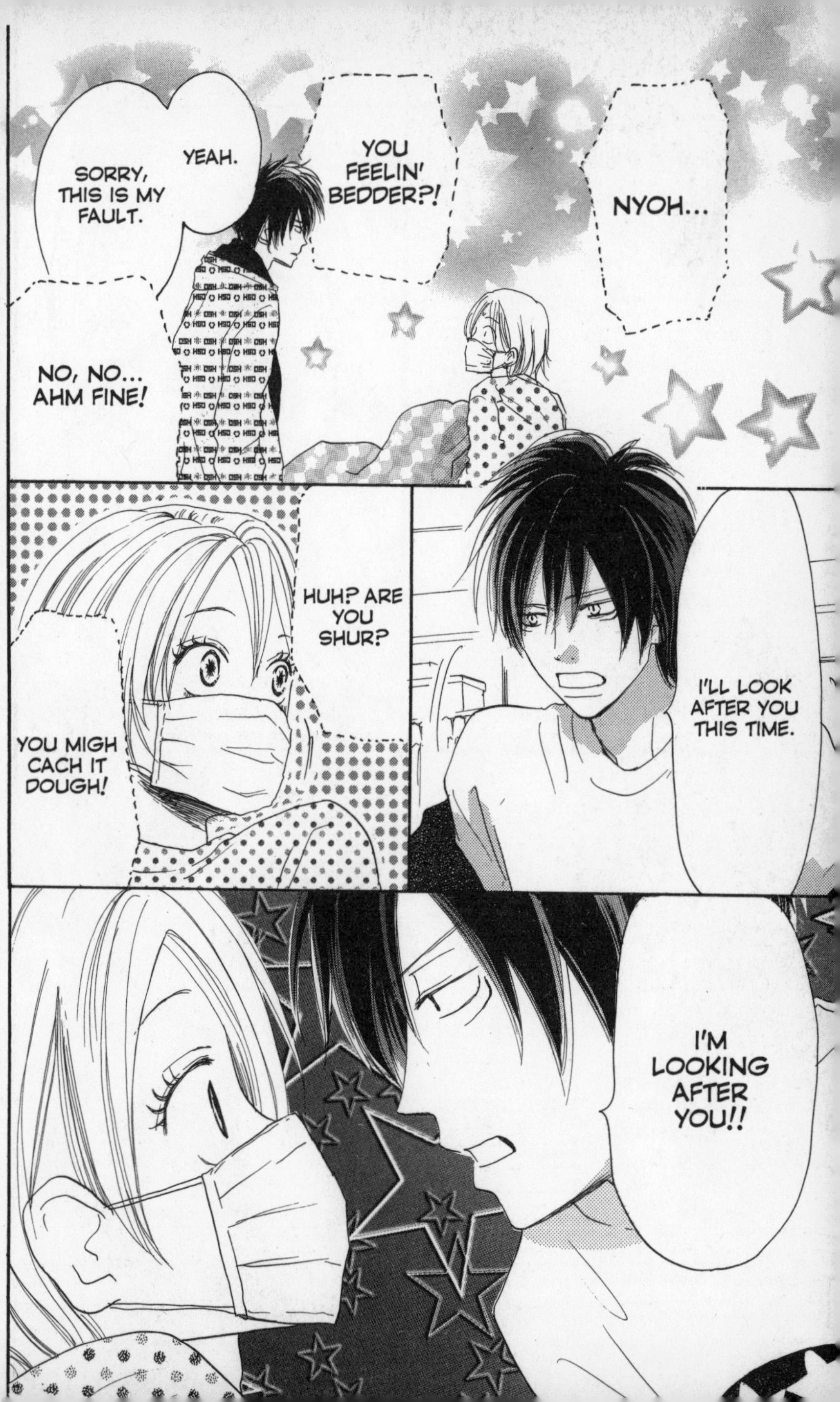
NYOH...
YOU FEELIN' BEDDER?!
YEAH.
SORRY, THIS IS MY FAULT.
NO, NO... AHM FINE!
I'LL LOOK AFTER YOU THIS TIME.
HUH? ARE YOU SHUR?
YOU MIGH CACH IT DOUGH!
I'M LOOKING AFTER YOU!!

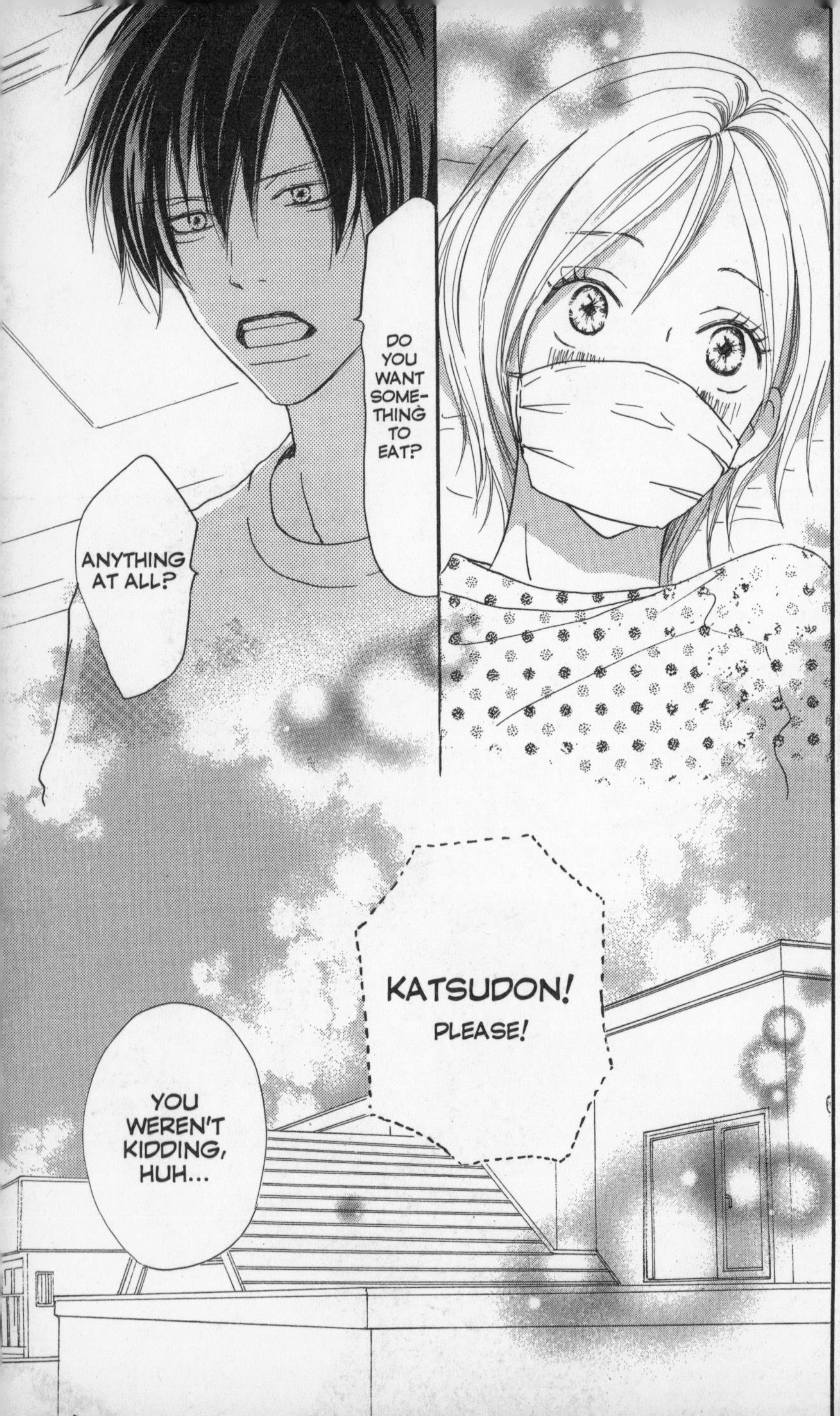
DO YOU WANT SOME-THING TO EAT?
ANYTHING AT ALL?
KATSUDON! PLEASE!
YOU WEREN'T KIDDING, HUH...

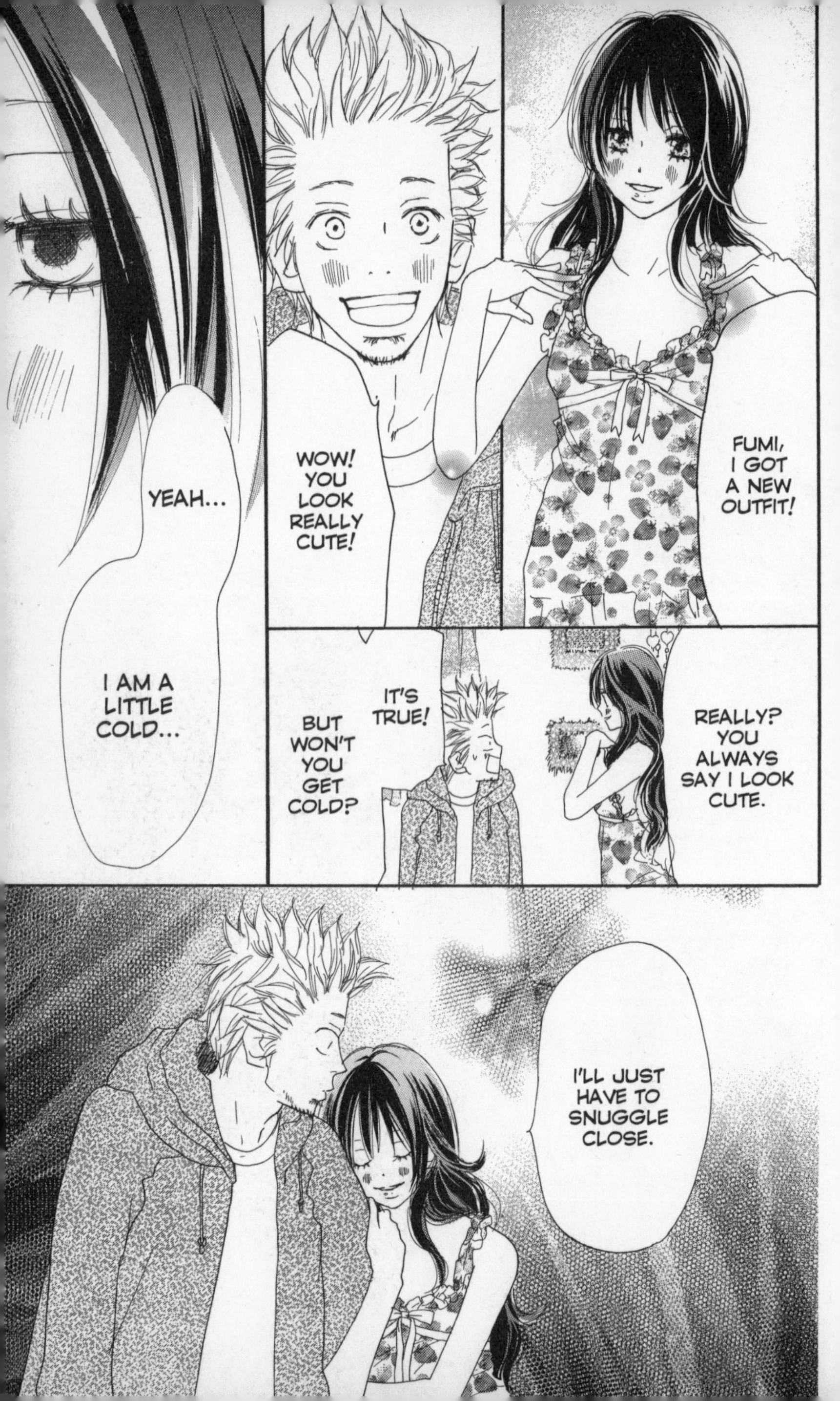

FUMI, I GOT A NEW OUTFIT!
WOW! YOU LOOK REALLY CUTE!
REALLY? YOU ALWAYS SAY I LOOK CUTE.
IT'S TRUE!
BUT WON'T YOU GET COLD?
YEAH...
I AM A LITTLE COLD...
I'LL JUST HAVE TO SNUGGLE CLOSE.

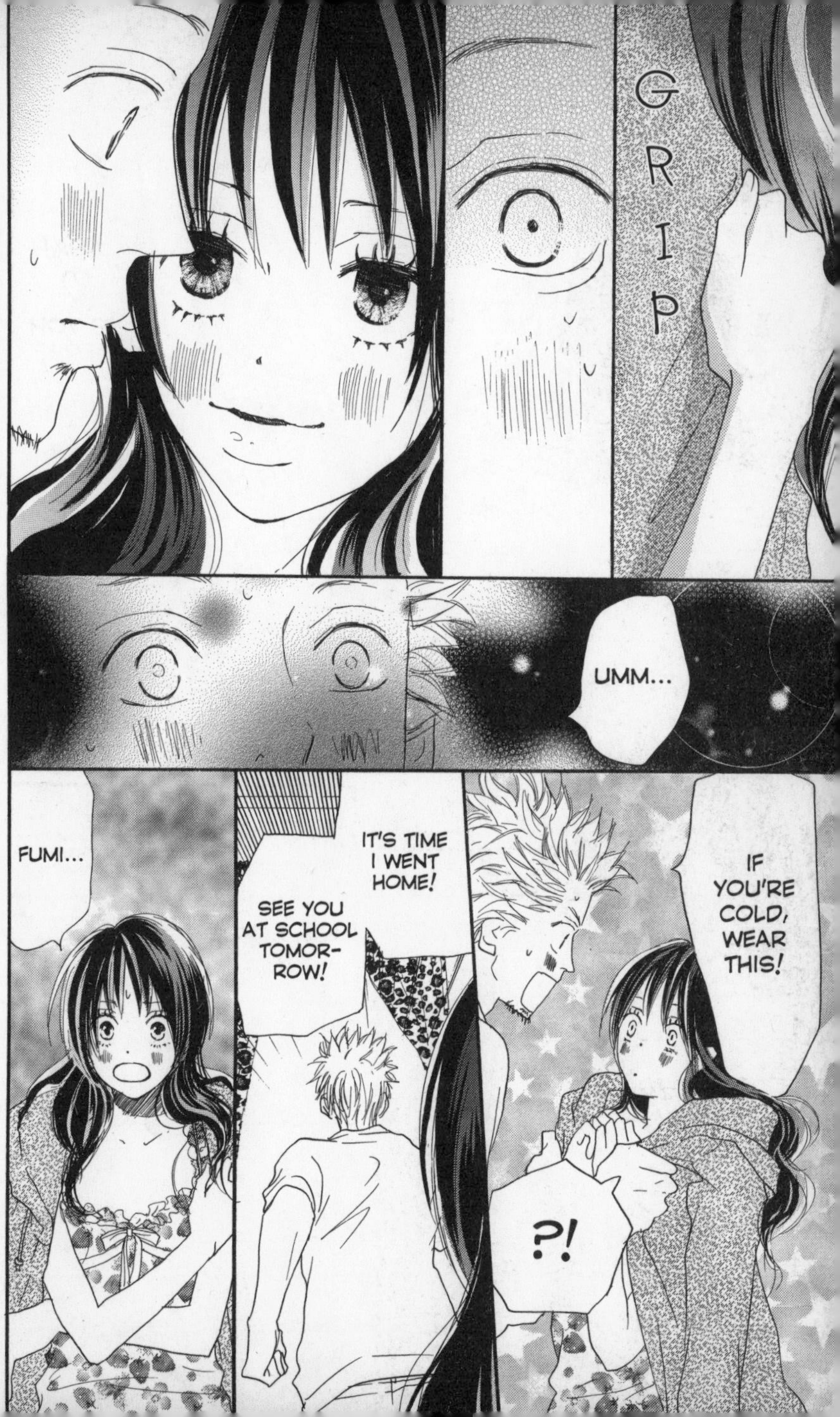
GRIP
UMM...
IF YOU'RE COLD, WEAR THIS!
?!
IT'S TIME I WENT HOME!
SEE YOU AT SCHOOL TOMOR-ROW!
FUMI...

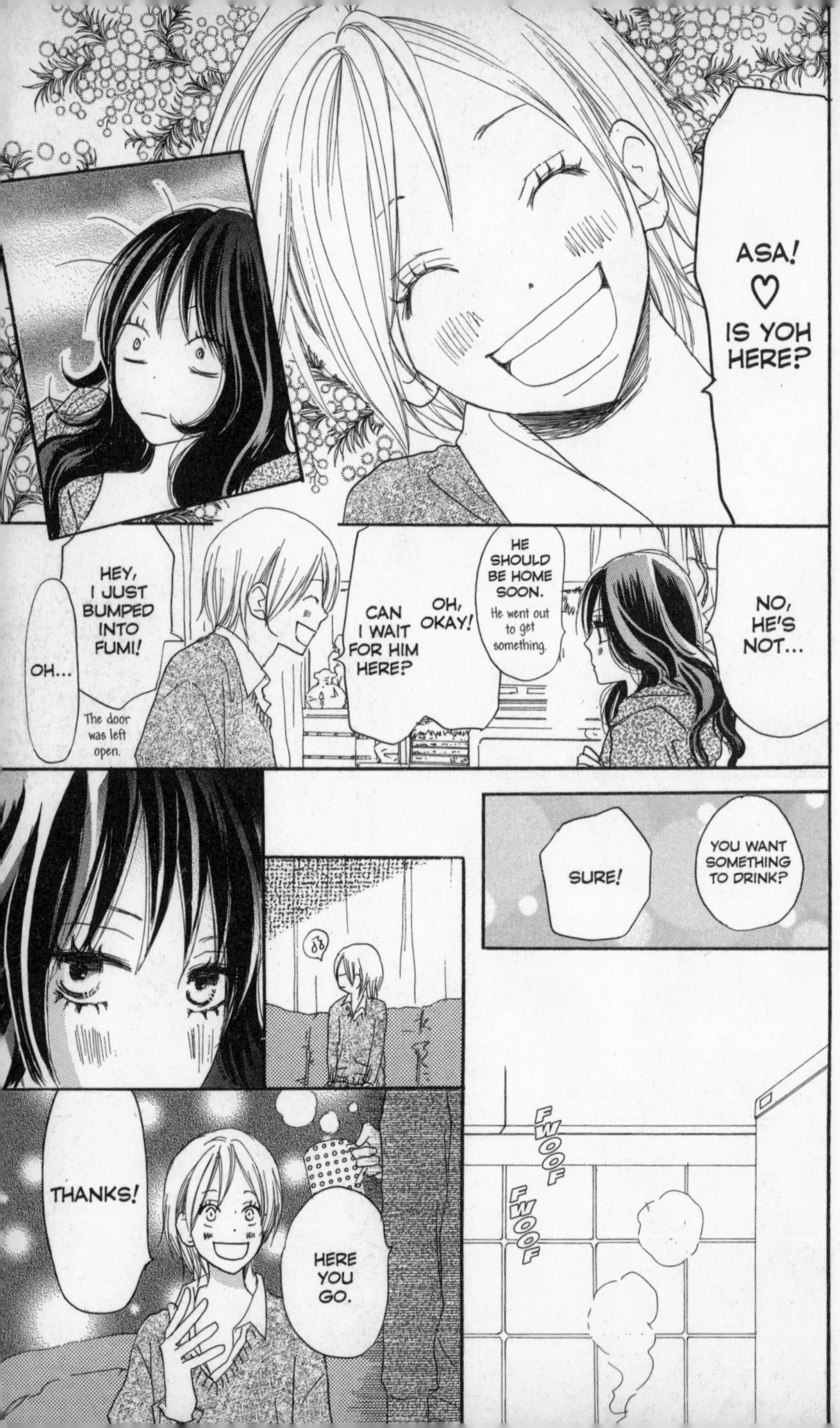
ASA! ♡ IS YOH HERE?
NO, HE'S NOT...
HE SHOULD BE HOME SOON.
He went out to get something.
OH, OKAY!
CAN I WAIT FOR HIM HERE?
HEY, I JUST BUMPED INTO FUMI!
OH...
The door was left open.
YOU WANT SOMETHING TO DRINK?
SURE!
FWOOF
FWOOF
HERE YOU GO.
THANKS!

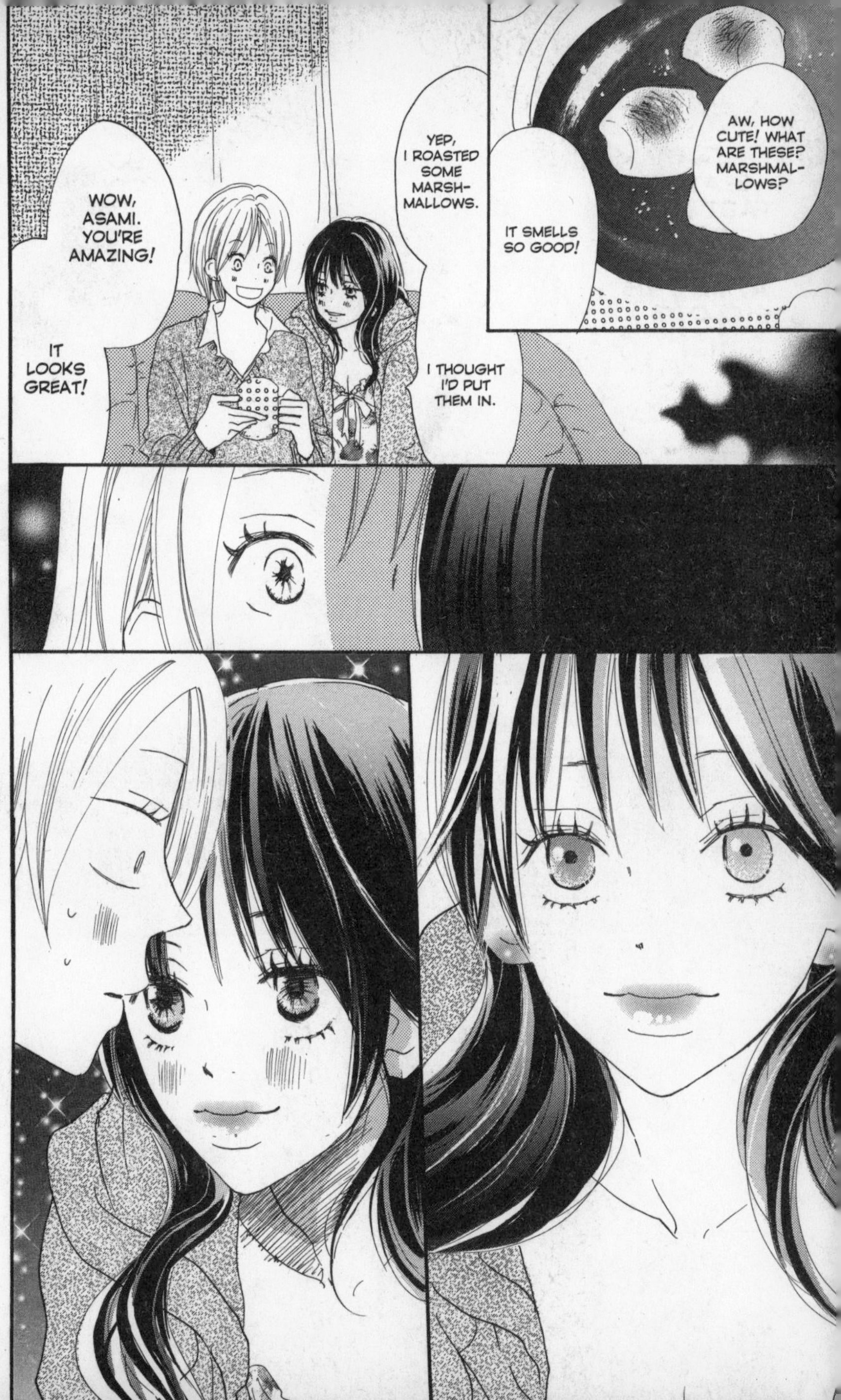
AW, HOW CUTE! WHAT ARE THESE? MARSHMAL-LOWS?
IT SMELLS SO GOOD!
YEP, I ROASTED SOME MARSH-MALLOWS.
I THOUGHT I'D PUT THEM IN.
WOW, ASAMI. YOU'RE AMAZING!
IT LOOKS GREAT!

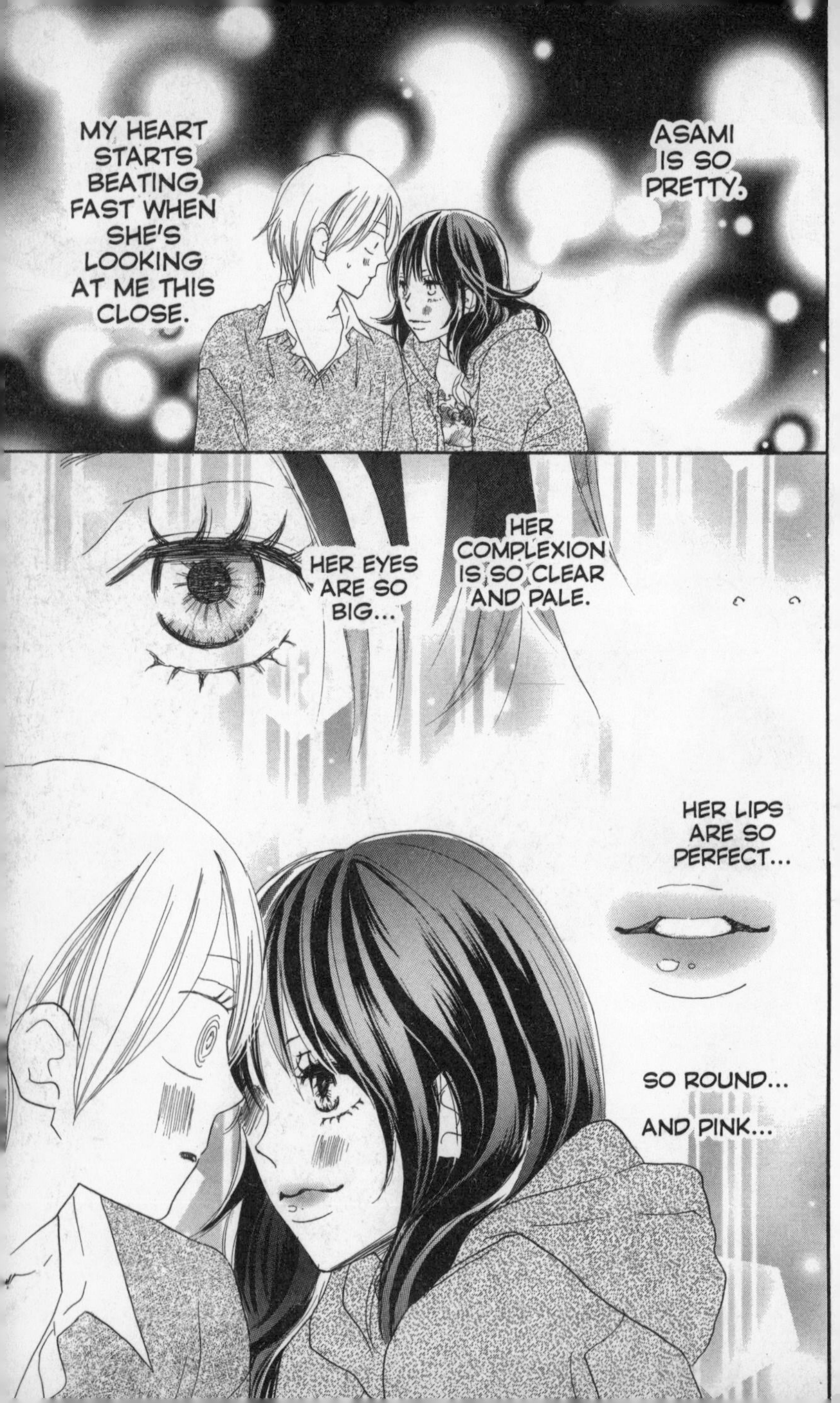
ASAMI IS SO PRETTY.
MY HEART STARTS BEATING FAST WHEN SHE'S LOOKING AT ME THIS CLOSE.
HER COMPLEXION IS SO CLEAR AND PALE.
HER EYES ARE SO BIG...
HER LIPS ARE SO PERFECT...
SO ROUND...
AND PINK...

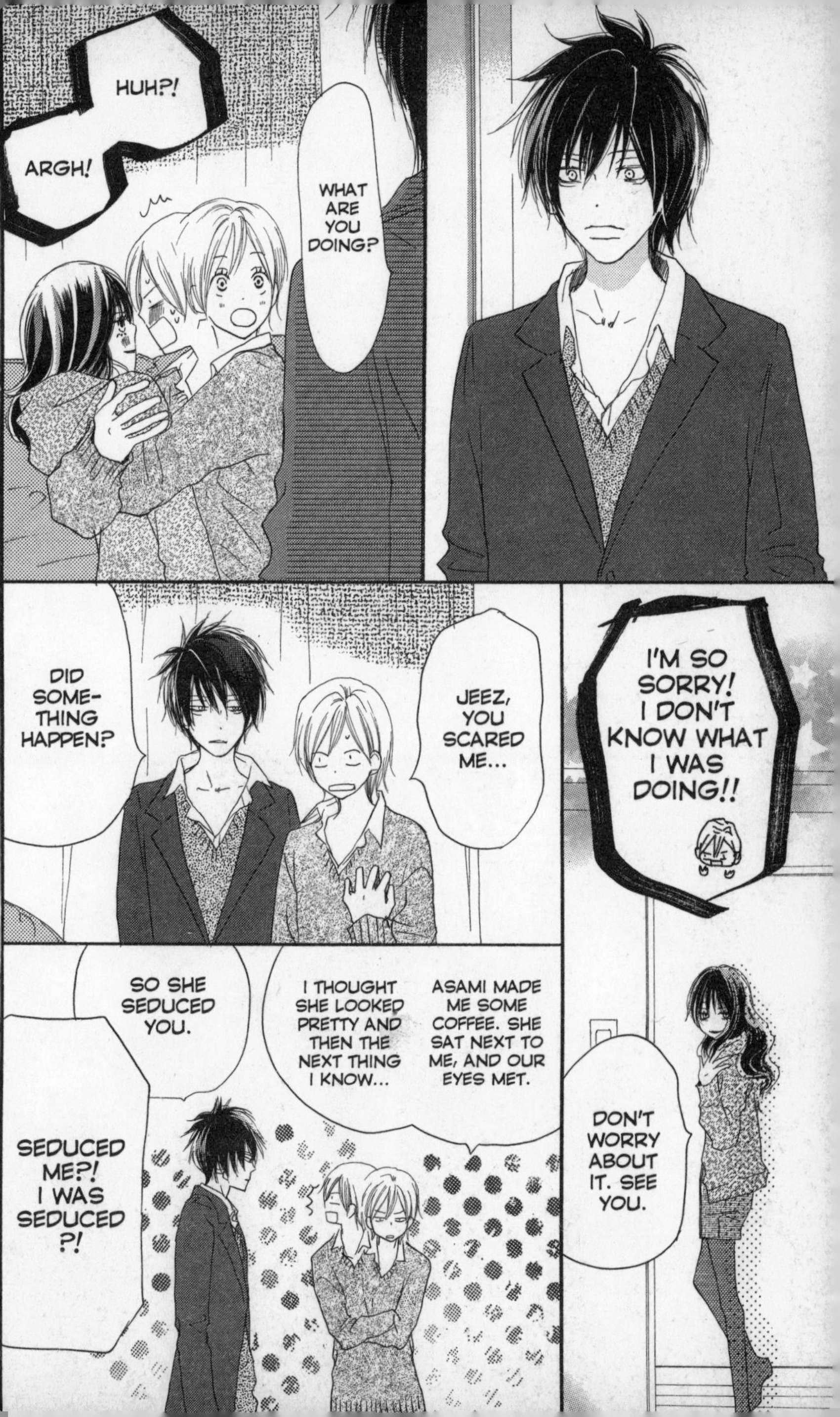
WHAT ARE YOU DOING?
HUH?!
ARGH!
I'M SO SORRY! I DON'T KNOW WHAT I WAS DOING!!
DON'T WORRY ABOUT IT. SEE YOU.
JEEZ, YOU SCARED ME...
DID SOME-THING HAPPEN?
ASAMI MADE ME SOME COFFEE. SHE SAT NEXT TO ME, AND OUR EYES MET.
I THOUGHT SHE LOOKED PRETTY AND THEN THE NEXT THING I KNOW...
SO SHE SEDUCED YOU.
SEDUCED ME?! I WAS SEDUCED ?!

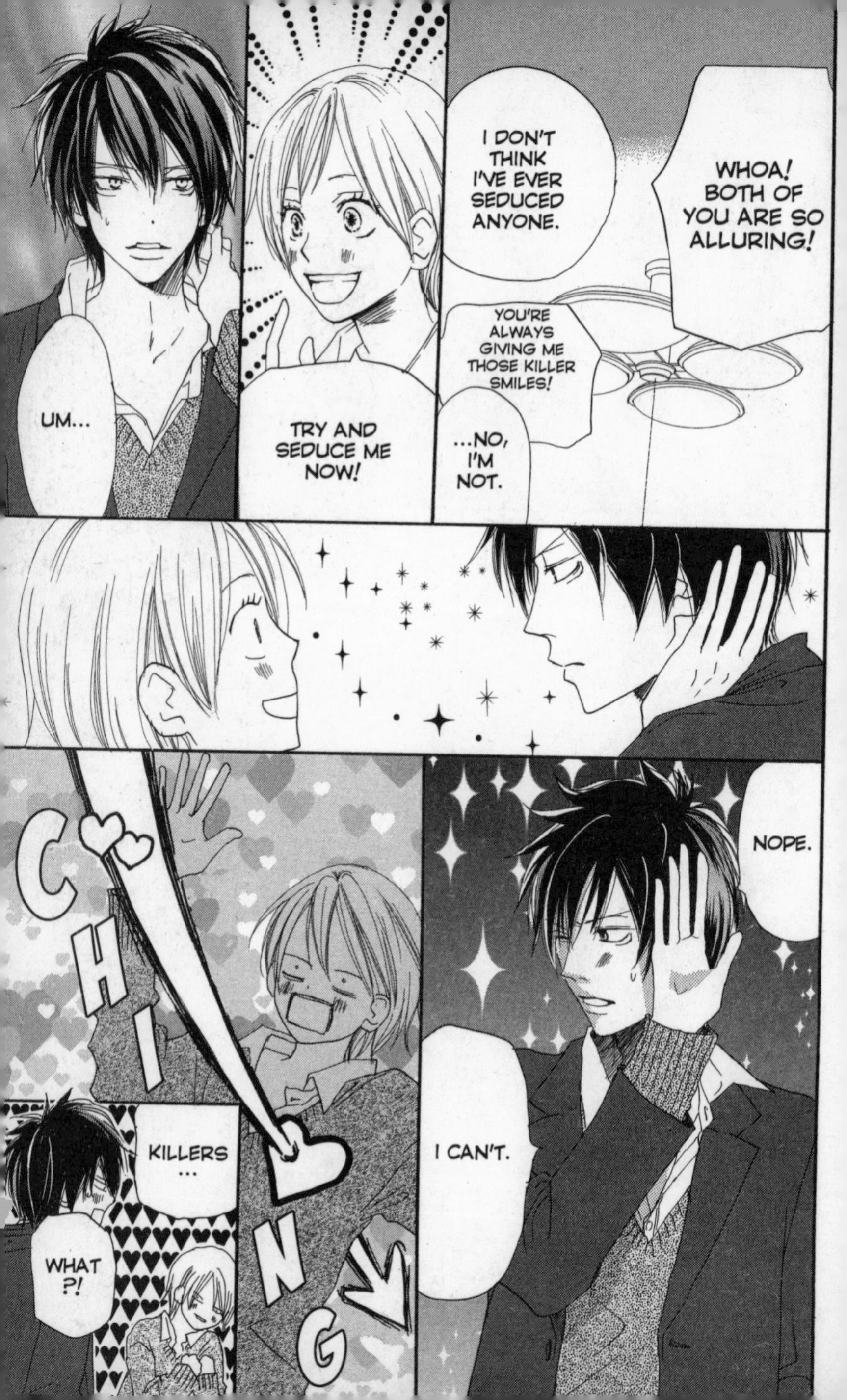
WHOA! BOTH OF YOU ARE SO ALLURING!
YOU'RE ALWAYS GIVING ME THOSE KILLER SMILES!
...NO, I'M NOT.
I DON'T THINK I'VE EVER SEDUCED ANYONE.
TRY AND SEDUCE ME NOW!
UM...
NOPE.
I CAN'T.
CHING
KILLERS ...
WHAT ?!

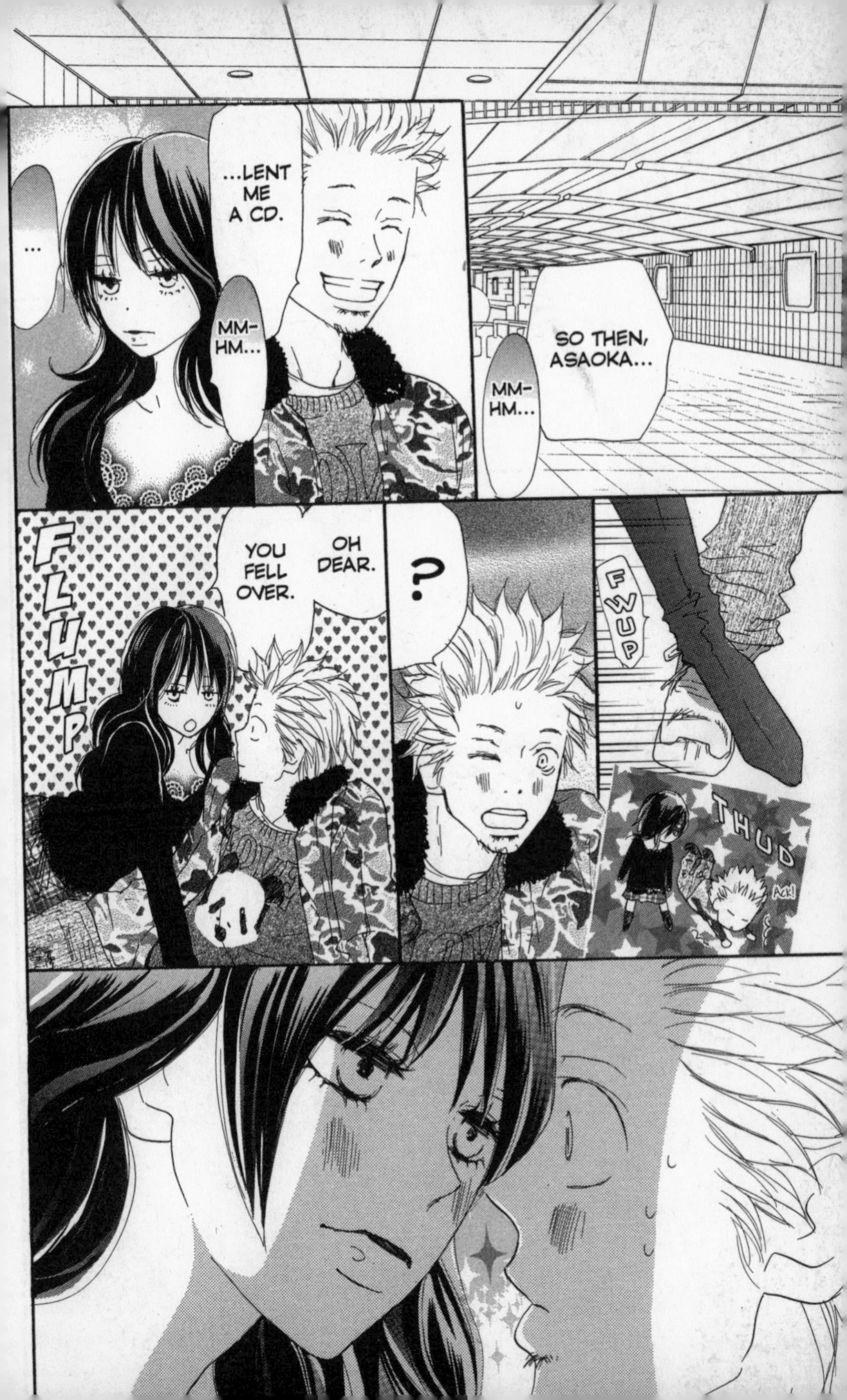
SO THEN, ASAOKA...
MM-HM...
...LENT ME A CD.
MM-HM...
...
FWUP
THUD
Ack!
?
OH DEAR.
YOU FELL OVER.
FLUMP

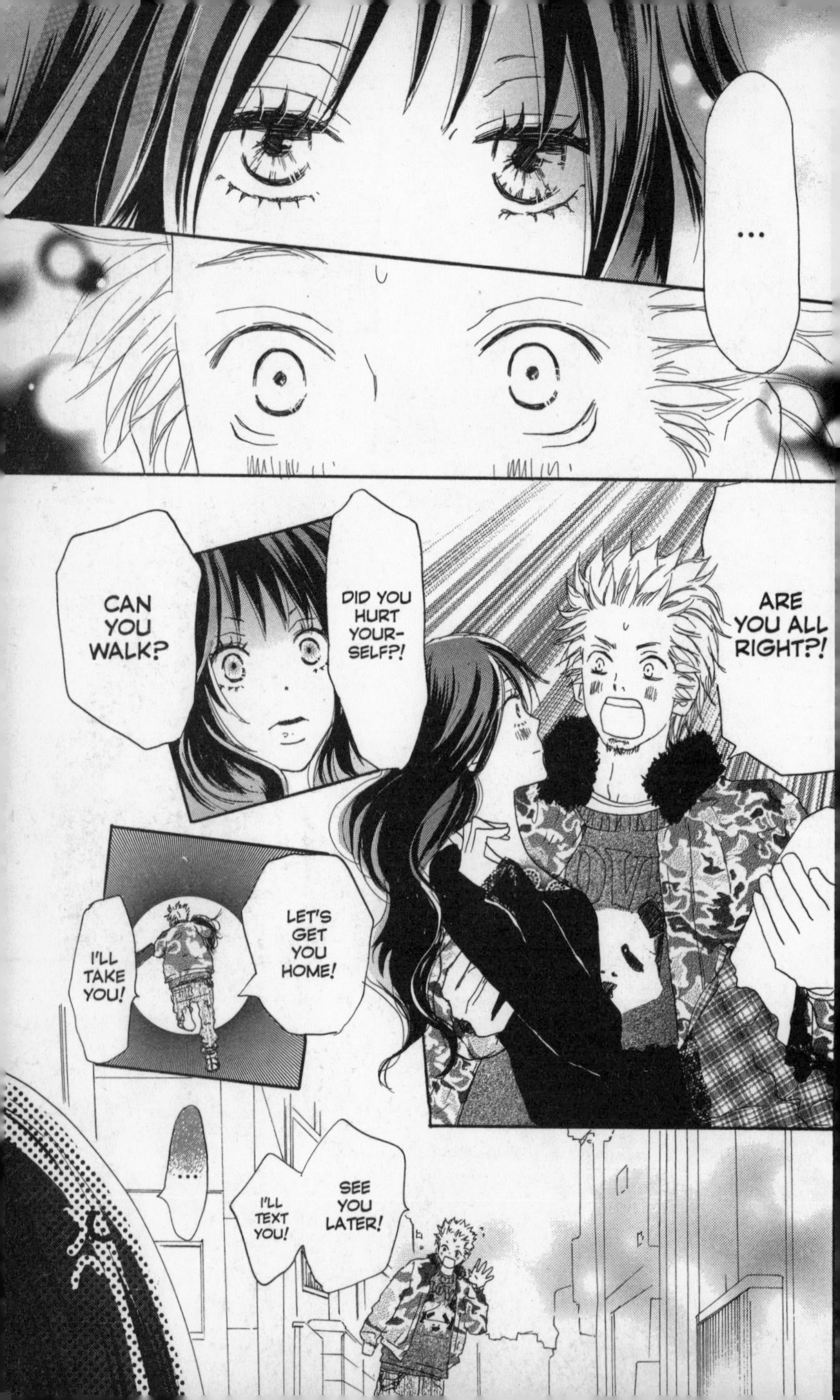
...
ARE YOU ALL RIGHT?!
DID YOU HURT YOURSELF?!
CAN YOU WALK?
LET'S GET YOU HOME!
I'LL TAKE YOU!
SEE YOU LATER!
I'LL TEXT YOU!
...

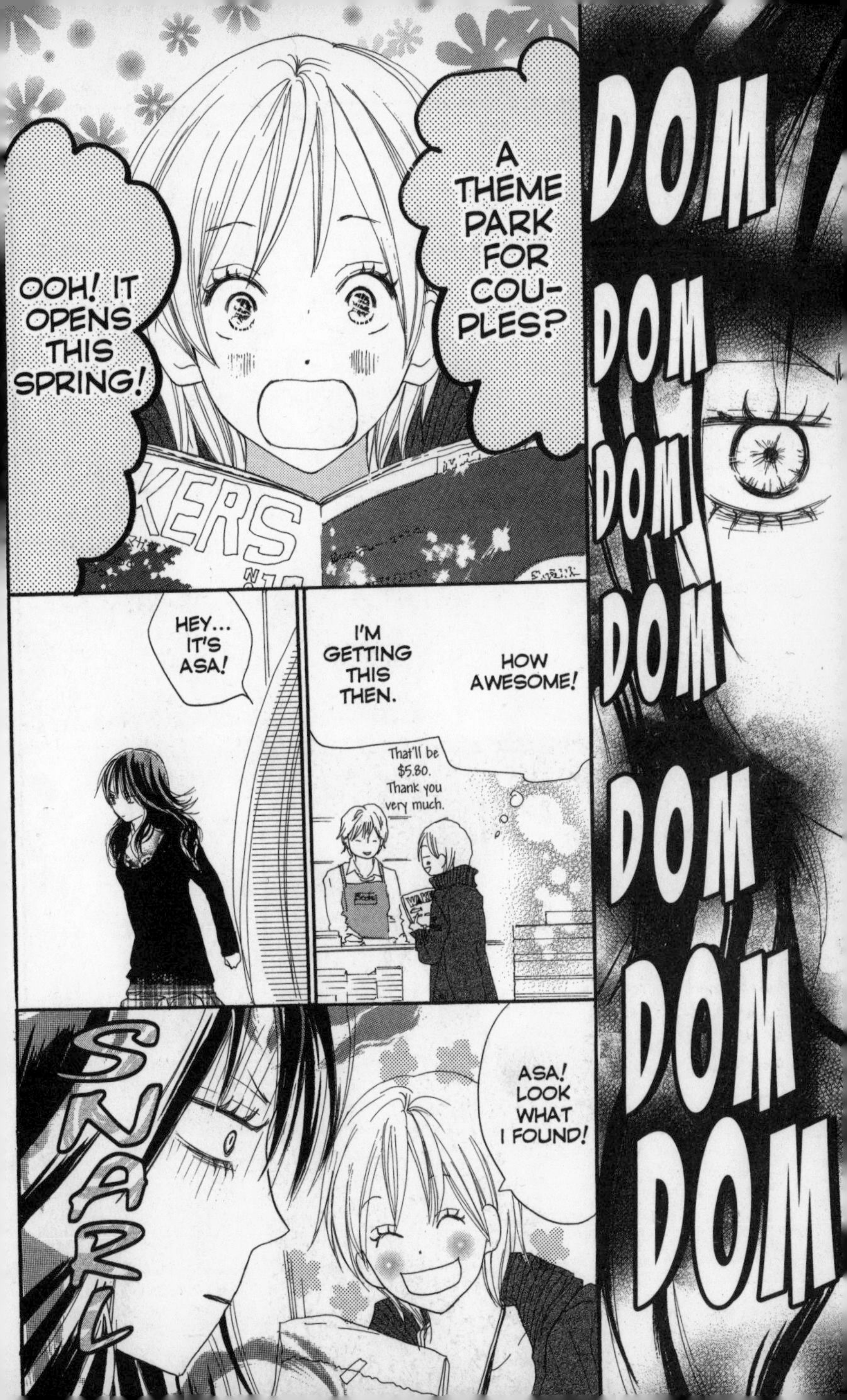
A THEME PARK FOR COU-PLES?
OOH! IT OPENS THIS SPRING!
HOW AWESOME!
I'M GETTING THIS THEN.
That'll be $5.80. Thank you very much.
HEY... IT'S ASA!
ASA! LOOK WHAT I FOUND!
SNARL
DOM DOM DOM DOM DOM DOM DOM

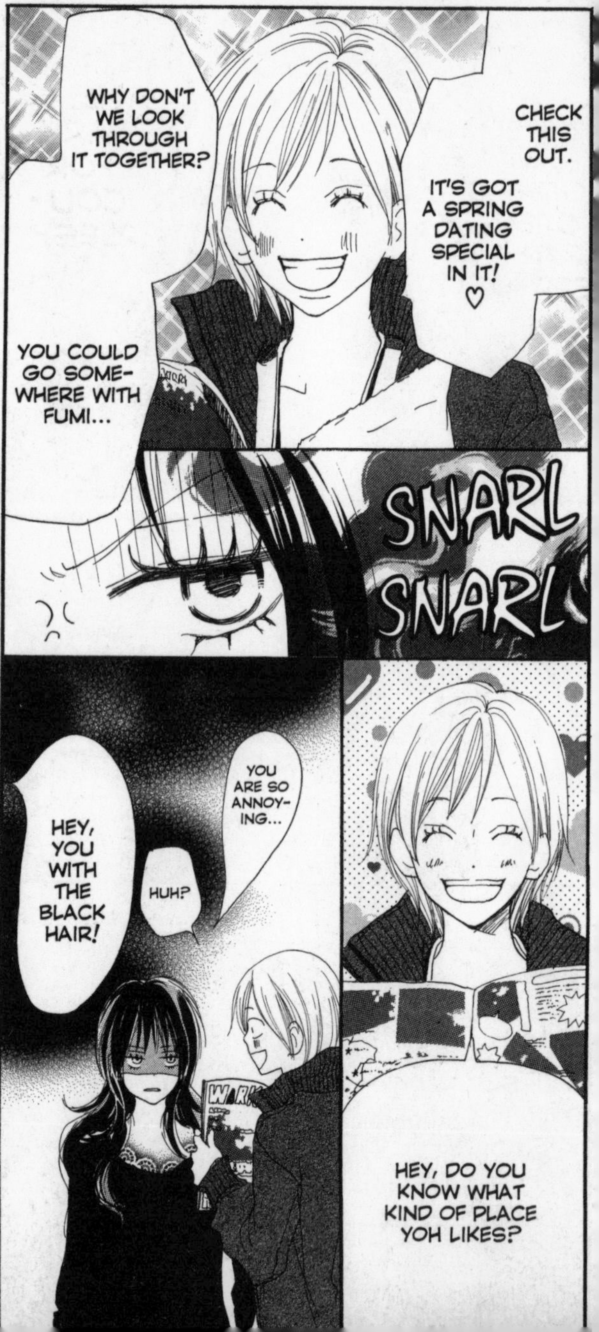
CHECK THIS OUT.
IT'S GOT A SPRING DATING SPECIAL IN IT! ♡
WHY DON'T WE LOOK THROUGH IT TOGETHER?
YOU COULD GO SOMEWHERE WITH FUMI...
SNARL SNARL
HEY, DO YOU KNOW WHAT KIND OF PLACE YOH LIKES?
YOU ARE SO ANNOYING...
HUH?
HEY, YOU WITH THE BLACK HAIR!

2

I've been working nonstop and finally my PC gave out. When I turned it on today, I got this:

> ⓧ
> A serious error has occurred.

I had no idea what to do! Well there wasn't much else to do but to go shopping.

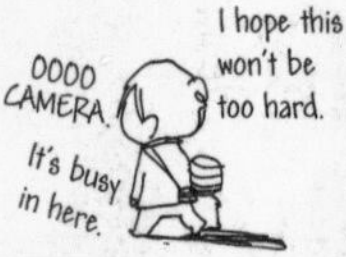
I hope this won't be too hard.
OOOO CAMERA.
It's busy in here.

Anyway, I've become so ditzy recently I've forgotten how old I am. I'm probably ●● years old. I know there are lots of things you can get to help your brain.

I think a serious error has occurred in my brain though.

At least I always know what year it is because I write it so often! It's 2006! It is...right? Right...?

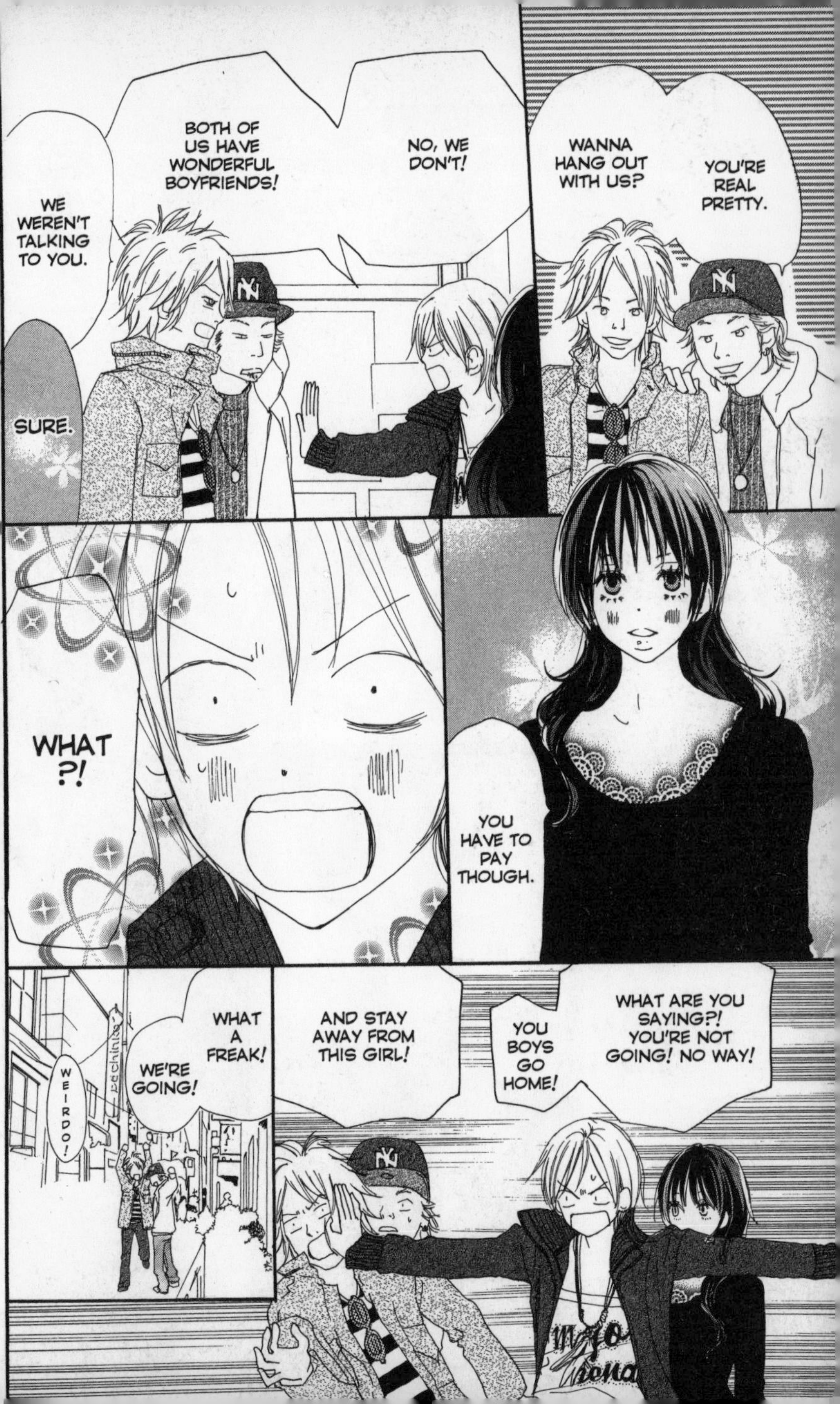
YOU'RE REAL PRETTY.
WANNA HANG OUT WITH US?
NO, WE DON'T!
BOTH OF US HAVE WONDERFUL BOYFRIENDS!
WE WEREN'T TALKING TO YOU.
SURE.
YOU HAVE TO PAY THOUGH.
WHAT ?!
WHAT ARE YOU SAYING?! YOU'RE NOT GOING! NO WAY!
YOU BOYS GO HOME!
AND STAY AWAY FROM THIS GIRL!
WHAT A FREAK!
WE'RE GOING!
WEIRDO!

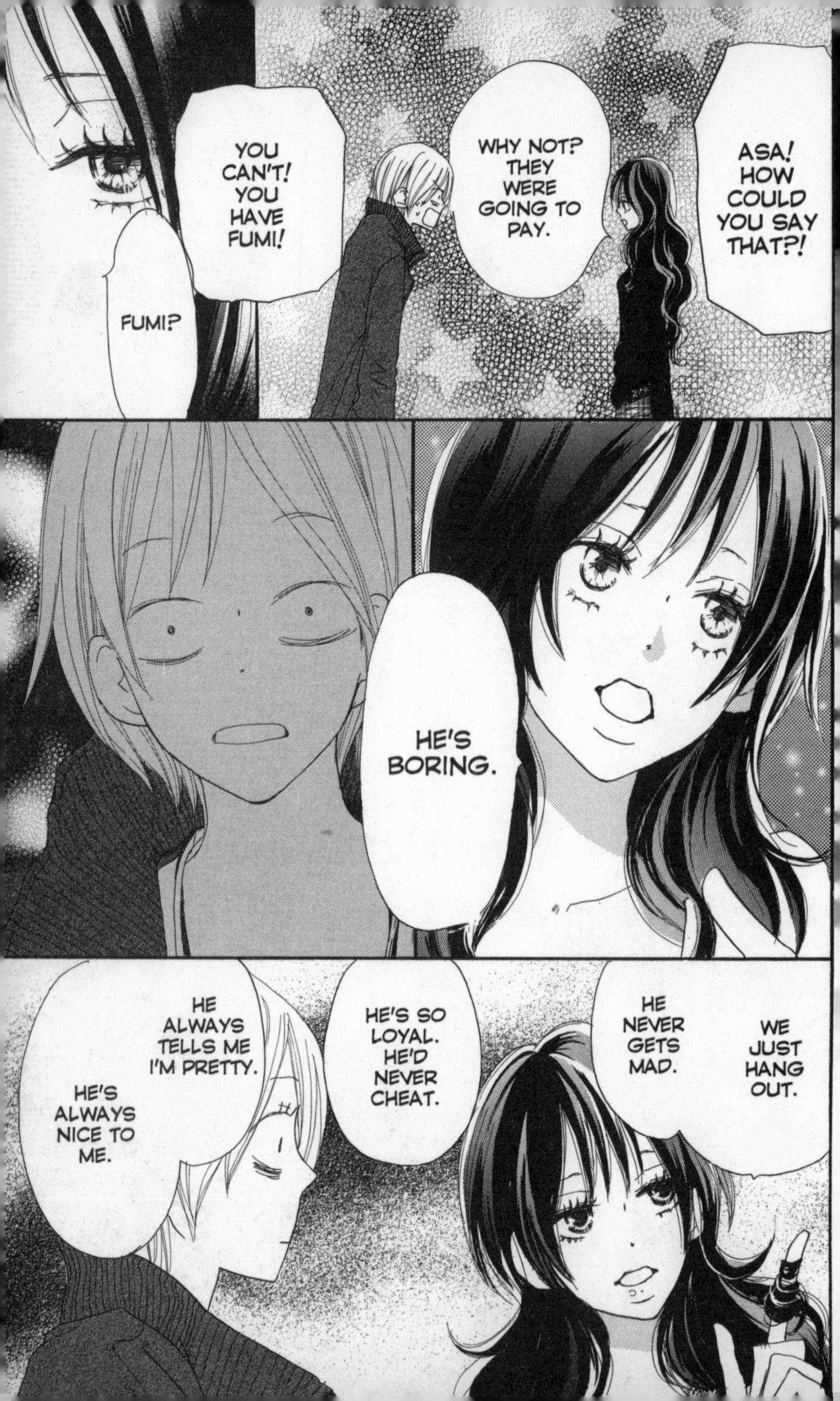
ASA! HOW COULD YOU SAY THAT?!
WHY NOT? THEY WERE GOING TO PAY.
YOU CAN'T! YOU HAVE FUMI!
FUMI?
HE'S BORING.
WE JUST HANG OUT.
HE NEVER GETS MAD.
HE'S SO LOYAL. HE'D NEVER CHEAT.
HE ALWAYS TELLS ME I'M PRETTY.
HE'S ALWAYS NICE TO ME.

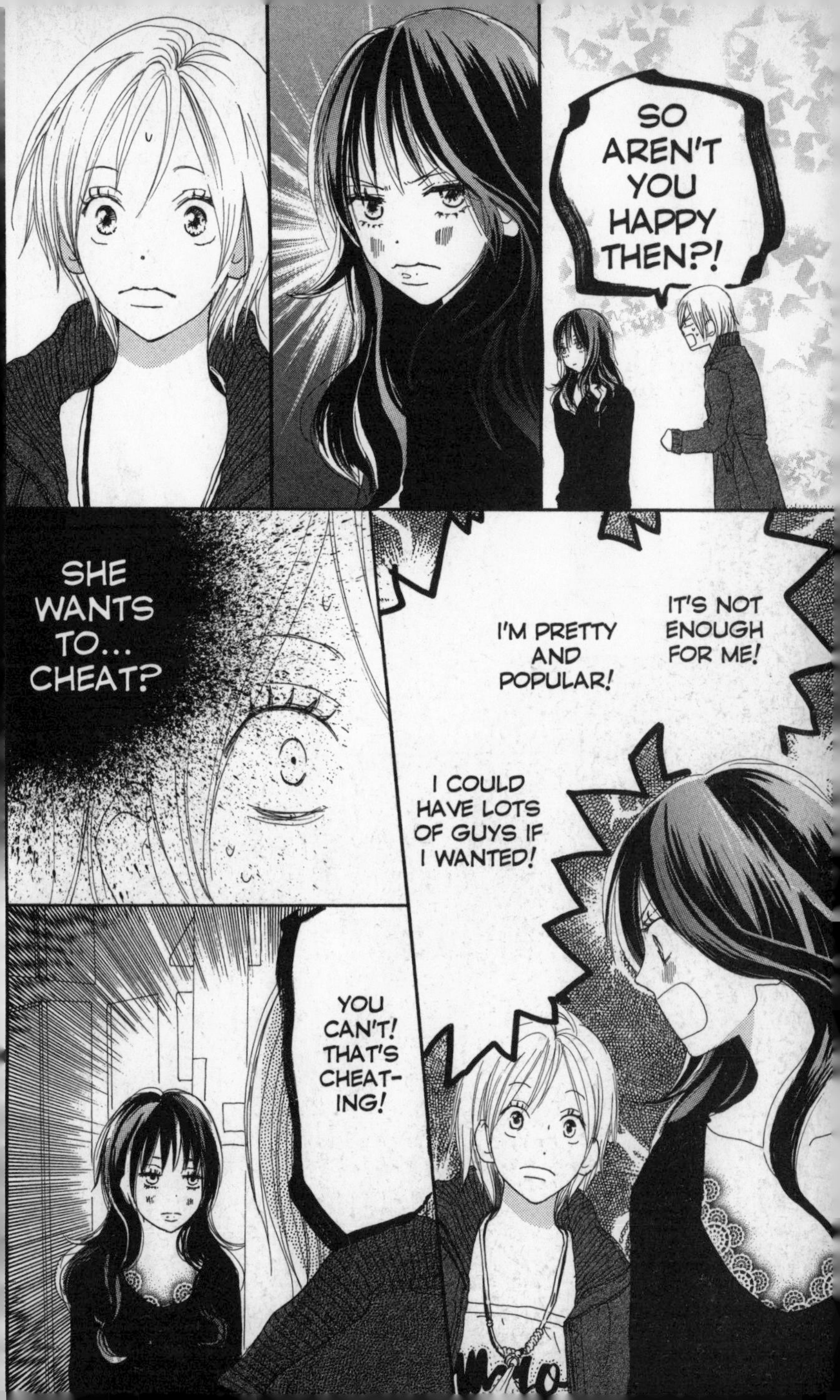
SO AREN'T YOU HAPPY THEN?!
IT'S NOT ENOUGH FOR ME!
I'M PRETTY AND POPULAR!
I COULD HAVE LOTS OF GUYS IF I WANTED!
SHE WANTS TO... CHEAT?
YOU CAN'T! THAT'S CHEAT-ING!

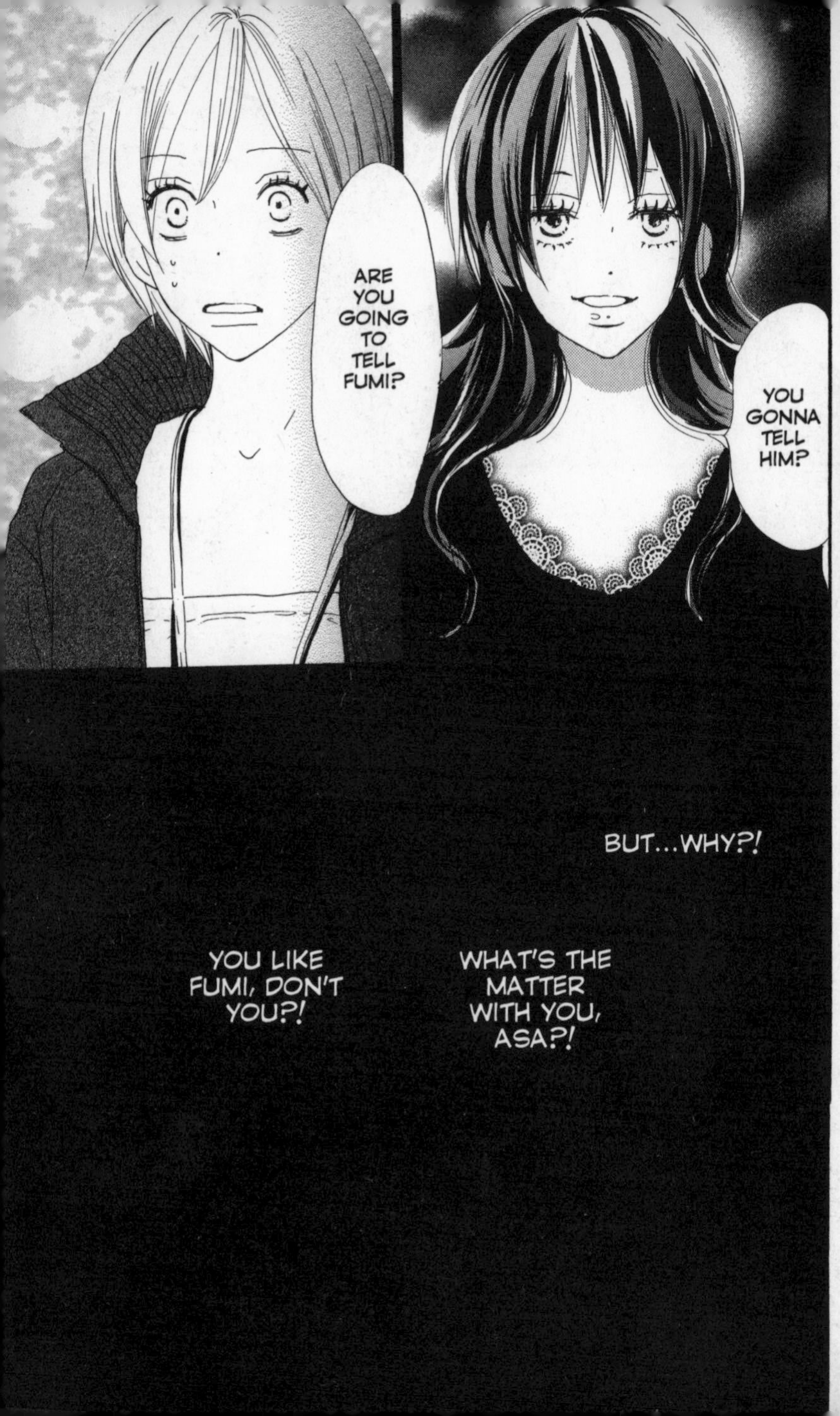
YOU GONNA TELL HIM?
ARE YOU GOING TO TELL FUMI?
BUT...WHY?!
WHAT'S THE MATTER WITH YOU, ASA?!
YOU LIKE FUMI, DON'T YOU?!

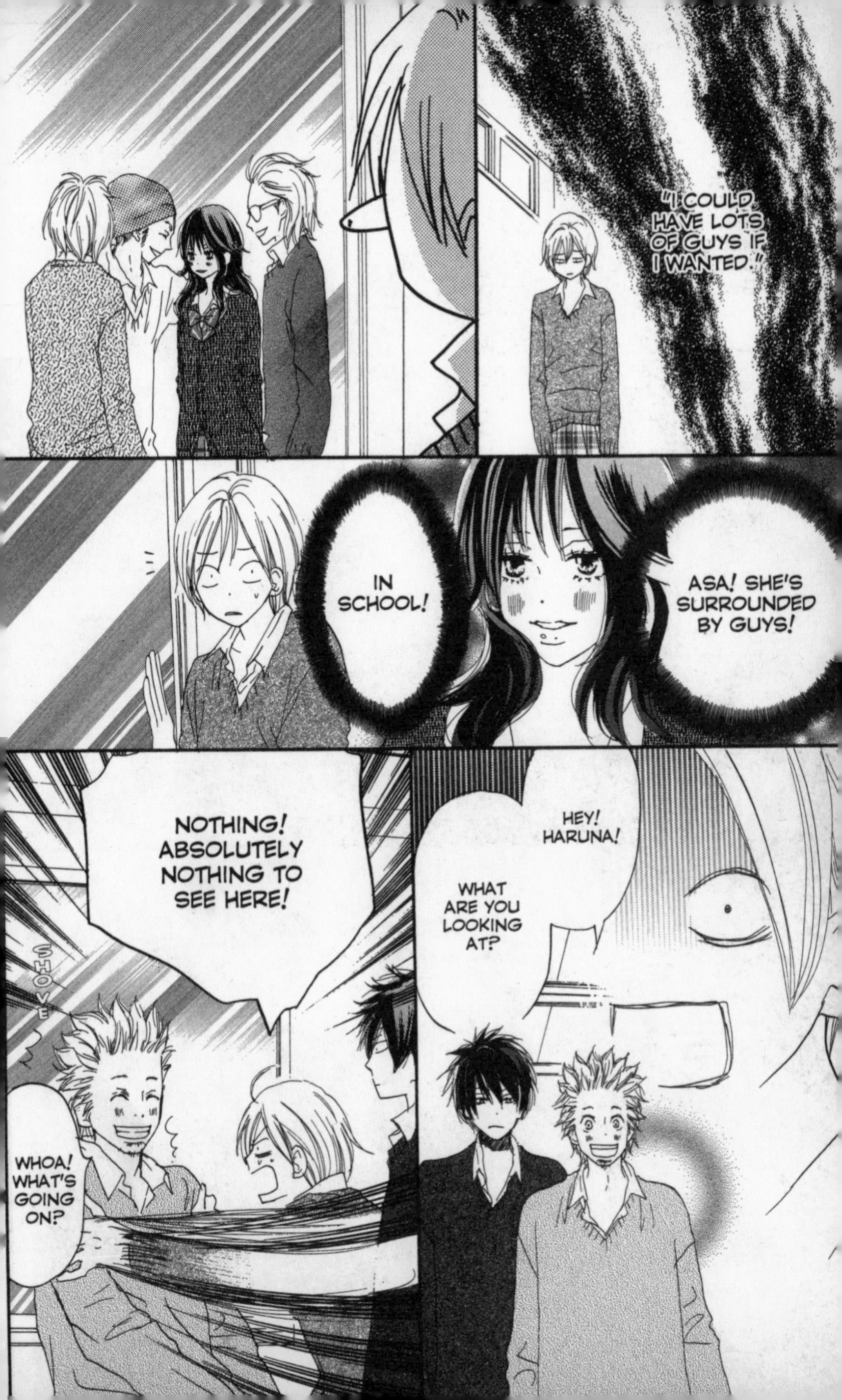
"I COULD HAVE LOTS OF GUYS IF I WANTED."
ASA! SHE'S SURROUNDED BY GUYS!
IN SCHOOL!
HEY! HARUNA!
WHAT ARE YOU LOOKING AT?
NOTHING! ABSOLUTELY NOTHING TO SEE HERE!
SHOVE
WHOA! WHAT'S GOING ON?

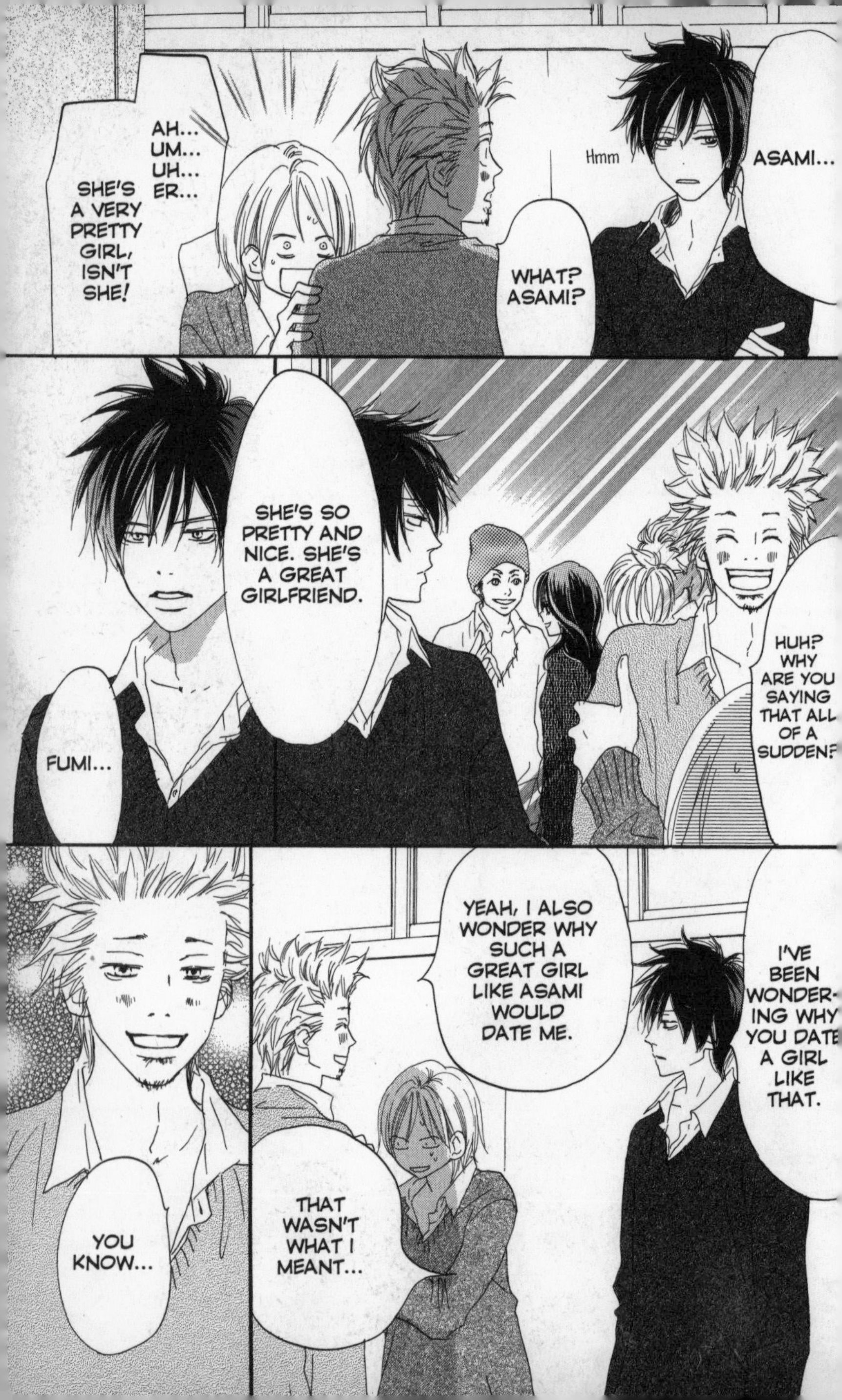
ASAMI...
Hmm
WHAT? ASAMI?
AH... UM... UH... ER...
SHE'S A VERY PRETTY GIRL, ISN'T SHE!
FUMI...
SHE'S SO PRETTY AND NICE. SHE'S A GREAT GIRLFRIEND.
HUH? WHY ARE YOU SAYING THAT ALL OF A SUDDEN?
I'VE BEEN WONDER-ING WHY YOU DATE A GIRL LIKE THAT.
YEAH, I ALSO WONDER WHY SUCH A GREAT GIRL LIKE ASAMI WOULD DATE ME.
THAT WASN'T WHAT I MEANT...
YOU KNOW...

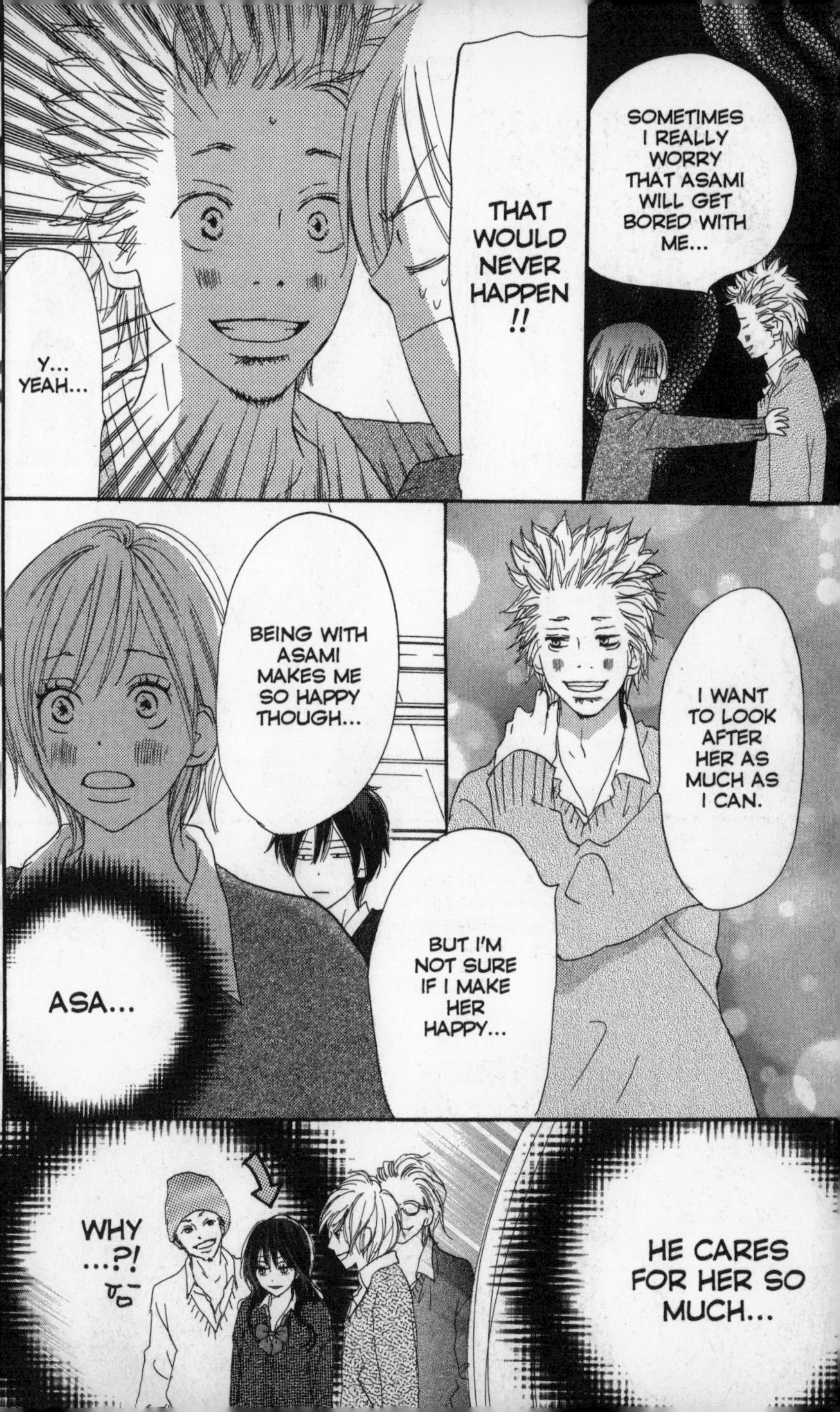
SOMETIMES I REALLY WORRY THAT ASAMI WILL GET BORED WITH ME...
THAT WOULD NEVER HAPPEN !!
Y... YEAH...
I WANT TO LOOK AFTER HER AS MUCH AS I CAN.
BUT I'M NOT SURE IF I MAKE HER HAPPY...
BEING WITH ASAMI MAKES ME SO HAPPY THOUGH...
ASA...
HE CARES FOR HER SO MUCH...
WHY ...?!

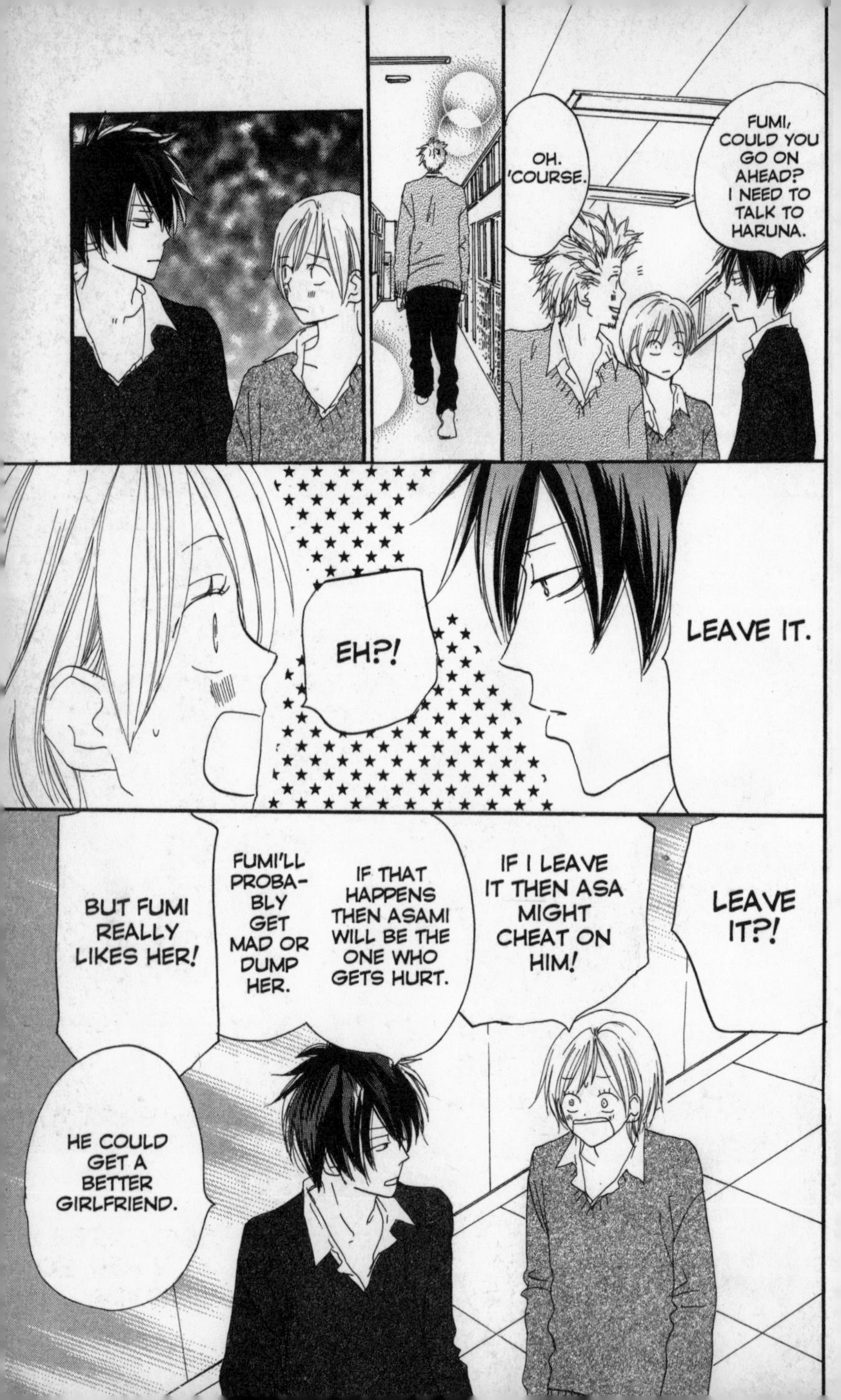
FUMI, COULD YOU GO ON AHEAD? I NEED TO TALK TO HARUNA.
OH. 'COURSE.
LEAVE IT.
EH?!
LEAVE IT?!
IF I LEAVE IT THEN ASA MIGHT CHEAT ON HIM!
IF THAT HAPPENS THEN ASAMI WILL BE THE ONE WHO GETS HURT.
FUMI'LL PROBA-BLY GET MAD OR DUMP HER.
BUT FUMI REALLY LIKES HER!
HE COULD GET A BETTER GIRLFRIEND.

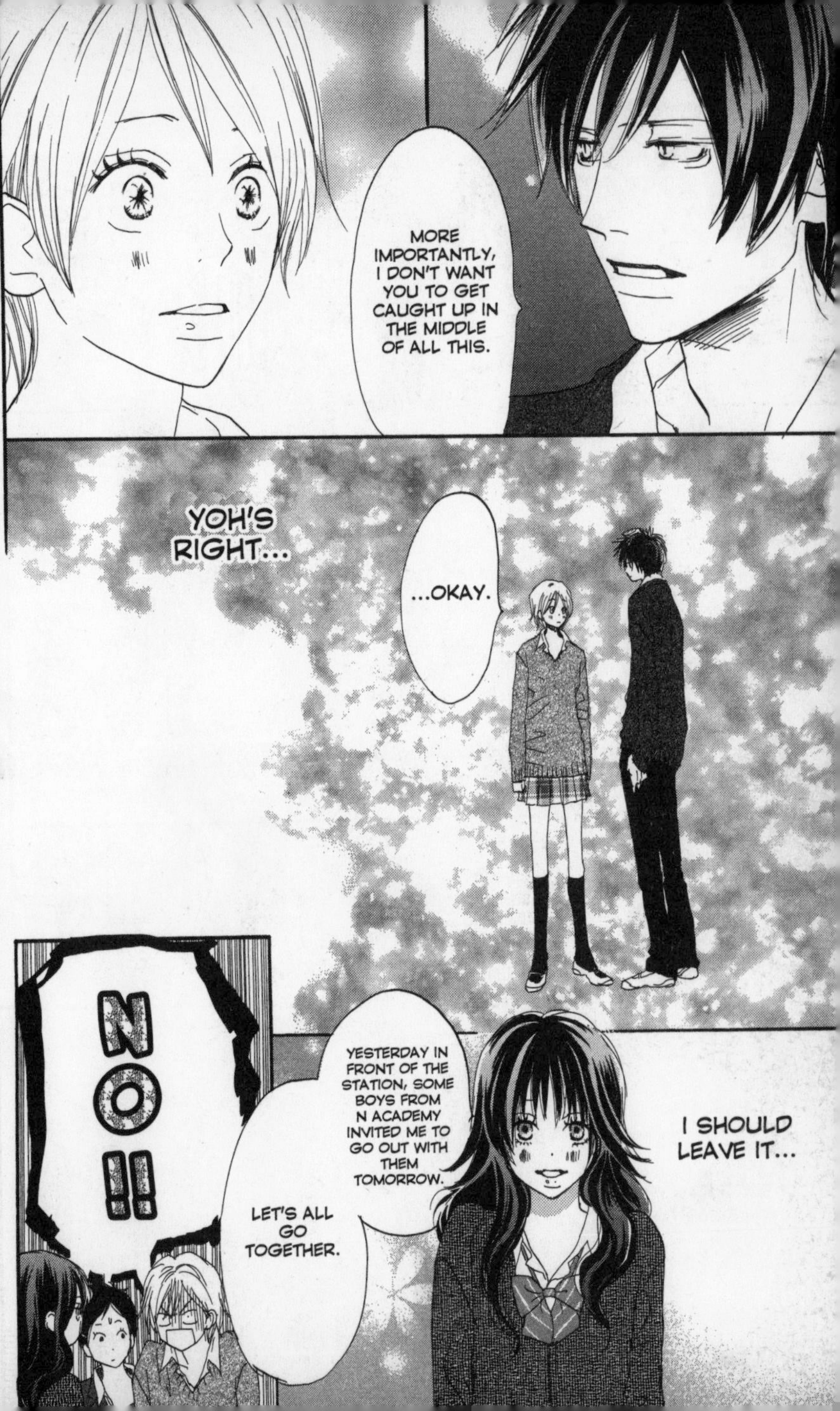
MORE IMPORTANTLY, I DON'T WANT YOU TO GET CAUGHT UP IN THE MIDDLE OF ALL THIS.
...OKAY.
YOH'S RIGHT...
I SHOULD LEAVE IT...
YESTERDAY IN FRONT OF THE STATION, SOME BOYS FROM N ACADEMY INVITED ME TO GO OUT WITH THEM TOMORROW.
LET'S ALL GO TOGETHER.
NO!!

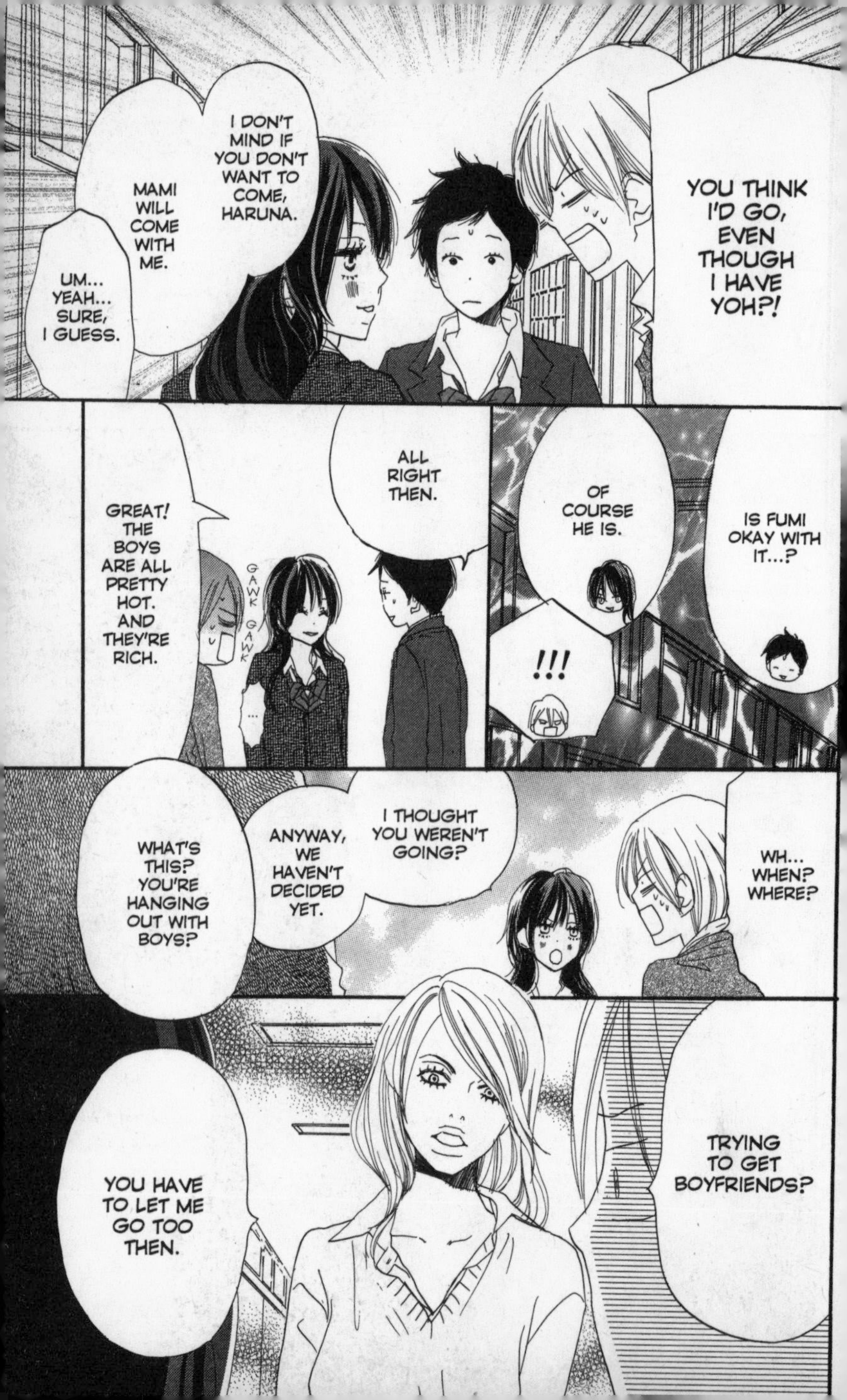
YOU THINK I'D GO, EVEN THOUGH I HAVE YOH?!
I DON'T MIND IF YOU DON'T WANT TO COME, HARUNA.
MAMI WILL COME WITH ME.
UM... YEAH... SURE, I GUESS.
IS FUMI OKAY WITH IT...?
OF COURSE HE IS.
!!!
ALL RIGHT THEN.
GREAT! THE BOYS ARE ALL PRETTY HOT. AND THEY'RE RICH.
GAWK GAWK
...
WH... WHEN? WHERE?
I THOUGHT YOU WEREN'T GOING?
ANYWAY, WE HAVEN'T DECIDED YET.
WHAT'S THIS? YOU'RE HANGING OUT WITH BOYS?
TRYING TO GET BOYFRIENDS?
YOU HAVE TO LET ME GO TOO THEN.

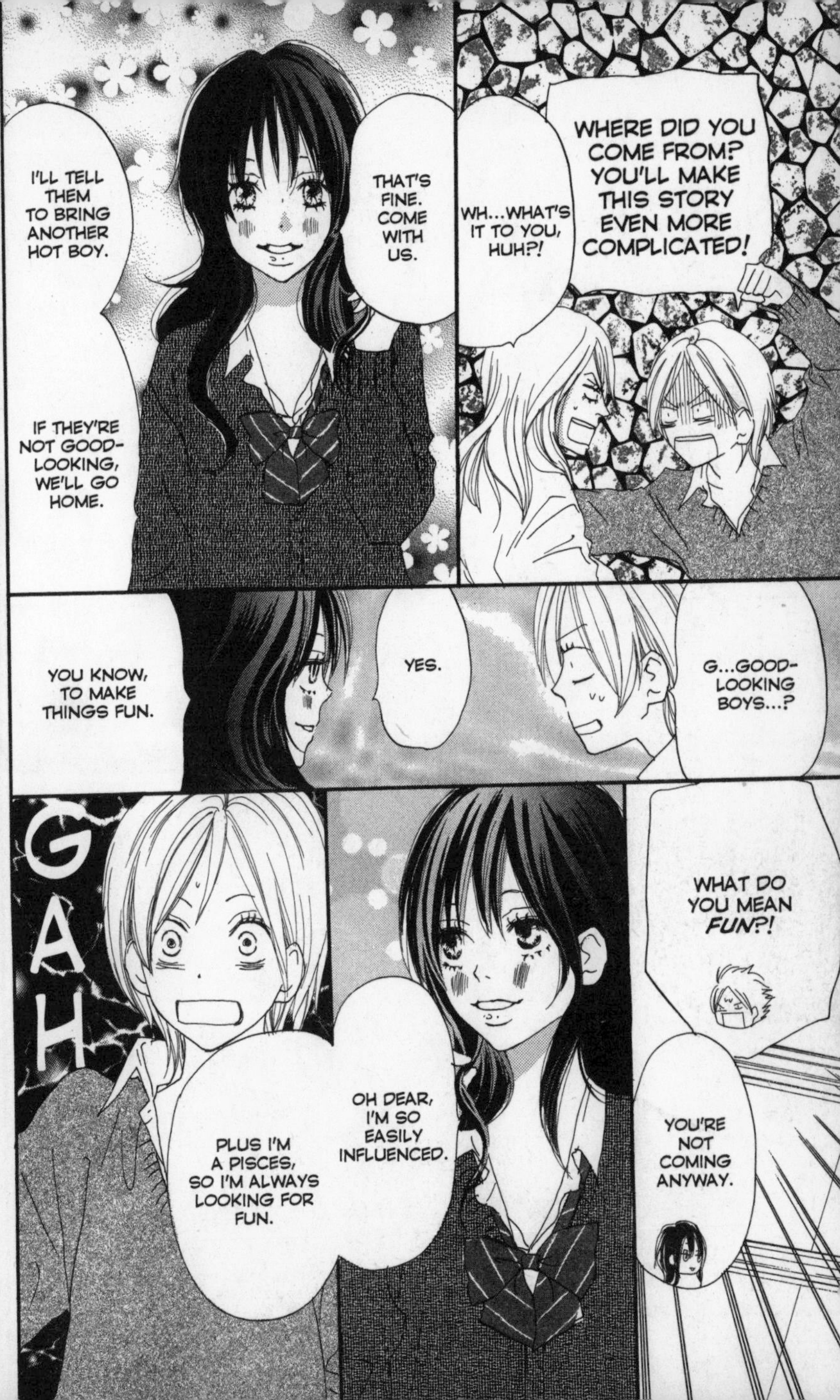
WHERE DID YOU COME FROM? YOU'LL MAKE THIS STORY EVEN MORE COMPLICATED!
WH...WHAT'S IT TO YOU, HUH?!
THAT'S FINE. COME WITH US.
I'LL TELL THEM TO BRING ANOTHER HOT BOY.
IF THEY'RE NOT GOOD-LOOKING, WE'LL GO HOME.
G...GOOD-LOOKING BOYS...?
YES.
YOU KNOW, TO MAKE THINGS FUN.
WHAT DO YOU MEAN *FUN*?!
YOU'RE NOT COMING ANYWAY.
OH DEAR, I'M SO EASILY INFLUENCED.
PLUS I'M A PISCES, SO I'M ALWAYS LOOKING FOR FUN.
GAH

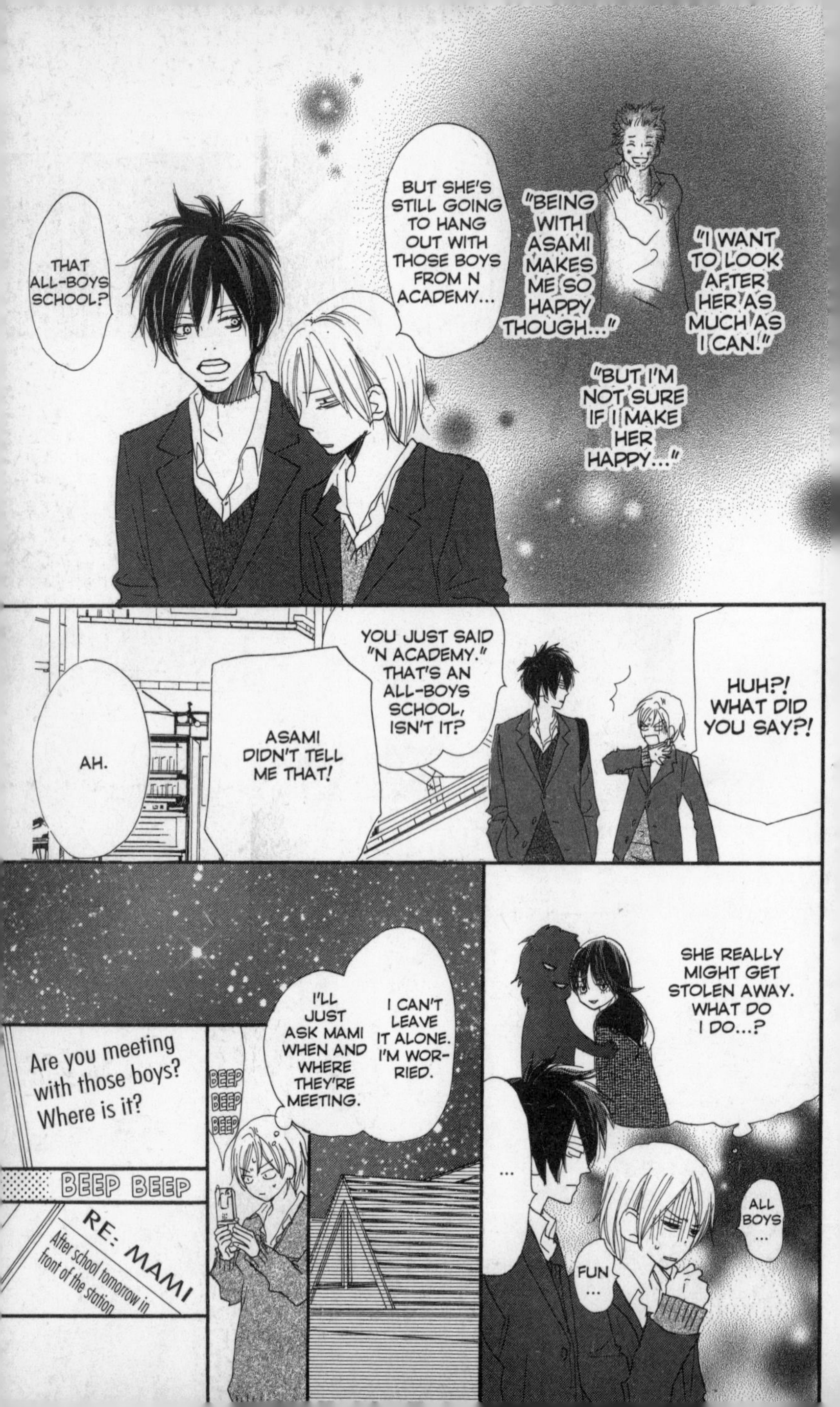

"BEING WITH ASAMI MAKES ME SO HAPPY THOUGH..."
"I WANT TO LOOK AFTER HER AS MUCH AS I CAN."
"BUT I'M NOT SURE IF I MAKE HER HAPPY..."
BUT SHE'S STILL GOING TO HANG OUT WITH THOSE BOYS FROM N ACADEMY...
THAT ALL-BOYS SCHOOL?
HUH?! WHAT DID YOU SAY?!
YOU JUST SAID "N ACADEMY." THAT'S AN ALL-BOYS SCHOOL, ISN'T IT?
ASAMI DIDN'T TELL ME THAT!
AH.
SHE REALLY MIGHT GET STOLEN AWAY. WHAT DO I DO...?
ALL BOYS...
FUN...
...
I CAN'T LEAVE IT ALONE. I'M WORRIED.
I'LL JUST ASK MAMI WHEN AND WHERE THEY'RE MEETING.
BEEP BEEP BEEP
Are you meeting with those boys? Where is it?
BEEP BEEP
RE: MAMI
After school tomorrow in front of the station

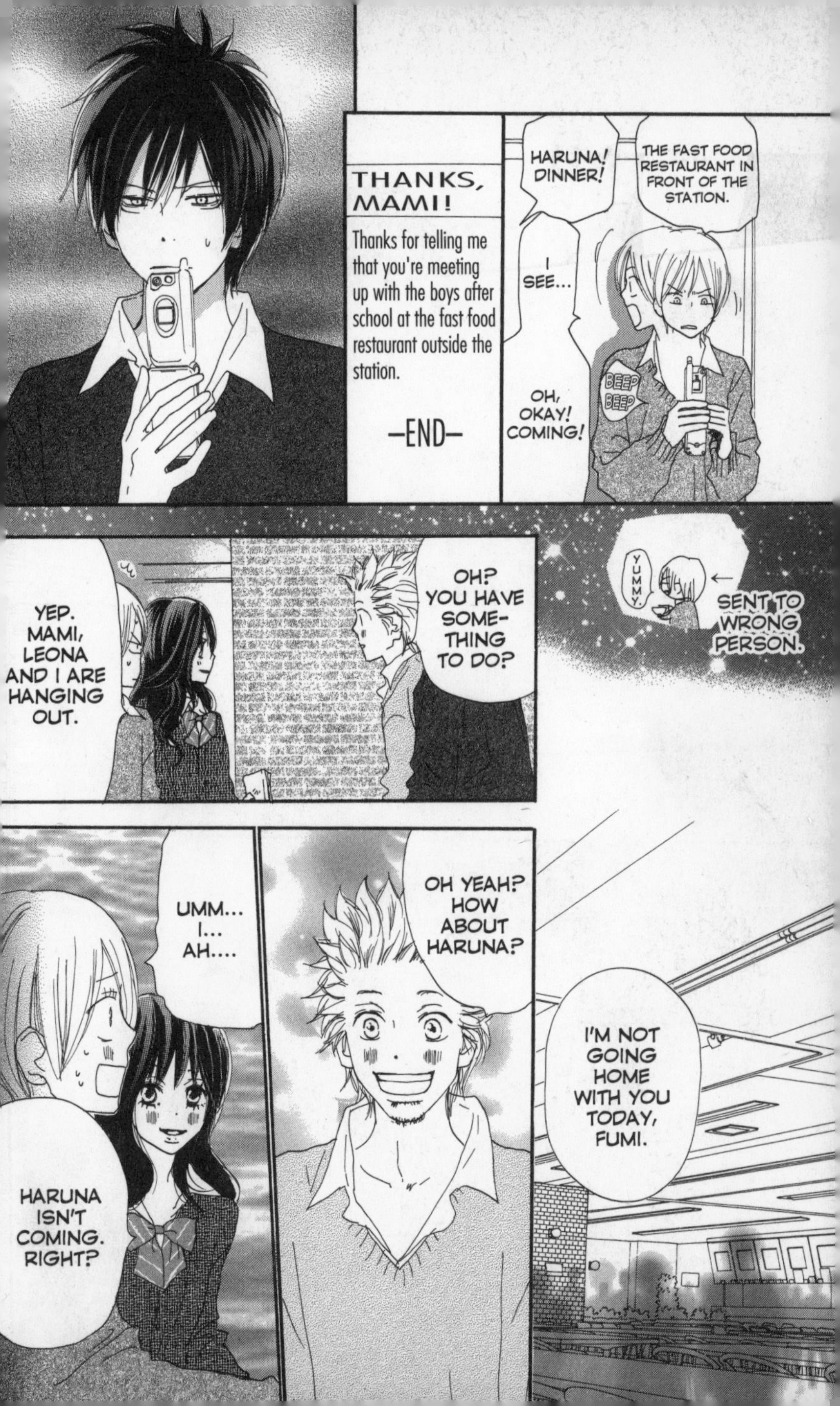
THE FAST FOOD RESTAURANT IN FRONT OF THE STATION.
HARUNA! DINNER!
I SEE...
BEEP BEEP
OH, OKAY! COMING!
THANKS, MAMI!
Thanks for telling me that you're meeting up with the boys after school at the fast food restaurant outside the station.
—END—
YUMMY.
SENT TO WRONG PERSON.
OH? YOU HAVE SOME-THING TO DO?
YEP. MAMI, LEONA AND I ARE HANGING OUT.
I'M NOT GOING HOME WITH YOU TODAY, FUMI.
OH YEAH? HOW ABOUT HARUNA?
UMM... I... AH....
HARUNA ISN'T COMING. RIGHT?

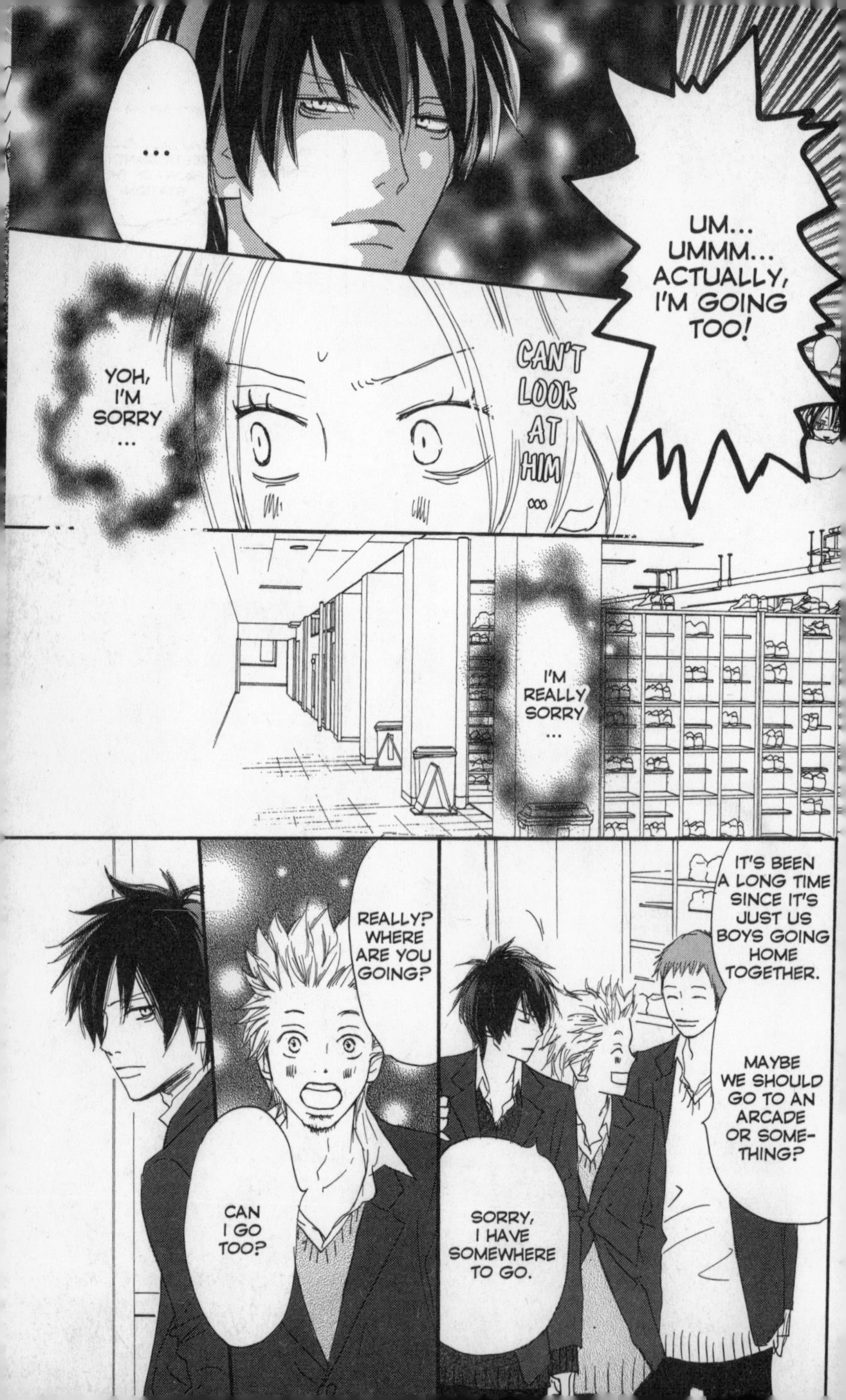
UM... UMMM... ACTUALLY, I'M GOING TOO!
...
CAN'T LOOK AT HIM...
YOH, I'M SORRY...
I'M REALLY SORRY...
IT'S BEEN A LONG TIME SINCE IT'S JUST US BOYS GOING HOME TOGETHER.
MAYBE WE SHOULD GO TO AN ARCADE OR SOME-THING?
SORRY, I HAVE SOMEWHERE TO GO.
REALLY? WHERE ARE YOU GOING?
CAN I GO TOO?

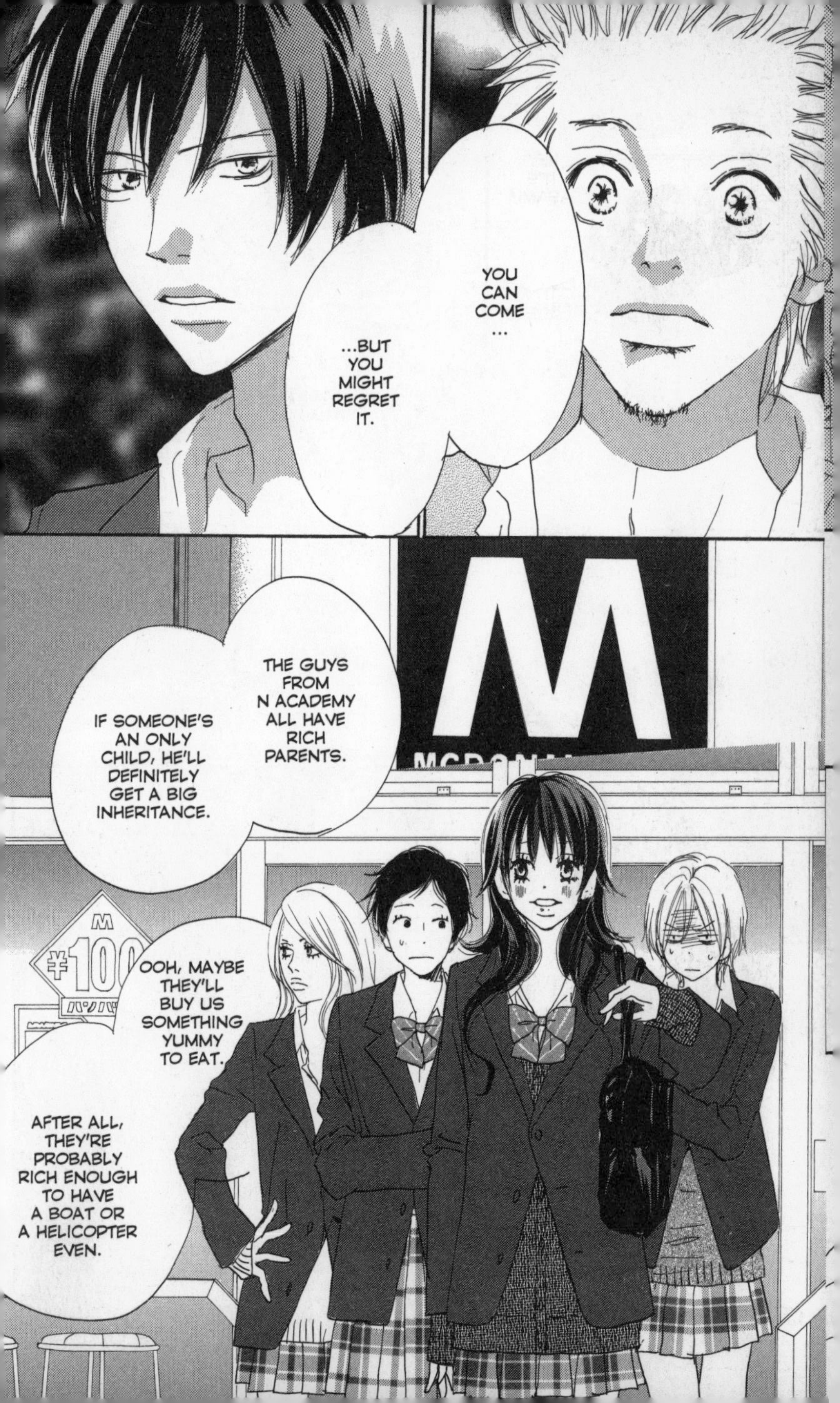
YOU CAN COME ...
...BUT YOU MIGHT REGRET IT.
THE GUYS FROM N ACADEMY ALL HAVE RICH PARENTS.
IF SOMEONE'S AN ONLY CHILD, HE'LL DEFINITELY GET A BIG INHERITANCE.
OOH, MAYBE THEY'LL BUY US SOMETHING YUMMY TO EAT.
AFTER ALL, THEY'RE PROBABLY RICH ENOUGH TO HAVE A BOAT OR A HELICOPTER EVEN.

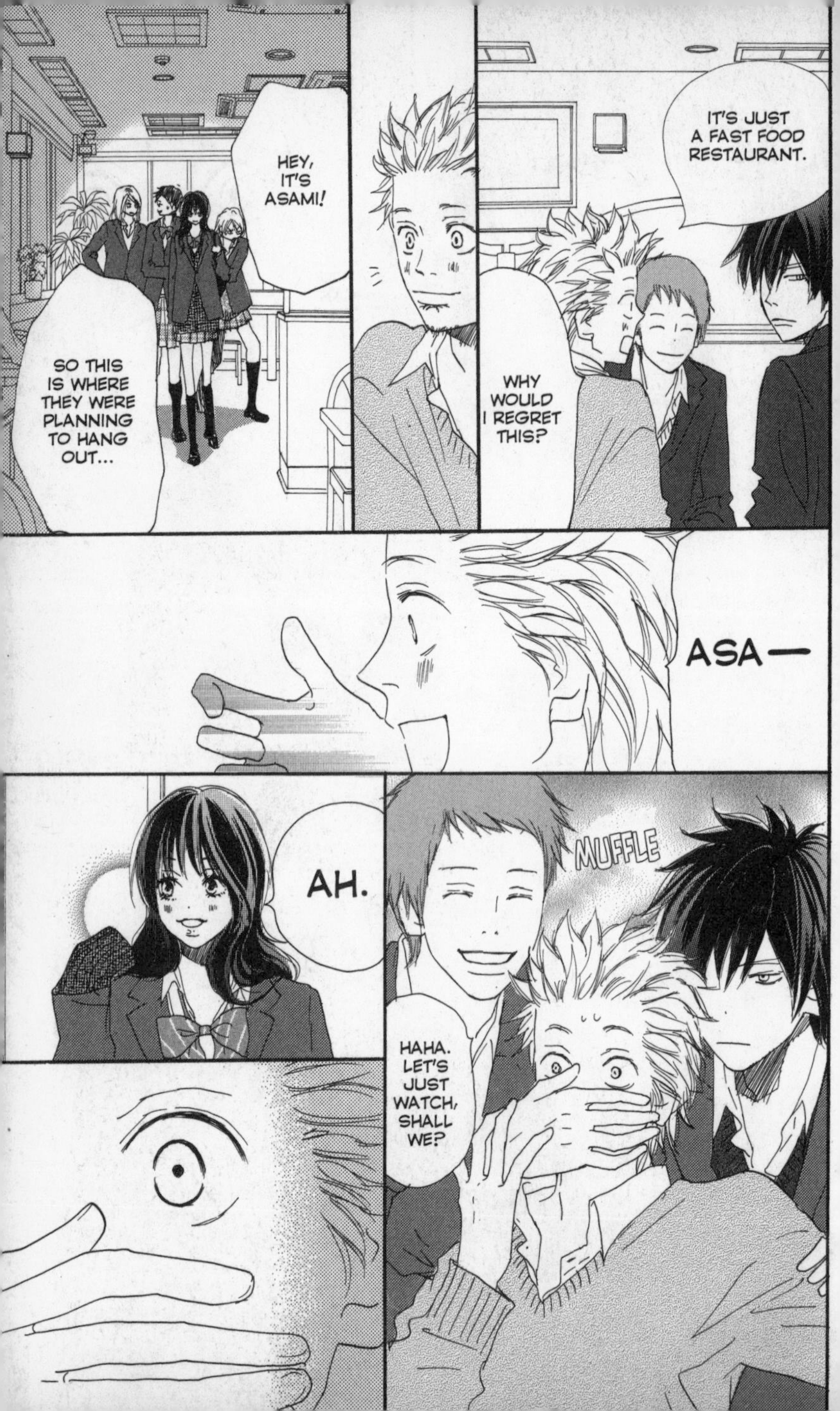
IT'S JUST A FAST FOOD RESTAURANT.
WHY WOULD I REGRET THIS?
HEY, IT'S ASAMI!
SO THIS IS WHERE THEY WERE PLANNING TO HANG OUT...
ASA—
MUFFLE
HAHA. LET'S JUST WATCH, SHALL WE?
AH.

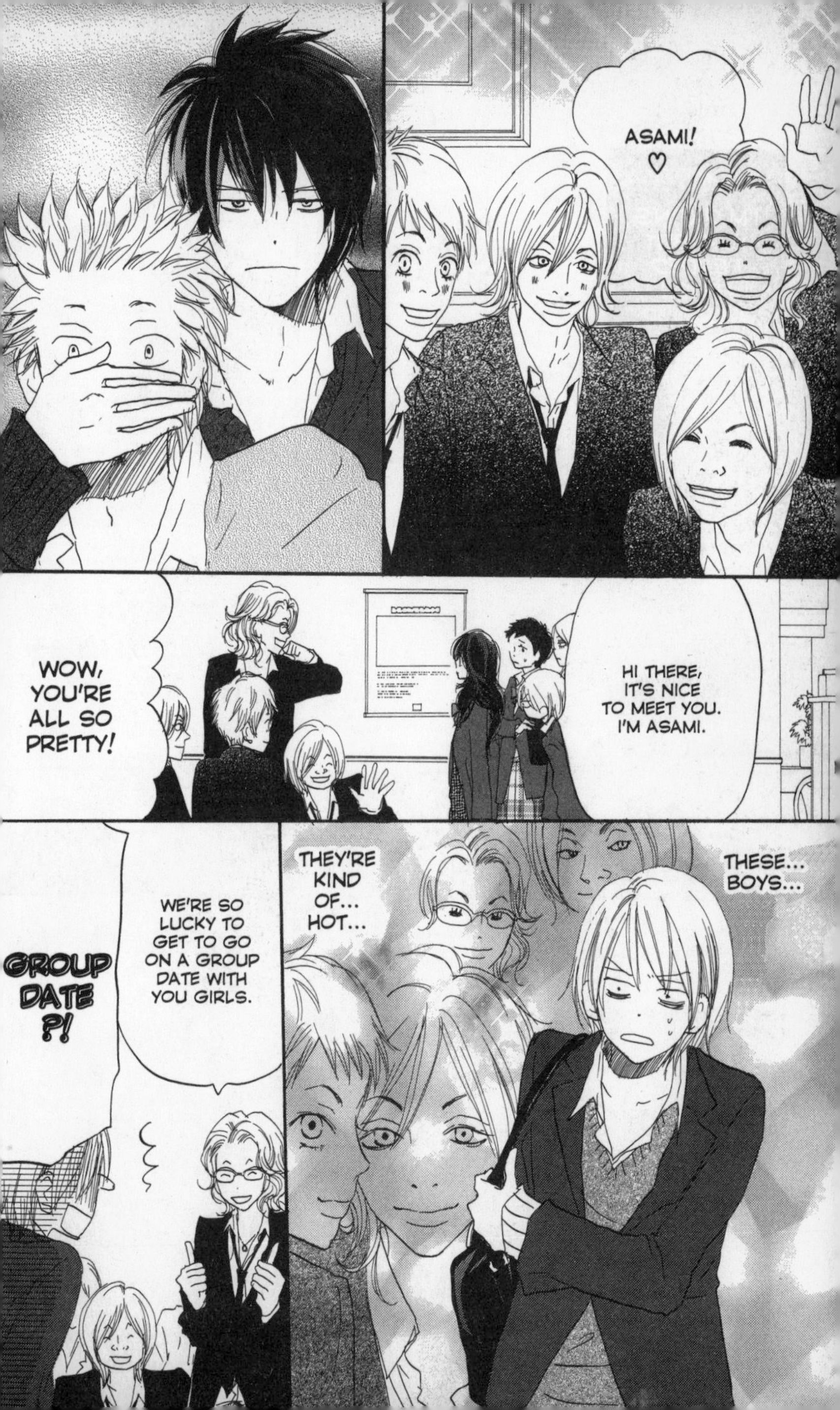
ASAMI! ♡
HI THERE, IT'S NICE TO MEET YOU. I'M ASAMI.
WOW, YOU'RE ALL SO PRETTY!
THESE... BOYS...
THEY'RE KIND OF... HOT...
WE'RE SO LUCKY TO GET TO GO ON A GROUP DATE WITH YOU GIRLS.
GROUP DATE?!

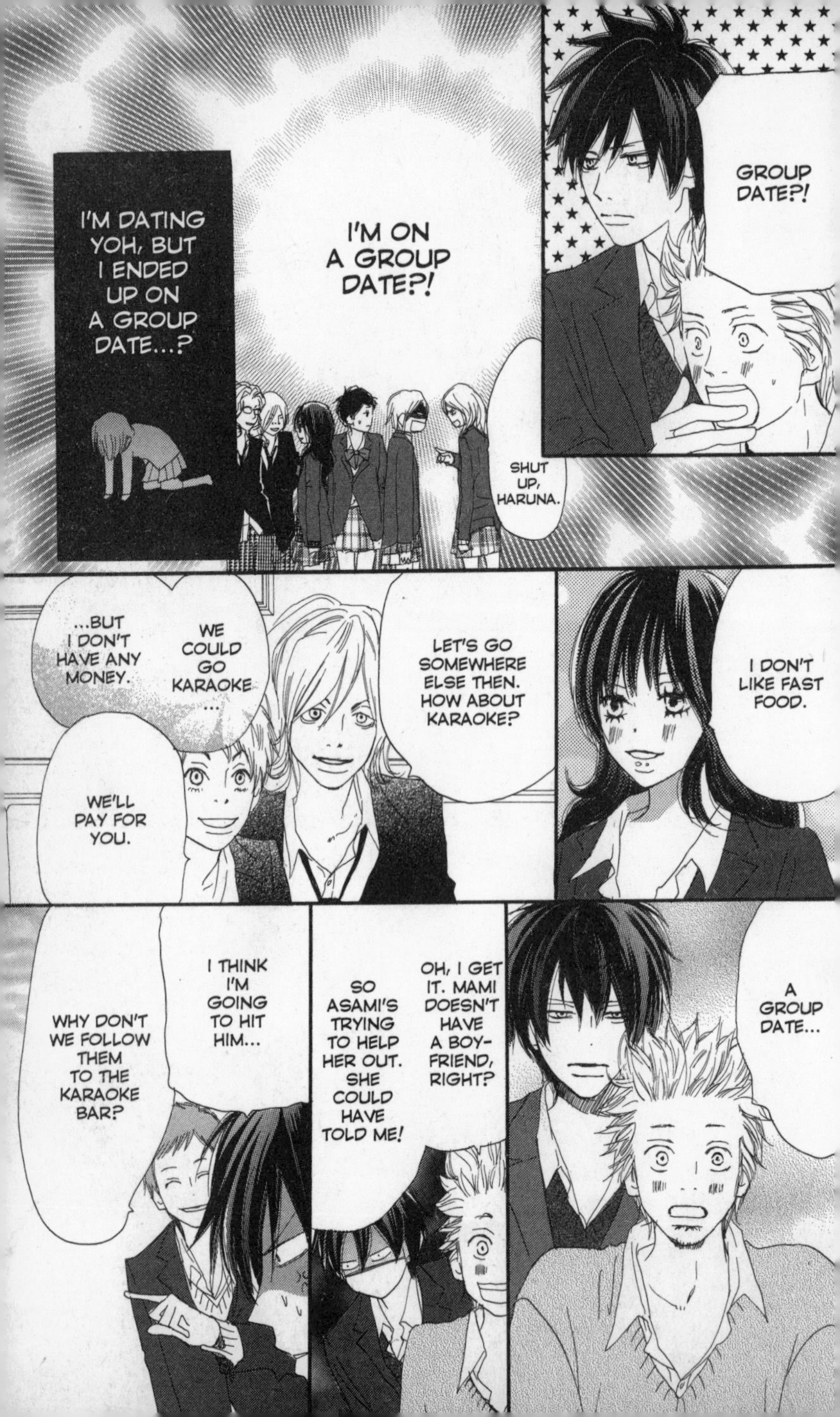
GROUP DATE?!
SHUT UP, HARUNA.
I'M ON A GROUP DATE?!
I'M DATING YOH, BUT I ENDED UP ON A GROUP DATE...?
I DON'T LIKE FAST FOOD.
LET'S GO SOMEWHERE ELSE THEN. HOW ABOUT KARAOKE?
WE COULD GO KARAOKE...
...BUT I DON'T HAVE ANY MONEY.
WE'LL PAY FOR YOU.
A GROUP DATE...
OH, I GET IT. MAMI DOESN'T HAVE A BOY-FRIEND, RIGHT?
SO ASAMI'S TRYING TO HELP HER OUT. SHE COULD HAVE TOLD ME!
I THINK I'M GOING TO HIT HIM...
WHY DON'T WE FOLLOW THEM TO THE KARAOKE BAR?

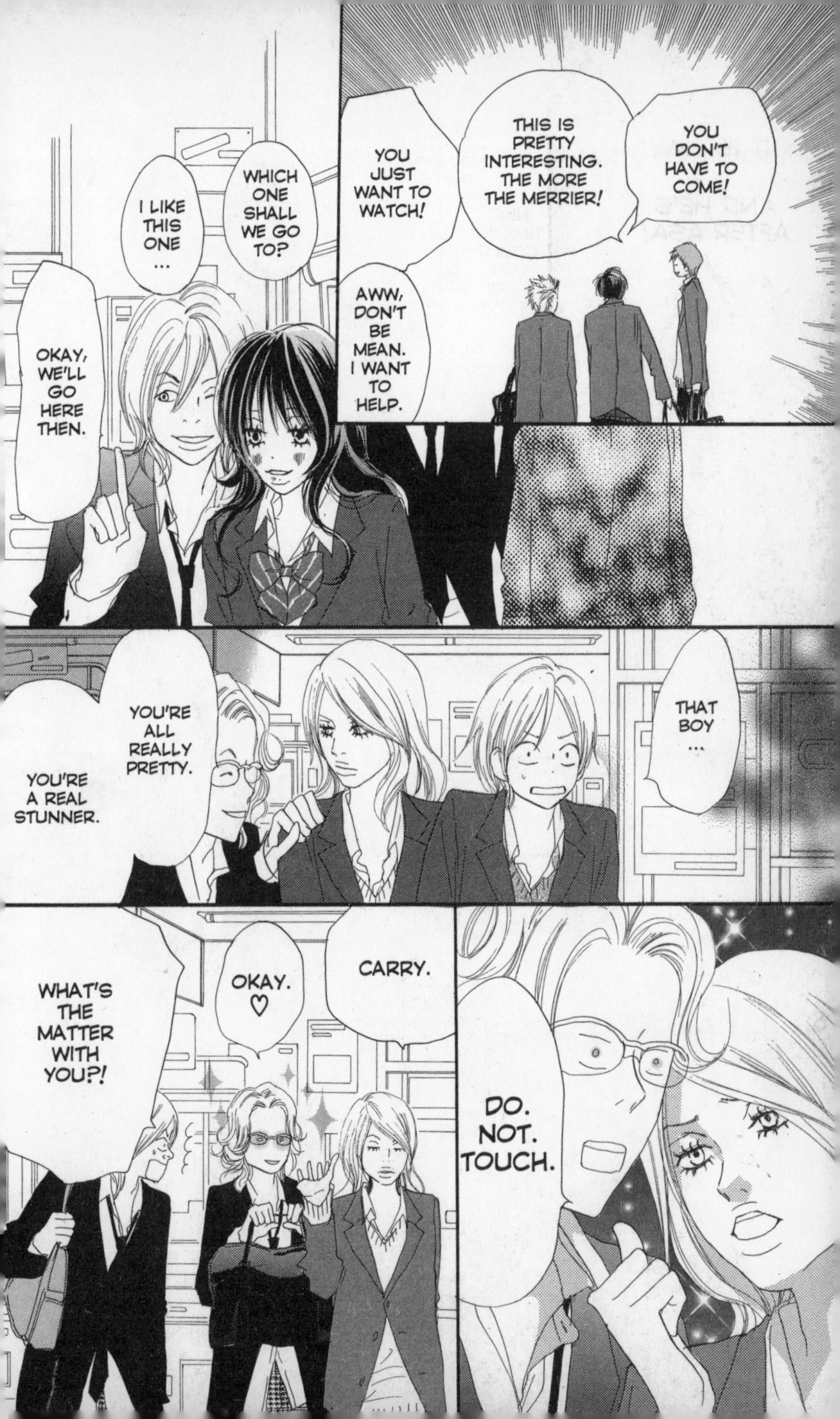
YOU DON'T HAVE TO COME!
THIS IS PRETTY INTERESTING. THE MORE THE MERRIER!
YOU JUST WANT TO WATCH!
AWW, DON'T BE MEAN. I WANT TO HELP.
WHICH ONE SHALL WE GO TO?
I LIKE THIS ONE ...
OKAY, WE'LL GO HERE THEN.
THAT BOY ...
YOU'RE ALL REALLY PRETTY.
YOU'RE A REAL STUNNER.
DO. NOT. TOUCH.
CARRY.
OKAY. ♡
WHAT'S THE MATTER WITH YOU?!

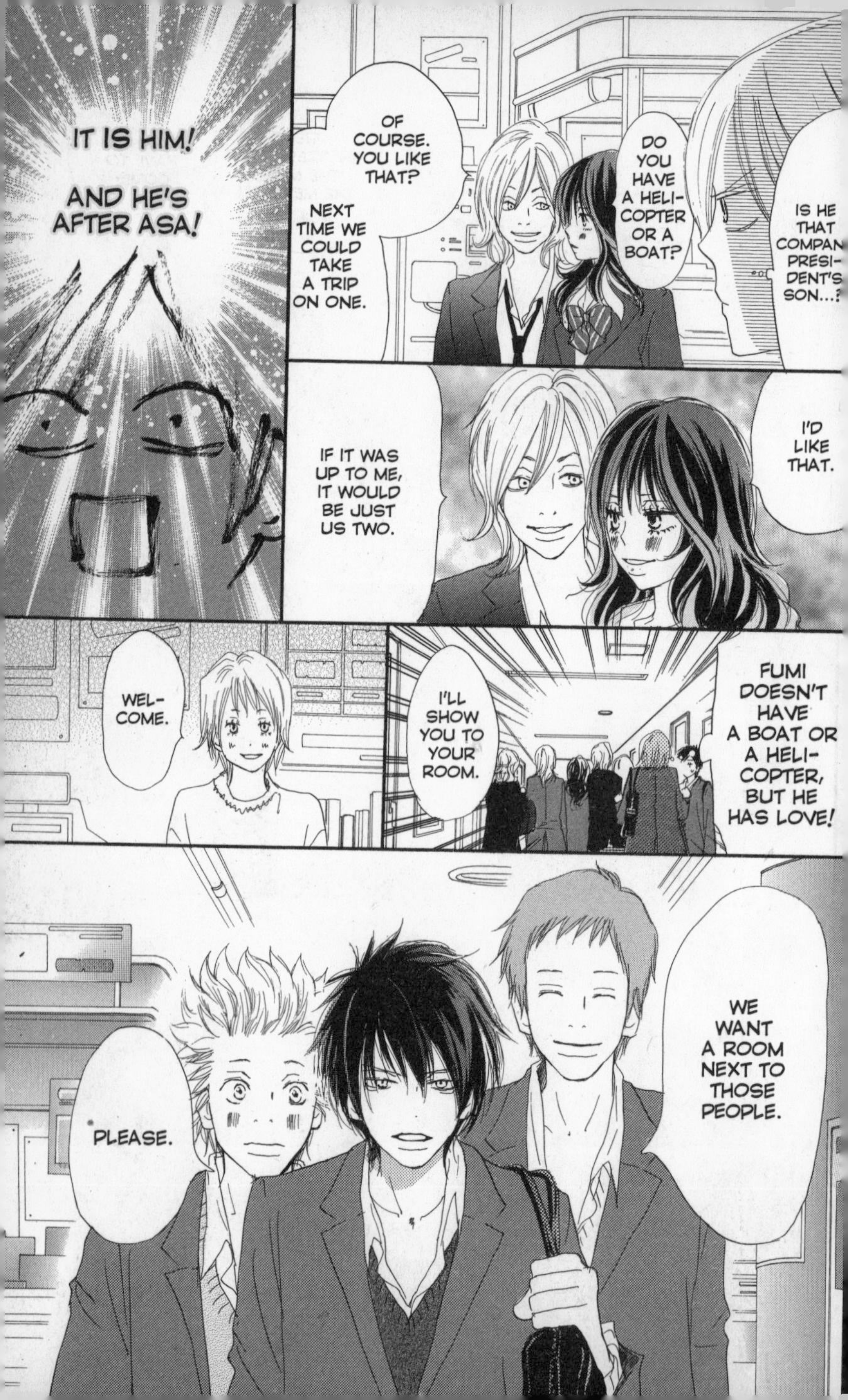
IS HE THAT COMPAN PRESI-DENT'S SON...?
DO YOU HAVE A HELI-COPTER OR A BOAT?
OF COURSE. YOU LIKE THAT?
NEXT TIME WE COULD TAKE A TRIP ON ONE.
I'D LIKE THAT.
IF IT WAS UP TO ME, IT WOULD BE JUST US TWO.
IT IS HIM!
AND HE'S AFTER ASA!
FUMI DOESN'T HAVE A BOAT OR A HELI-COPTER, BUT HE HAS LOVE!
I'LL SHOW YOU TO YOUR ROOM.
WEL-COME.
WE WANT A ROOM NEXT TO THOSE PEOPLE.
PLEASE.

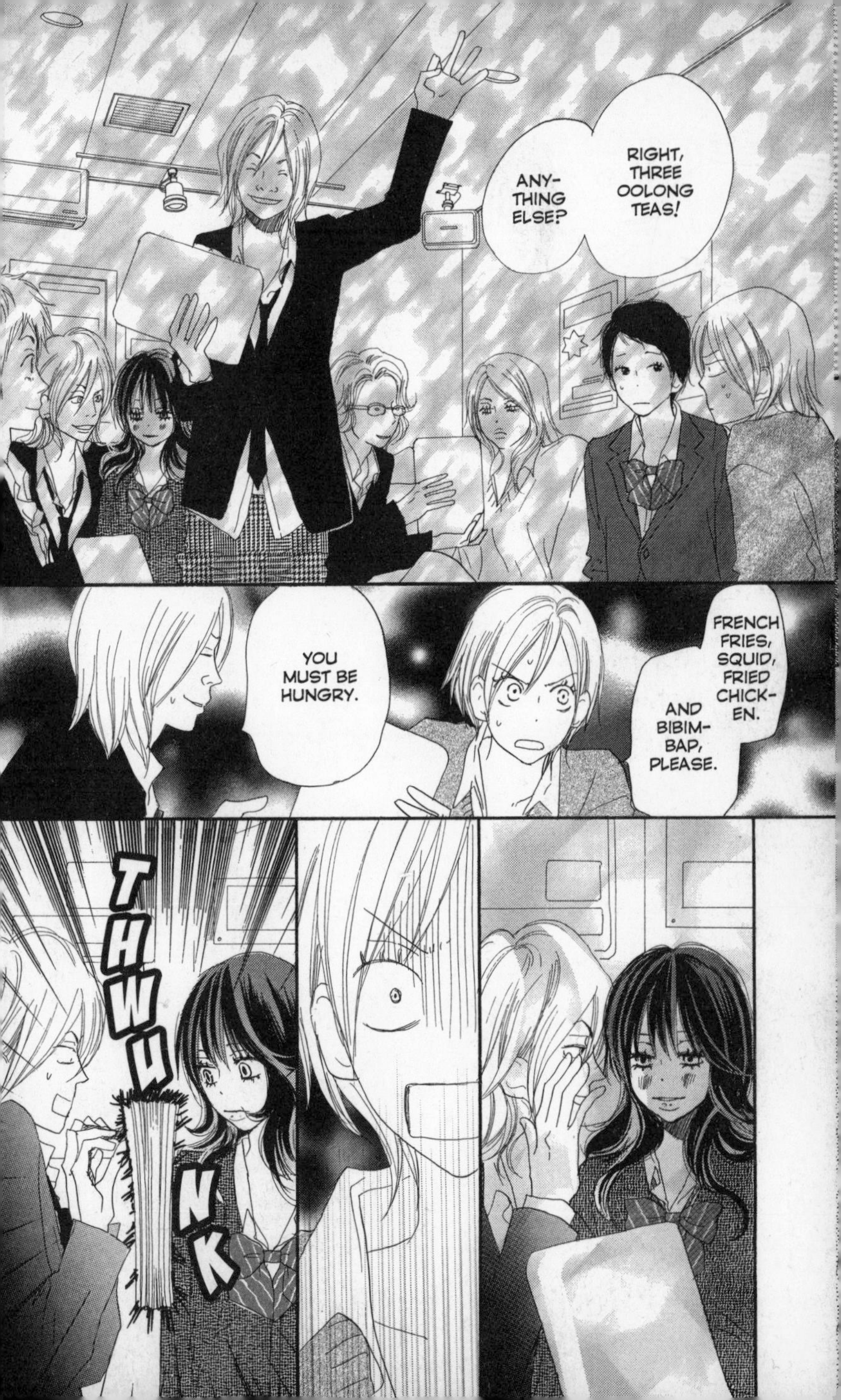
RIGHT, THREE OOLONG TEAS!
ANY-THING ELSE?
FRENCH FRIES, SQUID, FRIED CHICK-EN.
AND BIBIM-BAP, PLEASE.
YOU MUST BE HUNGRY.
THWUNK

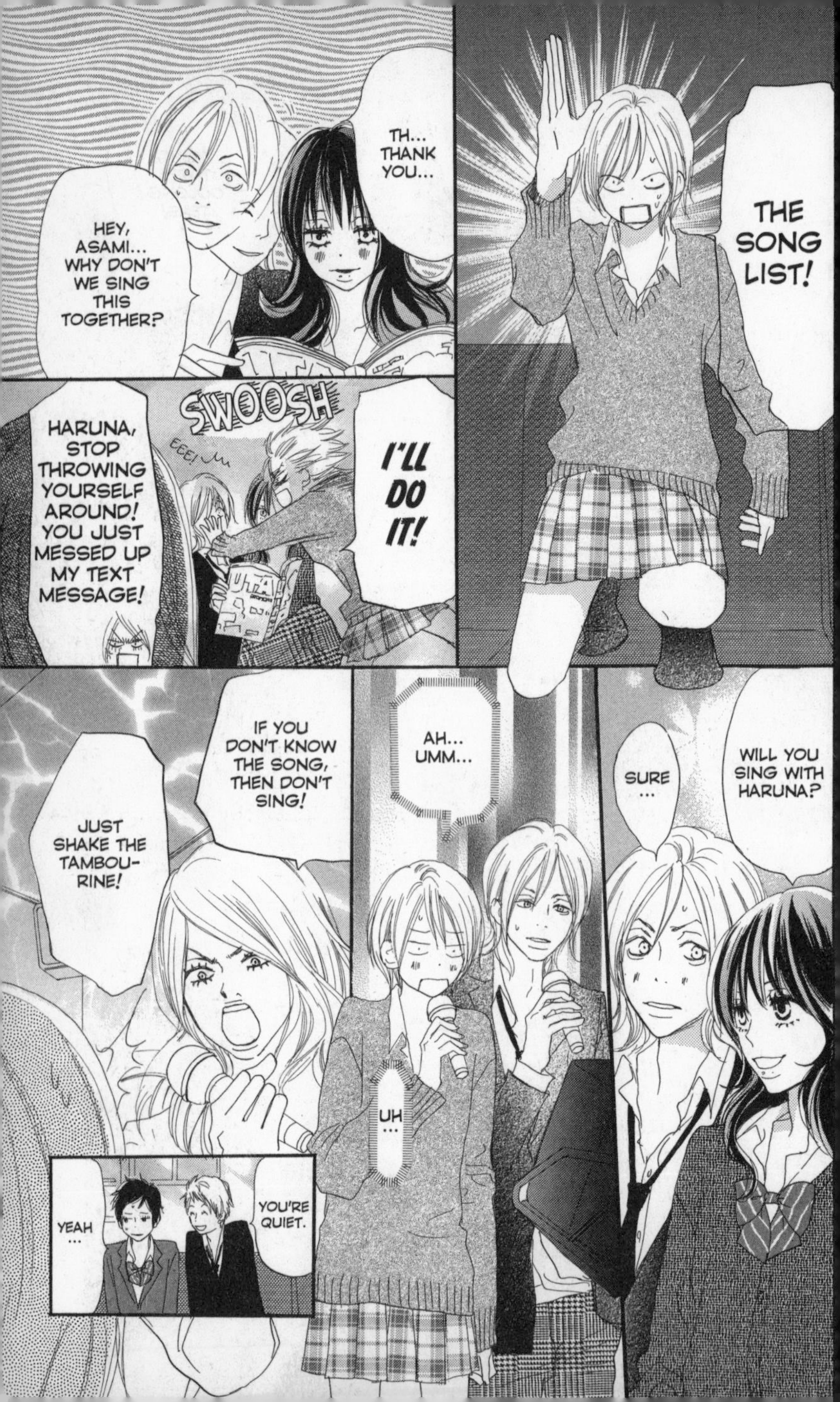
THE SONG LIST!
TH... THANK YOU...
HEY, ASAMI... WHY DON'T WE SING THIS TOGETHER?
I'LL DO IT!
SWOOSH
EEE!
HARUNA, STOP THROWING YOURSELF AROUND! YOU JUST MESSED UP MY TEXT MESSAGE!
WILL YOU SING WITH HARUNA?
SURE...
AH... UMM...
UH...
IF YOU DON'T KNOW THE SONG, THEN DON'T SING!
JUST SHAKE THE TAMBOU-RINE!
YOU'RE QUIET.
YEAH...

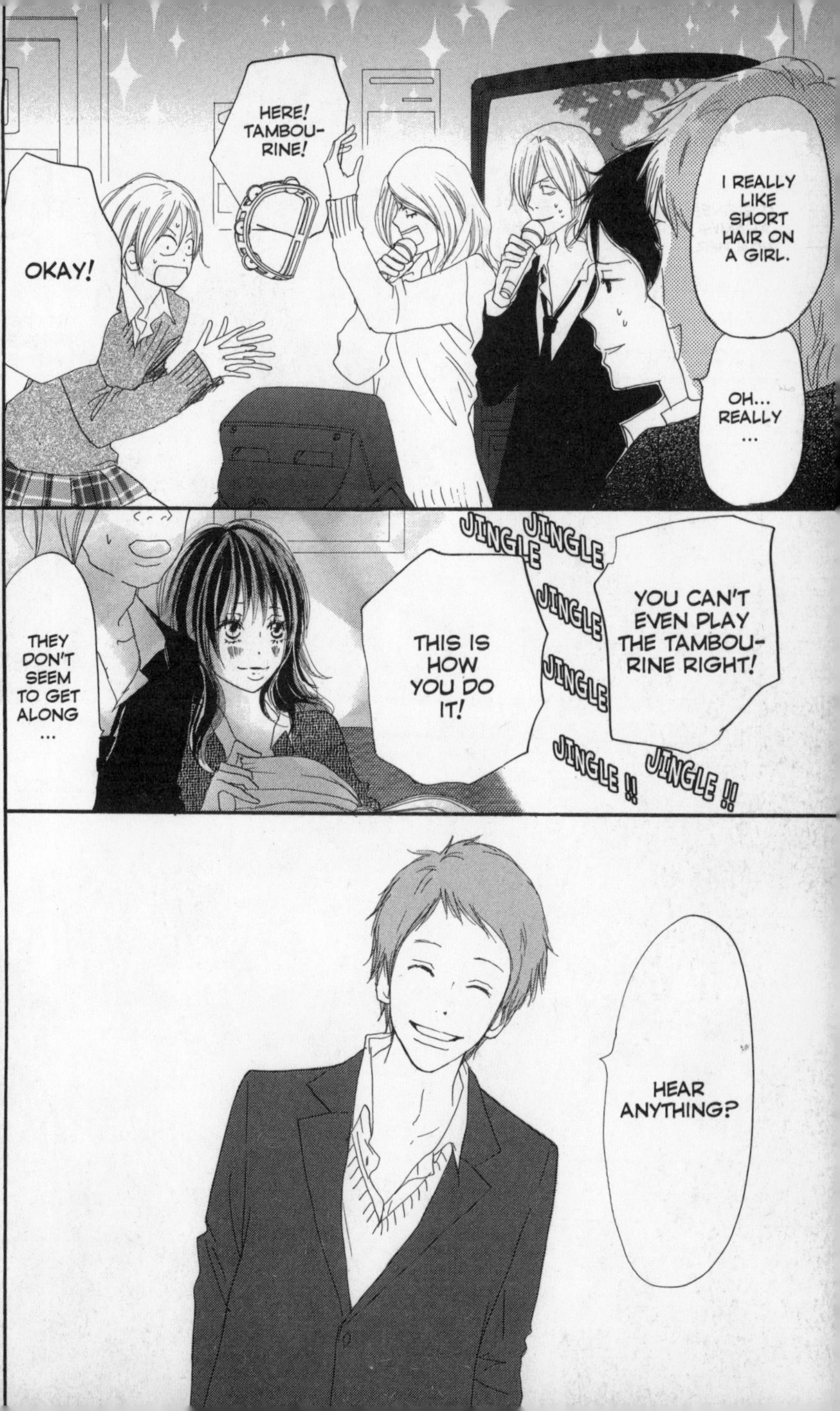
I REALLY LIKE SHORT HAIR ON A GIRL.
OH... REALLY ...
HERE! TAMBOU-RINE!
OKAY!
YOU CAN'T EVEN PLAY THE TAMBOU-RINE RIGHT!
JINGLE JINGLE
JINGLE
JINGLE
JINGLE !!
JINGLE !!
THIS IS HOW YOU DO IT!
THEY DON'T SEEM TO GET ALONG ...
HEAR ANYTHING?

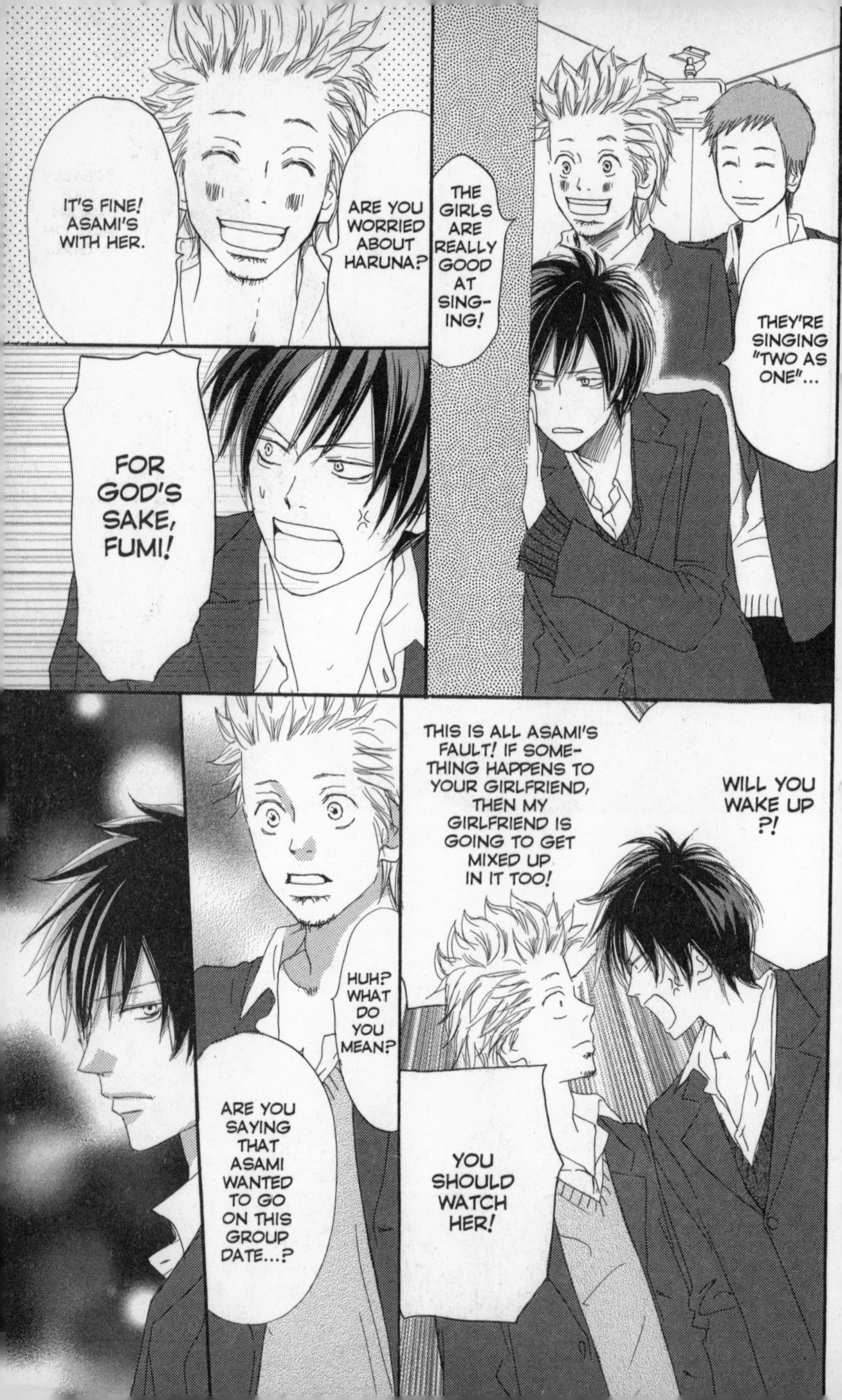
THE GIRLS ARE REALLY GOOD AT SINGING!
THEY'RE SINGING "TWO AS ONE"...
ARE YOU WORRIED ABOUT HARUNA?
IT'S FINE! ASAMI'S WITH HER.
FOR GOD'S SAKE, FUMI!
WILL YOU WAKE UP?!
THIS IS ALL ASAMI'S FAULT! IF SOMETHING HAPPENS TO YOUR GIRLFRIEND, THEN MY GIRLFRIEND IS GOING TO GET MIXED UP IN IT TOO!
YOU SHOULD WATCH HER!
HUH? WHAT DO YOU MEAN?
ARE YOU SAYING THAT ASAMI WANTED TO GO ON THIS GROUP DATE...?

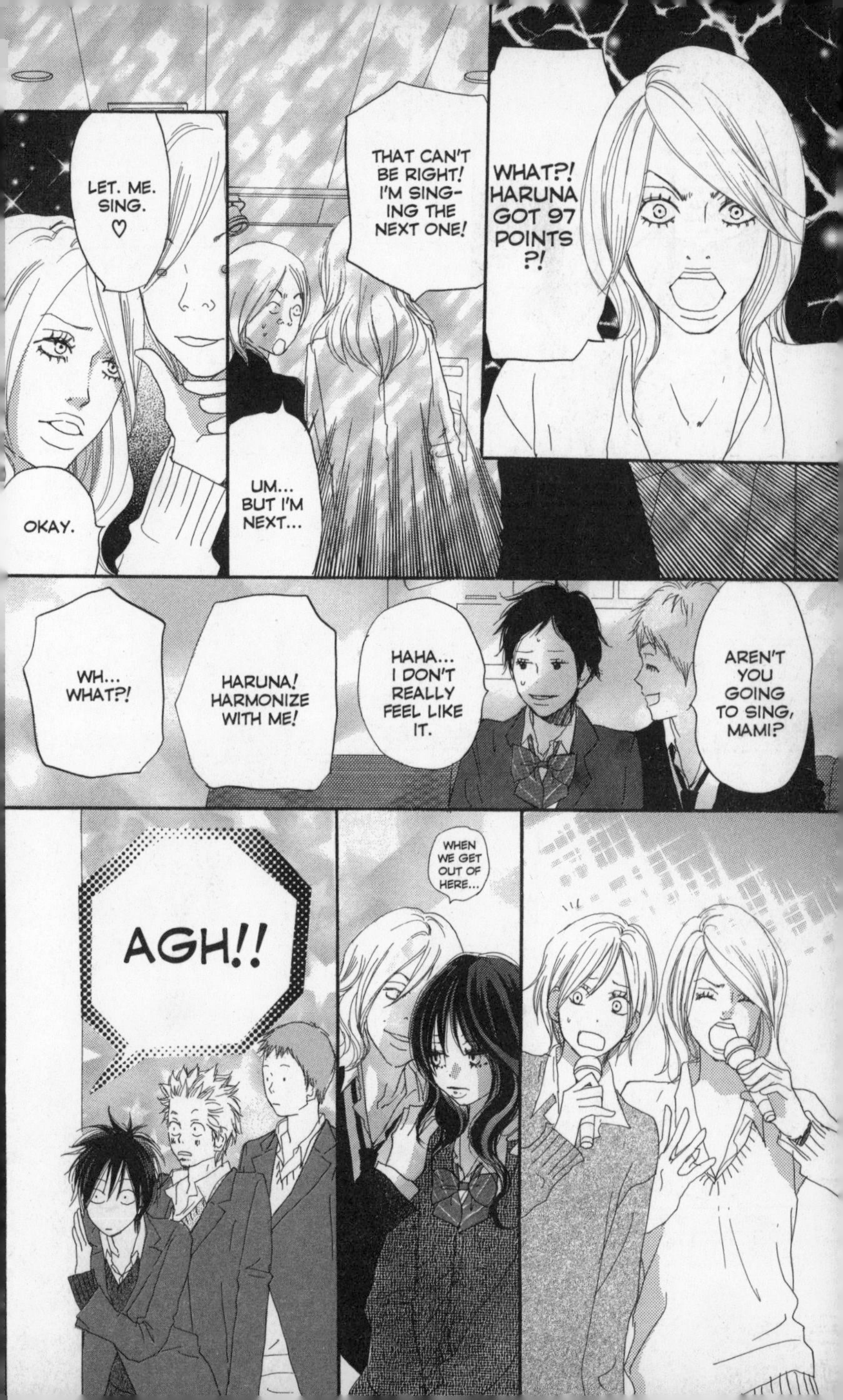
WHAT?! HARUNA GOT 97 POINTS ?!
THAT CAN'T BE RIGHT! I'M SING-ING THE NEXT ONE!
UM... BUT I'M NEXT...
LET. ME. SING. ♡
OKAY.
AREN'T YOU GOING TO SING, MAMI?
HAHA... I DON'T REALLY FEEL LIKE IT.
HARUNA! HARMONIZE WITH ME!
WH... WHAT?!
WHEN WE GET OUT OF HERE...
AGH!!

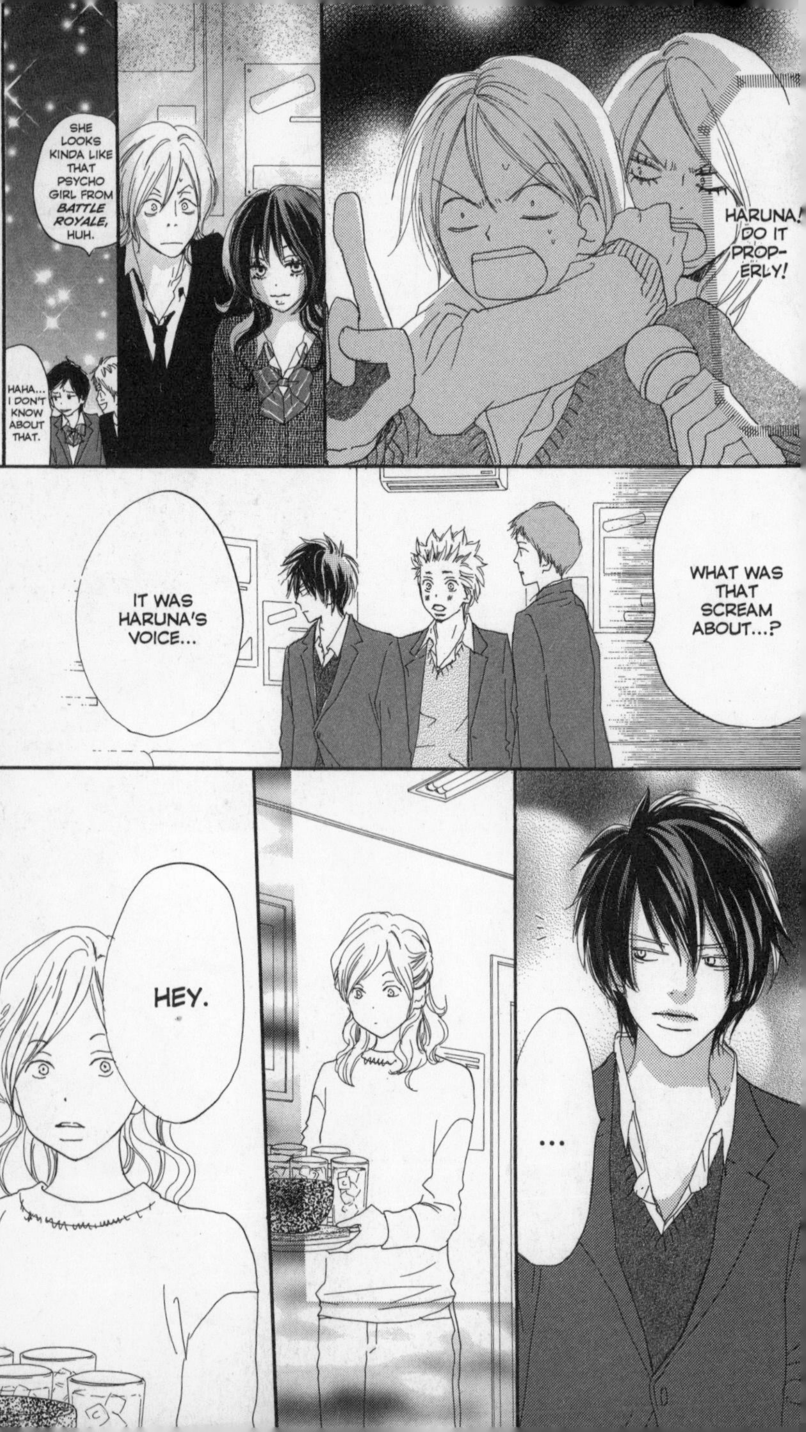
HARUNA! DO IT PROPERLY!
SHE LOOKS KINDA LIKE THAT PSYCHO GIRL FROM *BATTLE ROYALE*, HUH.
HAHA... I DON'T KNOW ABOUT THAT.
WHAT WAS THAT SCREAM ABOUT...?
IT WAS HARUNA'S VOICE...
...
HEY.

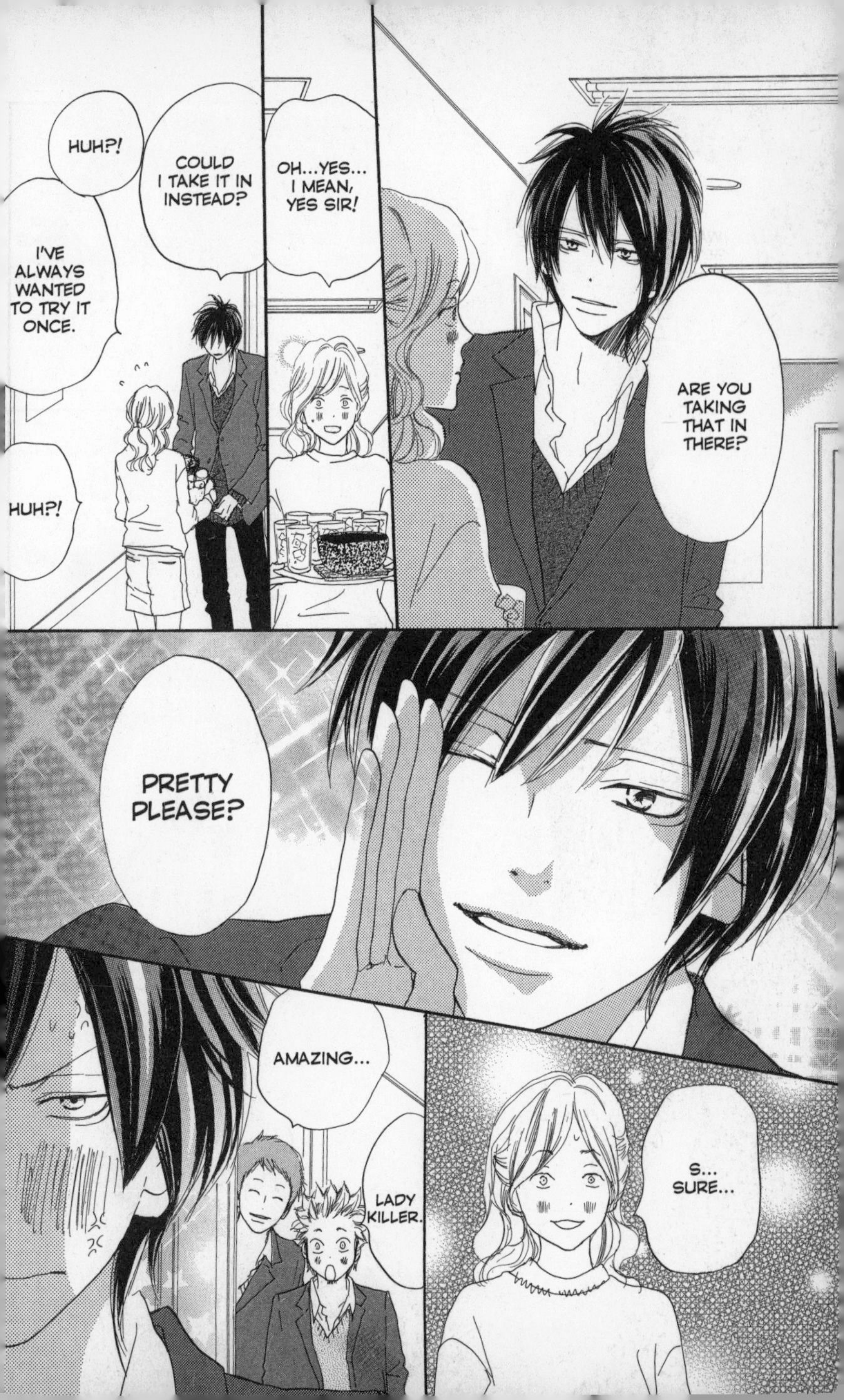
ARE YOU TAKING THAT IN THERE?
OH...YES... I MEAN, YES SIR!
COULD I TAKE IT IN INSTEAD?
HUH?!
I'VE ALWAYS WANTED TO TRY IT ONCE.
HUH?!
PRETTY PLEASE?
S... SURE...
AMAZING...
LADY KILLER.

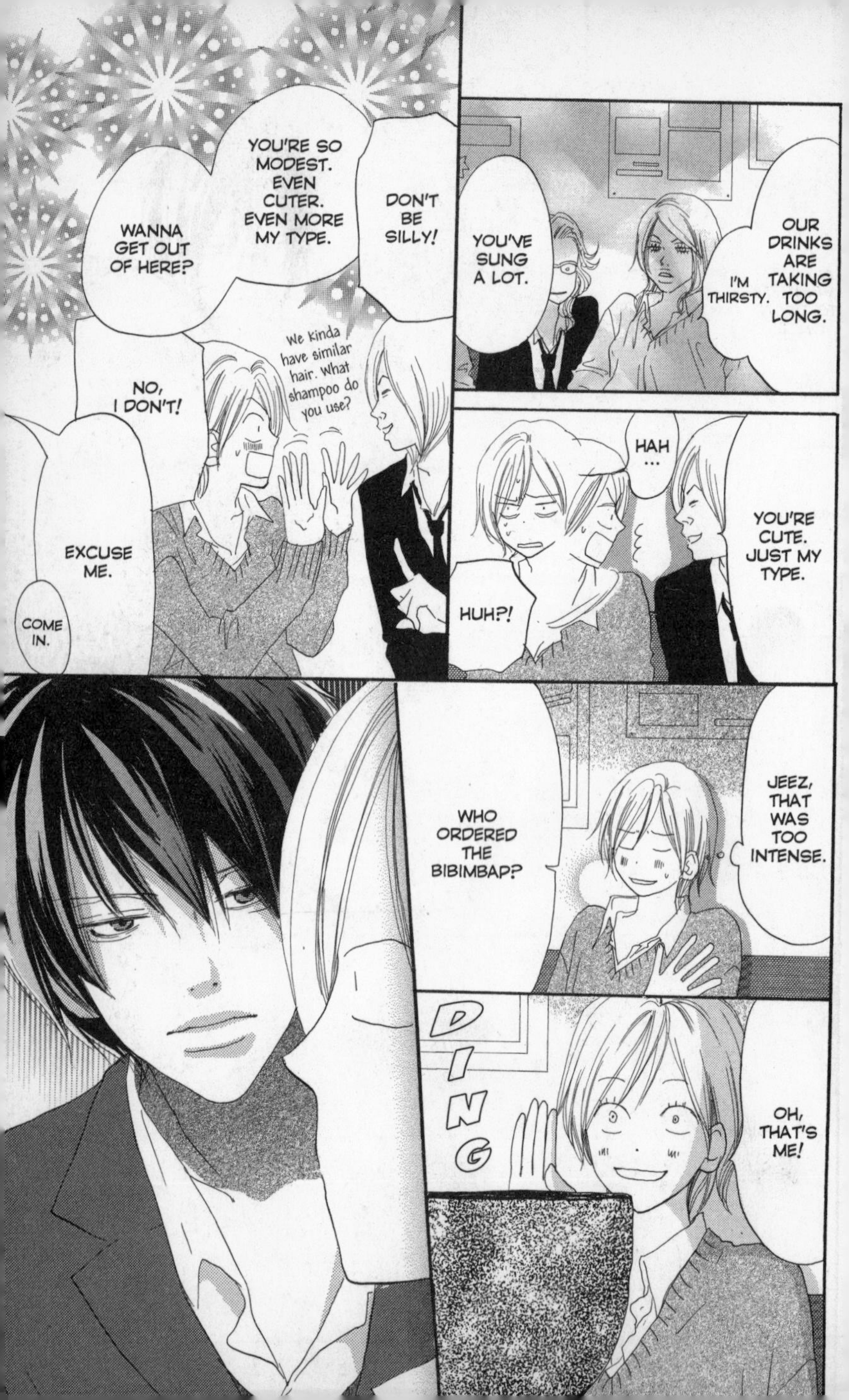
OUR DRINKS ARE TAKING TOO LONG.
I'M THIRSTY.
YOU'VE SUNG A LOT.
HAH...
YOU'RE CUTE. JUST MY TYPE.
HUH?!
DON'T BE SILLY!
YOU'RE SO MODEST. EVEN CUTER. EVEN MORE MY TYPE.
WANNA GET OUT OF HERE?
We kinda have similar hair. What shampoo do you use?
NO, I DON'T!
EXCUSE ME.
COME IN.
JEEZ, THAT WAS TOO INTENSE.
WHO ORDERED THE BIBIMBAP?
OH, THAT'S ME!
DING

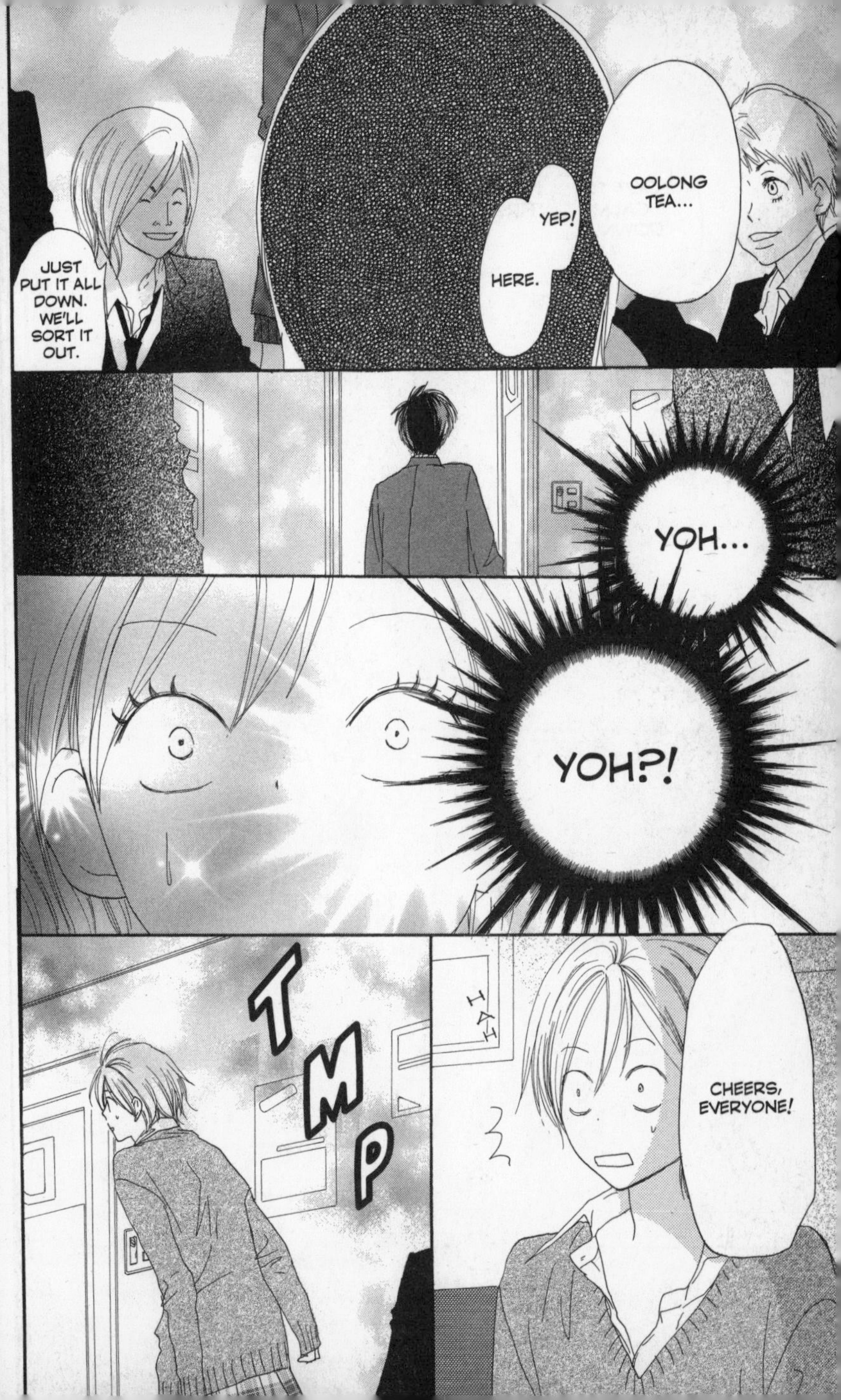
OOLONG TEA...
YEP!
HERE.
JUST PUT IT ALL DOWN. WE'LL SORT IT OUT.
YOH...
YOH?!
CHEERS, EVERYONE!
TMP

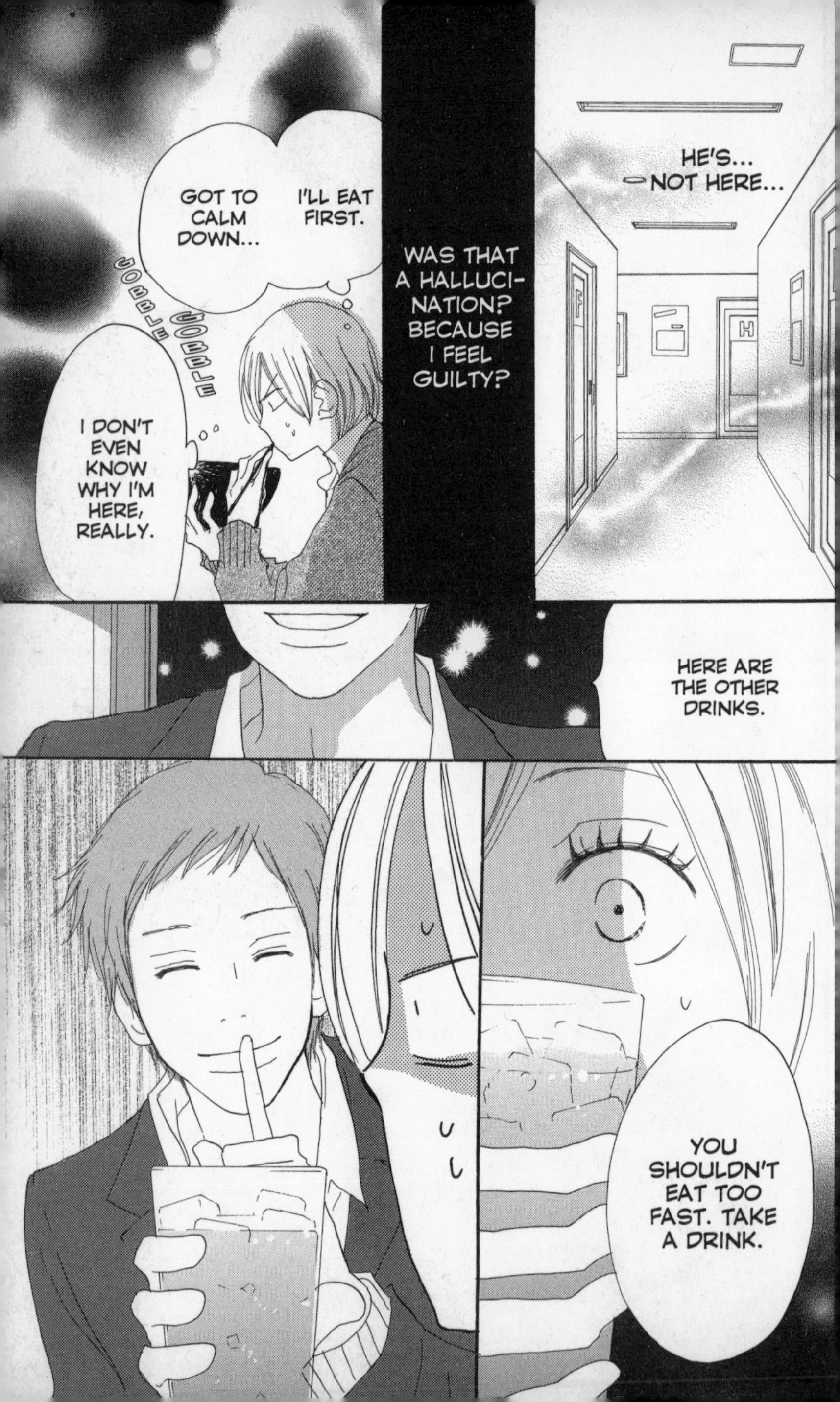
HE'S... NOT HERE...
WAS THAT A HALLUCI-NATION? BECAUSE I FEEL GUILTY?
I'LL EAT FIRST.
GOT TO CALM DOWN...
GOBBLE GOBBLE
I DON'T EVEN KNOW WHY I'M HERE, REALLY.
HERE ARE THE OTHER DRINKS.
YOU SHOULDN'T EAT TOO FAST. TAKE A DRINK.

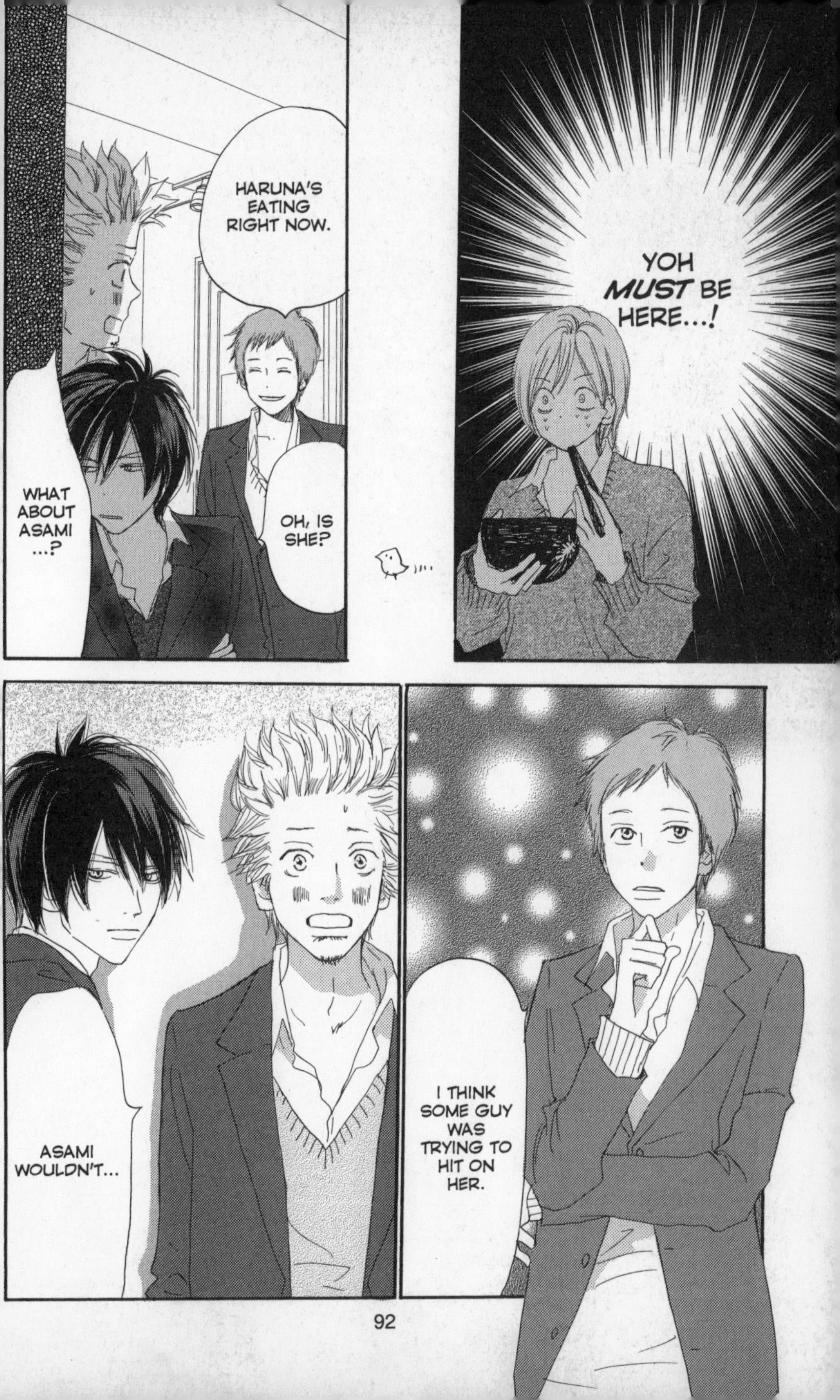
YOH *MUST* BE HERE...!
HARUNA'S EATING RIGHT NOW.
OH, IS SHE?
WHAT ABOUT ASAMI ...?
I THINK SOME GUY WAS TRYING TO HIT ON HER.
ASAMI WOULDN'T...

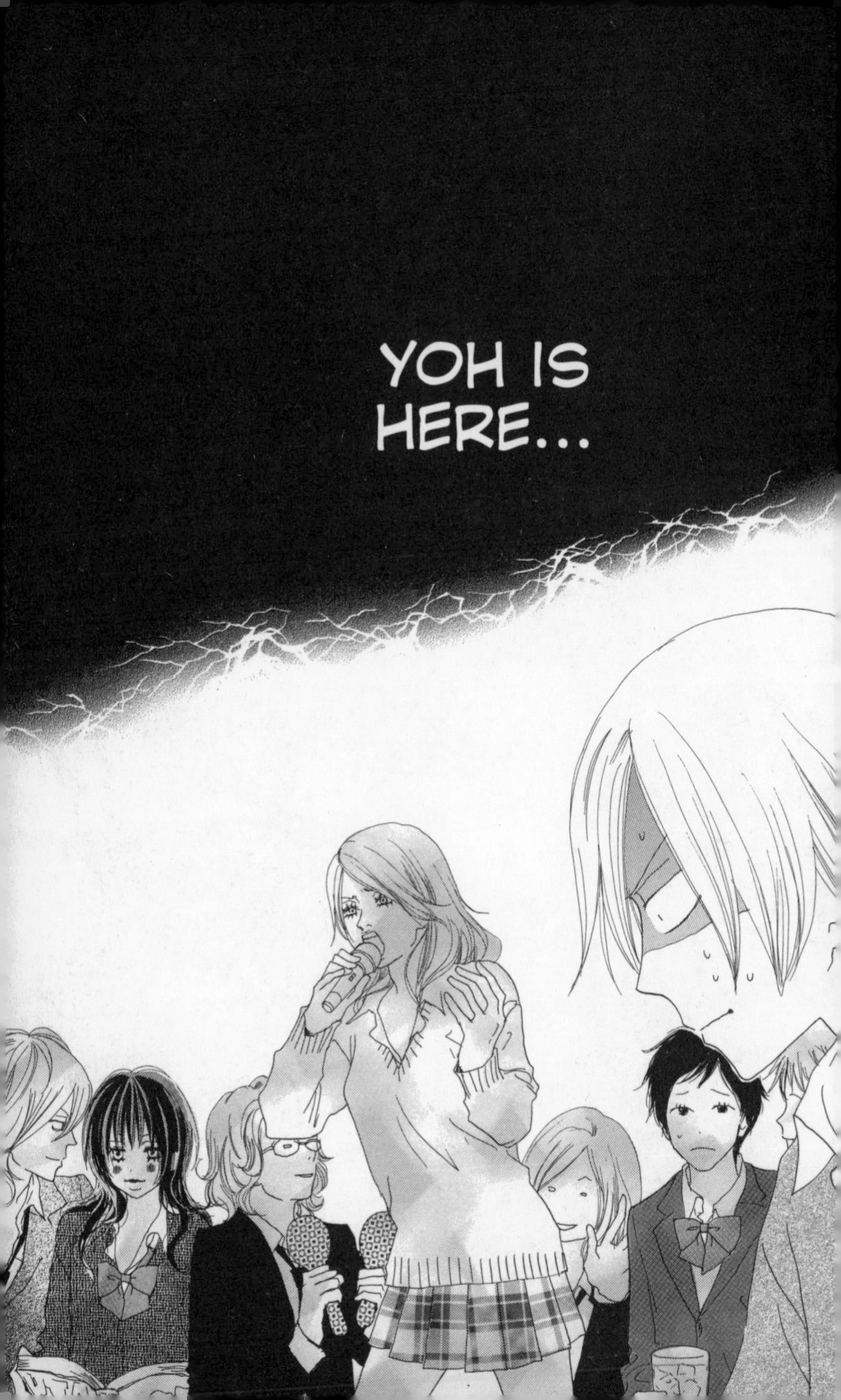
YOH IS
HERE...

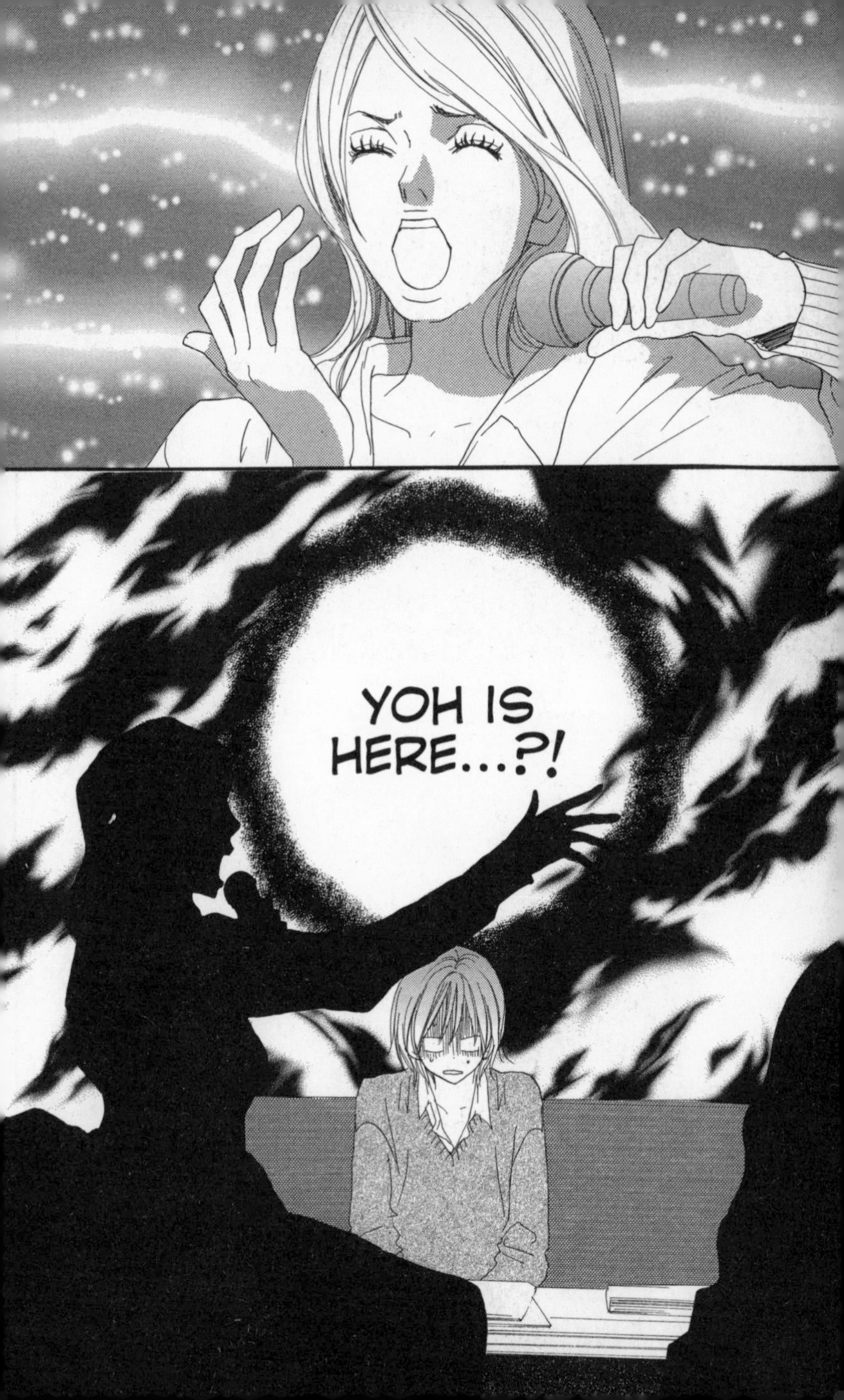
YOH IS HERE...?!

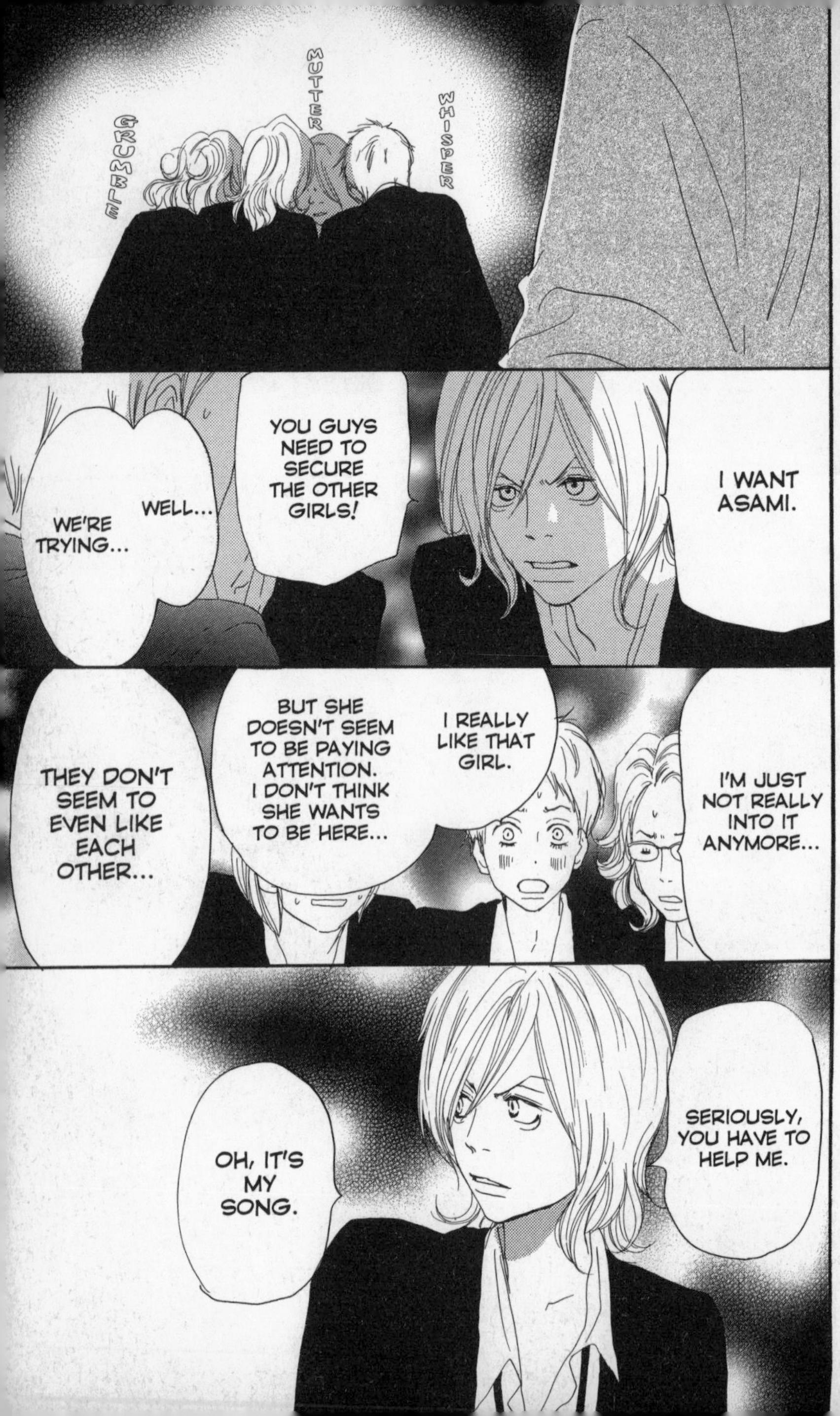
WHISPER
MUTTER
GRUMBLE
I WANT ASAMI.
YOU GUYS NEED TO SECURE THE OTHER GIRLS!
WELL...
WE'RE TRYING...
I'M JUST NOT REALLY INTO IT ANYMORE...
I REALLY LIKE THAT GIRL.
BUT SHE DOESN'T SEEM TO BE PAYING ATTENTION. I DON'T THINK SHE WANTS TO BE HERE...
THEY DON'T SEEM TO EVEN LIKE EACH OTHER...
SERIOUSLY, YOU HAVE TO HELP ME.
OH, IT'S MY SONG.

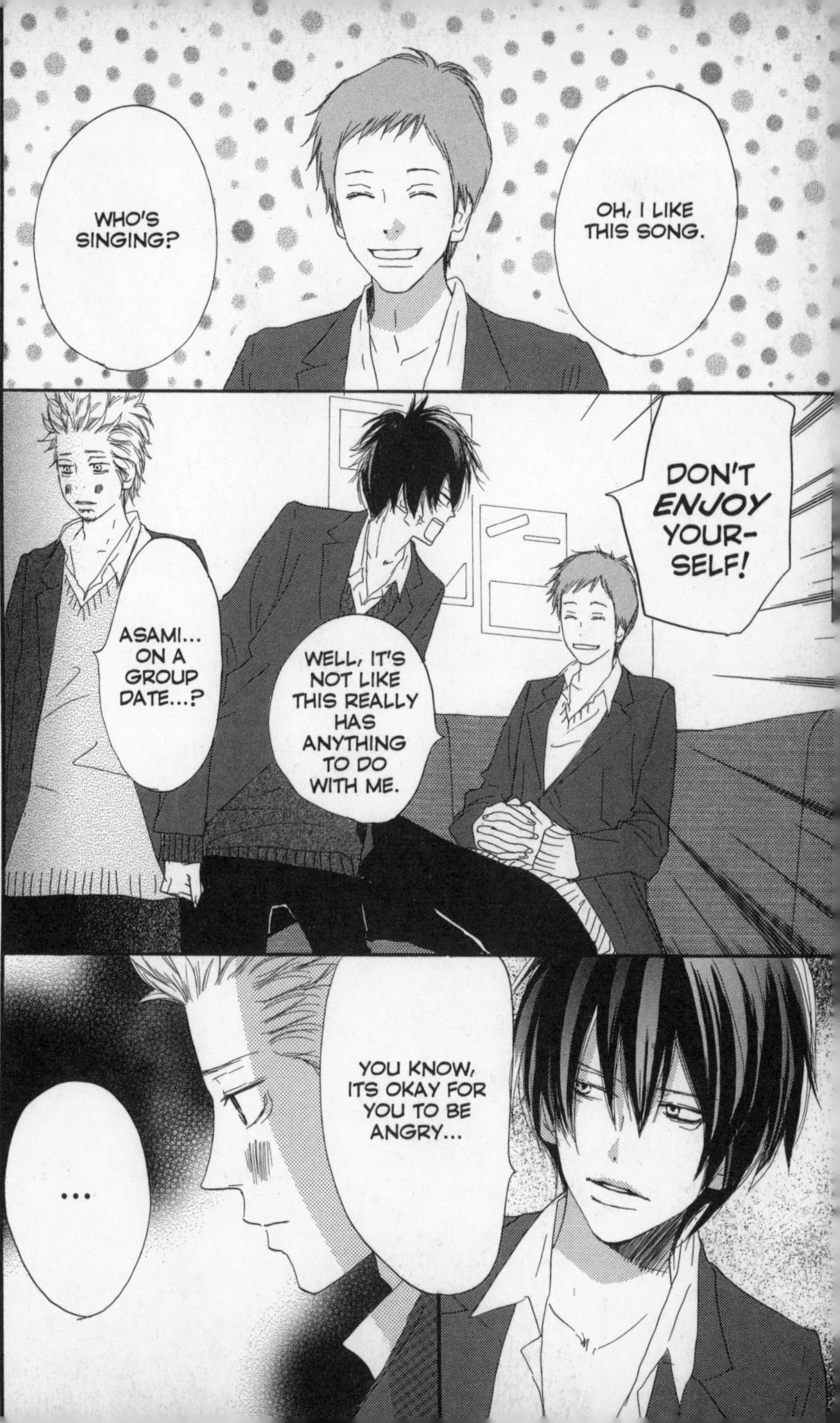
OH, I LIKE THIS SONG.
WHO'S SINGING?
DON'T *ENJOY* YOUR-SELF!
WELL, IT'S NOT LIKE THIS REALLY HAS ANYTHING TO DO WITH ME.
ASAMI... ON A GROUP DATE...?
YOU KNOW, ITS OKAY FOR YOU TO BE ANGRY...
...

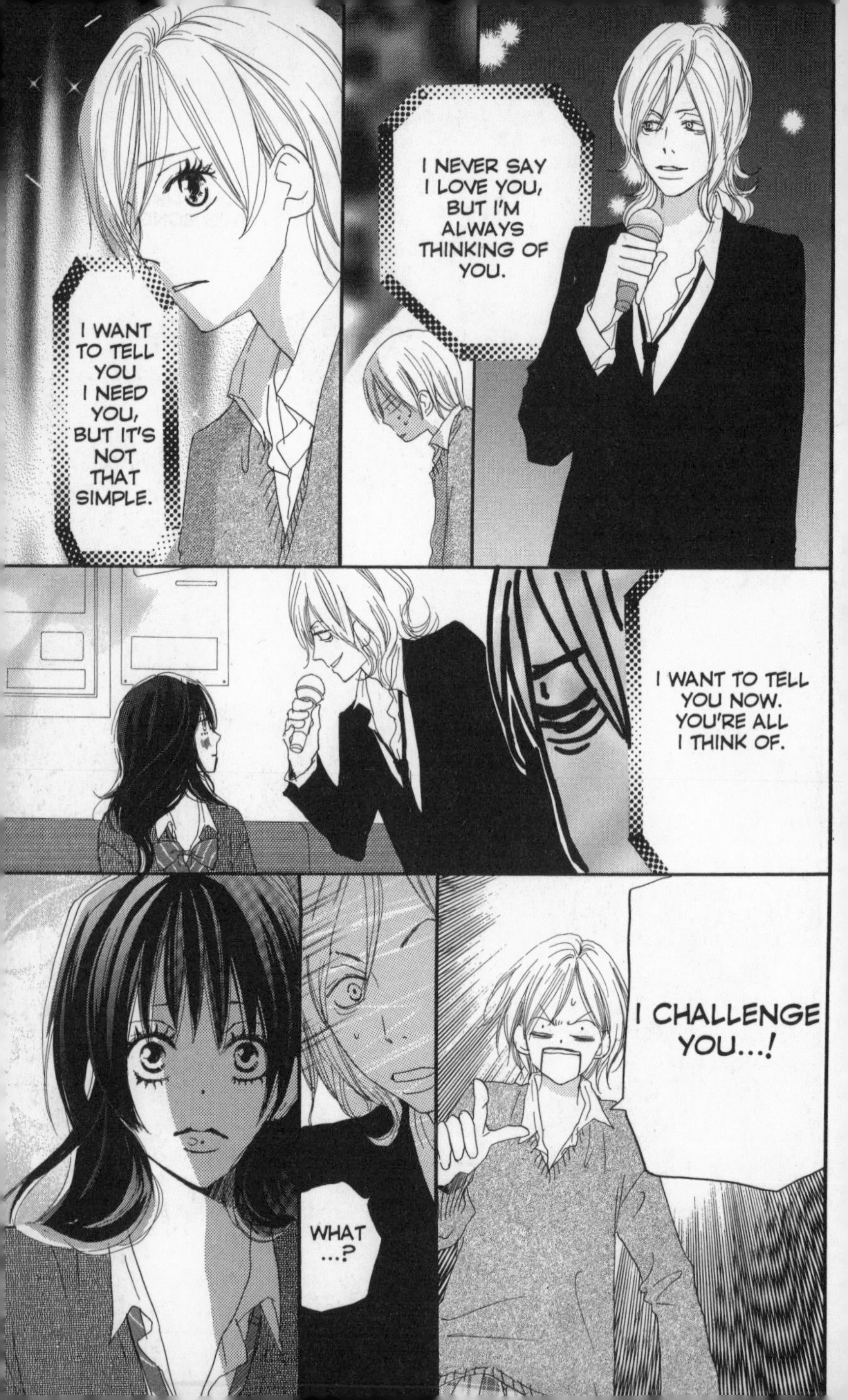
I NEVER SAY I LOVE YOU, BUT I'M ALWAYS THINKING OF YOU.
I WANT TO TELL YOU I NEED YOU, BUT IT'S NOT THAT SIMPLE.
I WANT TO TELL YOU NOW. YOU'RE ALL I THINK OF.
I CHALLENGE YOU...!
WHAT ...?

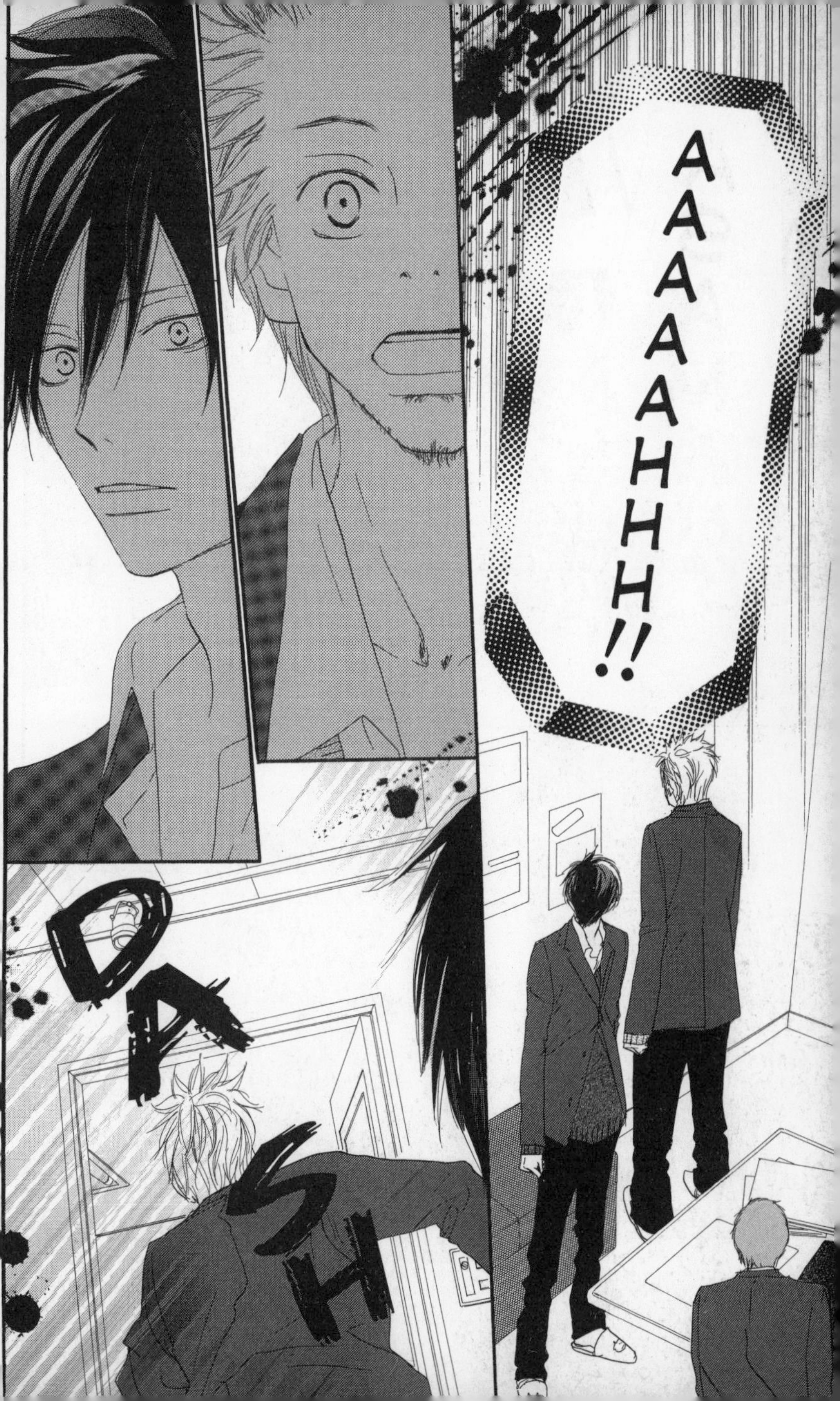
AAAAAHHH!!
DASH

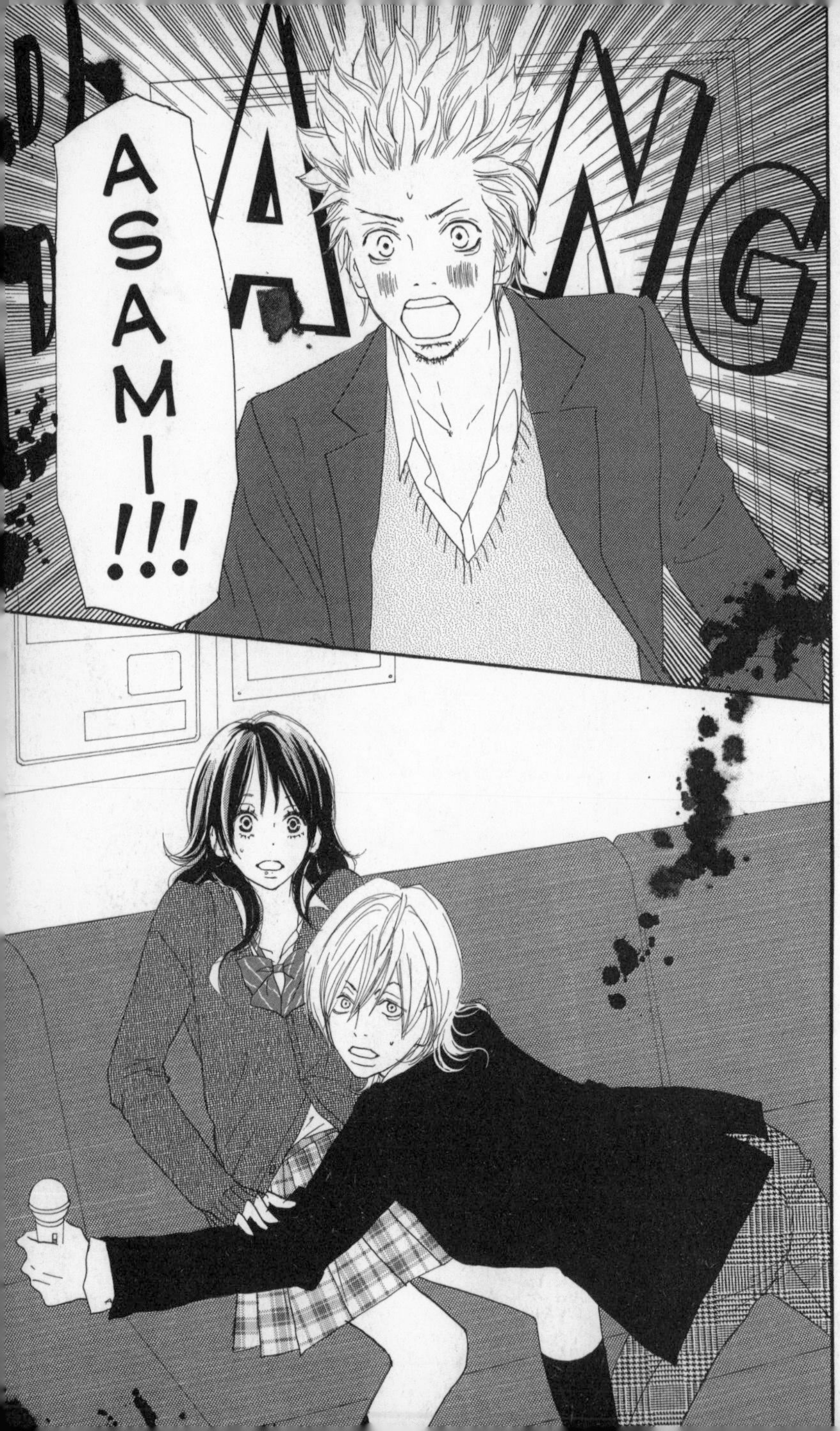
DHANG
ASAMI!!!

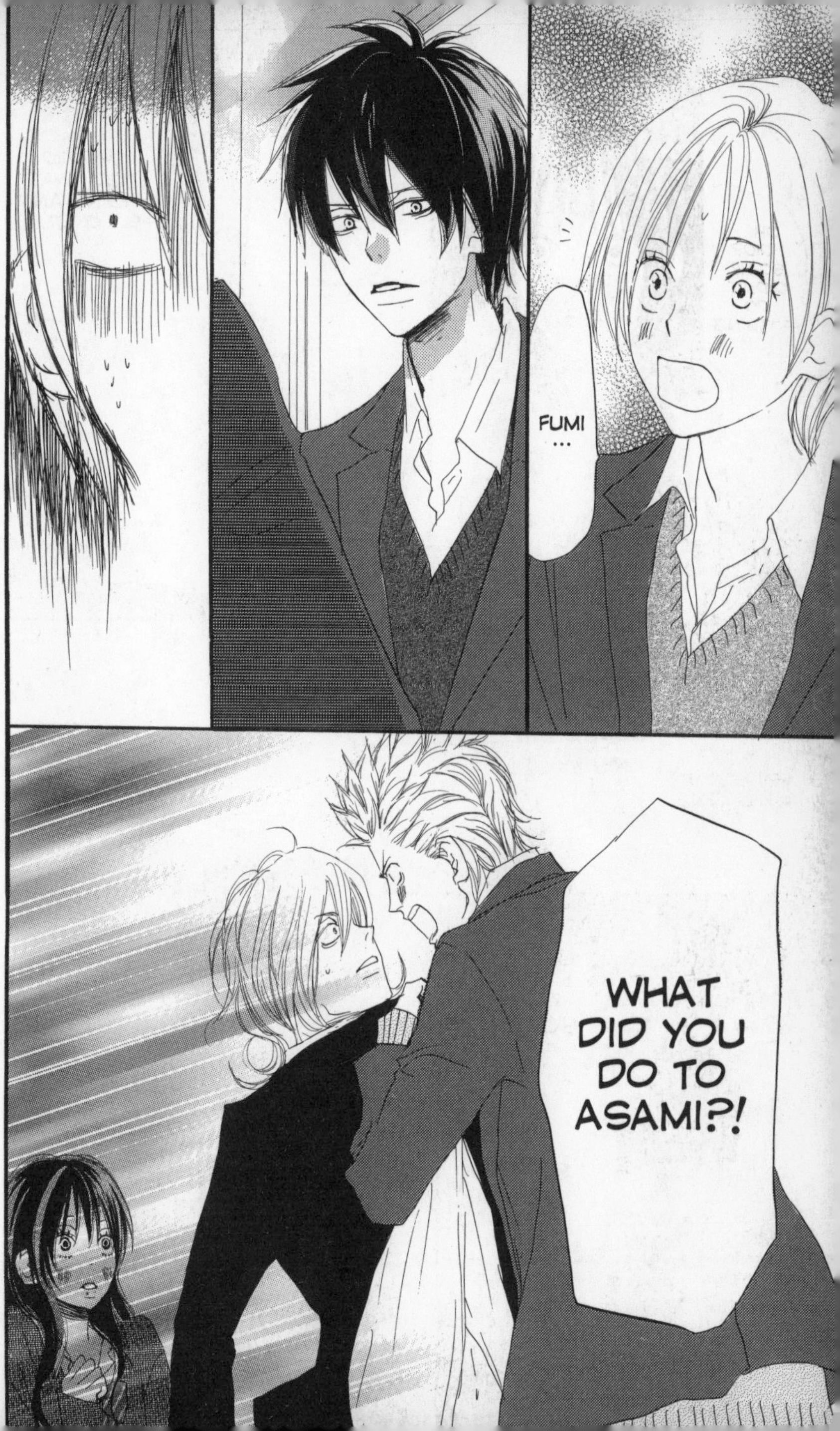
FUMI ...
WHAT DID YOU DO TO ASAMI?!

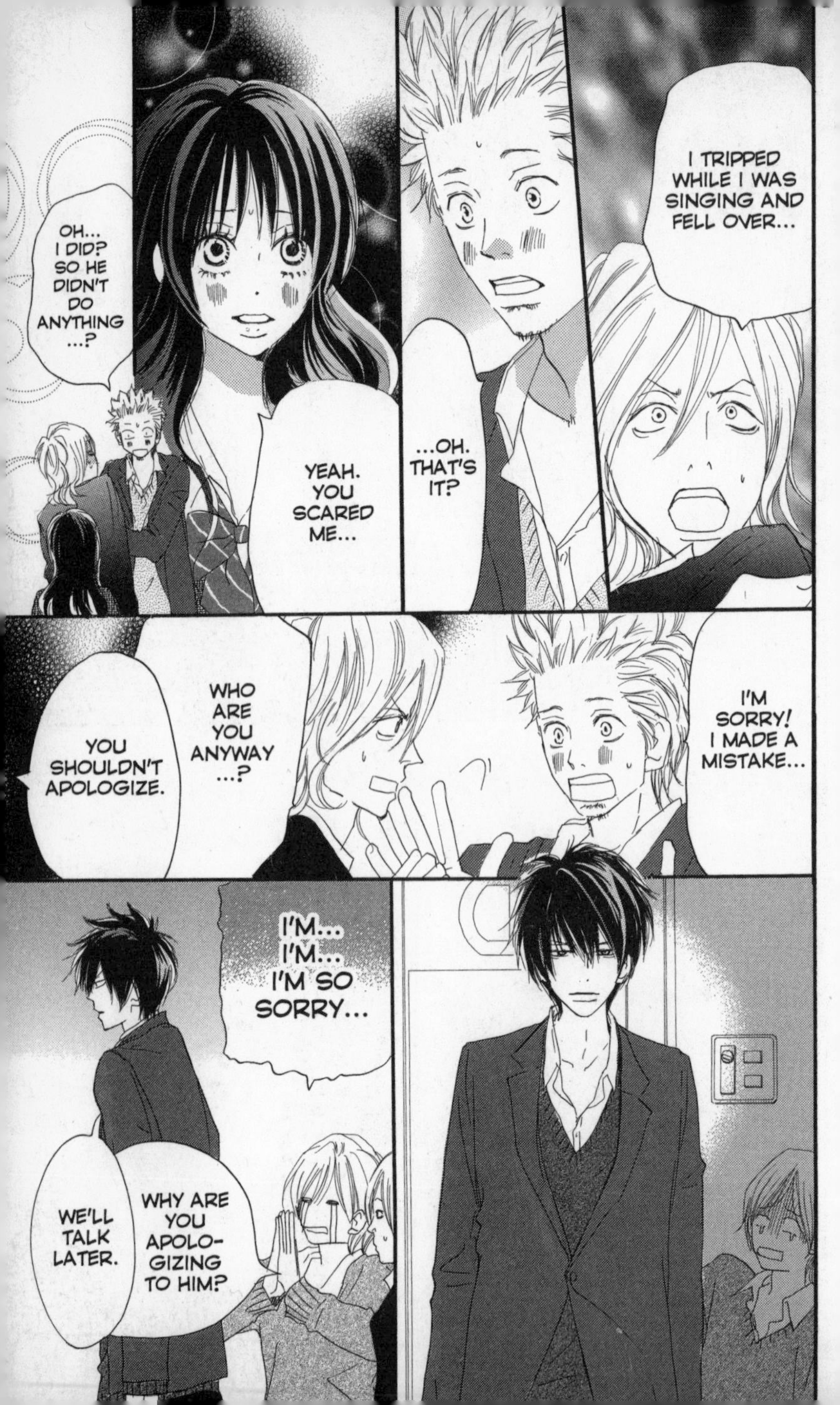
I TRIPPED WHILE I WAS SINGING AND FELL OVER...
...OH. THAT'S IT?
YEAH. YOU SCARED ME...
OH... I DID? SO HE DIDN'T DO ANYTHING ...?
I'M SORRY! I MADE A MISTAKE...
WHO ARE YOU ANYWAY ...?
YOU SHOULDN'T APOLOGIZE.
I'M... I'M... I'M SO SORRY...
WHY ARE YOU APOLO-GIZING TO HIM?
WE'LL TALK LATER.

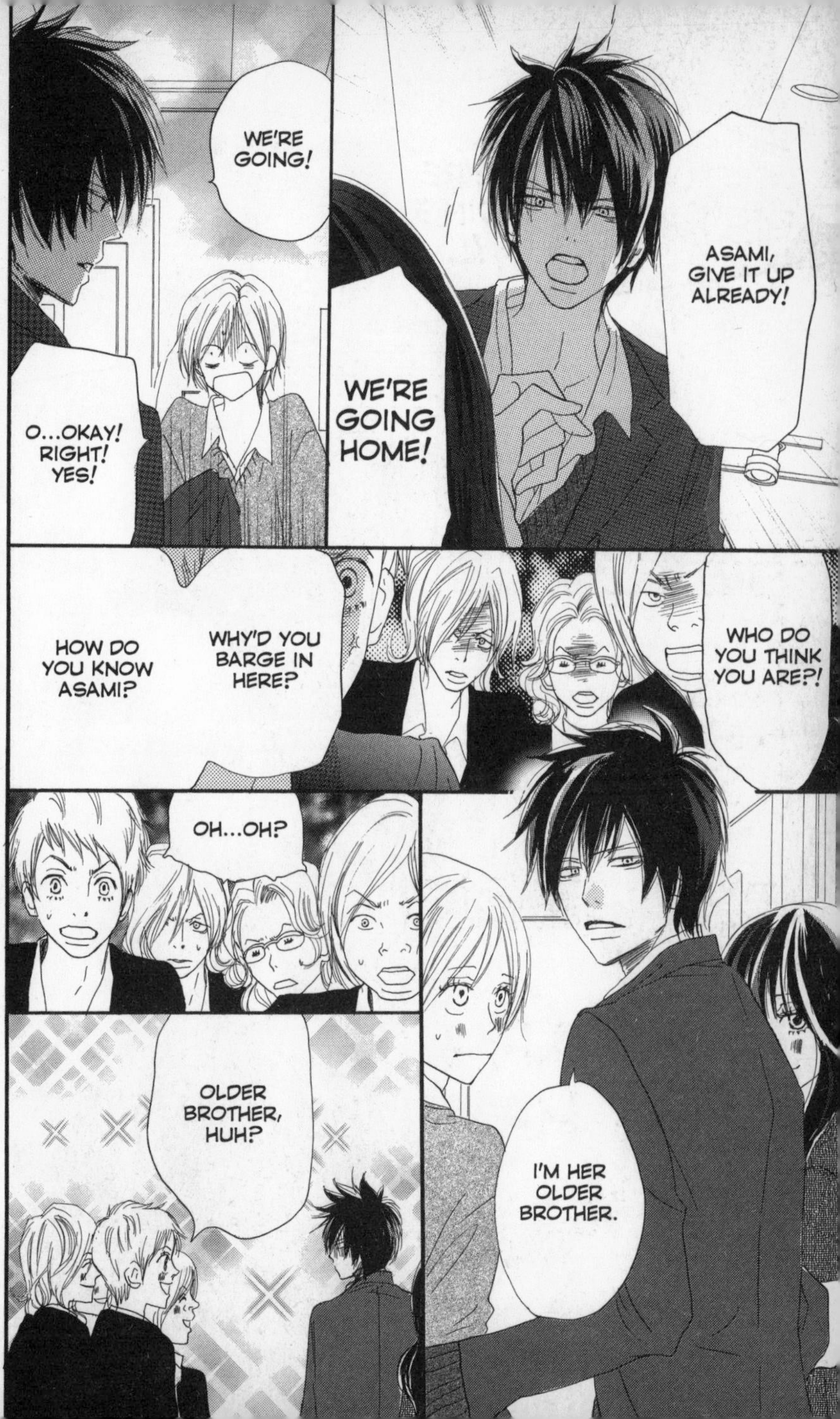
ASAMI, GIVE IT UP ALREADY!
WE'RE GOING HOME!
WE'RE GOING!
O...OKAY! RIGHT! YES!
WHO DO YOU THINK YOU ARE?!
WHY'D YOU BARGE IN HERE?
HOW DO YOU KNOW ASAMI?
I'M HER OLDER BROTHER.
OH...OH?
OLDER BROTHER, HUH?

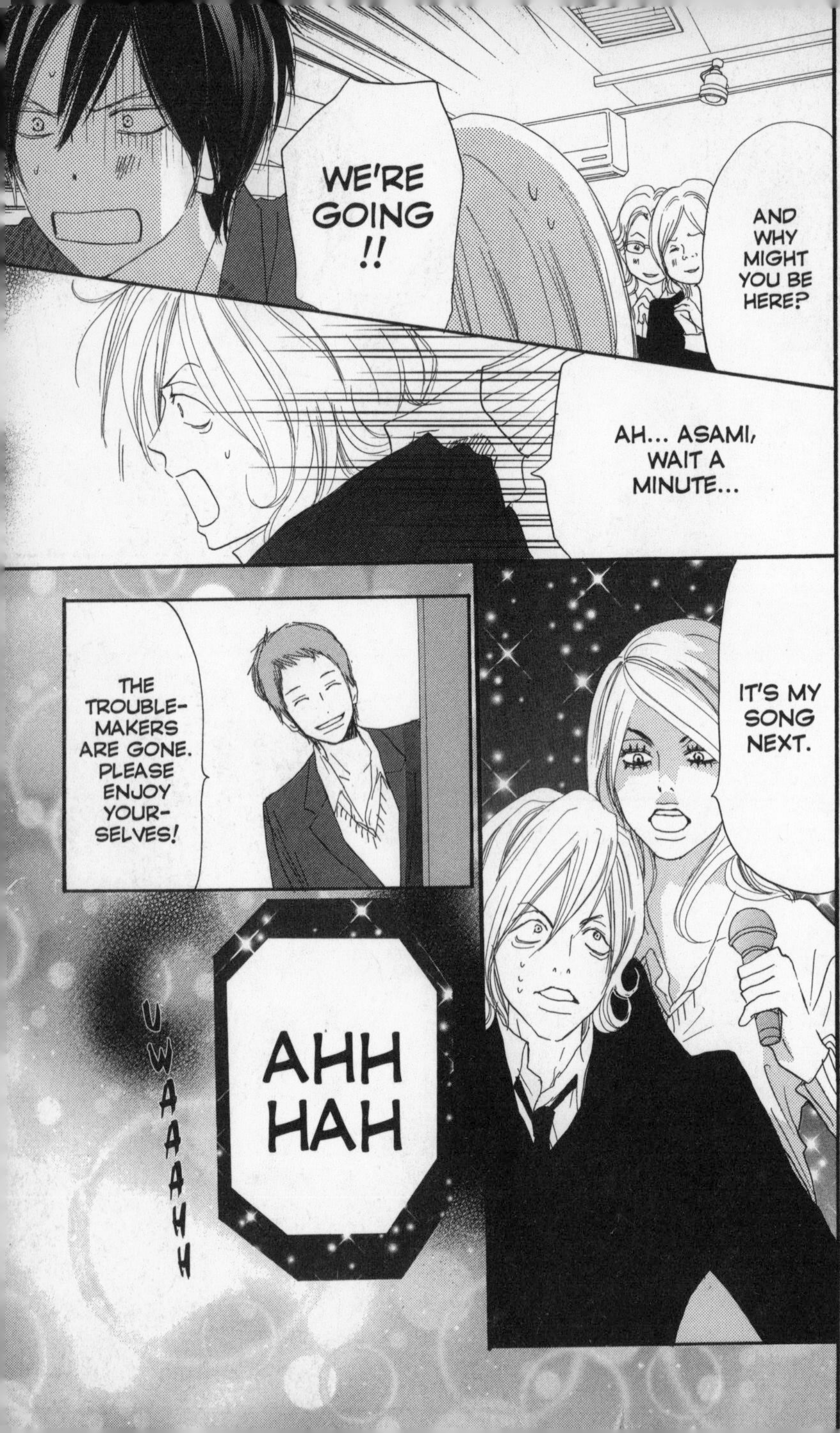
AND WHY MIGHT YOU BE HERE?
WE'RE GOING!!
AH... ASAMI, WAIT A MINUTE...
IT'S MY SONG NEXT.
THE TROUBLE-MAKERS ARE GONE. PLEASE ENJOY YOUR-SELVES!
AHH HAH
UWAAAHH

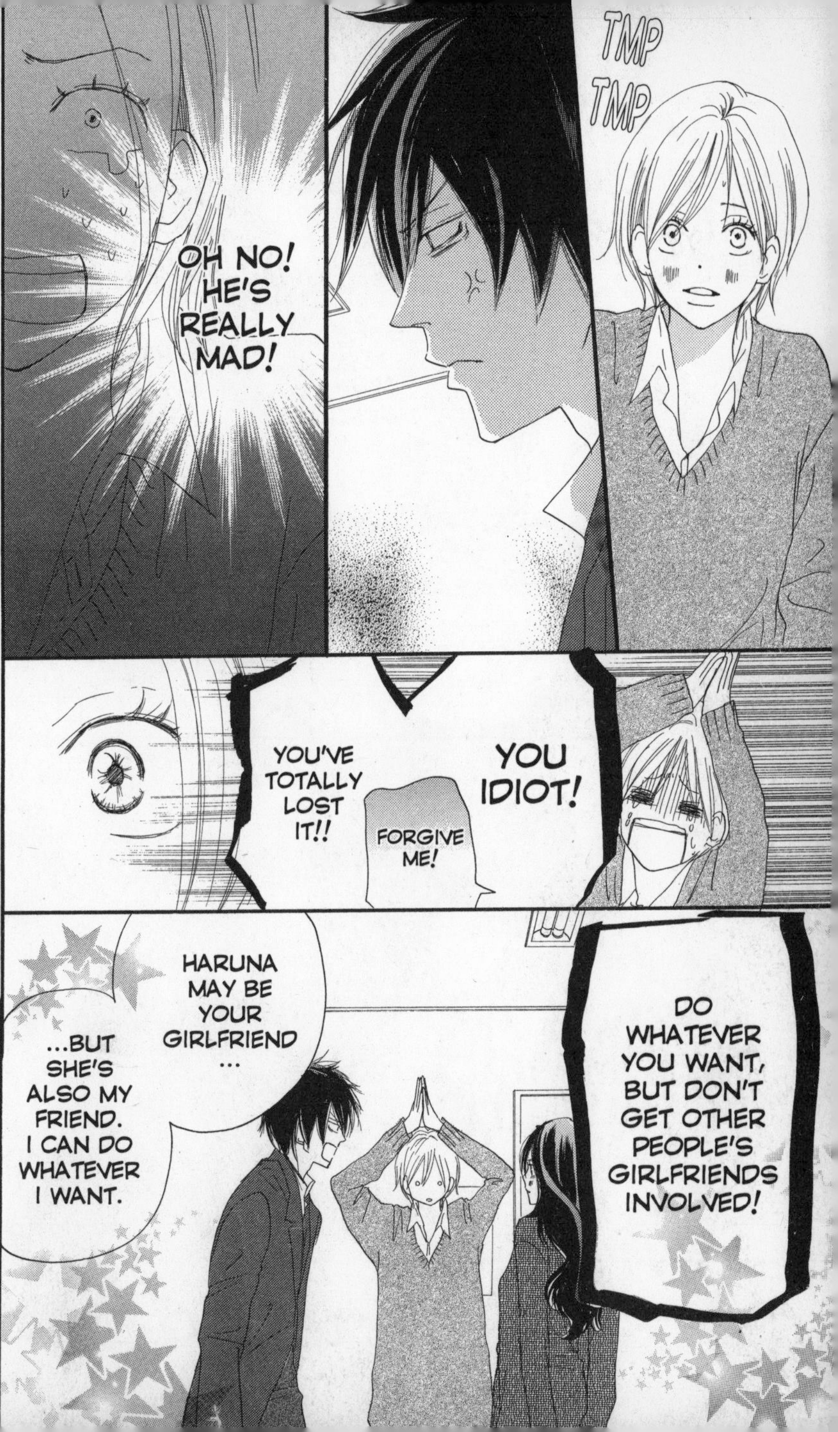
TMP TMP
OH NO! HE'S REALLY MAD!
YOU IDIOT!
YOU'VE TOTALLY LOST IT!!
FORGIVE ME!
DO WHATEVER YOU WANT, BUT DON'T GET OTHER PEOPLE'S GIRLFRIENDS INVOLVED!
HARUNA MAY BE YOUR GIRLFRIEND ...
...BUT SHE'S ALSO MY FRIEND. I CAN DO WHATEVER I WANT.

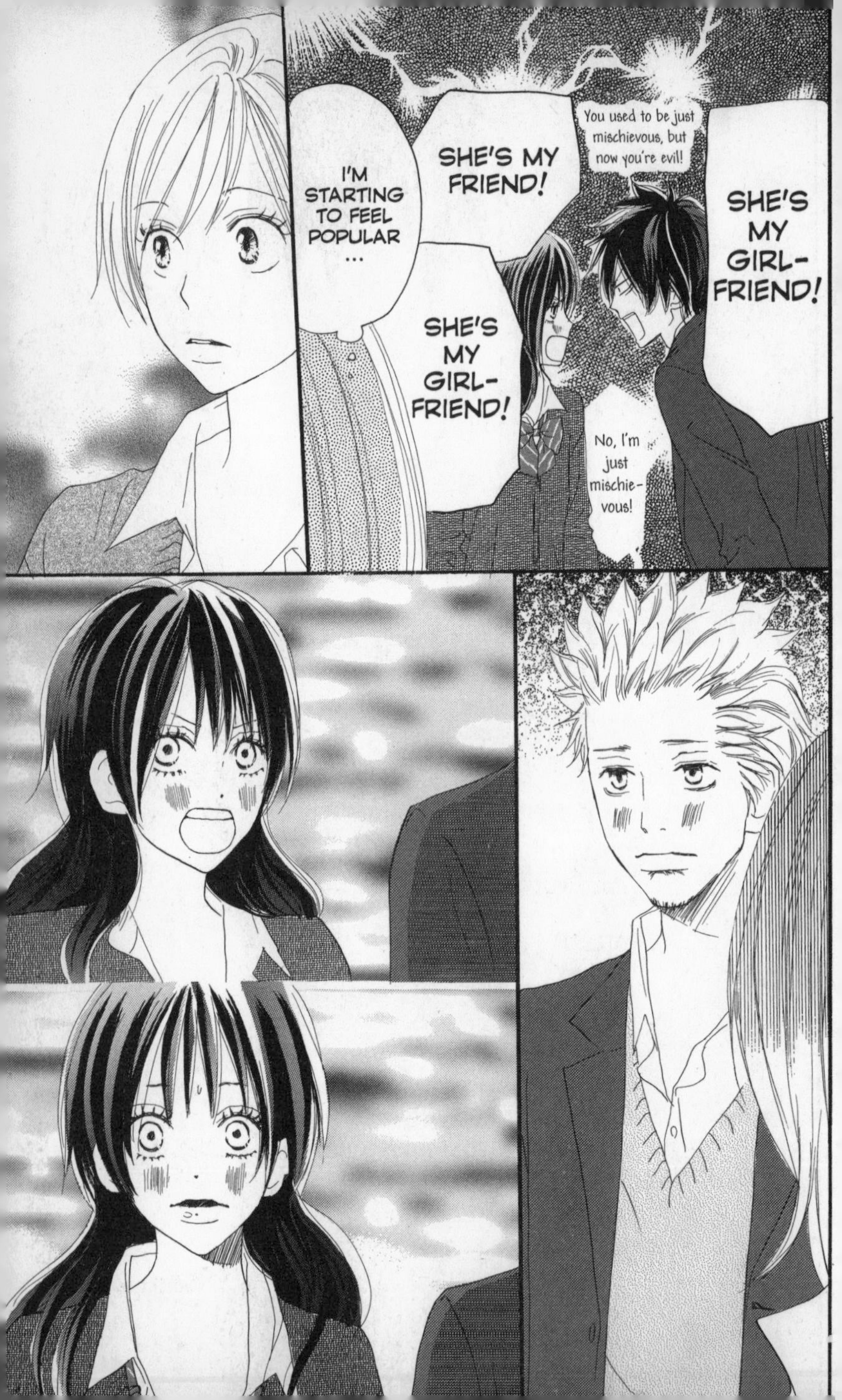
SHE'S MY GIRL-FRIEND!
You used to be just mischievous, but now you're evil!
SHE'S MY FRIEND!
I'M STARTING TO FEEL POPULAR ...
SHE'S MY GIRL-FRIEND!
No, I'm just mischie-vous!

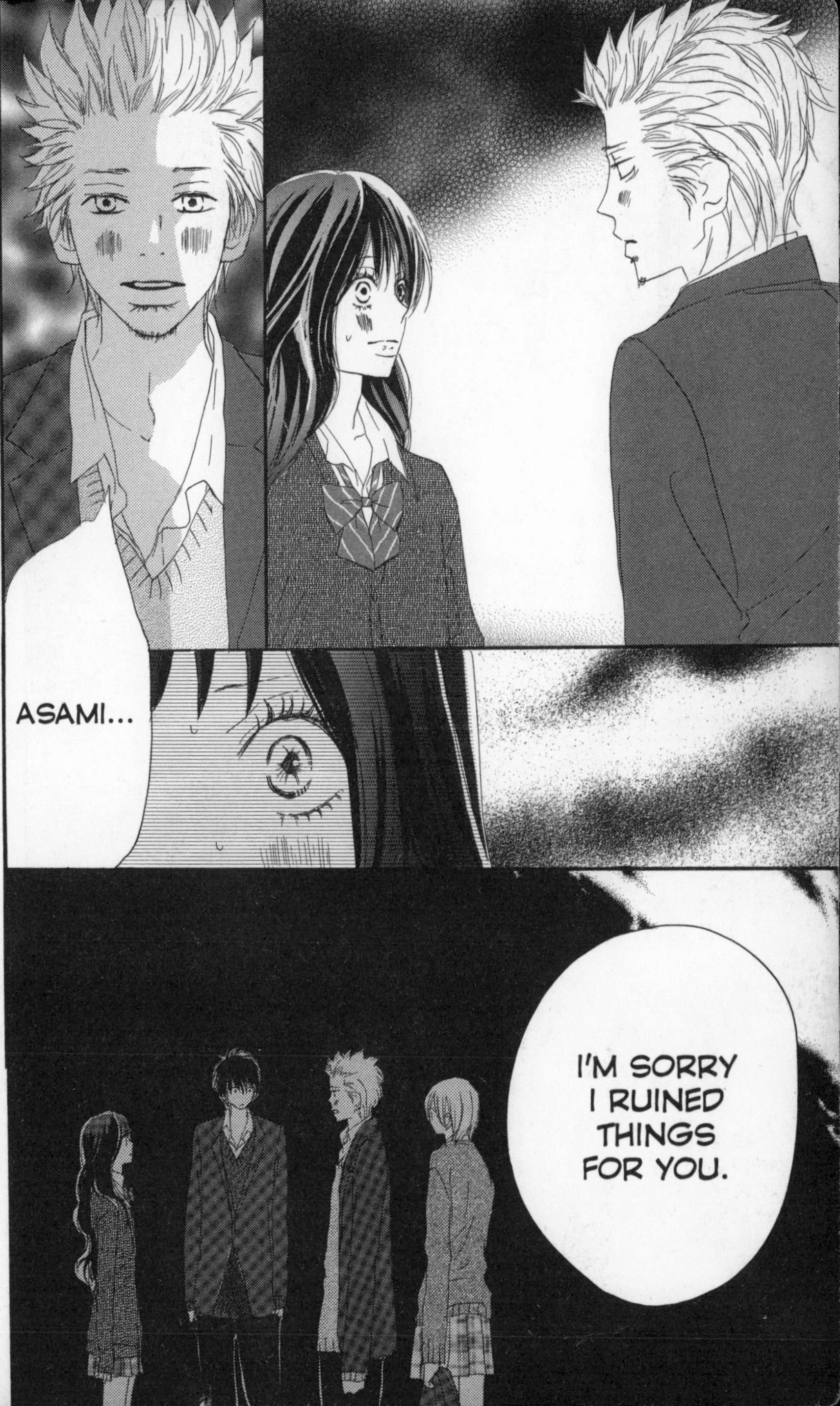
ASAMI...
I'M SORRY I RUINED THINGS FOR YOU.

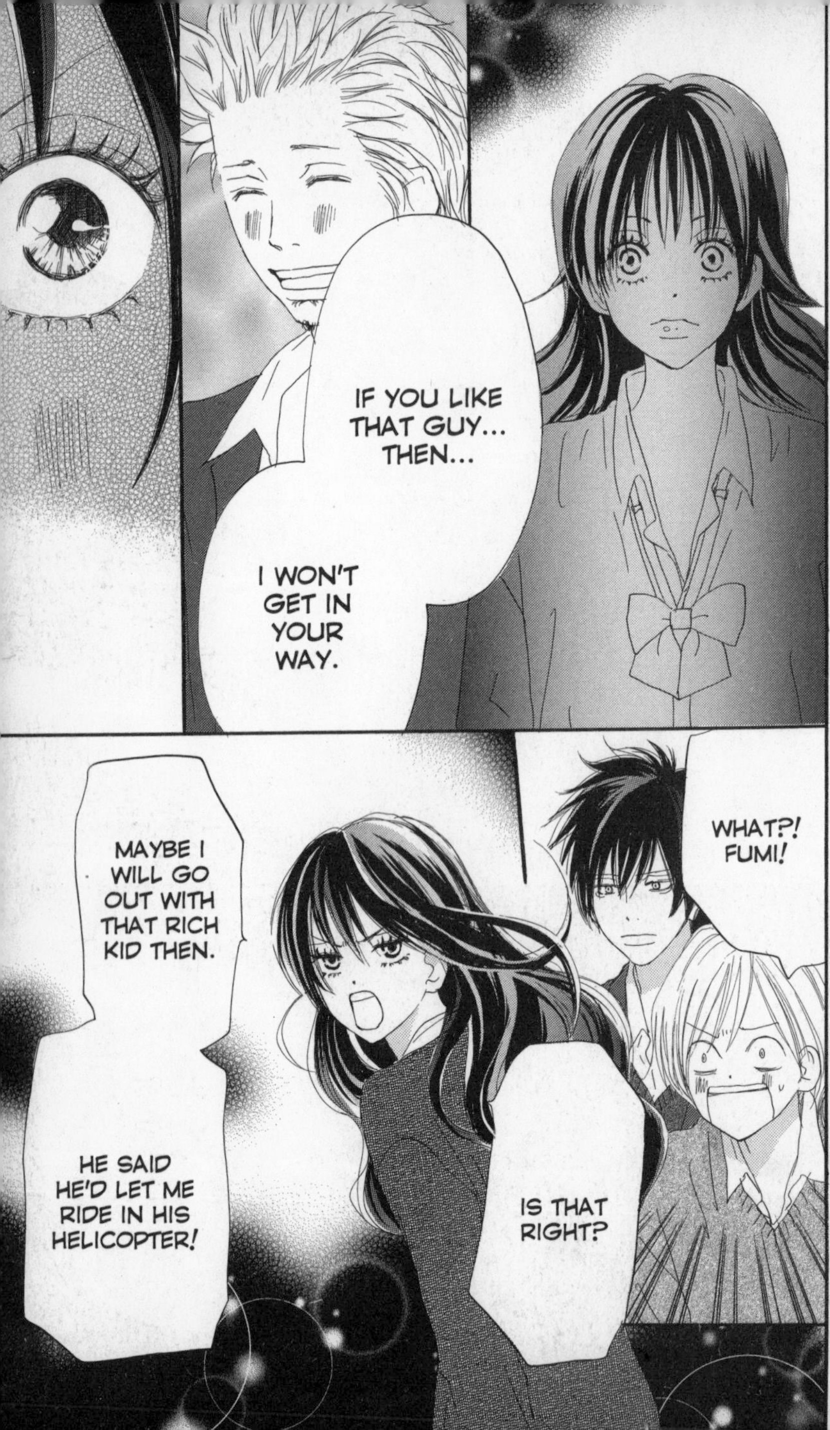
IF YOU LIKE THAT GUY... THEN...
I WON'T GET IN YOUR WAY.
WHAT?! FUMI!
MAYBE I WILL GO OUT WITH THAT RICH KID THEN.
HE SAID HE'D LET ME RIDE IN HIS HELICOPTER!
IS THAT RIGHT?

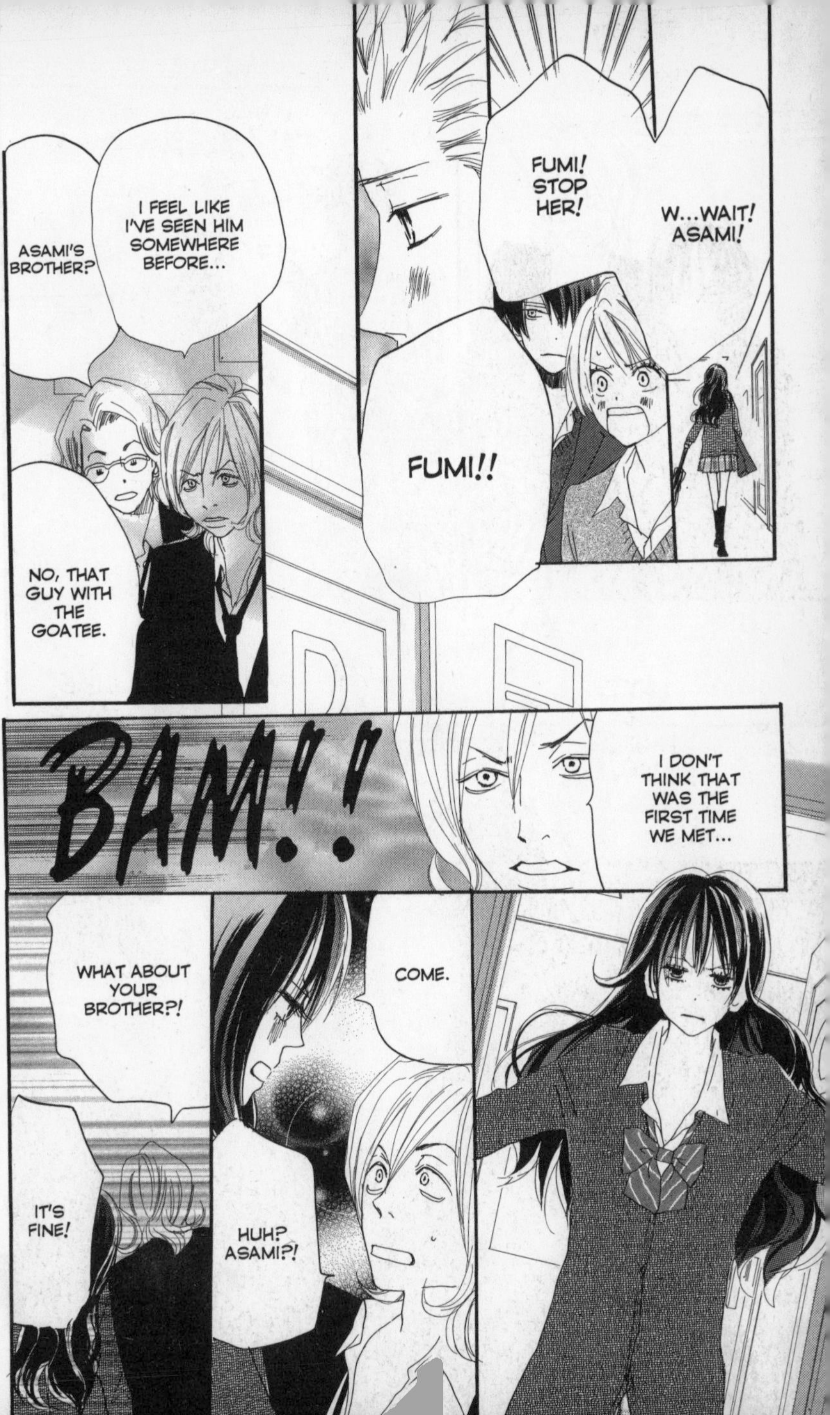
W...WAIT! ASAMI!
FUMI! STOP HER!
FUMI!!
I FEEL LIKE I'VE SEEN HIM SOMEWHERE BEFORE...
ASAMI'S BROTHER?
NO, THAT GUY WITH THE GOATEE.
I DON'T THINK THAT WAS THE FIRST TIME WE MET...
BAM!!
COME.
HUH? ASAMI?!
WHAT ABOUT YOUR BROTHER?!
IT'S FINE!

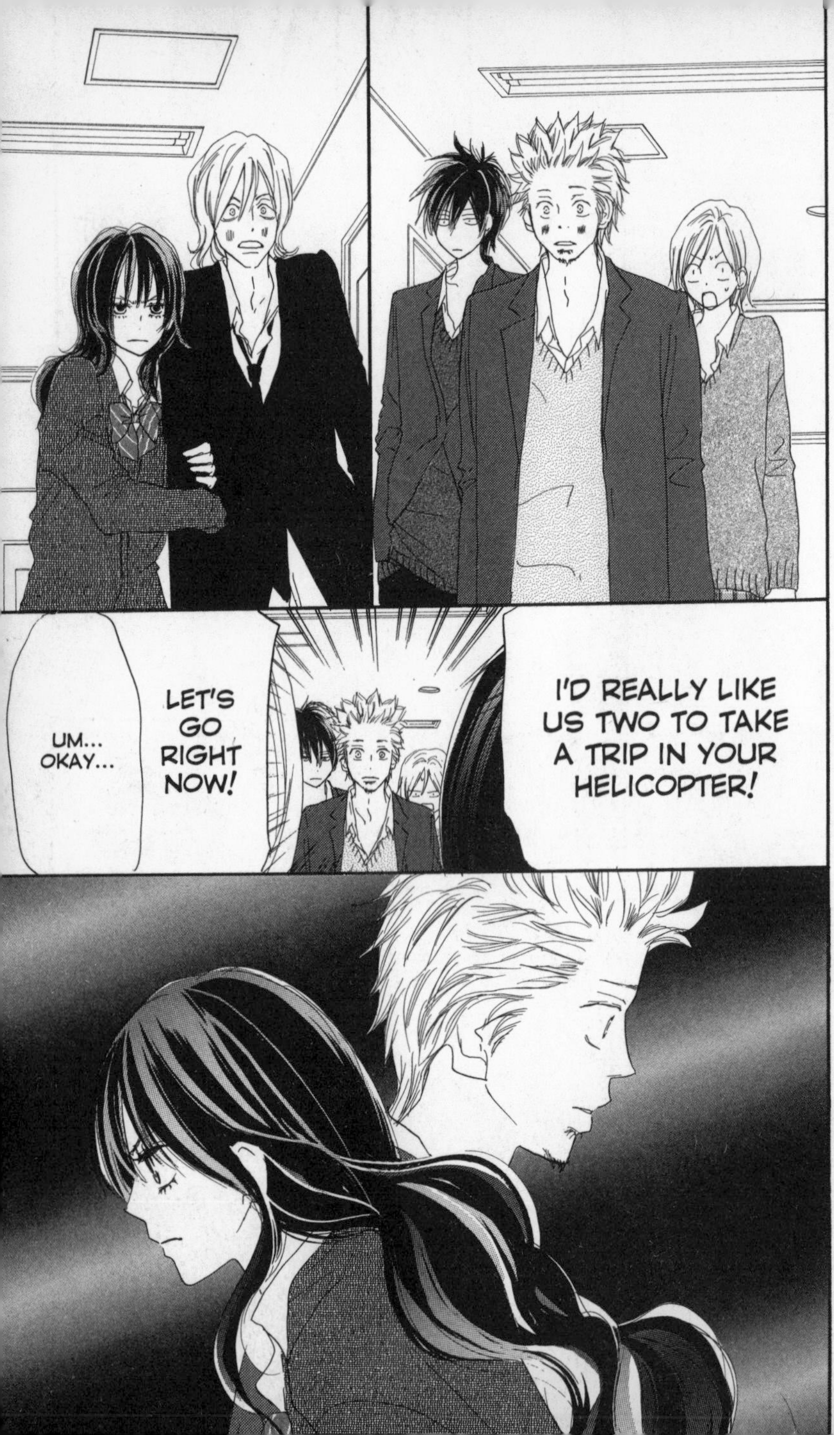
I'D REALLY LIKE US TWO TO TAKE A TRIP IN YOUR HELICOPTER!
LET'S GO RIGHT NOW!
UM... OKAY...

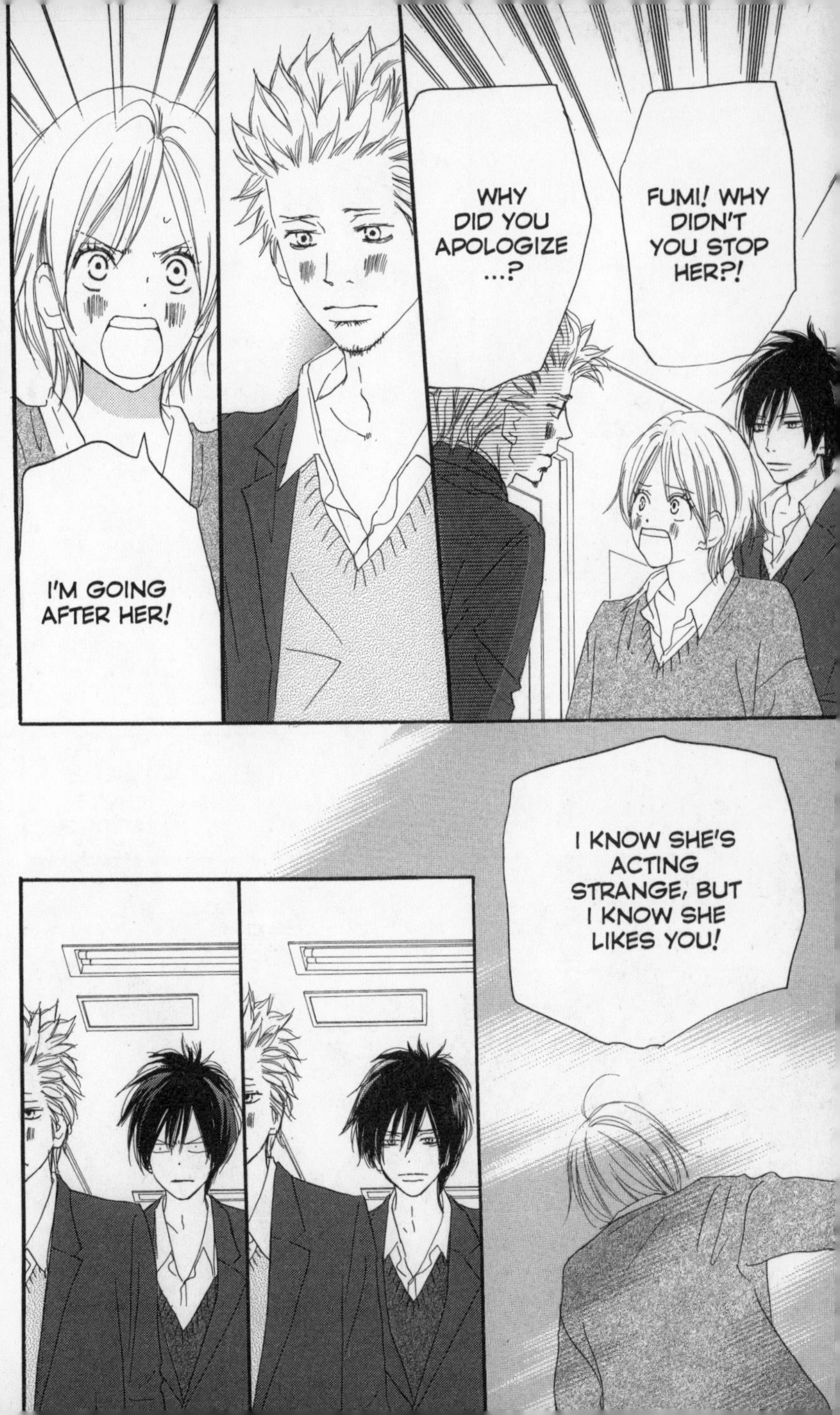
FUMI! WHY DIDN'T YOU STOP HER?!
WHY DID YOU APOLOGIZE ...?
I'M GOING AFTER HER!
I KNOW SHE'S ACTING STRANGE, BUT I KNOW SHE LIKES YOU!

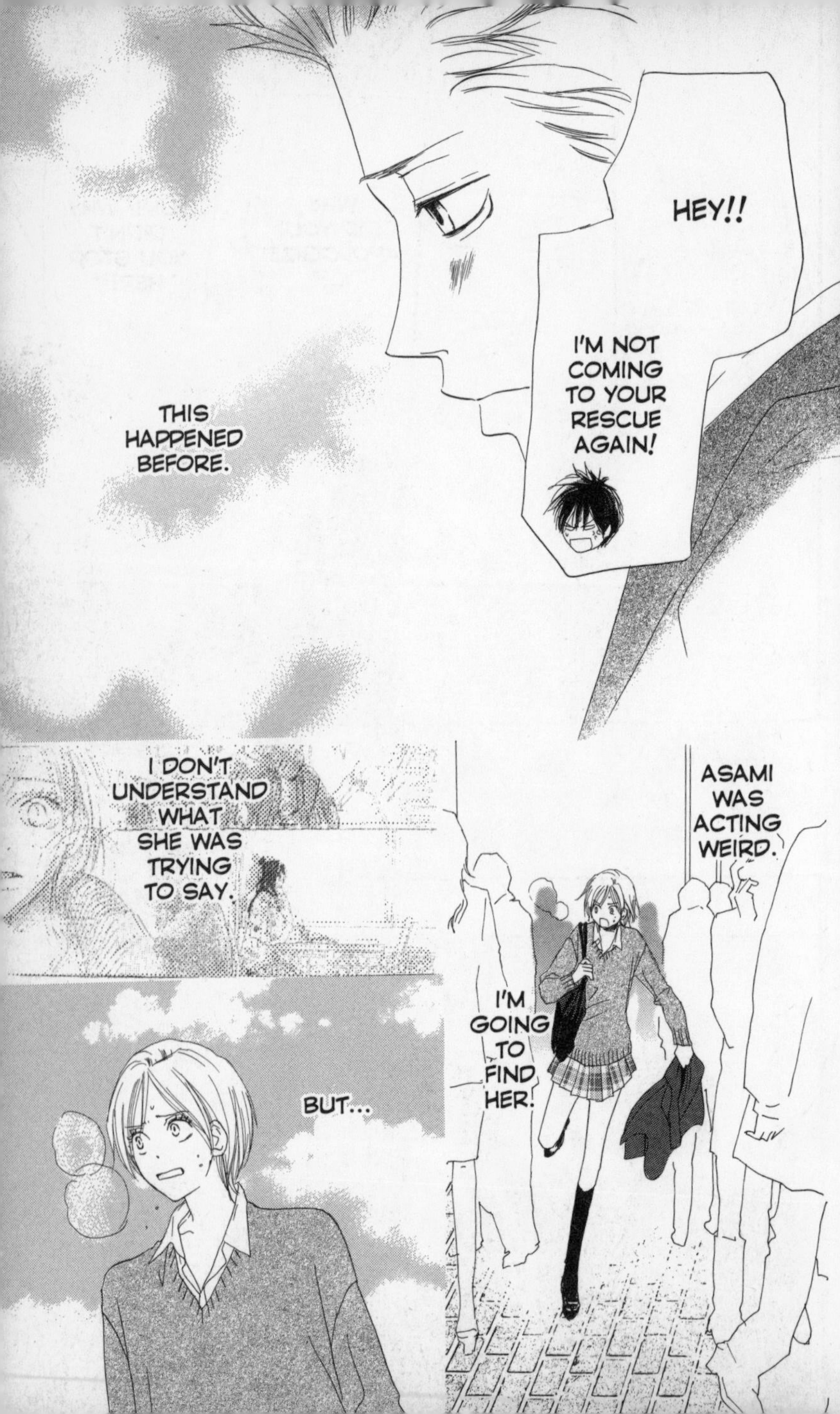
HEY!!
I'M NOT COMING TO YOUR RESCUE AGAIN!
THIS HAPPENED BEFORE.
ASAMI WAS ACTING WEIRD.
I'M GOING TO FIND HER.
I DON'T UNDERSTAND WHAT SHE WAS TRYING TO SAY.
BUT...

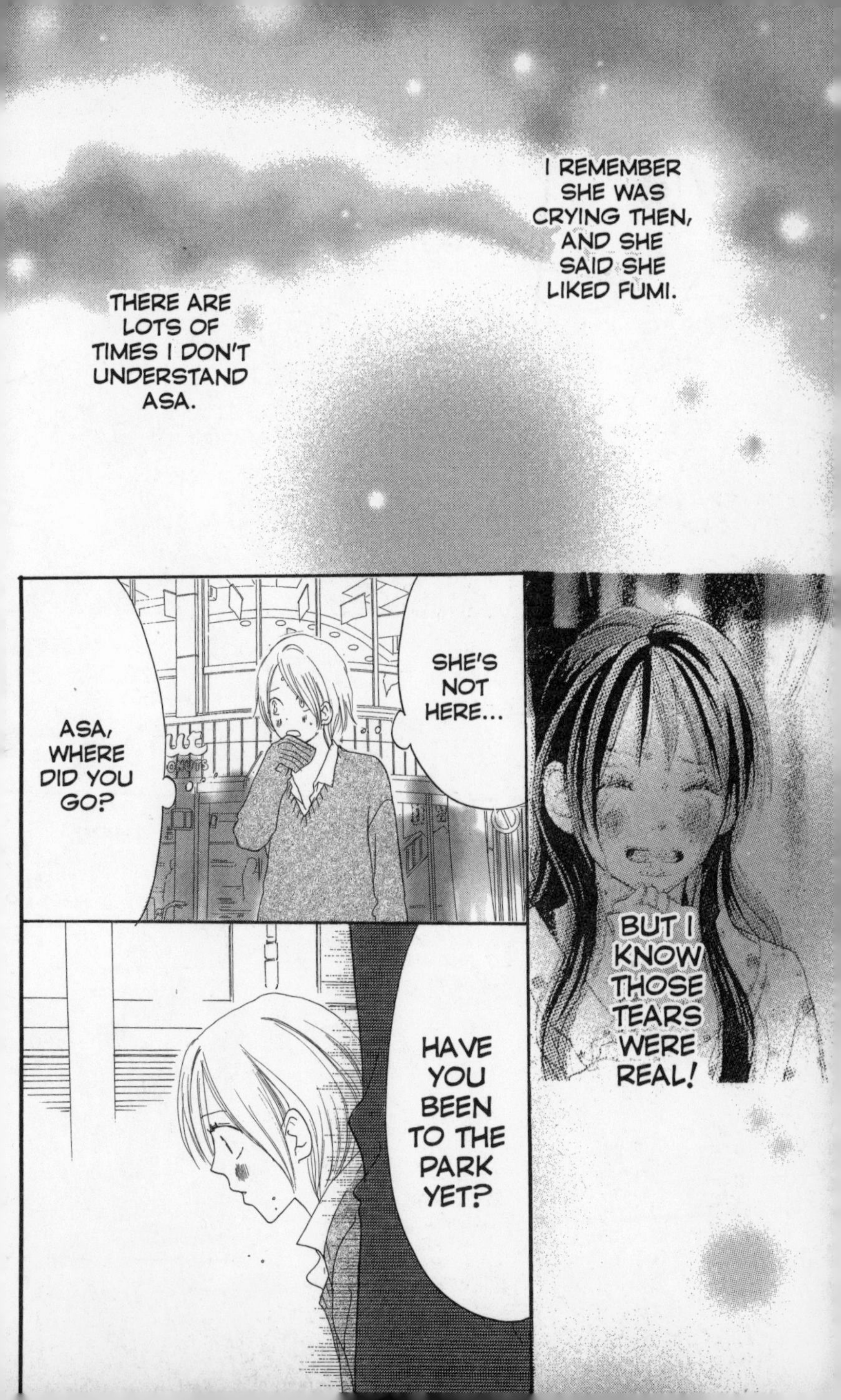
I REMEMBER SHE WAS CRYING THEN, AND SHE SAID SHE LIKED FUMI.
THERE ARE LOTS OF TIMES I DON'T UNDERSTAND ASA.
BUT I KNOW THOSE TEARS WERE REAL!
SHE'S NOT HERE...
ASA, WHERE DID YOU GO?
HAVE YOU BEEN TO THE PARK YET?

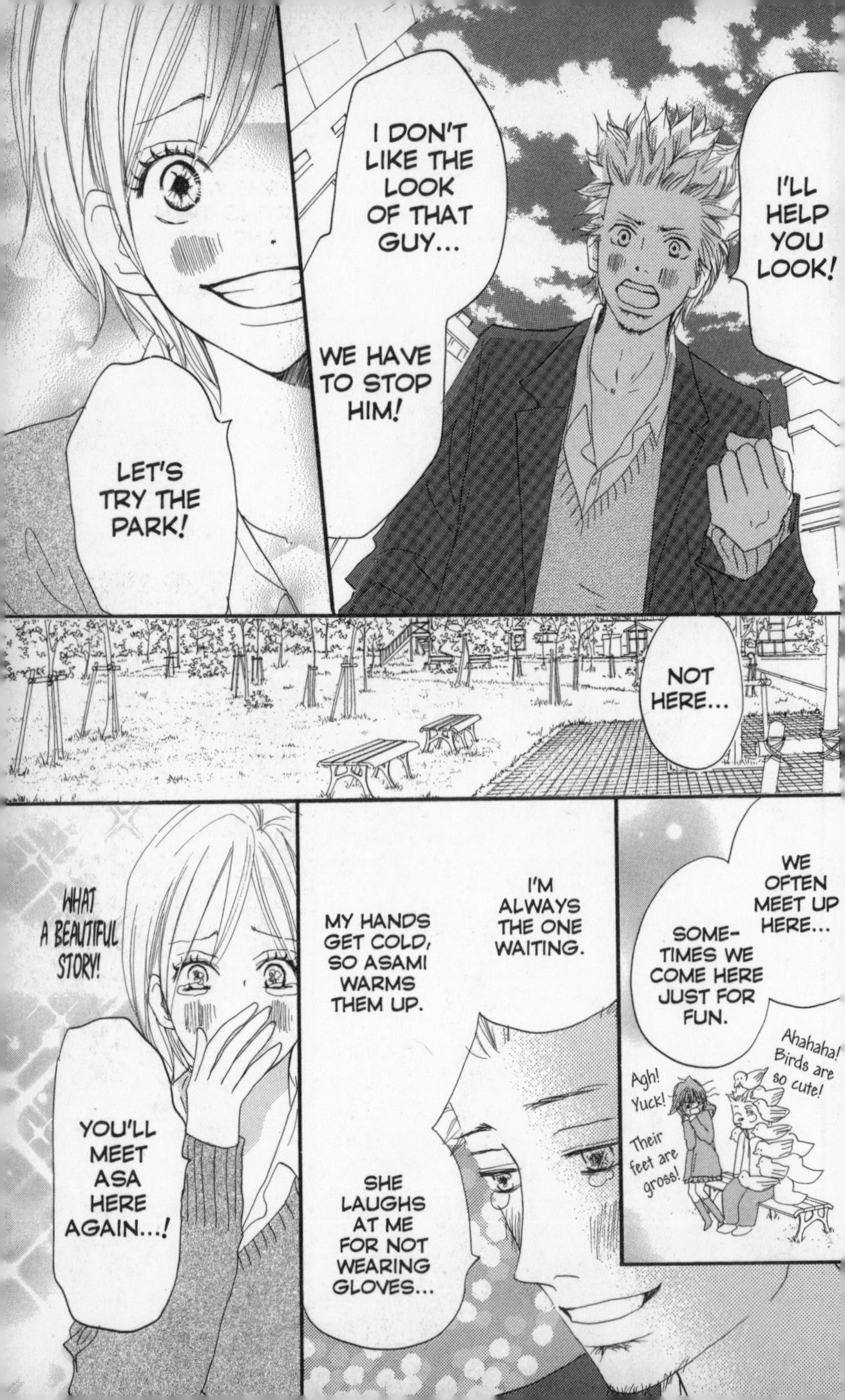
I'LL HELP YOU LOOK!
I DON'T LIKE THE LOOK OF THAT GUY...
WE HAVE TO STOP HIM!
LET'S TRY THE PARK!
NOT HERE...
WE OFTEN MEET UP HERE...
SOME-TIMES WE COME HERE JUST FOR FUN.
Ahahaha! Birds are so cute!
Agh! Yuck!
Their feet are gross!
I'M ALWAYS THE ONE WAITING.
MY HANDS GET COLD, SO ASAMI WARMS THEM UP.
SHE LAUGHS AT ME FOR NOT WEARING GLOVES...
WHAT A BEAUTIFUL STORY!
YOU'LL MEET ASA HERE AGAIN...!

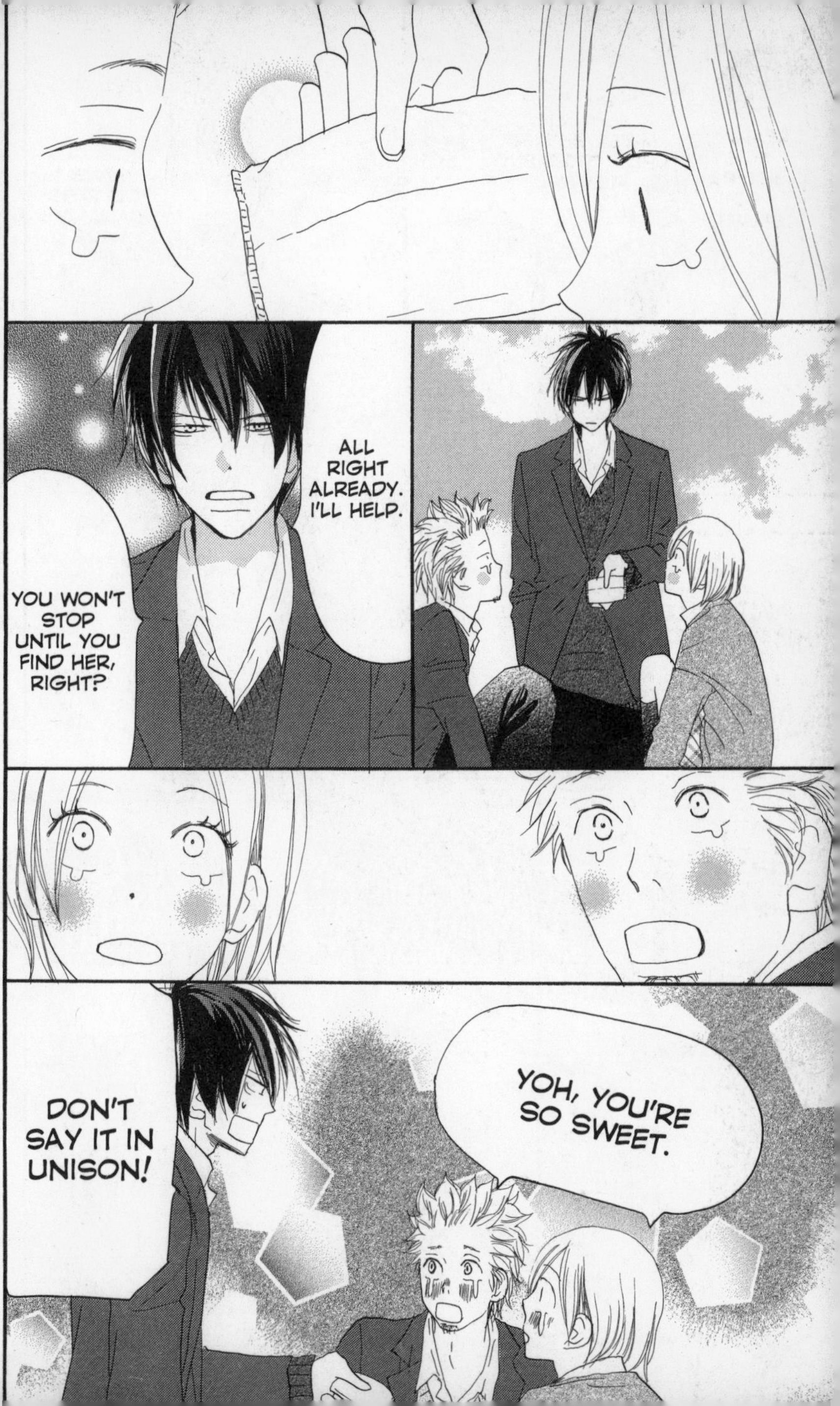

ALL RIGHT ALREADY. I'LL HELP.
YOU WON'T STOP UNTIL YOU FIND HER, RIGHT?
YOH, YOU'RE SO SWEET.
DON'T SAY IT IN UNISON!

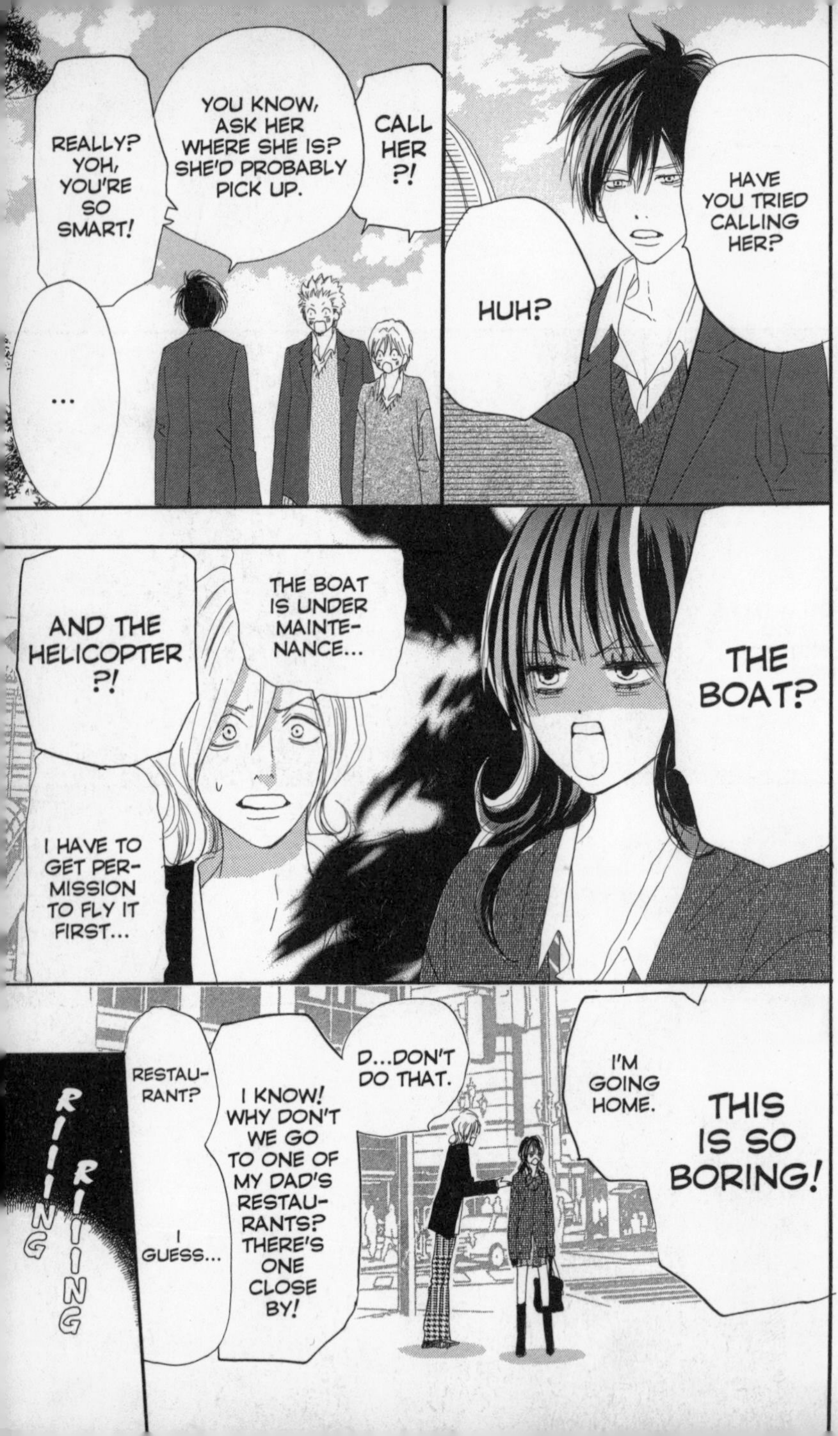
HAVE YOU TRIED CALLING HER?
HUH?
CALL HER ?!
YOU KNOW, ASK HER WHERE SHE IS? SHE'D PROBABLY PICK UP.
REALLY? YOH, YOU'RE SO SMART!
...
THE BOAT?
THE BOAT IS UNDER MAINTE- NANCE...
AND THE HELICOPTER ?!
I HAVE TO GET PER- MISSION TO FLY IT FIRST...
THIS IS SO BORING!
I'M GOING HOME.
D...DON'T DO THAT.
I KNOW! WHY DON'T WE GO TO ONE OF MY DAD'S RESTAU- RANTS? THERE'S ONE CLOSE BY!
RESTAU- RANT?
I GUESS...
RIIING RIIING

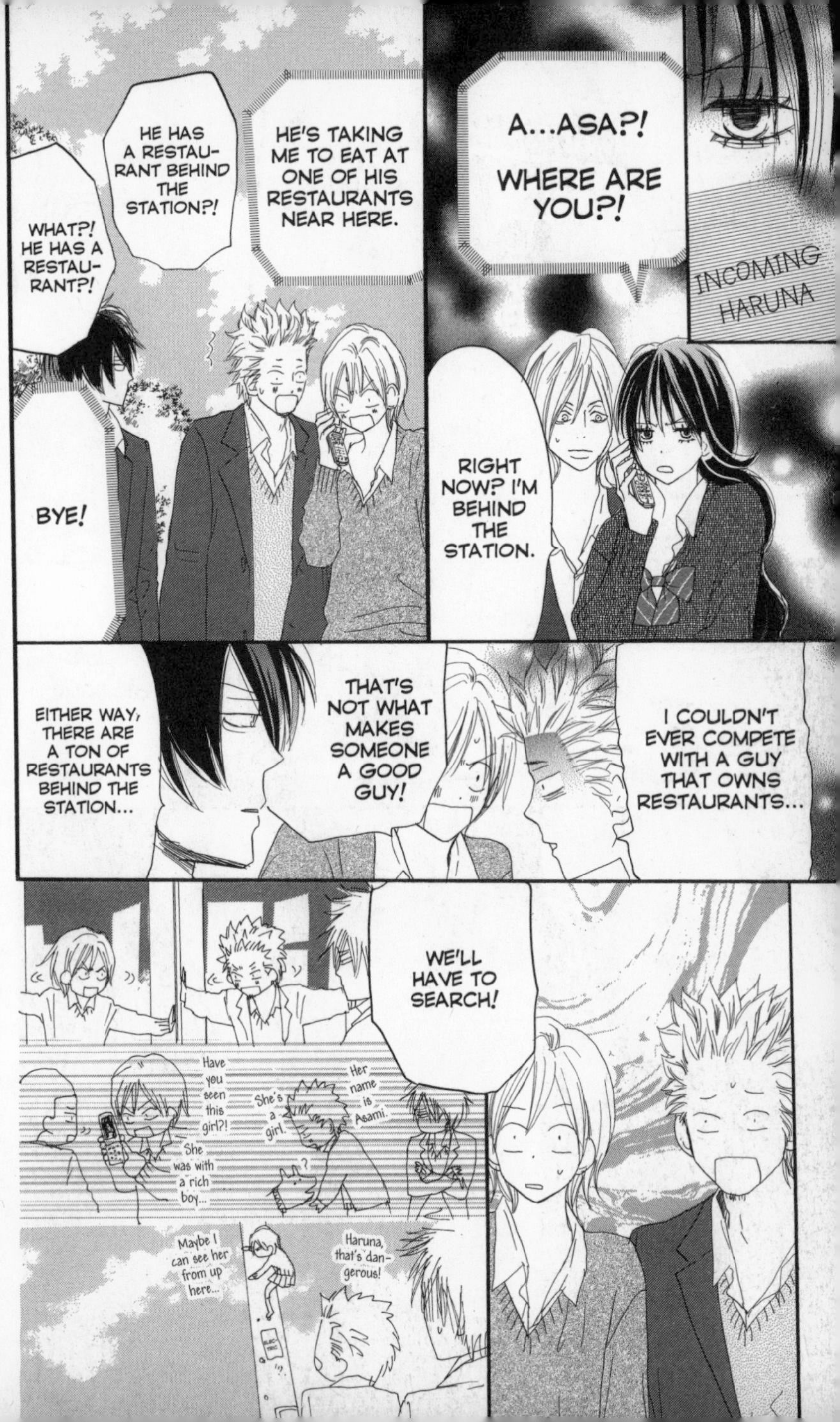
INCOMING HARUNA
A...ASA?! WHERE ARE YOU?!
RIGHT NOW? I'M BEHIND THE STATION.
HE'S TAKING ME TO EAT AT ONE OF HIS RESTAURANTS NEAR HERE.
HE HAS A RESTAURANT BEHIND THE STATION?!
WHAT?! HE HAS A RESTAURANT?!
BYE!
I COULDN'T EVER COMPETE WITH A GUY THAT OWNS RESTAURANTS...
THAT'S NOT WHAT MAKES SOMEONE A GOOD GUY!
EITHER WAY, THERE ARE A TON OF RESTAURANTS BEHIND THE STATION...
WE'LL HAVE TO SEARCH!
Her name is Asami.
She's a girl.
Have you seen this girl?!
She was with a rich boy...
Haruna, that's dangerous!
Maybe I can see her from up here...

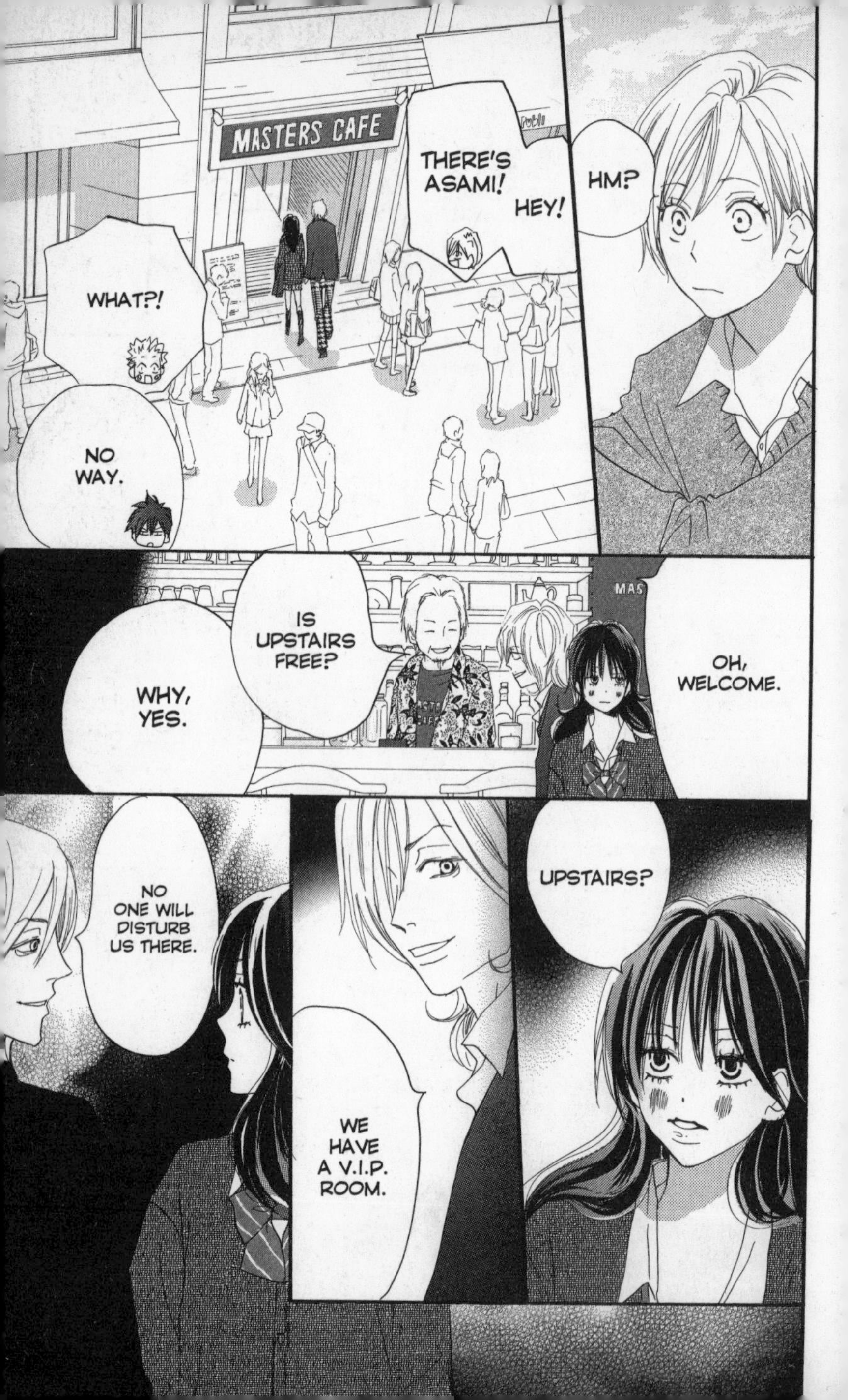
HM?
THERE'S ASAMI!
HEY!
MASTERS CAFE
WHAT?!
NO WAY.
OH, WELCOME.
IS UPSTAIRS FREE?
WHY, YES.
UPSTAIRS?
WE HAVE A V.I.P. ROOM.
NO ONE WILL DISTURB US THERE.

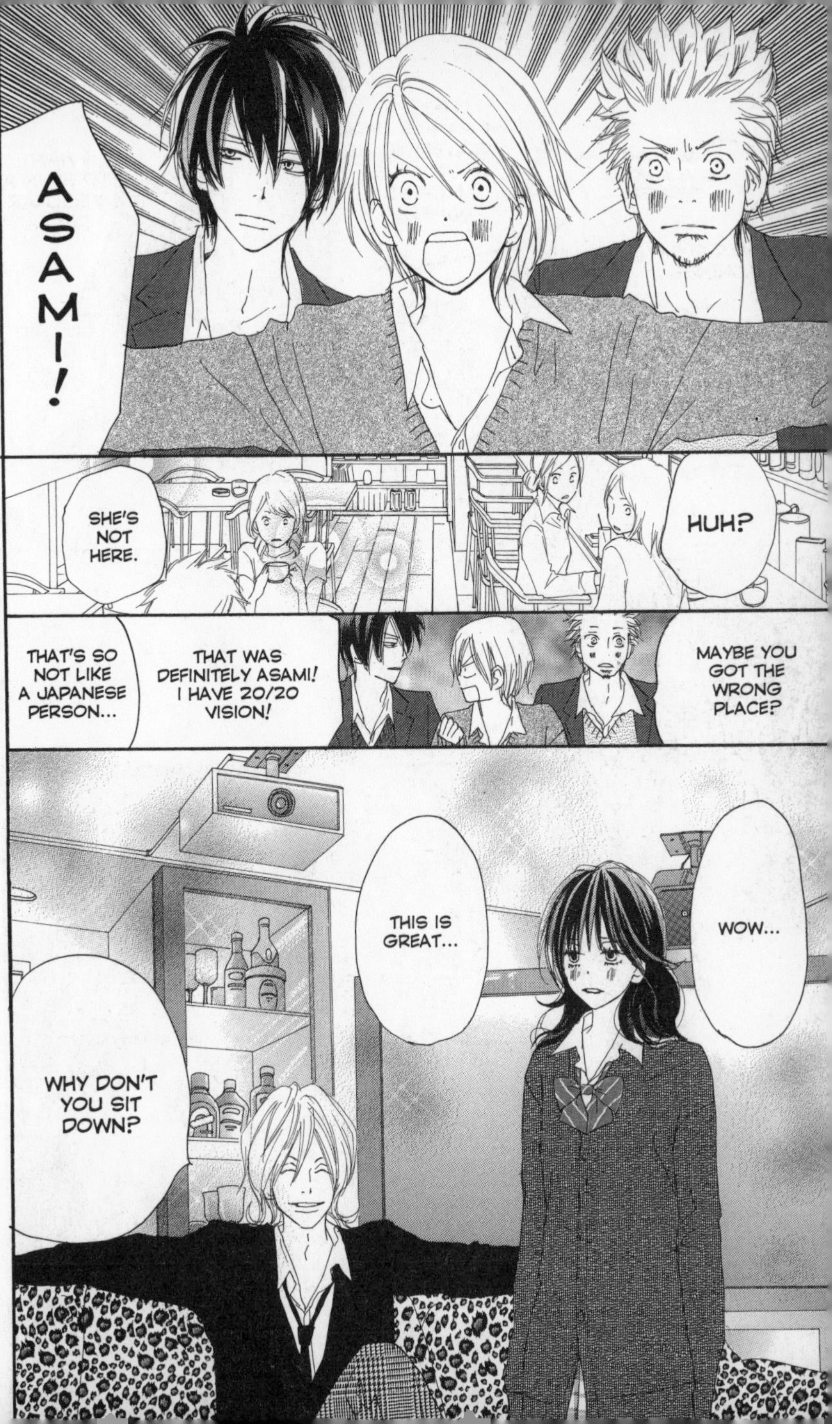
ASAMI!
HUH?
SHE'S NOT HERE.
MAYBE YOU GOT THE WRONG PLACE?
THAT WAS DEFINITELY ASAMI! I HAVE 20/20 VISION!
THAT'S SO NOT LIKE A JAPANESE PERSON...
WOW...
THIS IS GREAT...
WHY DON'T YOU SIT DOWN?

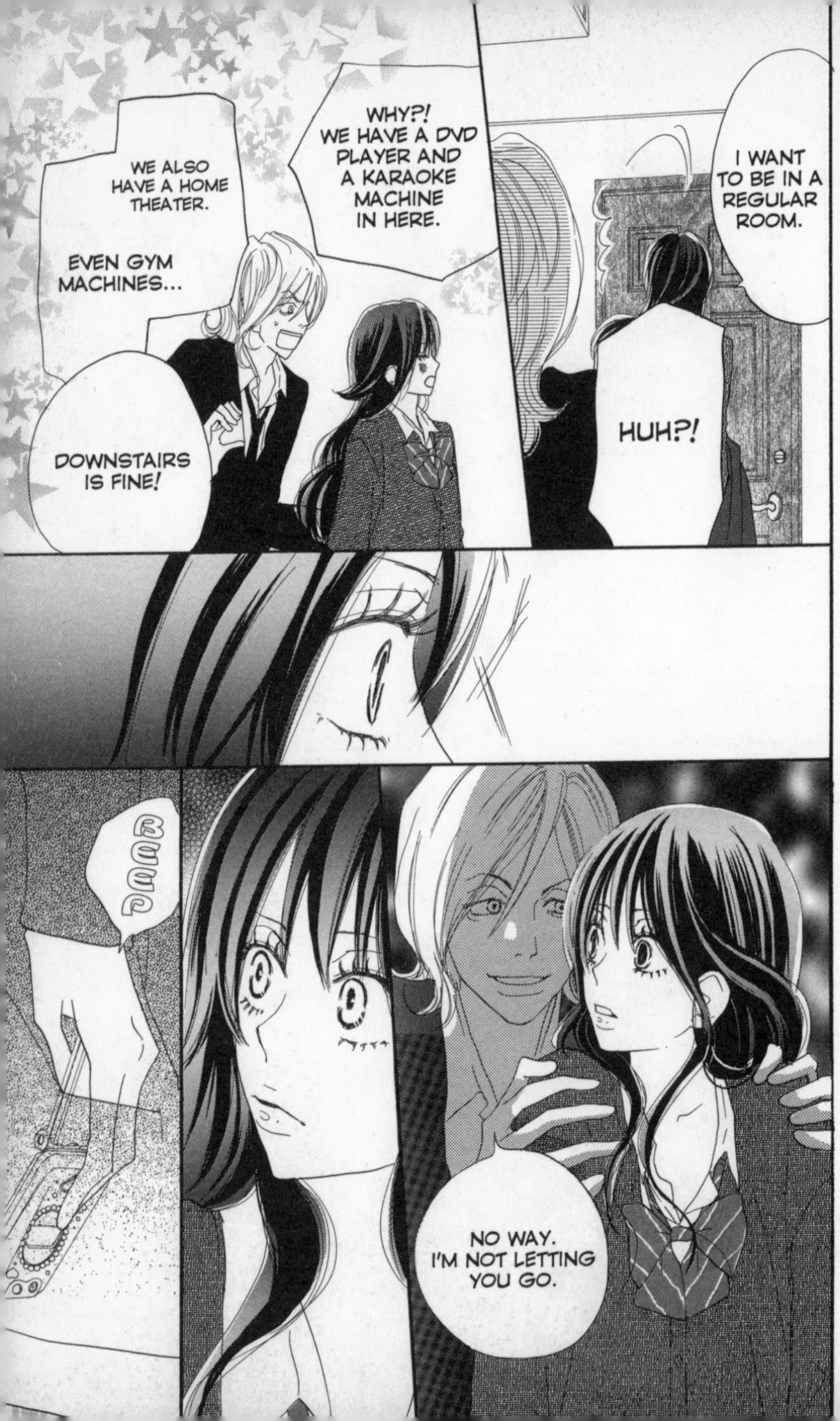
I WANT TO BE IN A REGULAR ROOM.
HUH?!
WHY?! WE HAVE A DVD PLAYER AND A KARAOKE MACHINE IN HERE.
WE ALSO HAVE A HOME THEATER.
EVEN GYM MACHINES...
DOWNSTAIRS IS FINE!
NO WAY. I'M NOT LETTING YOU GO.
BEEP

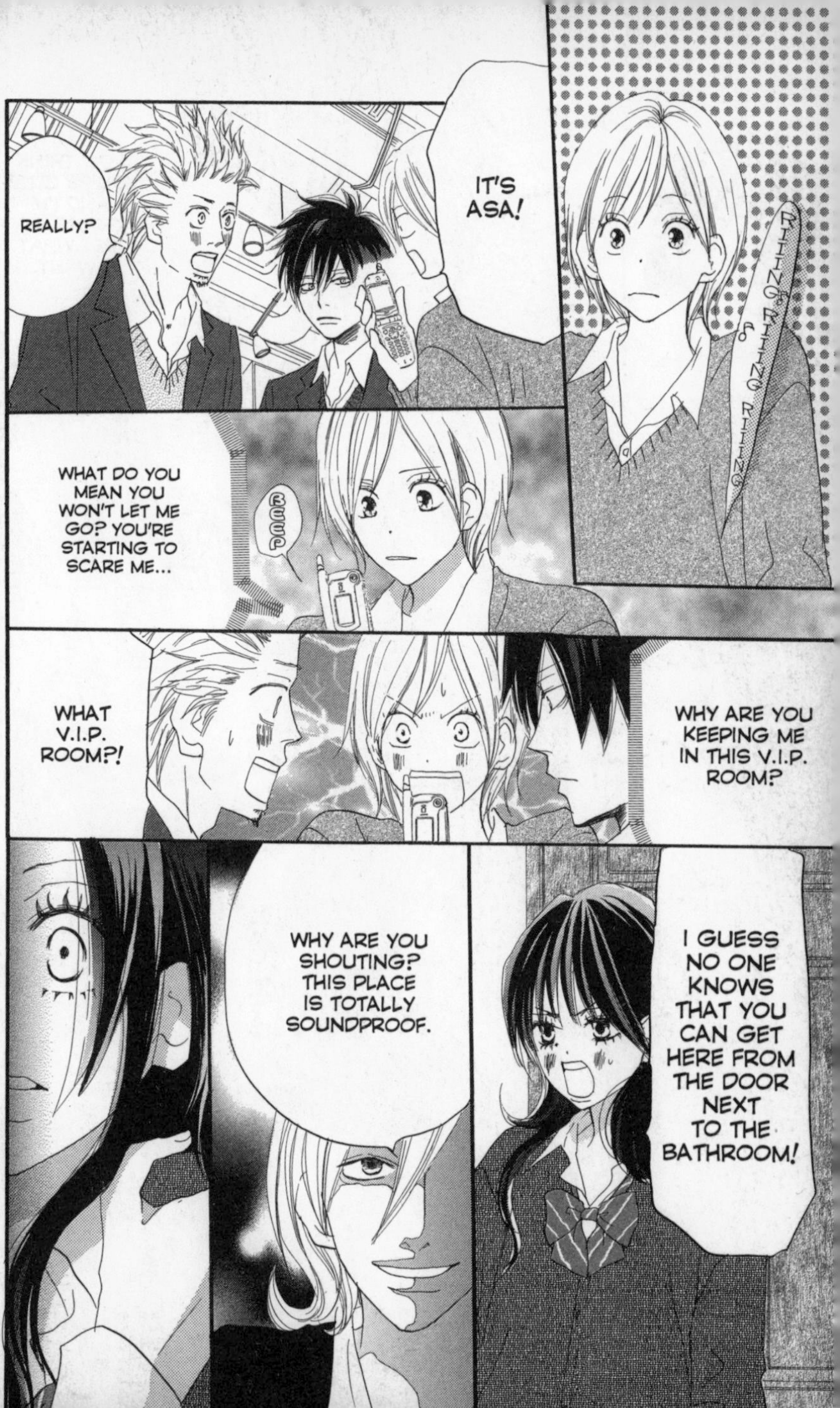
RIIING♪ RIIING RIIING
IT'S ASA!
REALLY?
BEEP
WHAT DO YOU MEAN YOU WON'T LET ME GO? YOU'RE STARTING TO SCARE ME...
WHY ARE YOU KEEPING ME IN THIS V.I.P. ROOM?
WHAT V.I.P. ROOM?!
I GUESS NO ONE KNOWS THAT YOU CAN GET HERE FROM THE DOOR NEXT TO THE BATHROOM!
WHY ARE YOU SHOUTING? THIS PLACE IS TOTALLY SOUNDPROOF.

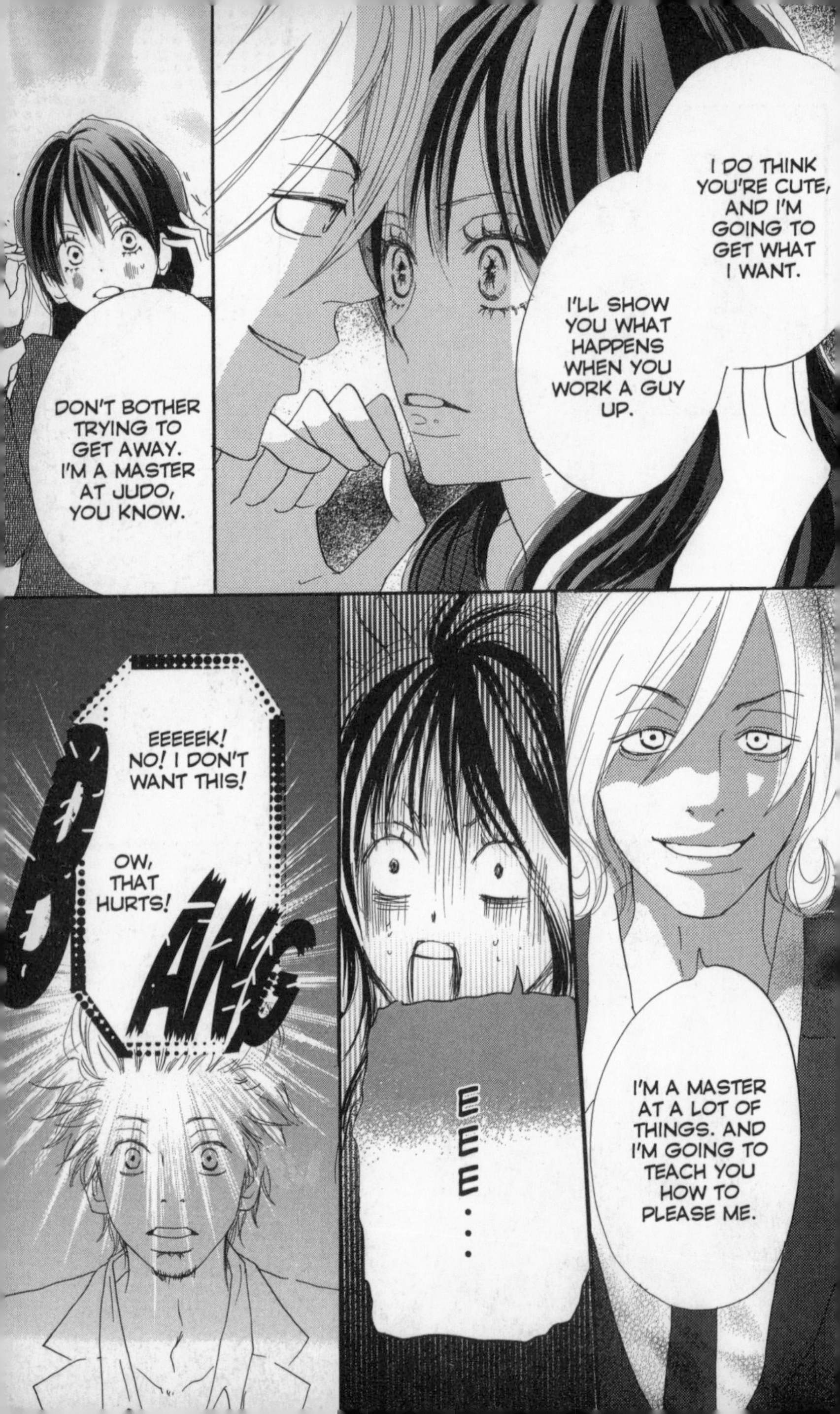
I DO THINK YOU'RE CUTE, AND I'M GOING TO GET WHAT I WANT.
I'LL SHOW YOU WHAT HAPPENS WHEN YOU WORK A GUY UP.
DON'T BOTHER TRYING TO GET AWAY. I'M A MASTER AT JUDO, YOU KNOW.
I'M A MASTER AT A LOT OF THINGS. AND I'M GOING TO TEACH YOU HOW TO PLEASE ME.
EEE...
EEEEEK! NO! I DON'T WANT THIS!
OW, THAT HURTS!
BANG

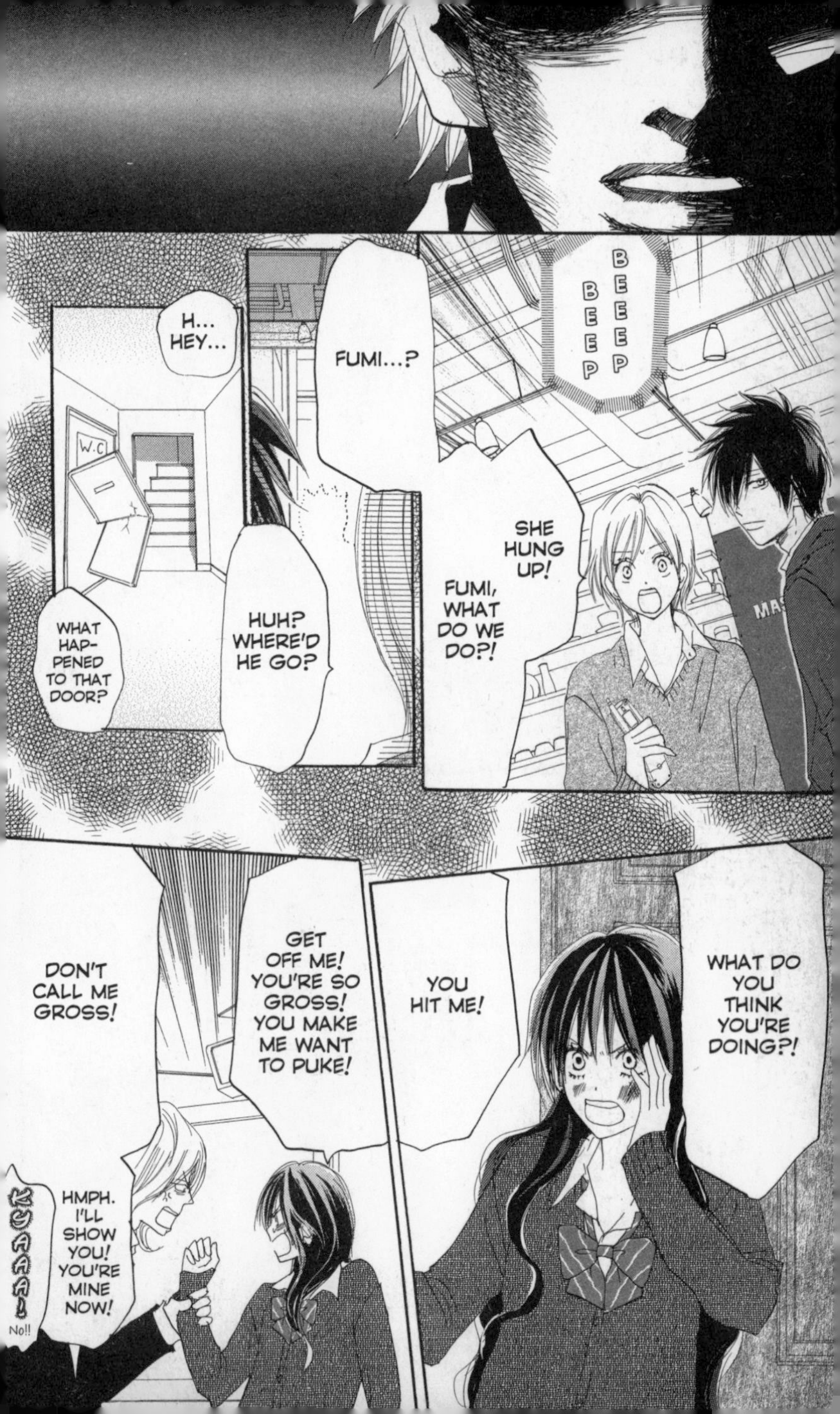
BEEP BEEP
SHE HUNG UP!
FUMI, WHAT DO WE DO?!
FUMI...?
HUH? WHERE'D HE GO?
H... HEY...
WHAT HAPPENED TO THAT DOOR?
WHAT DO YOU THINK YOU'RE DOING?!
YOU HIT ME!
GET OFF ME! YOU'RE SO GROSS! YOU MAKE ME WANT TO PUKE!
DON'T CALL ME GROSS!
HMPH. I'LL SHOW YOU! YOU'RE MINE NOW!
KYAAA!
No!!

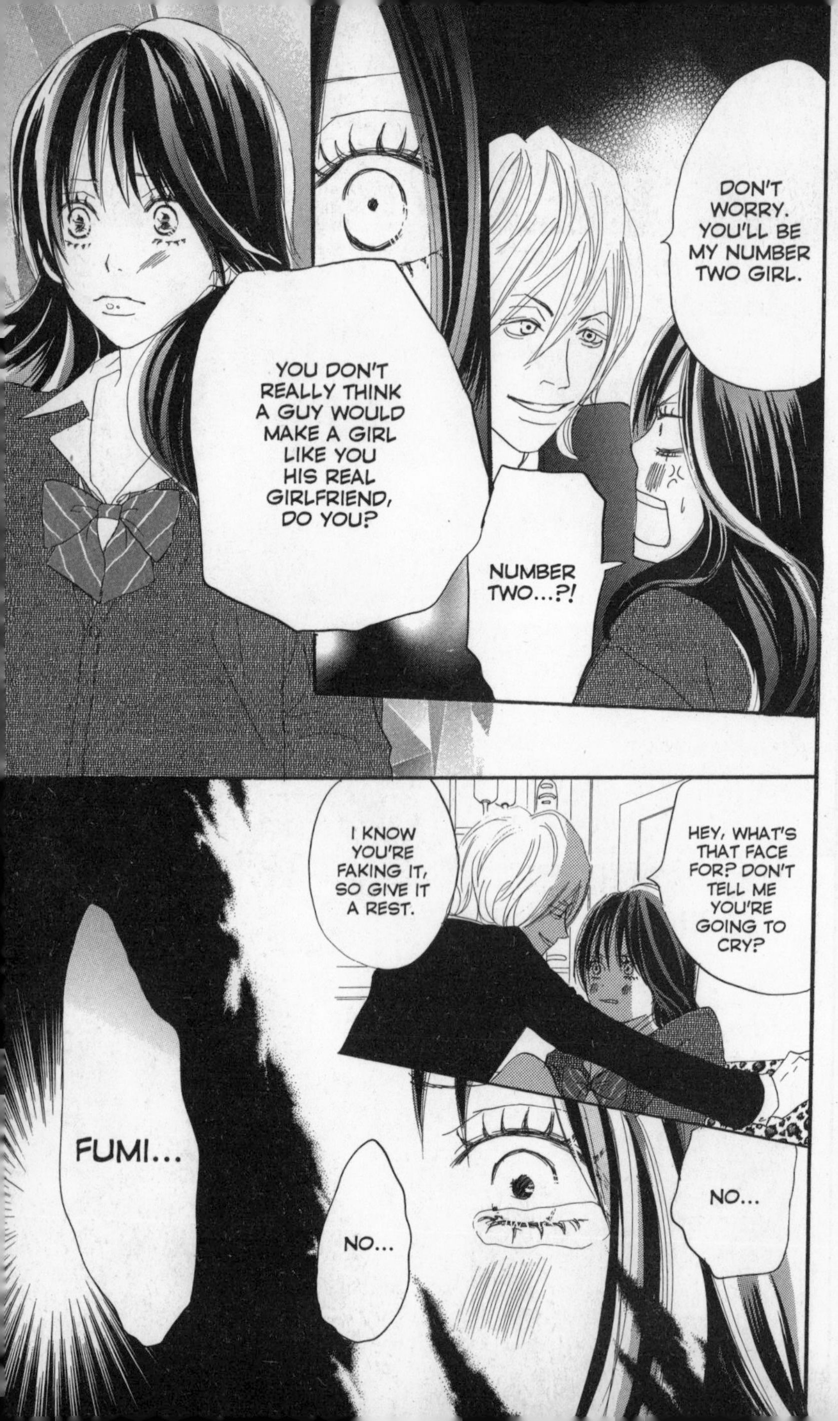
DON'T WORRY. YOU'LL BE MY NUMBER TWO GIRL.
NUMBER TWO...?!
YOU DON'T REALLY THINK A GUY WOULD MAKE A GIRL LIKE YOU HIS REAL GIRLFRIEND, DO YOU?
HEY, WHAT'S THAT FACE FOR? DON'T TELL ME YOU'RE GOING TO CRY?
I KNOW YOU'RE FAKING IT, SO GIVE IT A REST.
NO...
NO...
FUMI...

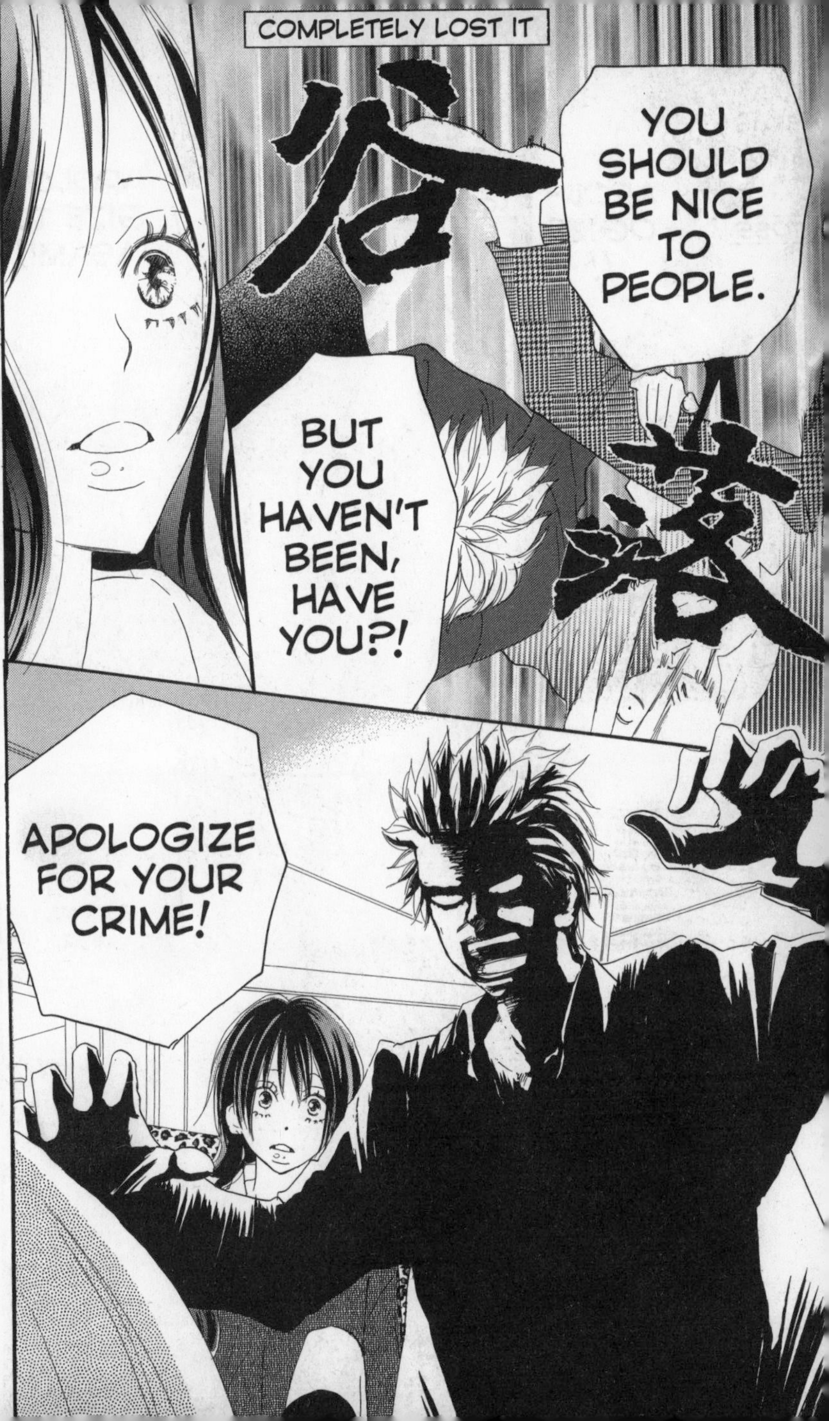
COMPLETELY LOST IT
YOU SHOULD BE NICE TO PEOPLE.
BUT YOU HAVEN'T BEEN, HAVE YOU?!
APOLOGIZE FOR YOUR CRIME!

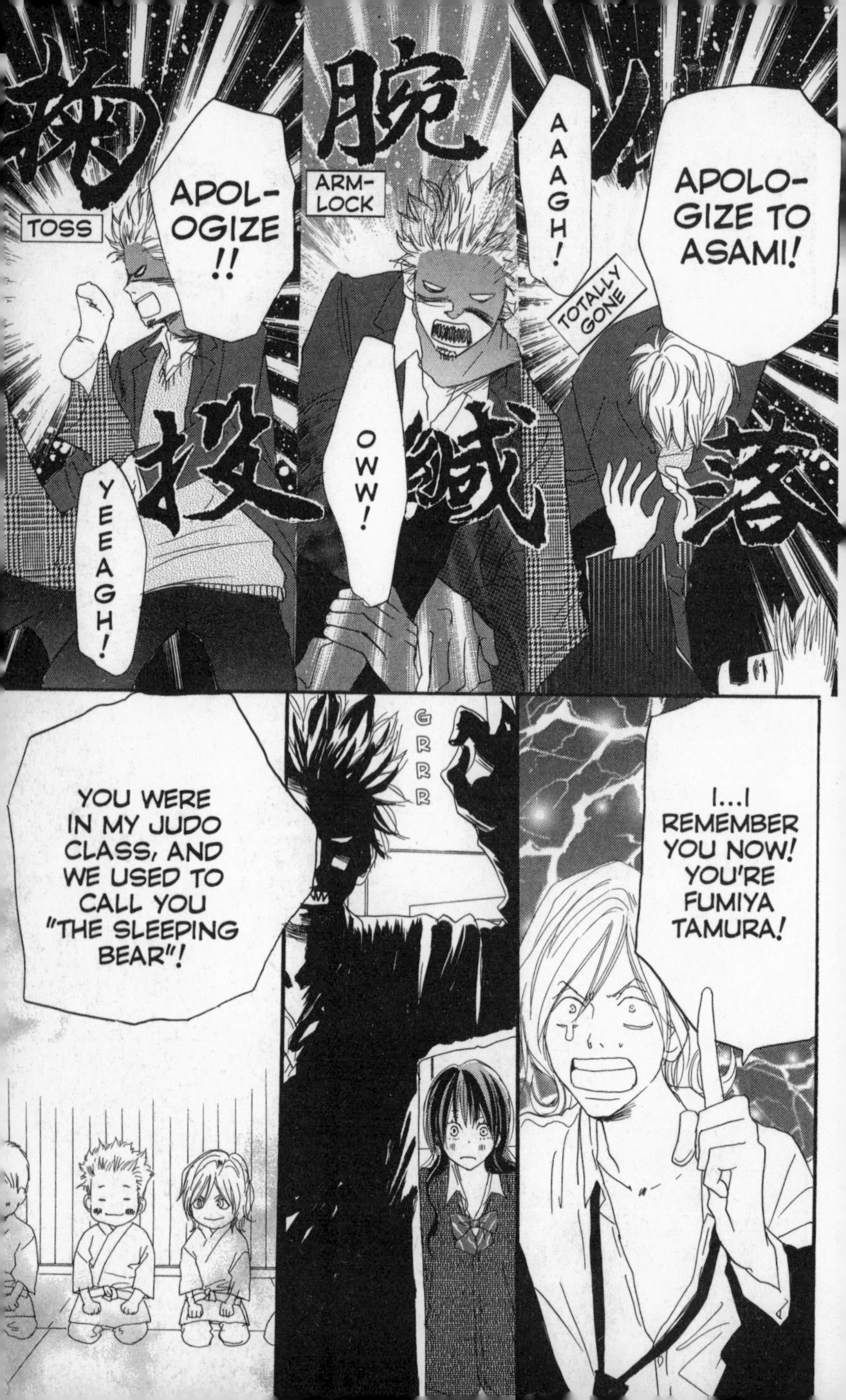
APOLOGIZE TO ASAMI!
AAAGH!
TOTALLY GONE
ARM-LOCK
OWW!
APOLOGIZE!!
TOSS
YEEAGH!
I...I REMEMBER YOU NOW! YOU'RE FUMIYA TAMURA!
GRRR
YOU WERE IN MY JUDO CLASS, AND WE USED TO CALL YOU "THE SLEEPING BEAR"!

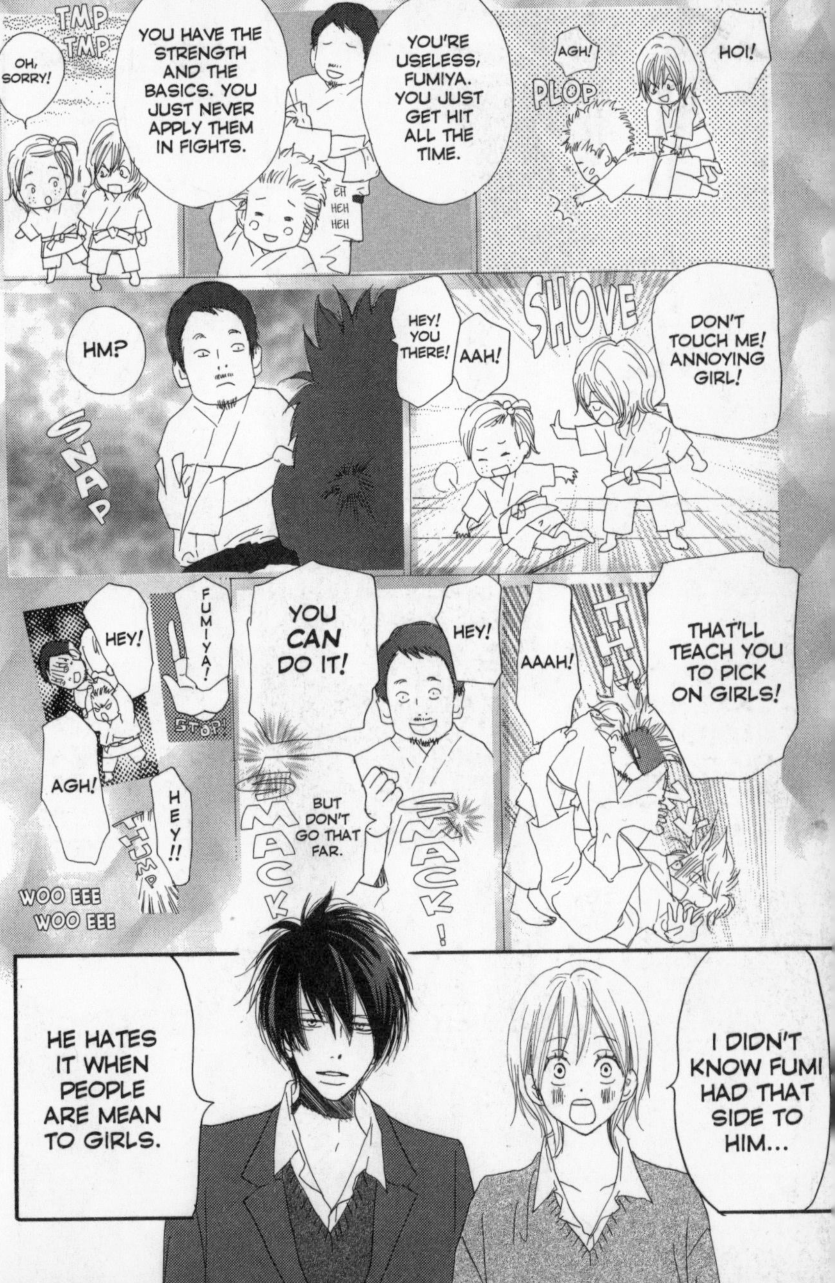
HOI!
AGH!
PLOP
YOU'RE USELESS, FUMIYA. YOU JUST GET HIT ALL THE TIME.
YOU HAVE THE STRENGTH AND THE BASICS. YOU JUST NEVER APPLY THEM IN FIGHTS.
EH HEH HEH
TMP TMP
OH, SORRY!
DON'T TOUCH ME! ANNOYING GIRL!
SHOVE
AAH!
HEY! YOU THERE!
HM?
SNAP
THAT'LL TEACH YOU TO PICK ON GIRLS!
AAAH!
HEY!
YOU CAN DO IT!
SMACK!
BUT DON'T GO THAT FAR.
SMACK
FUMIYA!
HEY!
STOP!
AGH!
HEY!!
THUMP
WOO EEE
WOO EEE
I DIDN'T KNOW FUMI HAD THAT SIDE TO HIM...
HE HATES IT WHEN PEOPLE ARE MEAN TO GIRLS.

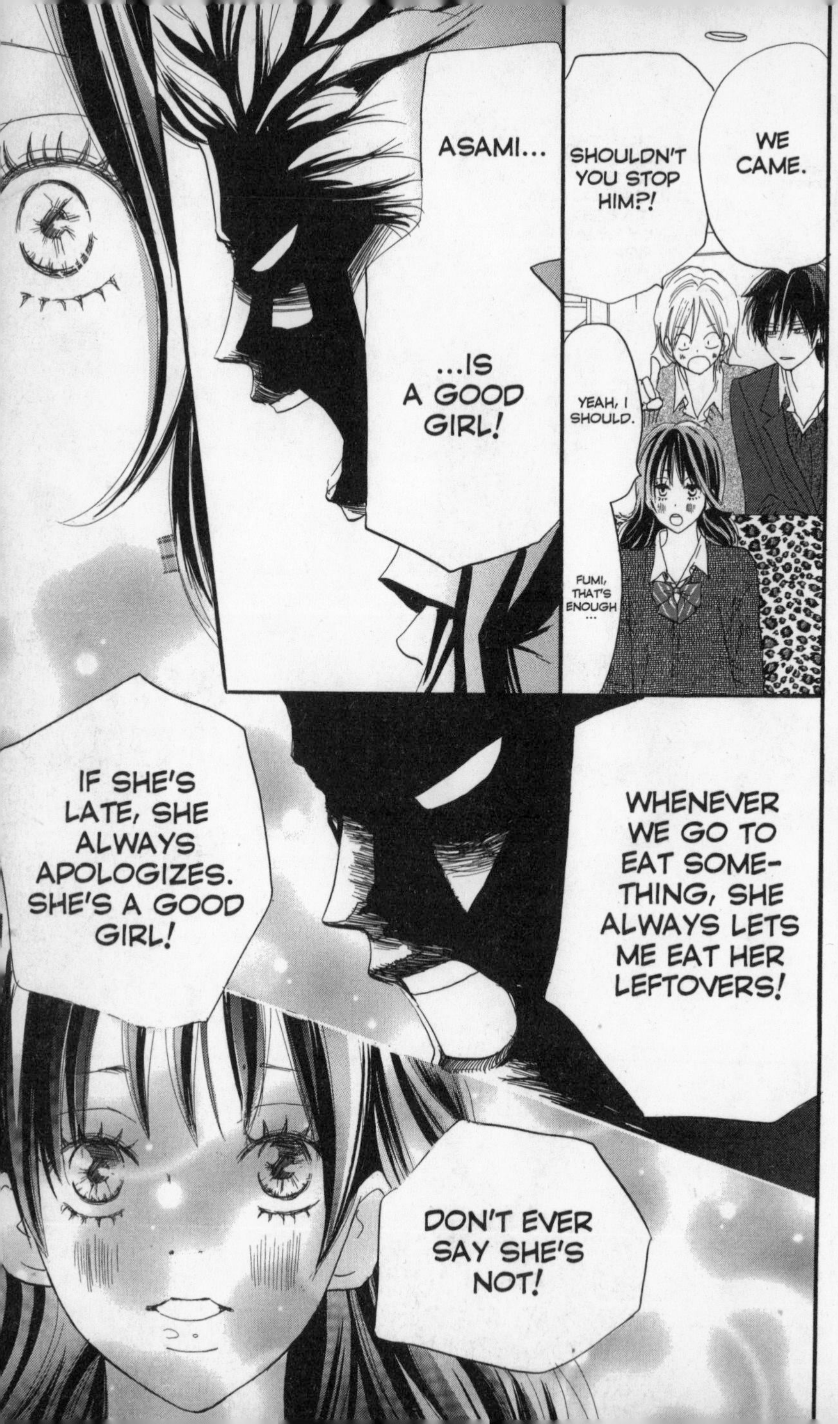
WE CAME.
SHOULDN'T YOU STOP HIM?!
YEAH, I SHOULD.
FUMI, THAT'S ENOUGH...
ASAMI...
...IS A GOOD GIRL!
WHENEVER WE GO TO EAT SOME-THING, SHE ALWAYS LETS ME EAT HER LEFTOVERS!
IF SHE'S LATE, SHE ALWAYS APOLOGIZES. SHE'S A GOOD GIRL!
DON'T EVER SAY SHE'S NOT!

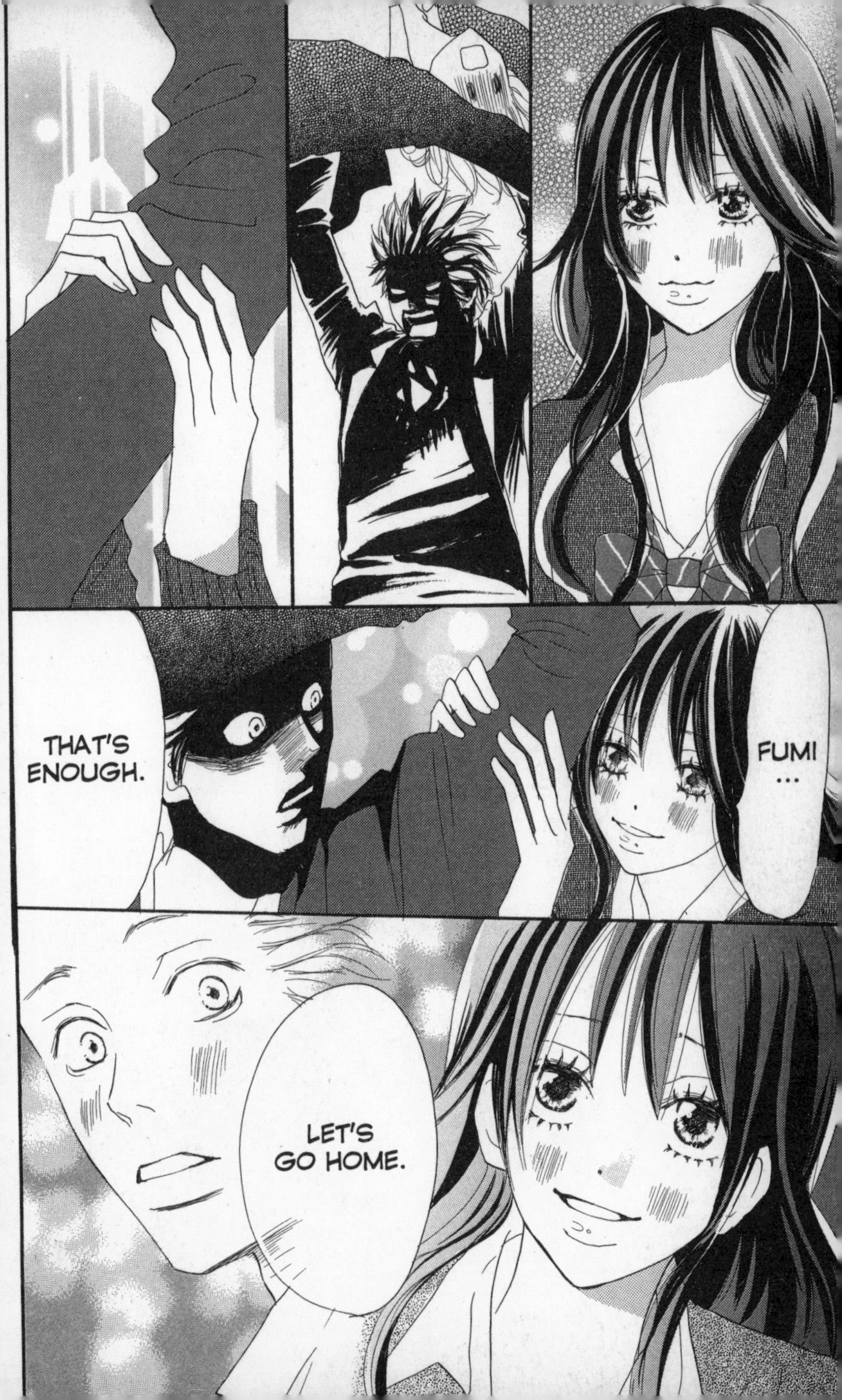
FUMI ...
THAT'S ENOUGH.
LET'S GO HOME.

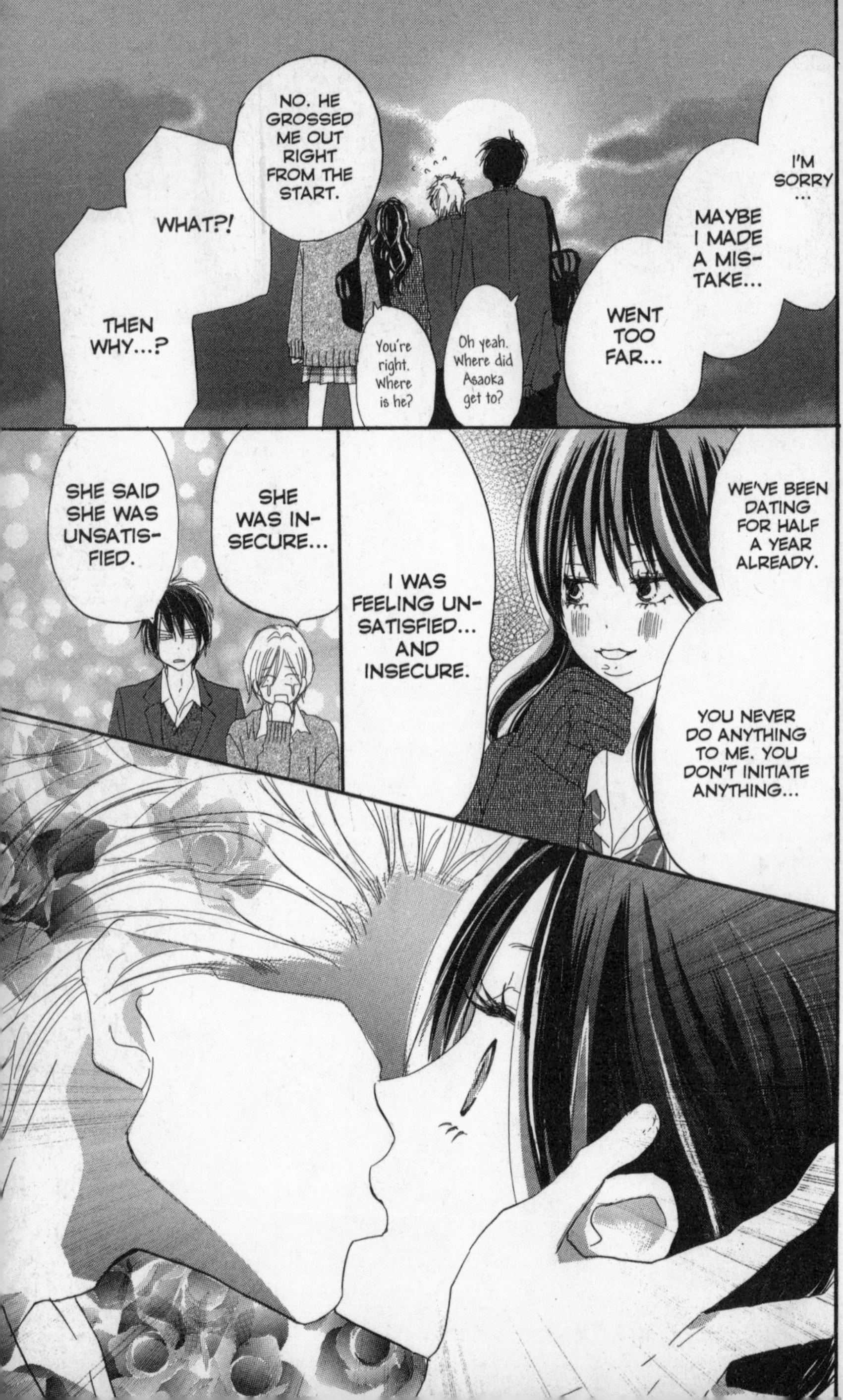
I'M SORRY ...
MAYBE I MADE A MIS-TAKE...
WENT TOO FAR...
Oh yeah. Where did Asaoka get to?
You're right. Where is he?
NO. HE GROSSED ME OUT RIGHT FROM THE START.
WHAT?!
THEN WHY...?
WE'VE BEEN DATING FOR HALF A YEAR ALREADY.
YOU NEVER DO ANYTHING TO ME. YOU DON'T INITIATE ANYTHING...
I WAS FEELING UN-SATISFIED... AND INSECURE.
SHE WAS IN-SECURE...
SHE SAID SHE WAS UNSATIS-FIED.

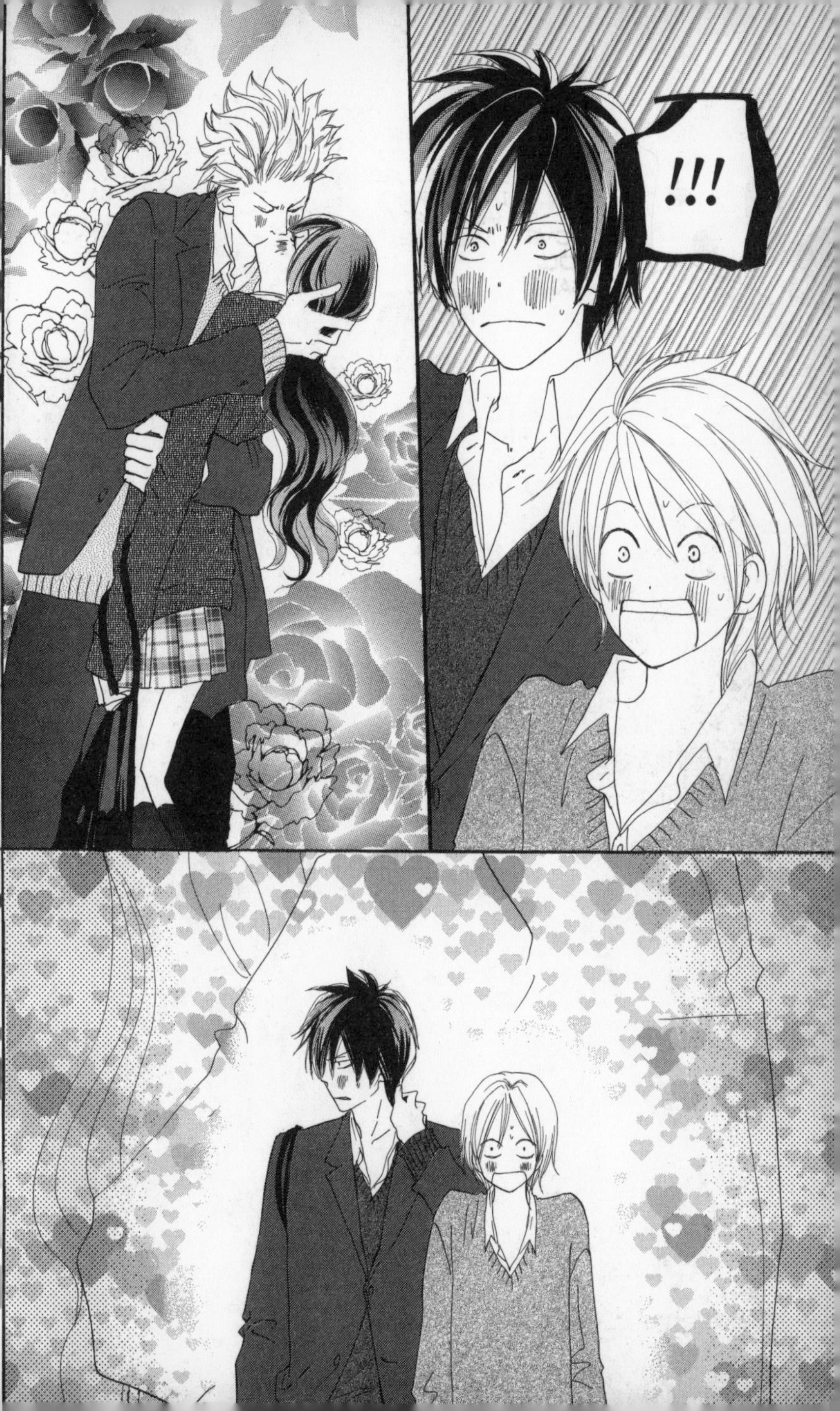
!!!

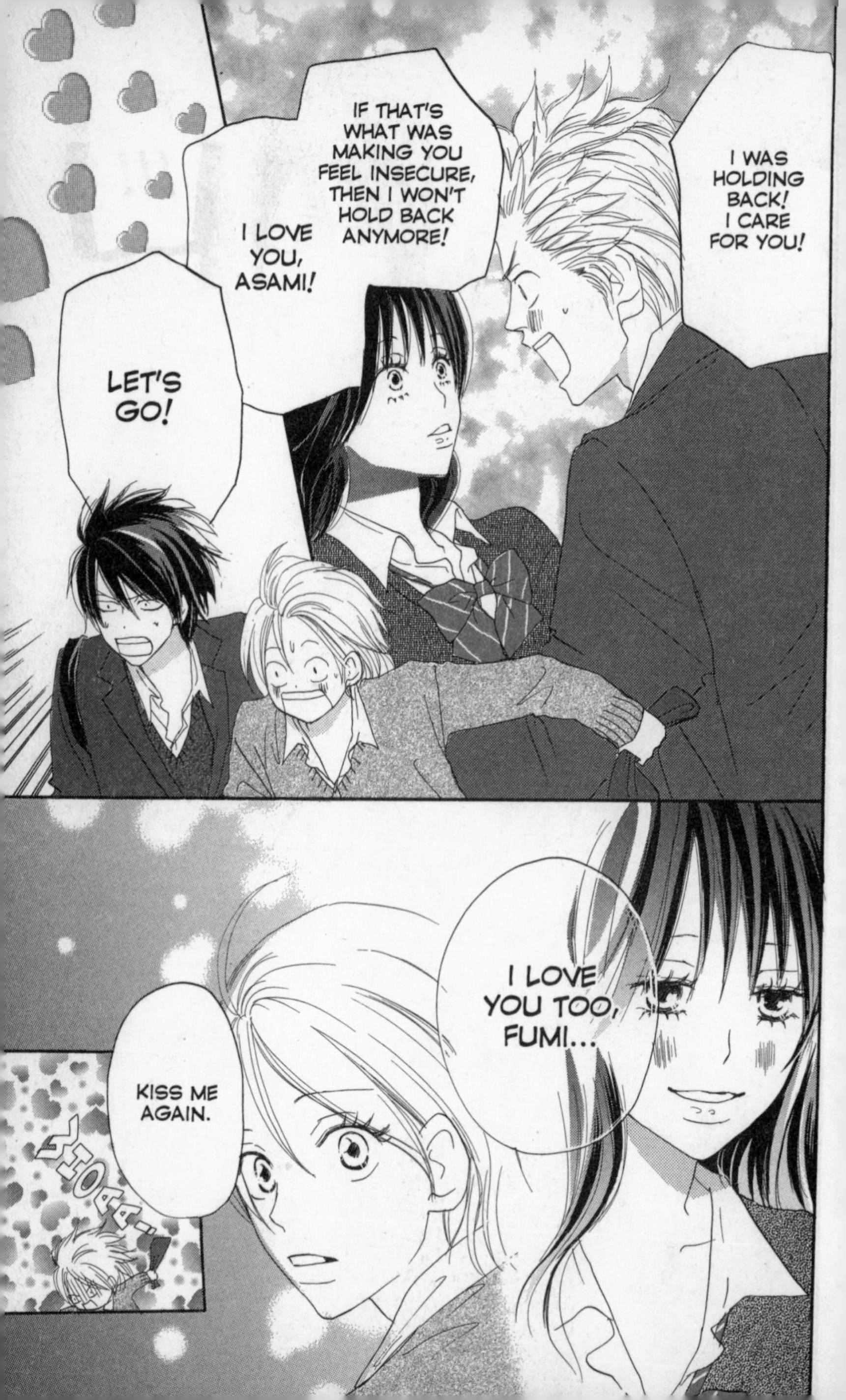

I WAS HOLDING BACK! I CARE FOR YOU!
IF THAT'S WHAT WAS MAKING YOU FEEL INSECURE, THEN I WON'T HOLD BACK ANYMORE!
I LOVE YOU, ASAMI!
LET'S GO!
I LOVE YOU TOO, FUMI...
KISS ME AGAIN.

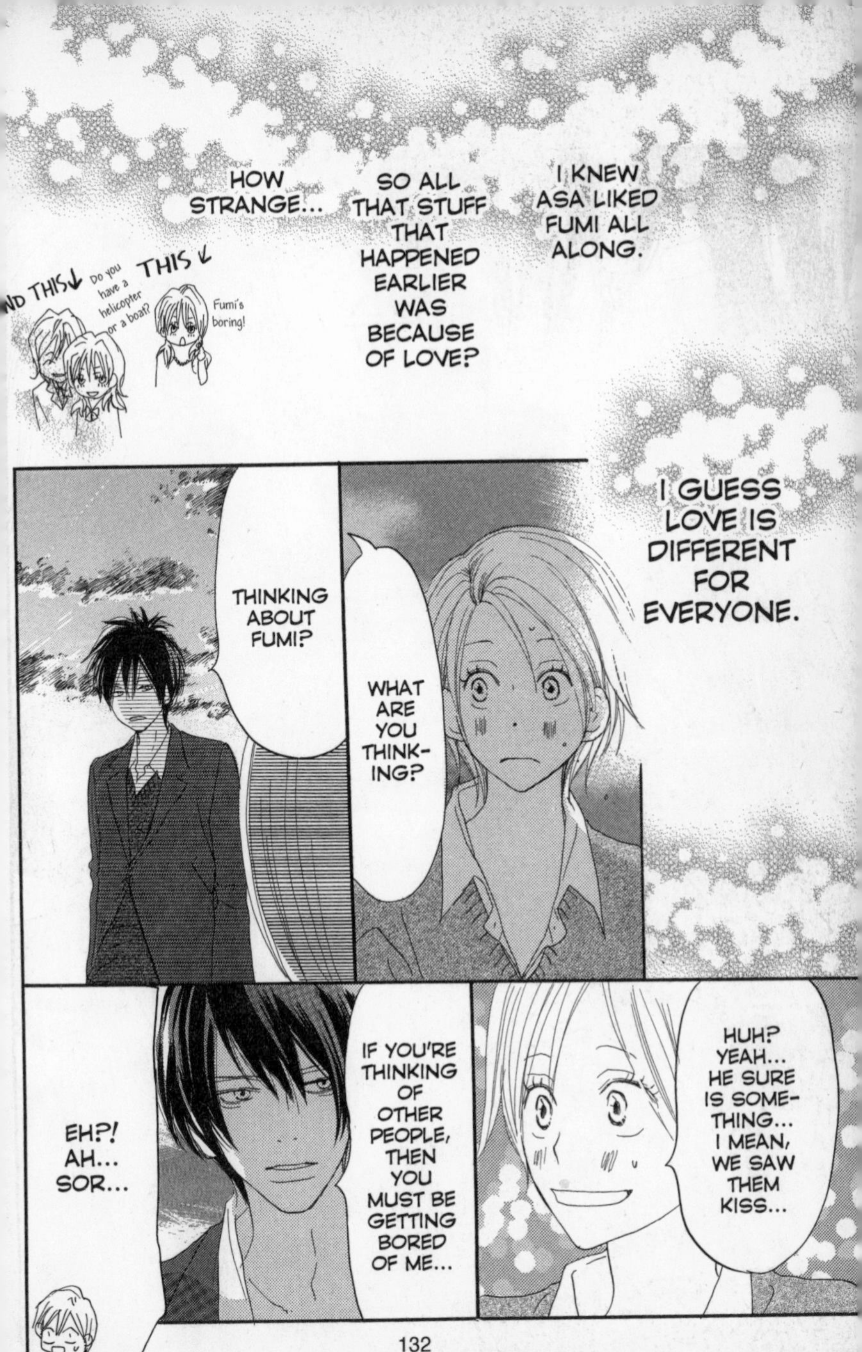
I KNEW ASA LIKED FUMI ALL ALONG.
SO ALL THAT STUFF THAT HAPPENED EARLIER WAS BECAUSE OF LOVE?
HOW STRANGE...
THIS ↙
Fumi's boring!
ND THIS↓
Do you have a helicopter or a boat?
I GUESS LOVE IS DIFFERENT FOR EVERYONE.
WHAT ARE YOU THINKING?
THINKING ABOUT FUMI?
HUH? YEAH... HE SURE IS SOMETHING... I MEAN, WE SAW THEM KISS...
IF YOU'RE THINKING OF OTHER PEOPLE, THEN YOU MUST BE GETTING BORED OF ME...
EH?! AH... SOR...

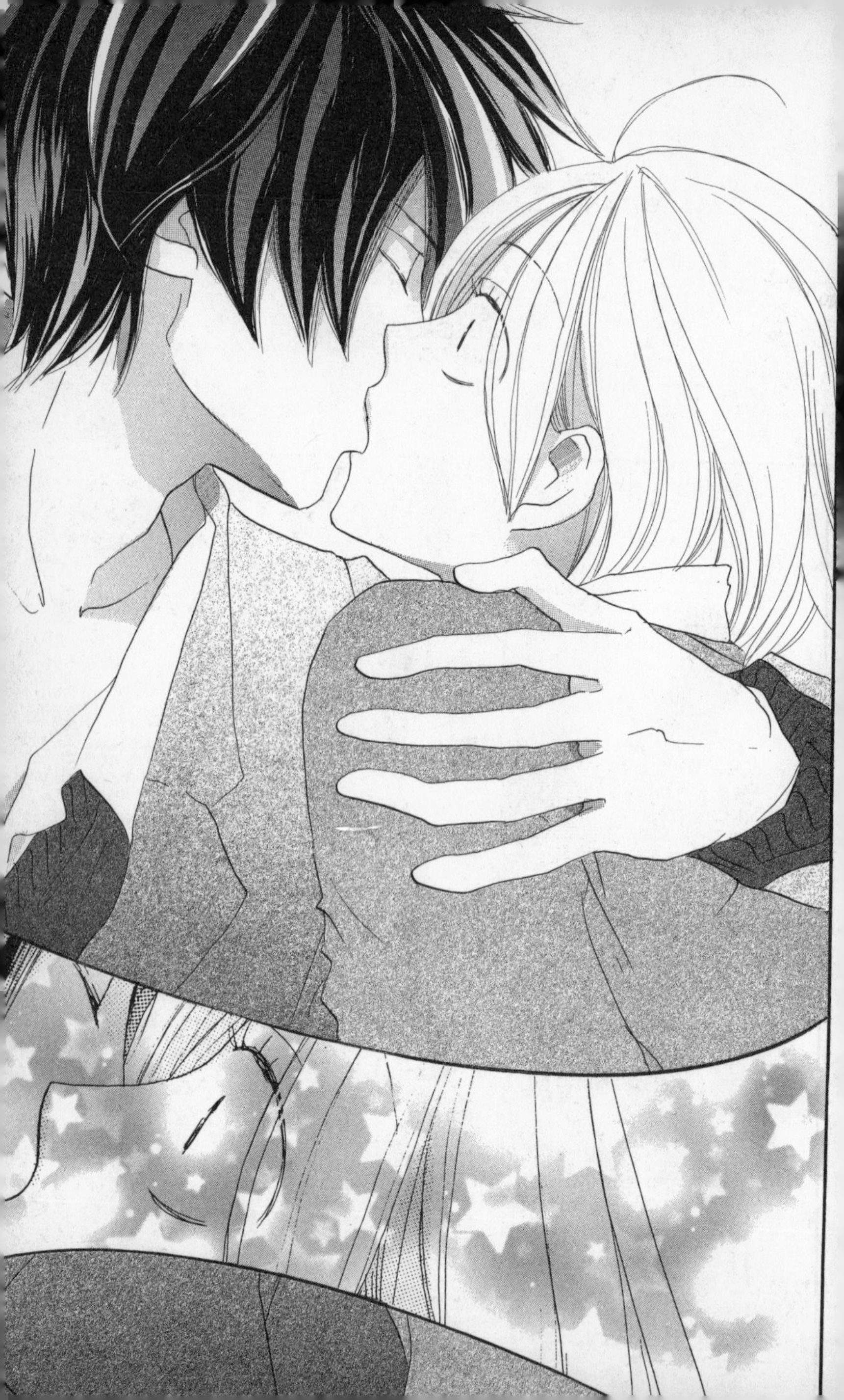

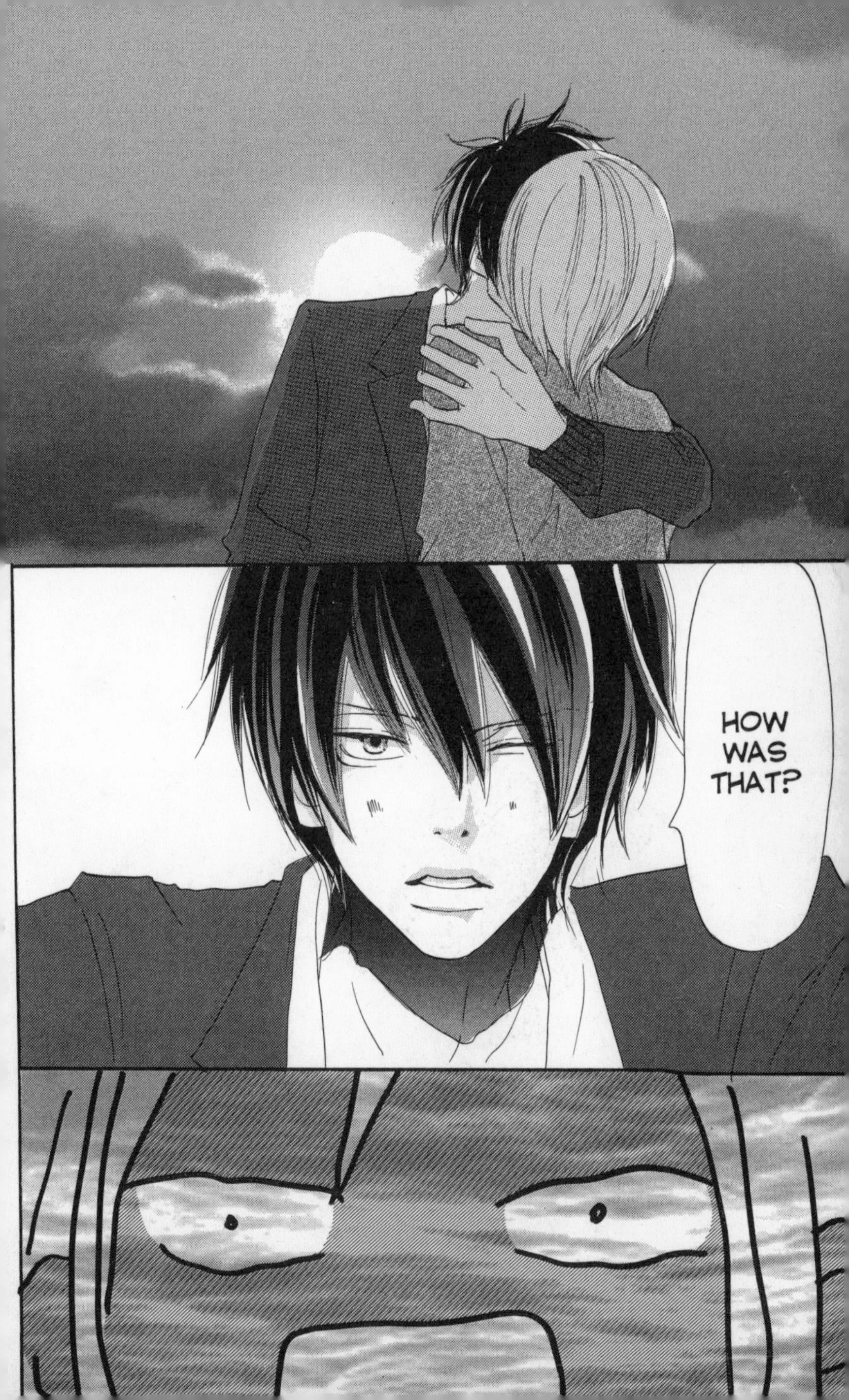
HOW WAS THAT?

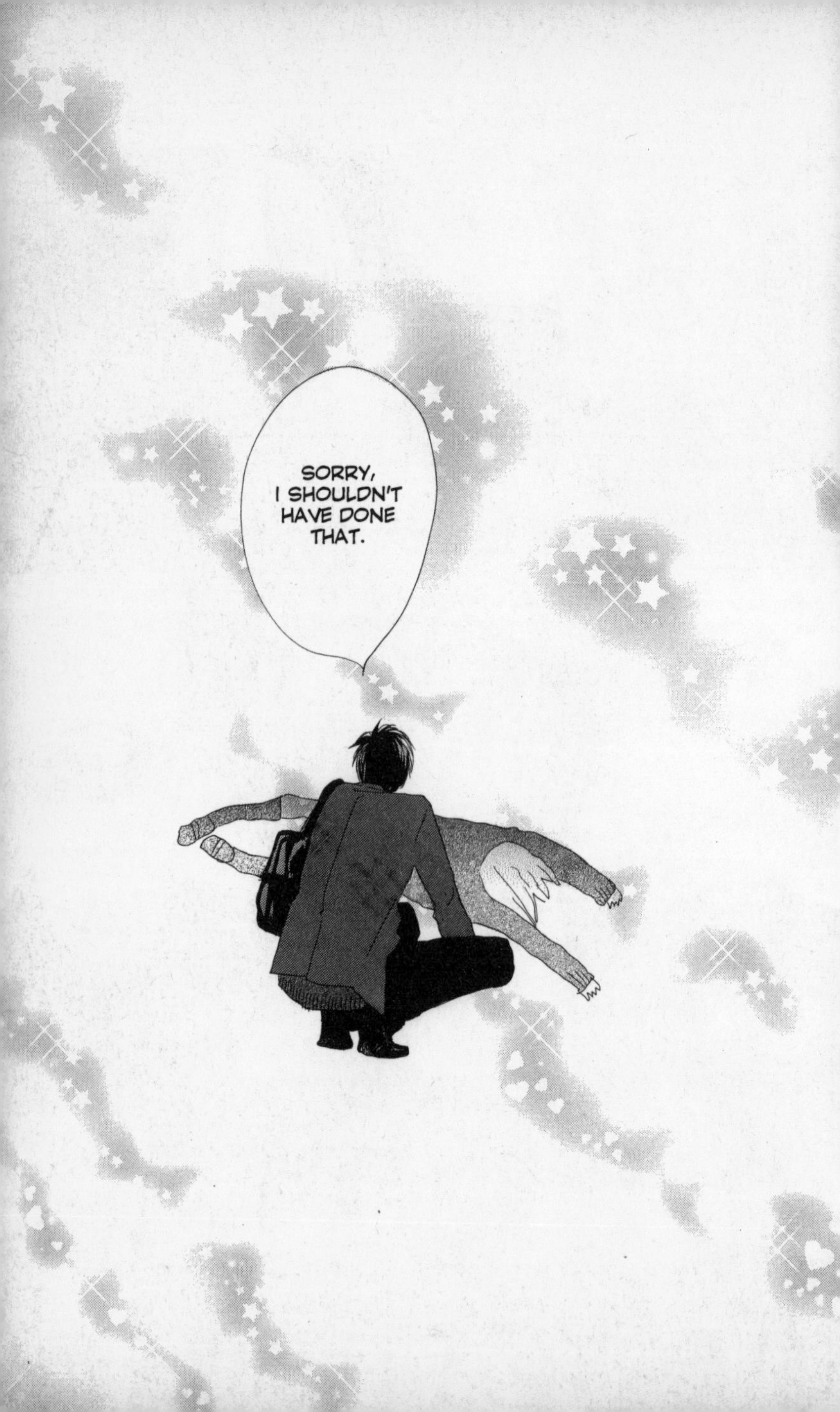
SORRY, I SHOULDN'T HAVE DONE THAT.

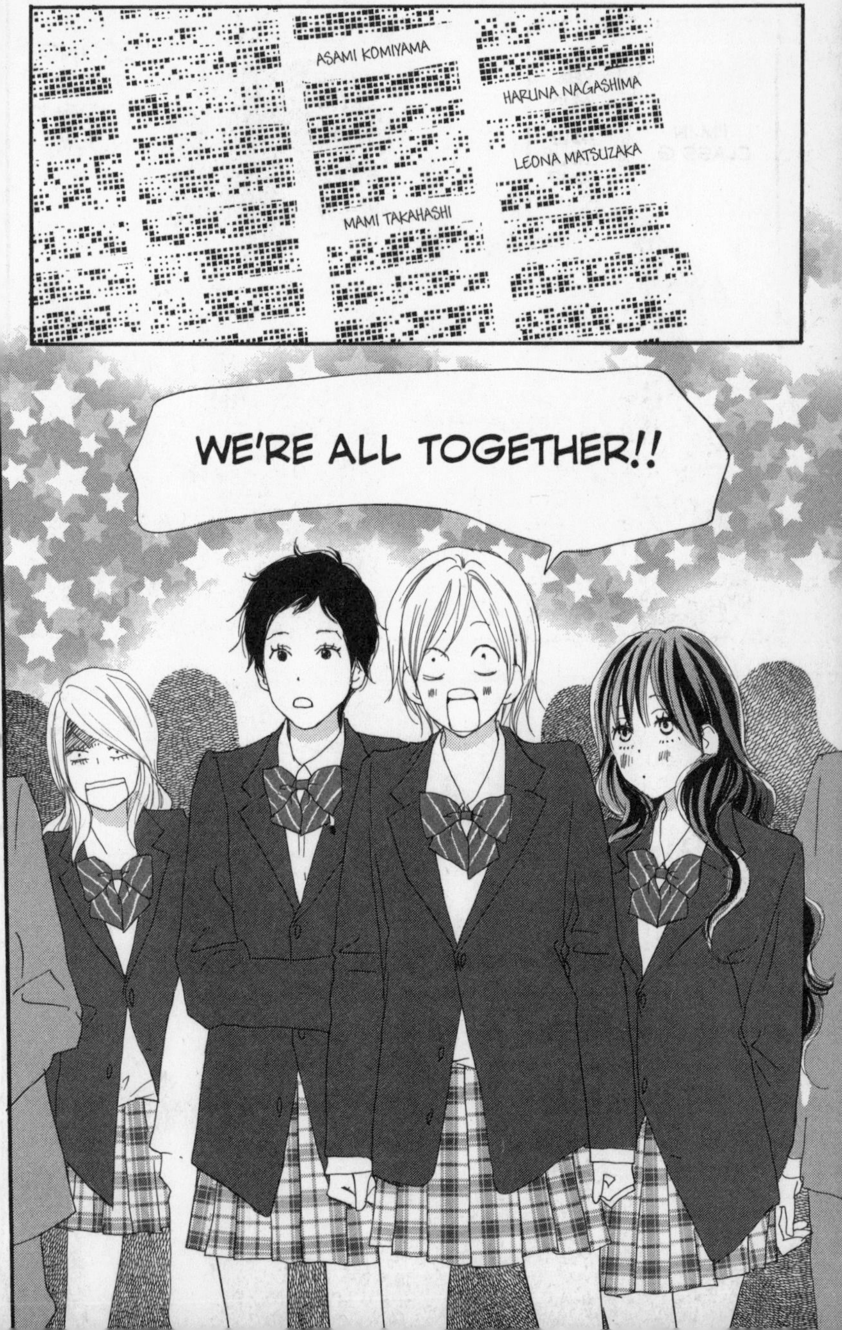
HARUNA NAGASHIMA
LEONA MATSUZAKA
ASAMI KOMIYAMA
MAMI TAKAHASHI
WE'RE ALL TOGETHER!!

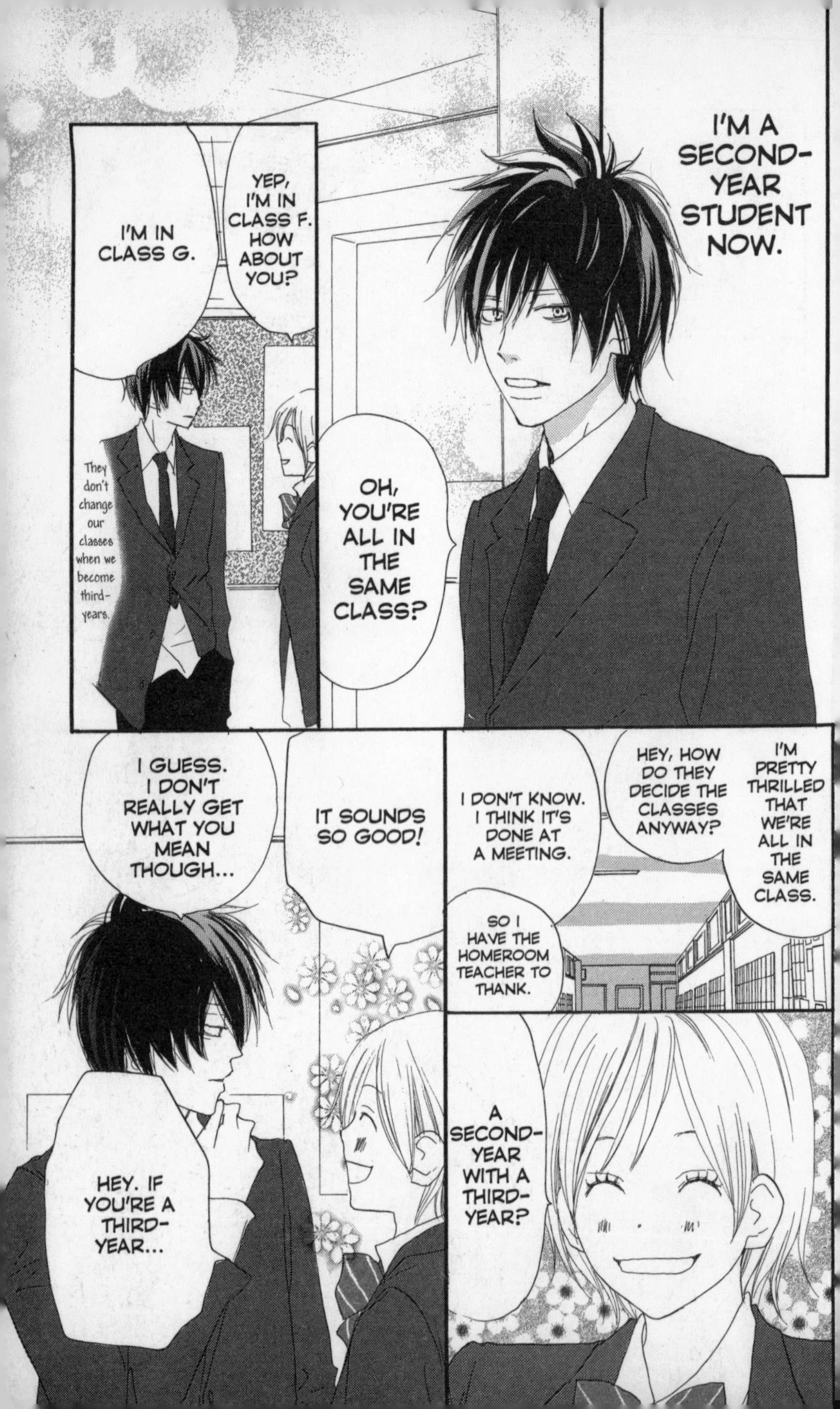
I'M A SECOND-YEAR STUDENT NOW.
OH, YOU'RE ALL IN THE SAME CLASS?
YEP, I'M IN CLASS F. HOW ABOUT YOU?
I'M IN CLASS G.
They don't change our classes when we become third-years.
I'M PRETTY THRILLED THAT WE'RE ALL IN THE SAME CLASS.
HEY, HOW DO THEY DECIDE THE CLASSES ANYWAY?
I DON'T KNOW. I THINK IT'S DONE AT A MEETING.
SO I HAVE THE HOMEROOM TEACHER TO THANK.
A SECOND-YEAR WITH A THIRD-YEAR?
IT SOUNDS SO GOOD!
I GUESS. I DON'T REALLY GET WHAT YOU MEAN THOUGH...
HEY. IF YOU'RE A THIRD-YEAR...

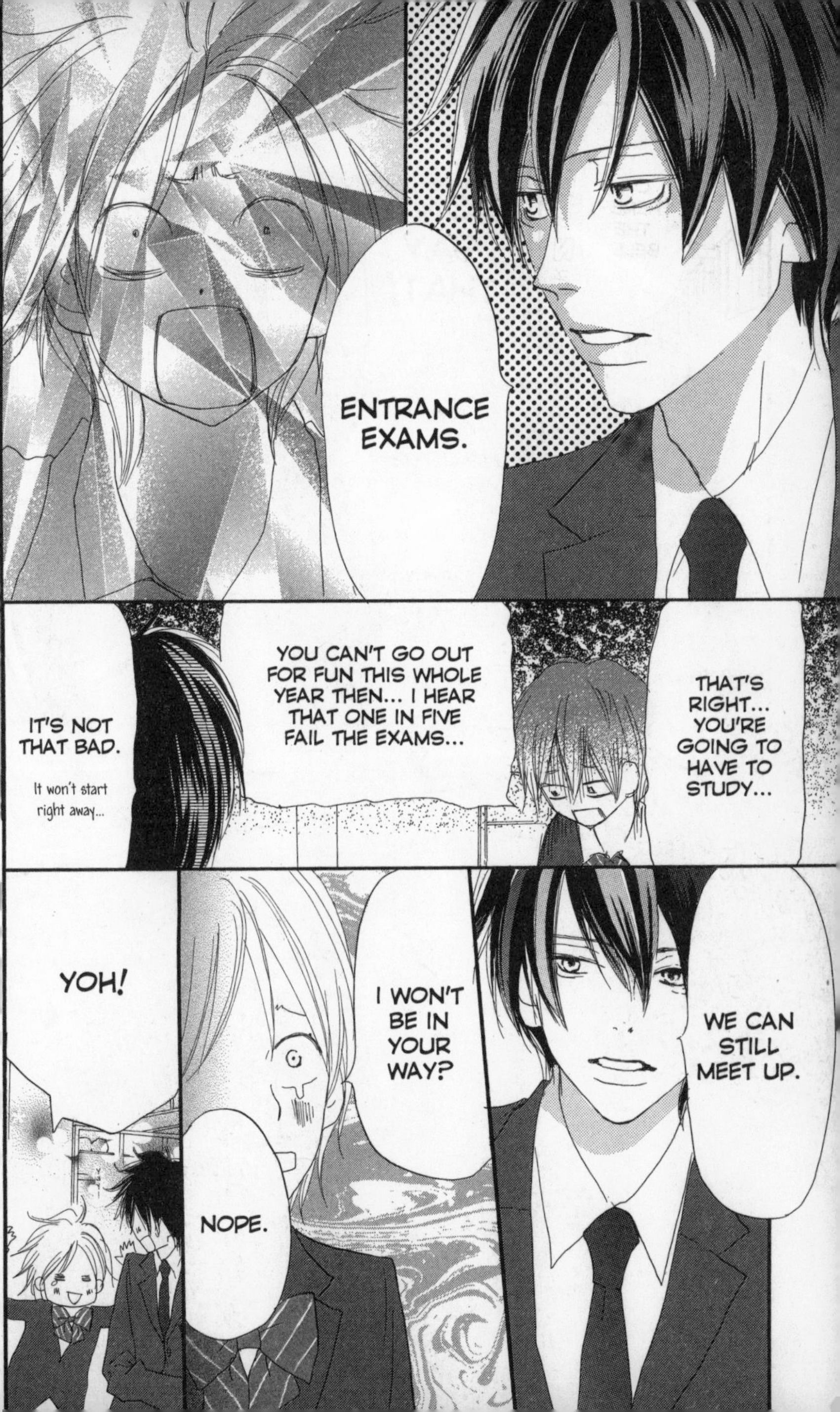
ENTRANCE EXAMS.
THAT'S RIGHT... YOU'RE GOING TO HAVE TO STUDY...
YOU CAN'T GO OUT FOR FUN THIS WHOLE YEAR THEN... I HEAR THAT ONE IN FIVE FAIL THE EXAMS...
IT'S NOT THAT BAD.
It won't start right away...
WE CAN STILL MEET UP.
I WON'T BE IN YOUR WAY?
NOPE.
YOH!

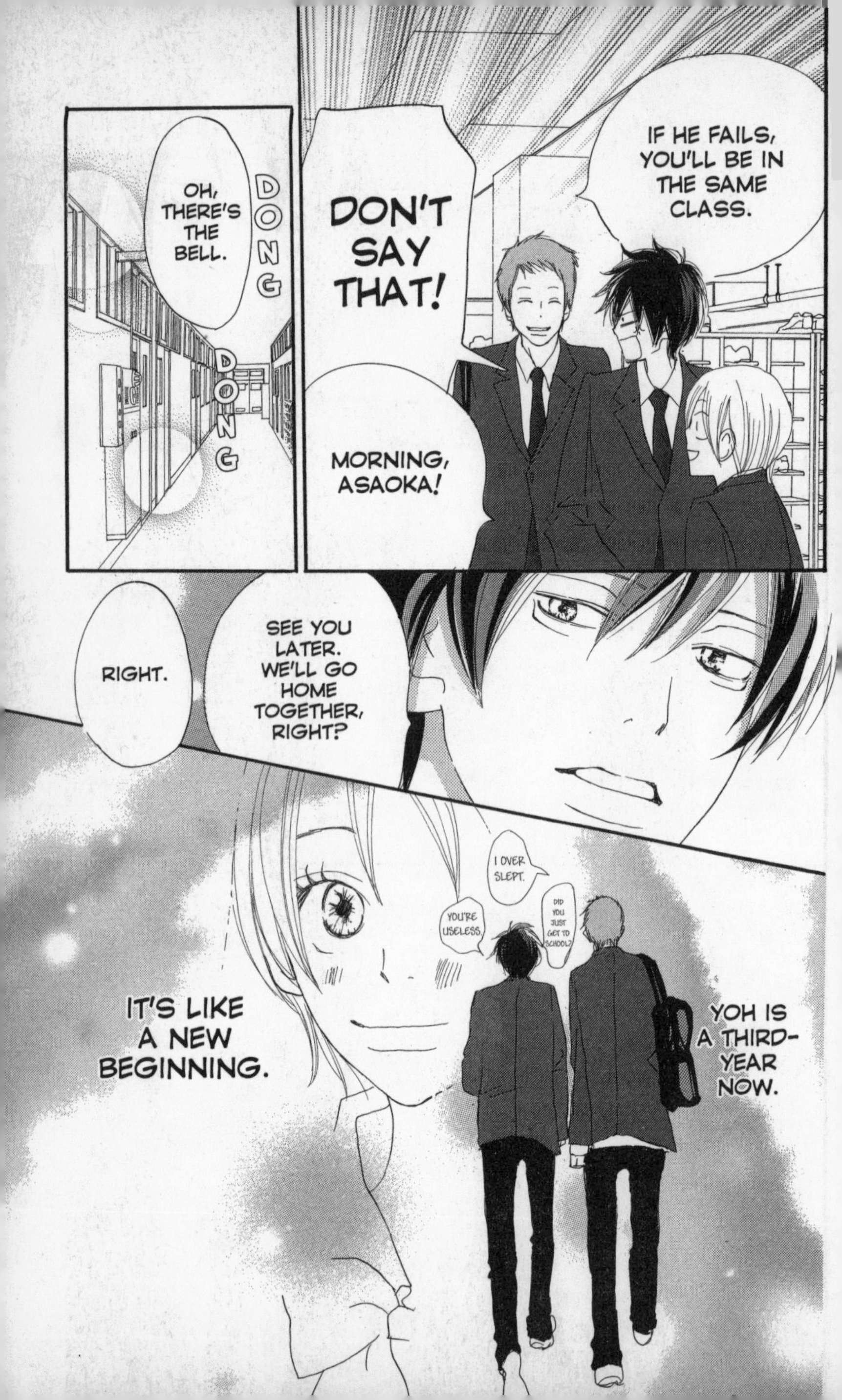
IF HE FAILS, YOU'LL BE IN THE SAME CLASS.
DON'T SAY THAT!
MORNING, ASAOKA!
DONG
DONG
OH, THERE'S THE BELL.
SEE YOU LATER. WE'LL GO HOME TOGETHER, RIGHT?
RIGHT.
YOH IS A THIRD-YEAR NOW.
DID YOU JUST GET TO SCHOOL?
I OVER SLEPT.
YOU'RE USELESS.
IT'S LIKE A NEW BEGINNING.

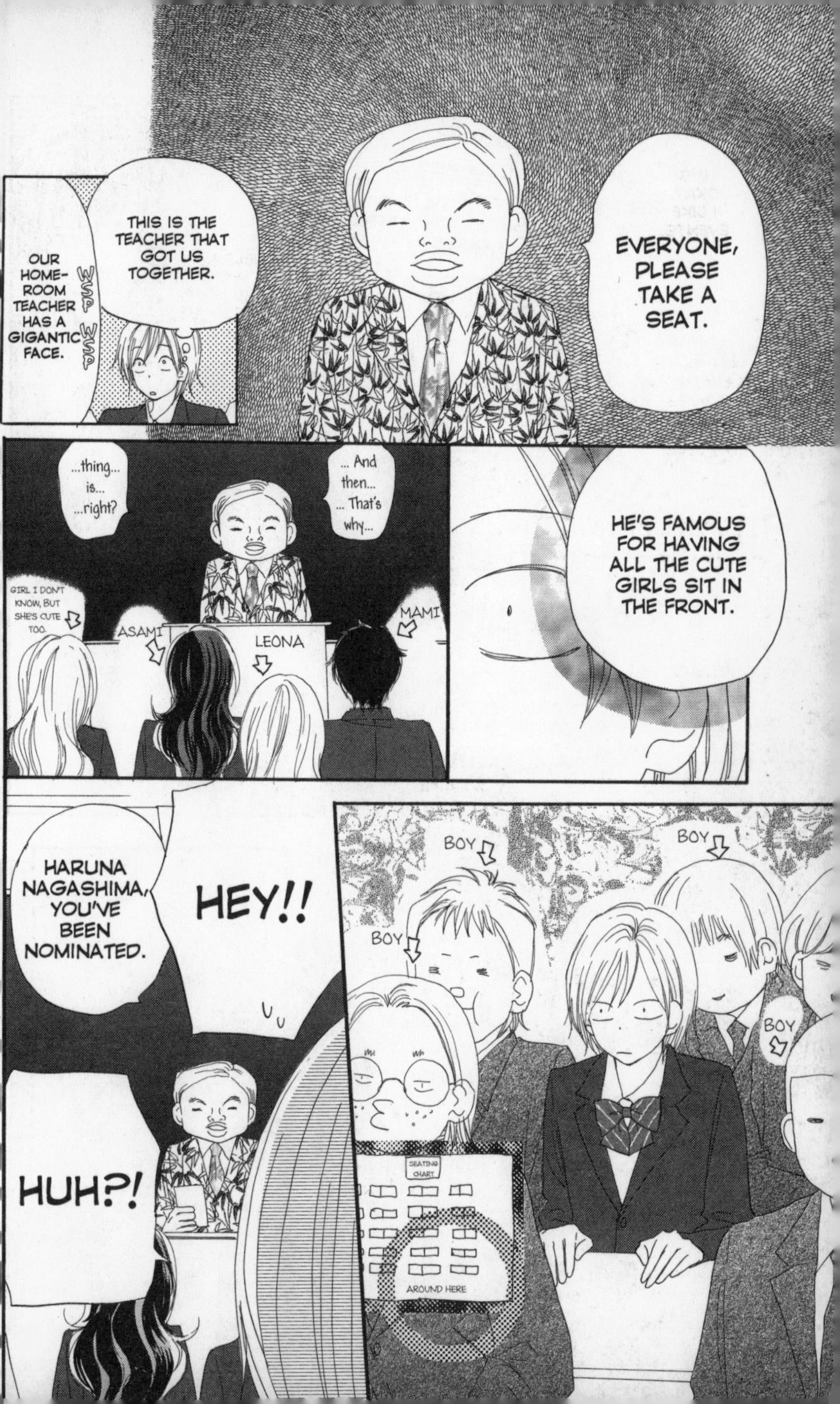
EVERYONE, PLEASE TAKE A SEAT.
THIS IS THE TEACHER THAT GOT US TOGETHER.
WSP WSP
OUR HOME-ROOM TEACHER HAS A GIGANTIC FACE.
HE'S FAMOUS FOR HAVING ALL THE CUTE GIRLS SIT IN THE FRONT.
... And then... ... That's why...
...thing... is... ...right?
MAMI
LEONA
ASAMI
GIRL I DON'T KNOW, BUT SHE'S CUTE TOO.
BOY
BOY
BOY
BOY
SEATING CHART
AROUND HERE
HARUNA NAGASHIMA, YOU'VE BEEN NOMINATED.
HEY!!
HUH?!

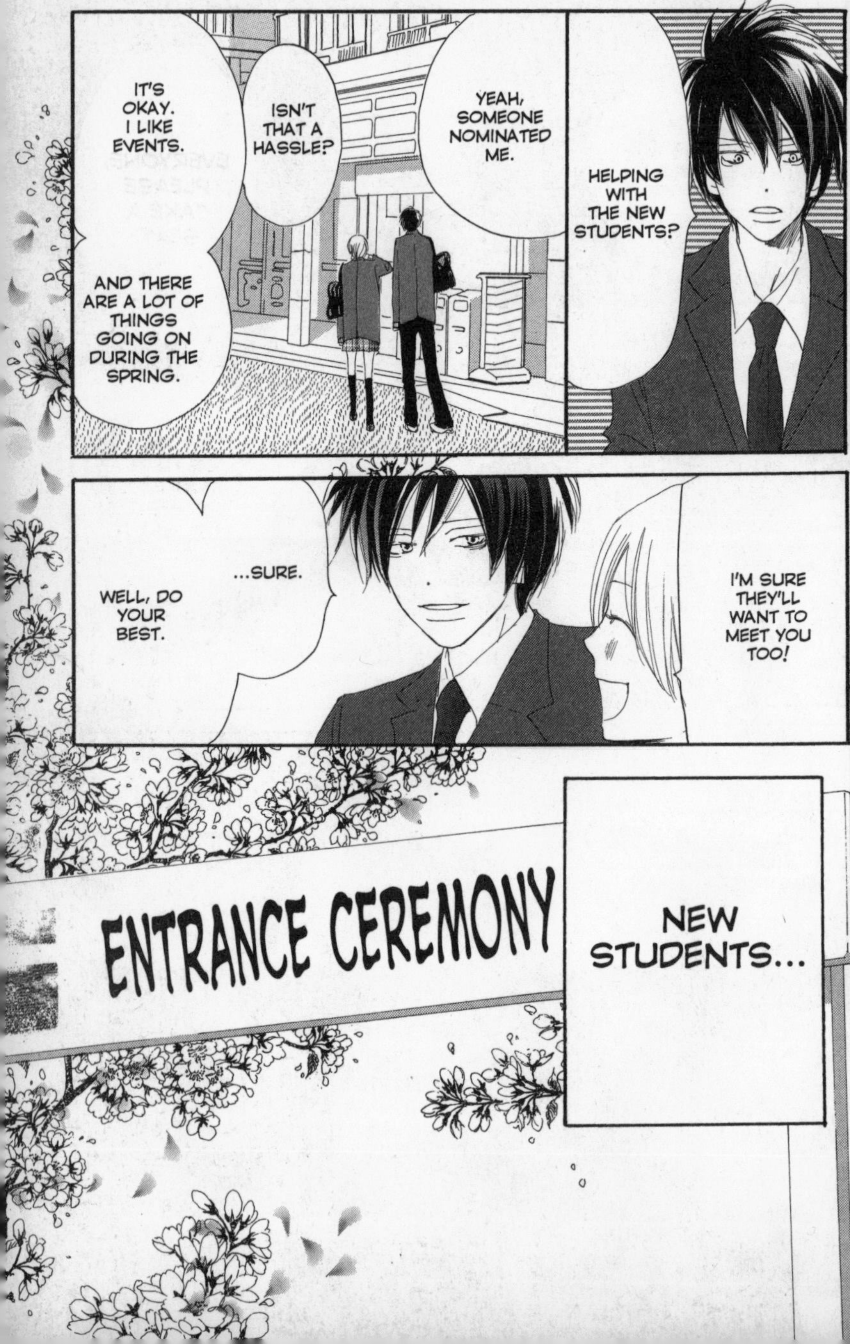
HELPING WITH THE NEW STUDENTS?
YEAH, SOMEONE NOMINATED ME.
ISN'T THAT A HASSLE?
IT'S OKAY. I LIKE EVENTS.
AND THERE ARE A LOT OF THINGS GOING ON DURING THE SPRING.
I'M SURE THEY'LL WANT TO MEET YOU TOO!
...SURE.
WELL, DO YOUR BEST.
NEW STUDENTS...
ENTRANCE CEREMONY

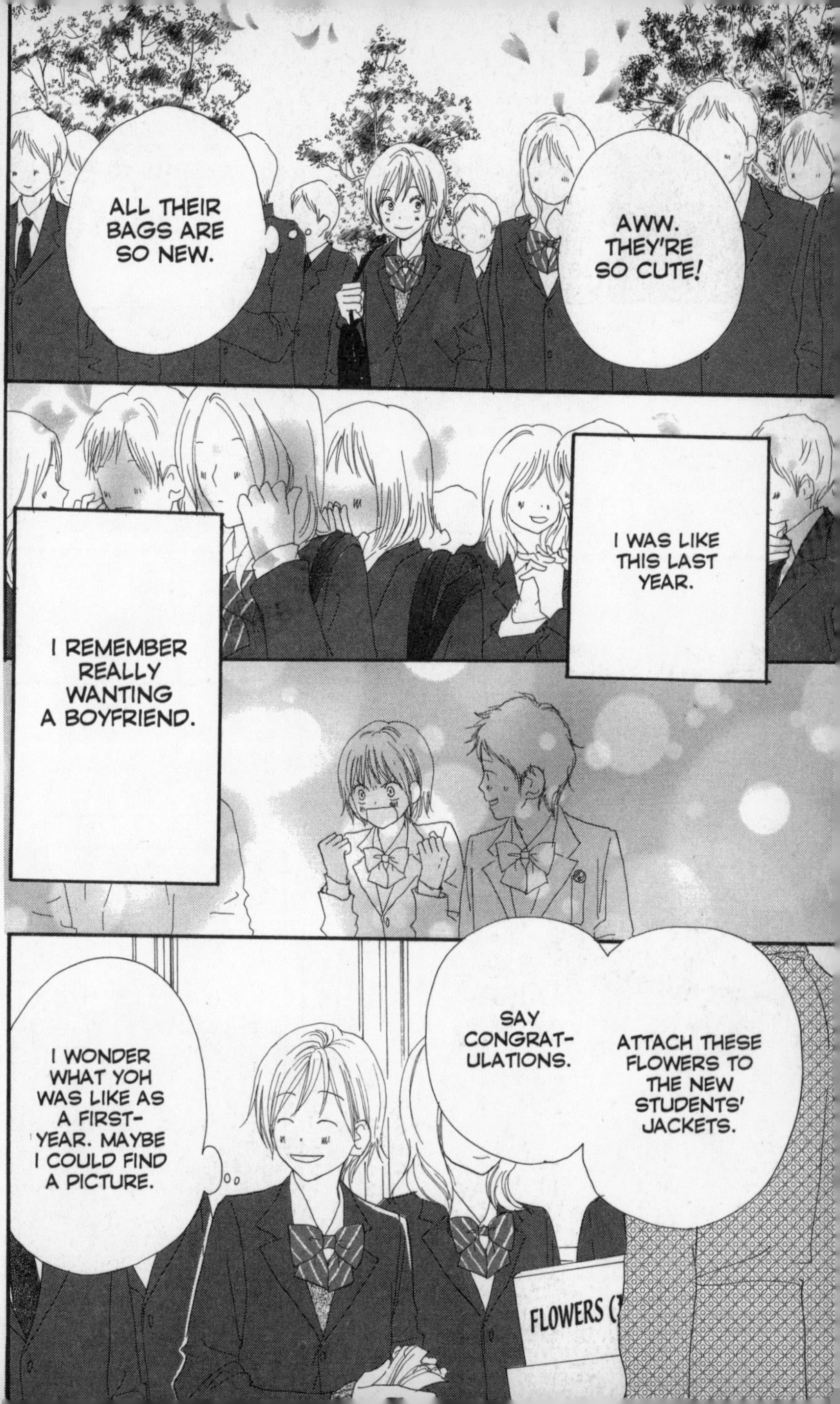
AWW. THEY'RE SO CUTE!
ALL THEIR BAGS ARE SO NEW.
I WAS LIKE THIS LAST YEAR.
I REMEMBER REALLY WANTING A BOYFRIEND.
ATTACH THESE FLOWERS TO THE NEW STUDENTS' JACKETS.
SAY CONGRAT-ULATIONS.
FLOWERS
I WONDER WHAT YOH WAS LIKE AS A FIRST-YEAR. MAYBE I COULD FIND A PICTURE.

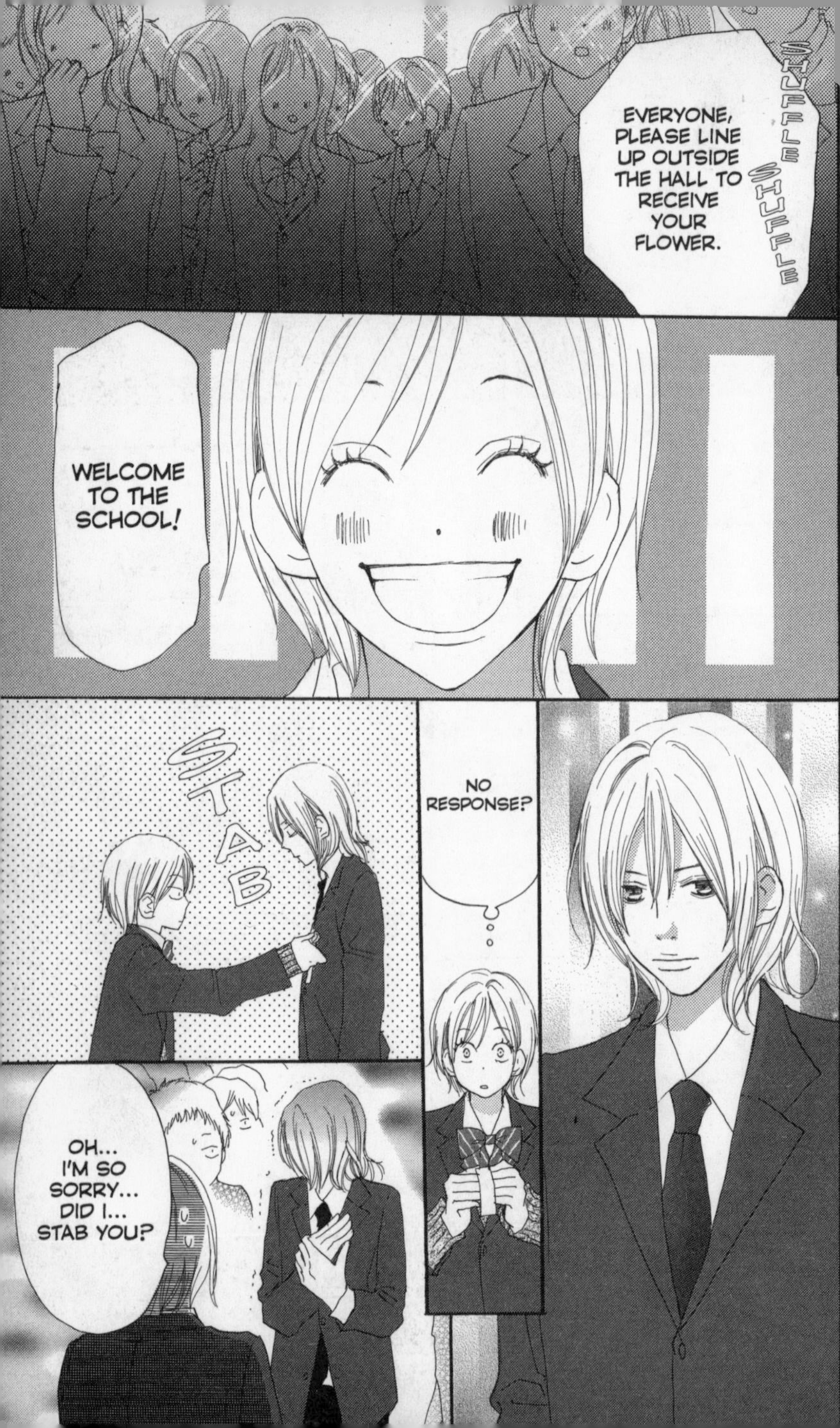
SHUFFLE
SHUFFLE
EVERYONE, PLEASE LINE UP OUTSIDE THE HALL TO RECEIVE YOUR FLOWER.
WELCOME TO THE SCHOOL!
NO RESPONSE?
STAB
OH... I'M SO SORRY... DID I... STAB YOU?

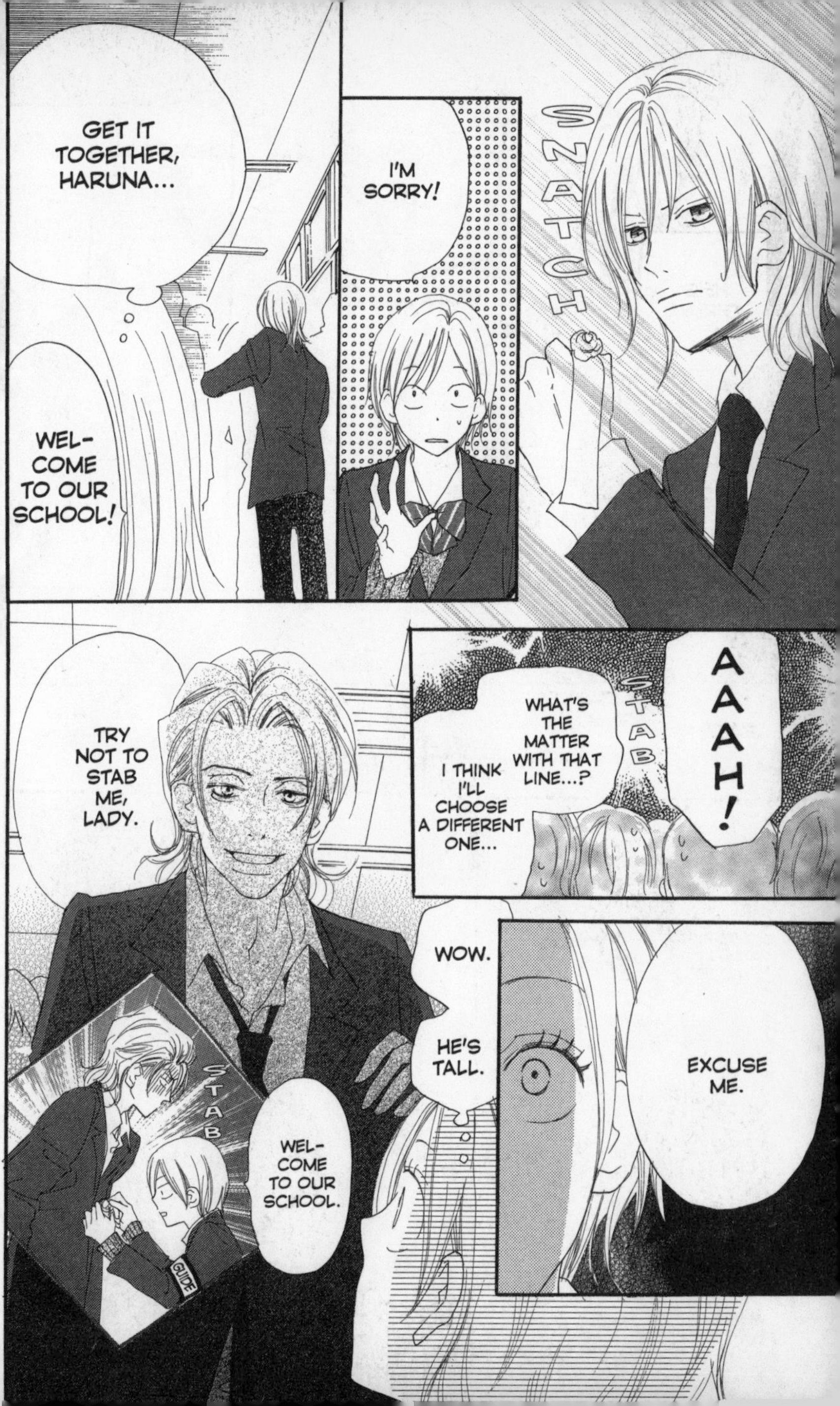
SNATCH
I'M SORRY!
GET IT TOGETHER, HARUNA...
WEL- COME TO OUR SCHOOL!
AAAH!
STAB
WHAT'S THE MATTER WITH THAT LINE...?
I THINK I'LL CHOOSE A DIFFERENT ONE...
EXCUSE ME.
WOW.
HE'S TALL.
TRY NOT TO STAB ME, LADY.
STAB
GUIDE
WEL- COME TO OUR SCHOOL.

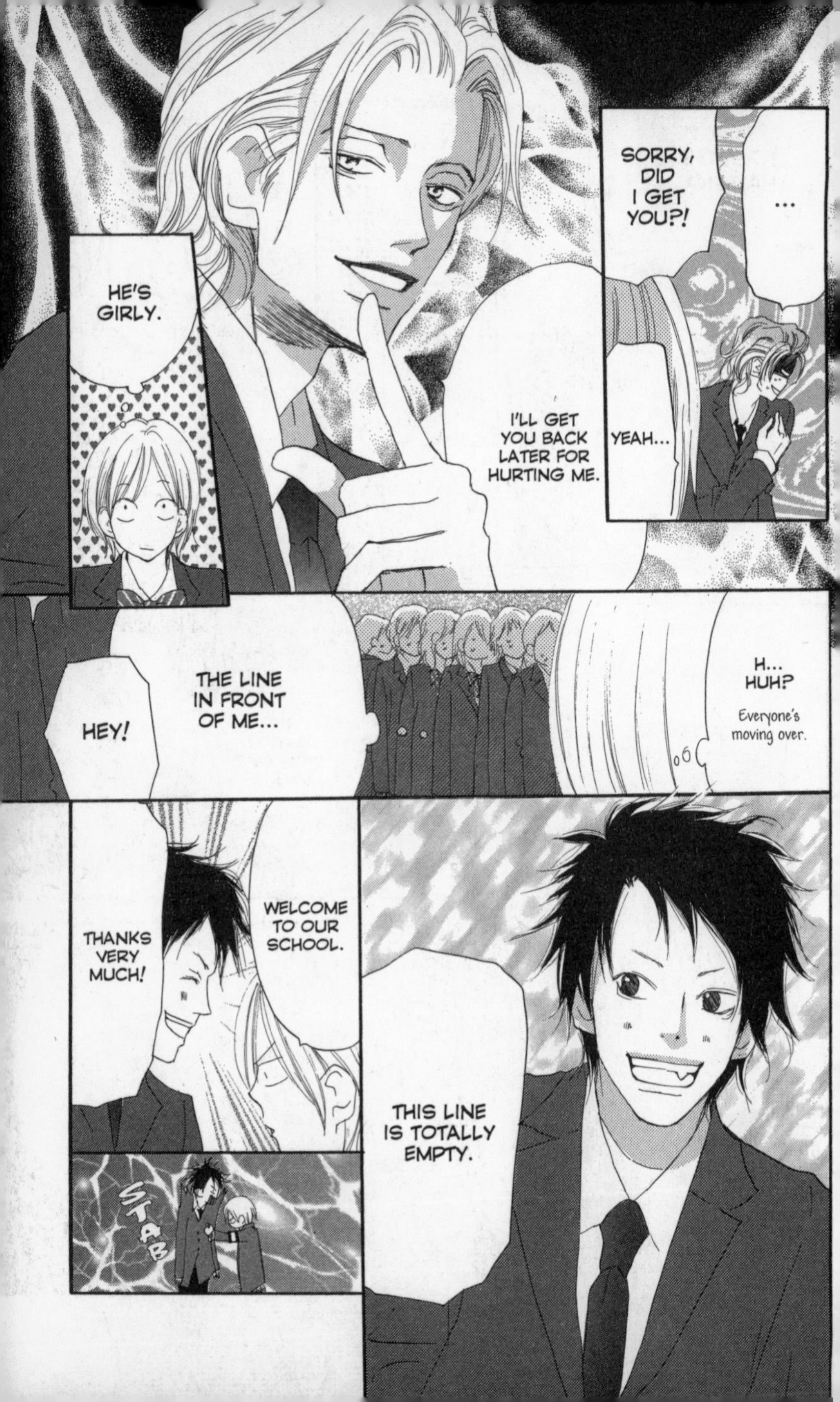
...
SORRY, DID I GET YOU?!
YEAH...
I'LL GET YOU BACK LATER FOR HURTING ME.
HE'S GIRLY.
H... HUH?
Everyone's moving over.
THE LINE IN FRONT OF ME...
HEY!
THIS LINE IS TOTALLY EMPTY.
WELCOME TO OUR SCHOOL.
THANKS VERY MUCH!
STAB

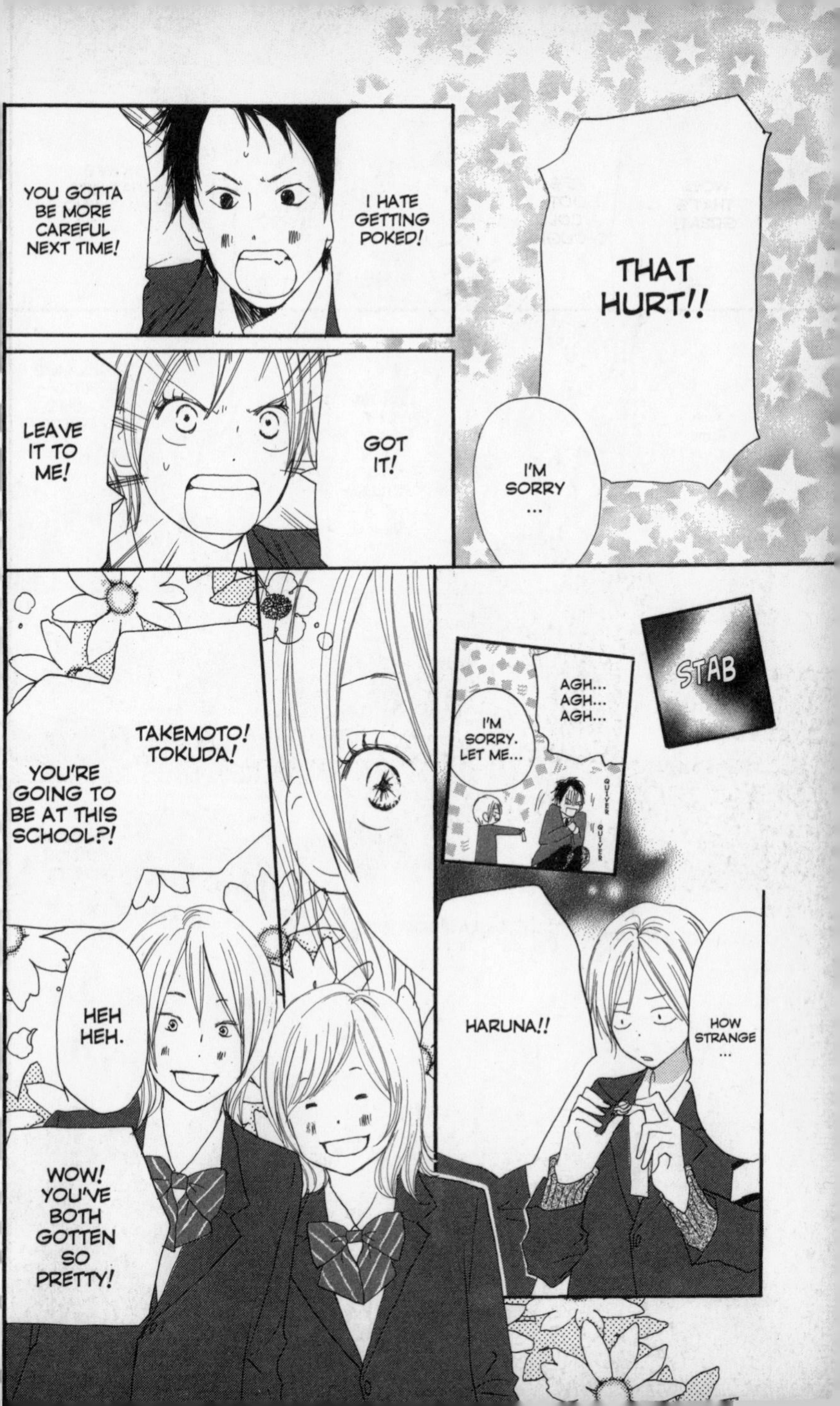
THAT HURT!!
I'M SORRY...
I HATE GETTING POKED!
YOU GOTTA BE MORE CAREFUL NEXT TIME!
GOT IT!
LEAVE IT TO ME!
STAB
AGH... AGH... AGH...
I'M SORRY. LET ME...
QUIVER QUIVER
HOW STRANGE...
HARUNA!!
TAKEMOTO! TOKUDA!
YOU'RE GOING TO BE AT THIS SCHOOL?!
HEH HEH.
WOW! YOU'VE BOTH GOTTEN SO PRETTY!

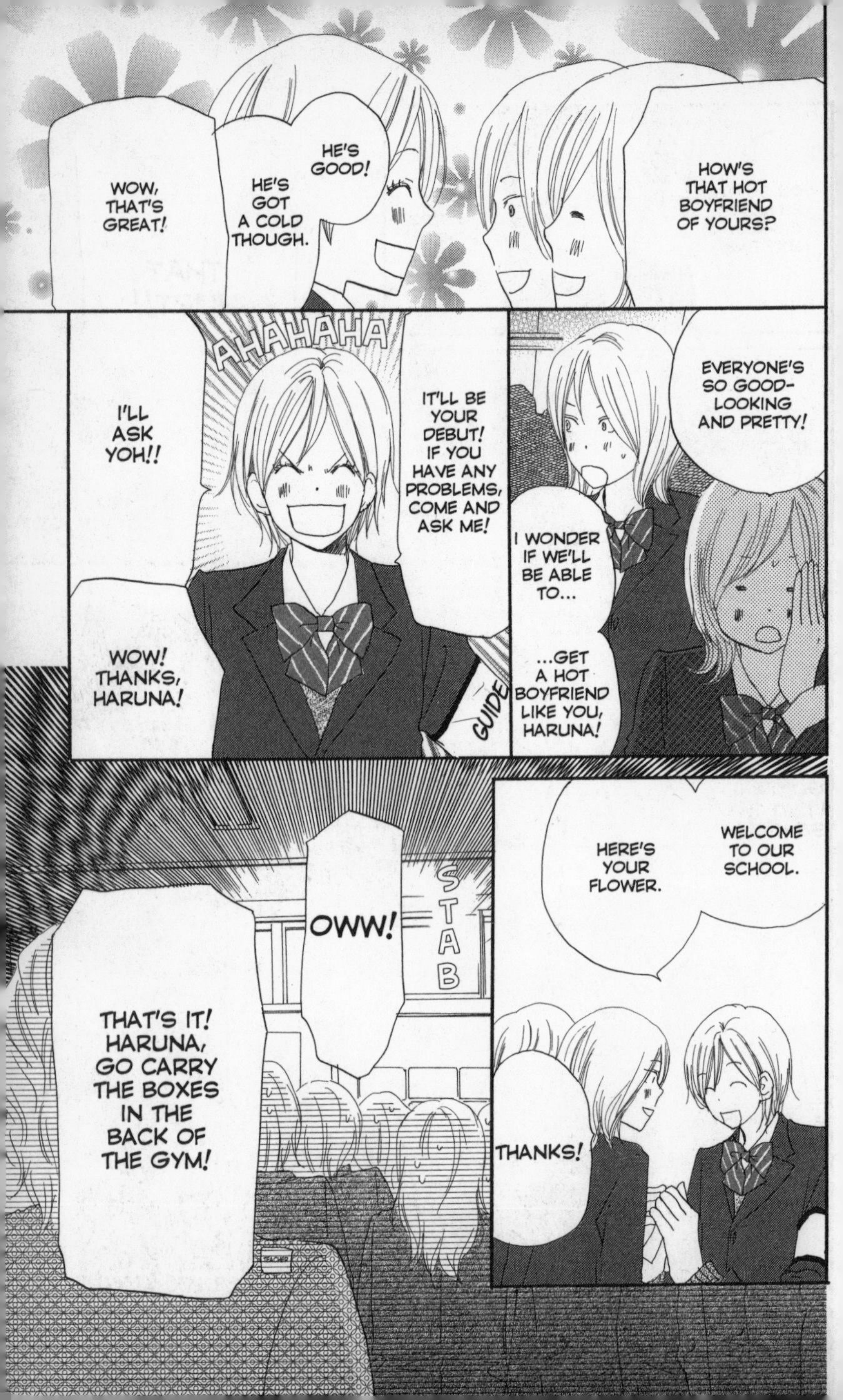
HOW'S THAT HOT BOYFRIEND OF YOURS?
HE'S GOOD!
HE'S GOT A COLD THOUGH.
WOW, THAT'S GREAT!
EVERYONE'S SO GOOD-LOOKING AND PRETTY!
I WONDER IF WE'LL BE ABLE TO...
...GET A HOT BOYFRIEND LIKE YOU, HARUNA!
AHAHAHA
IT'LL BE YOUR DEBUT! IF YOU HAVE ANY PROBLEMS, COME AND ASK ME!
I'LL ASK YOH!!
WOW! THANKS, HARUNA!
GUIDE
WELCOME TO OUR SCHOOL.
HERE'S YOUR FLOWER.
THANKS!
STAB
OWW!
THAT'S IT! HARUNA, GO CARRY THE BOXES IN THE BACK OF THE GYM!

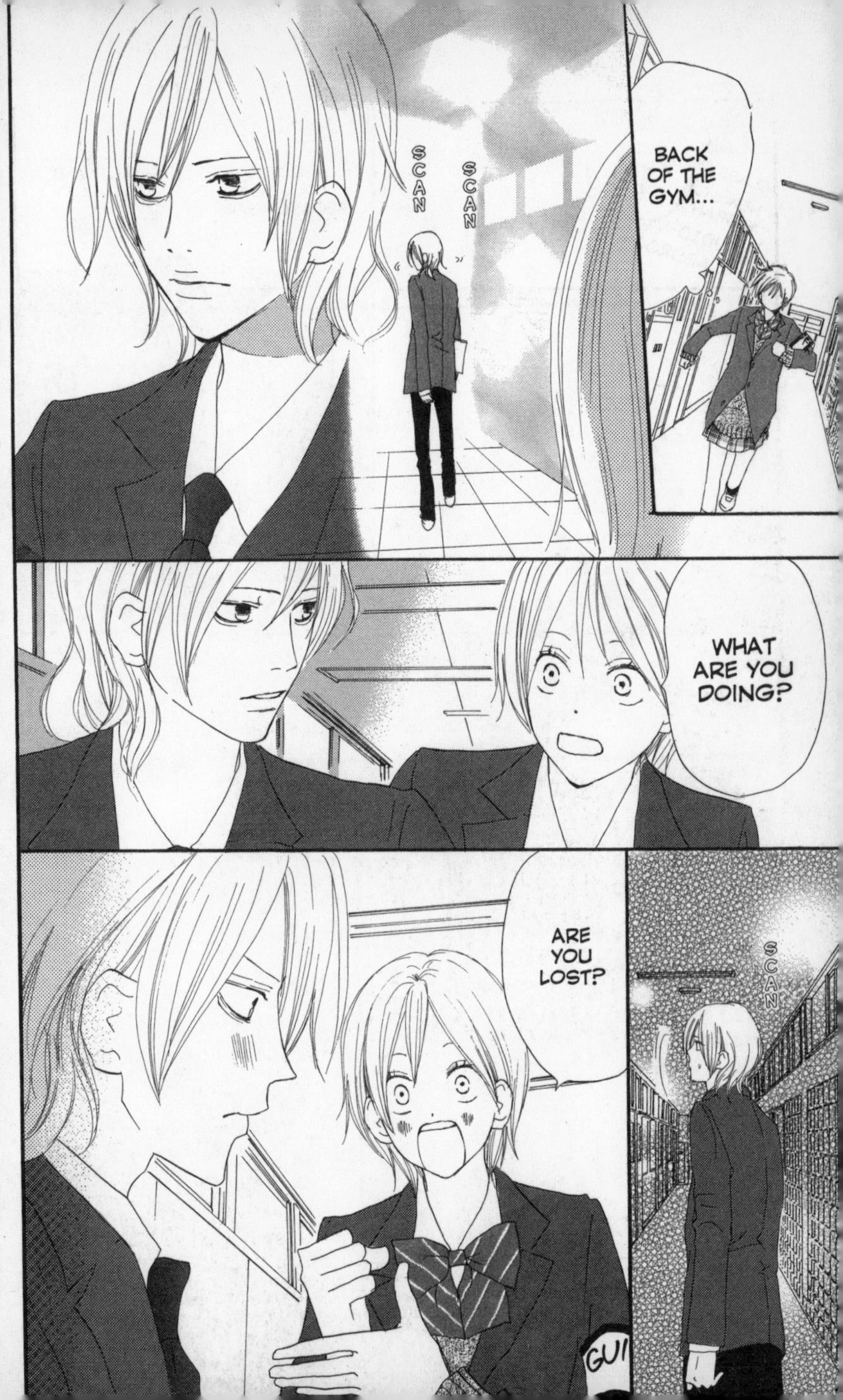
BACK OF THE GYM...
SCAN
SCAN
WHAT ARE YOU DOING?
SCAN
ARE YOU LOST?
GUI

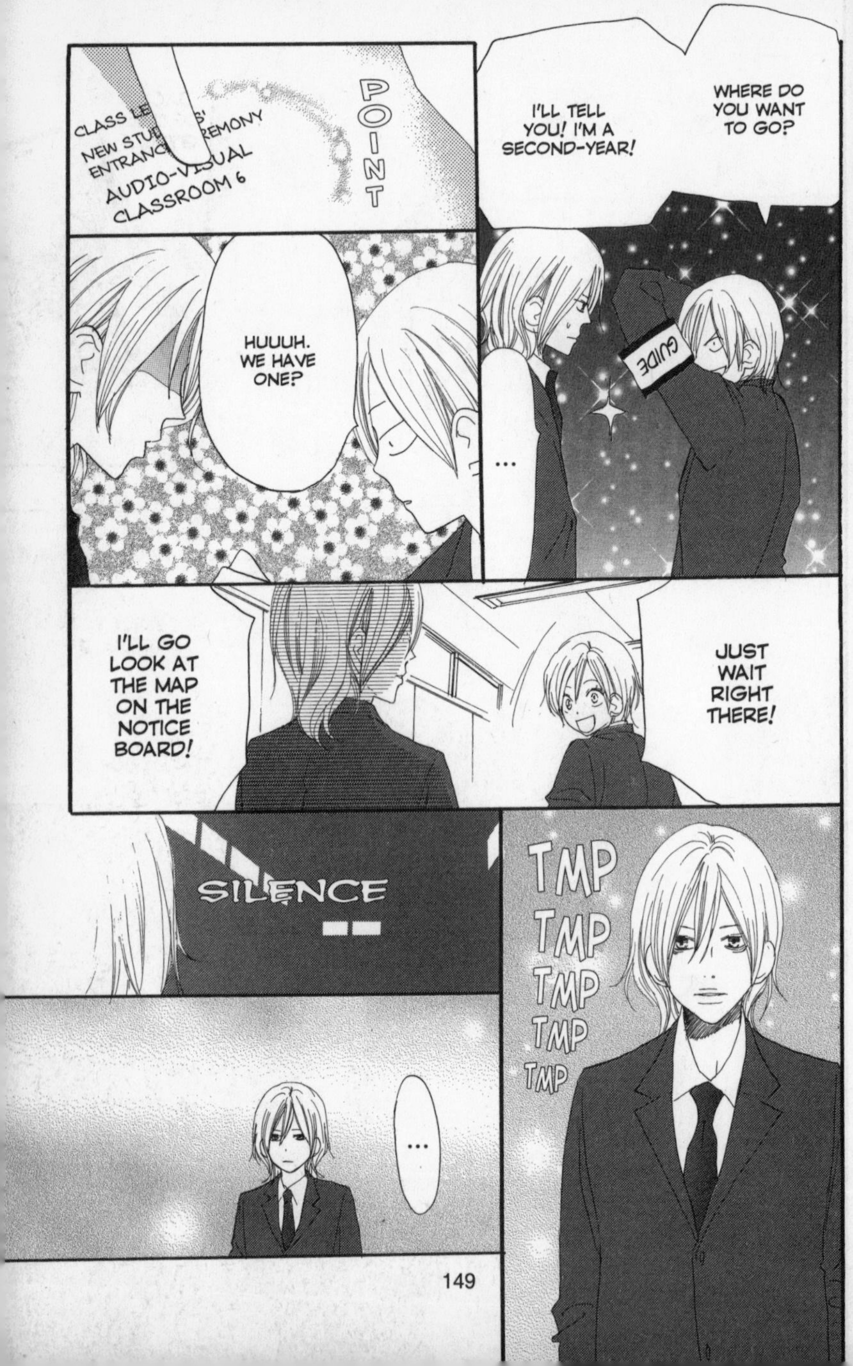
WHERE DO YOU WANT TO GO?
I'LL TELL YOU! I'M A SECOND-YEAR!
GUIDE
...
AUDIO-VISUAL CLASSROOM 6
POINT
HUUUH. WE HAVE ONE?
JUST WAIT RIGHT THERE!
I'LL GO LOOK AT THE MAP ON THE NOTICE BOARD!
TMP TMP TMP TMP TMP
SILENCE
...

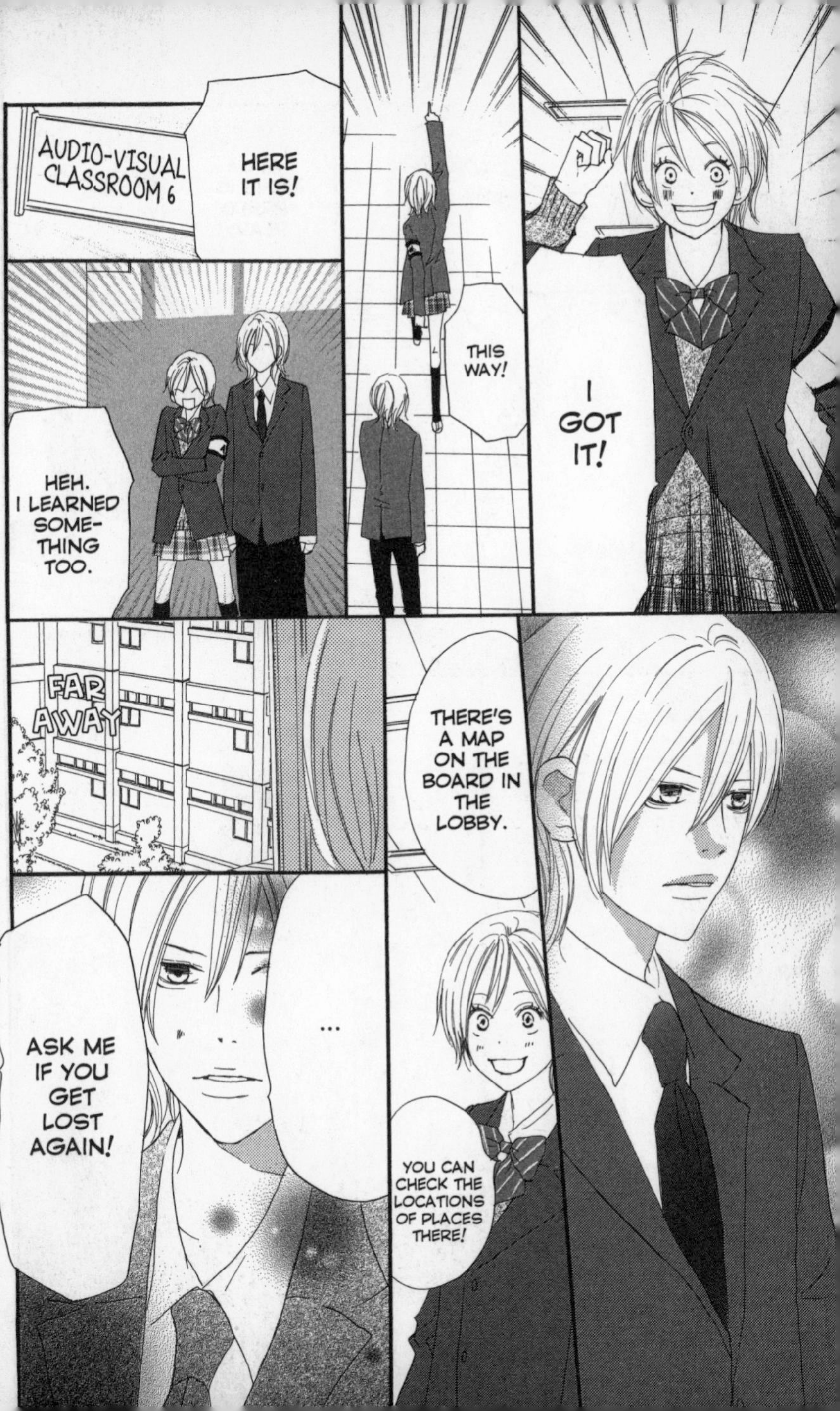
I GOT IT!
THIS WAY!
AUDIO-VISUAL CLASSROOM 6
HERE IT IS!
HEH. I LEARNED SOMETHING TOO.
THERE'S A MAP ON THE BOARD IN THE LOBBY.
YOU CAN CHECK THE LOCATIONS OF PLACES THERE!
FAR AWAY
...
ASK ME IF YOU GET LOST AGAIN!

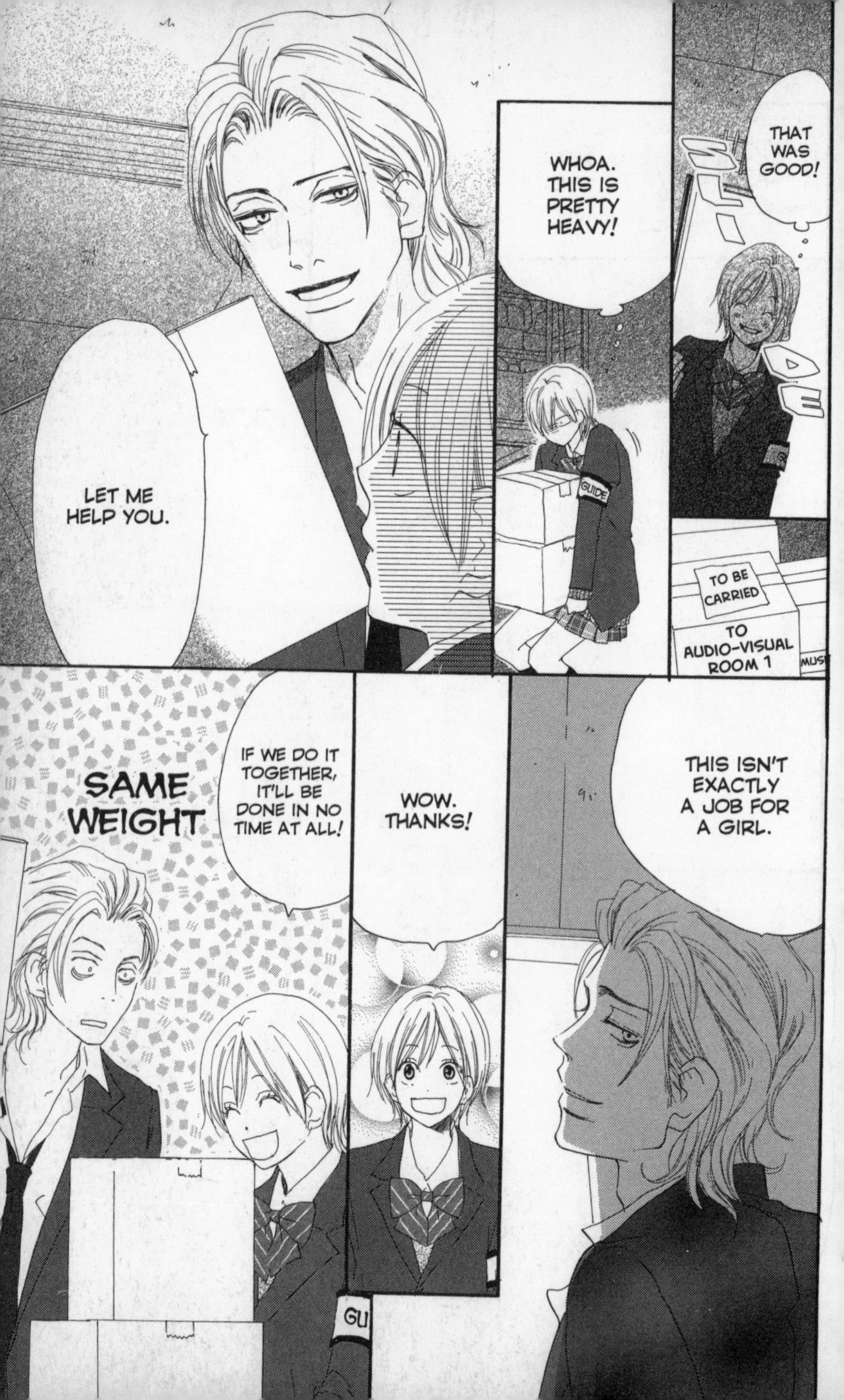
THAT WAS GOOD!
TO BE CARRIED
TO AUDIO-VISUAL ROOM 1
WHOA. THIS IS PRETTY HEAVY!
GUIDE
LET ME HELP YOU.
THIS ISN'T EXACTLY A JOB FOR A GIRL.
WOW. THANKS!
IF WE DO IT TOGETHER, IT'LL BE DONE IN NO TIME AT ALL!
SAME WEIGHT

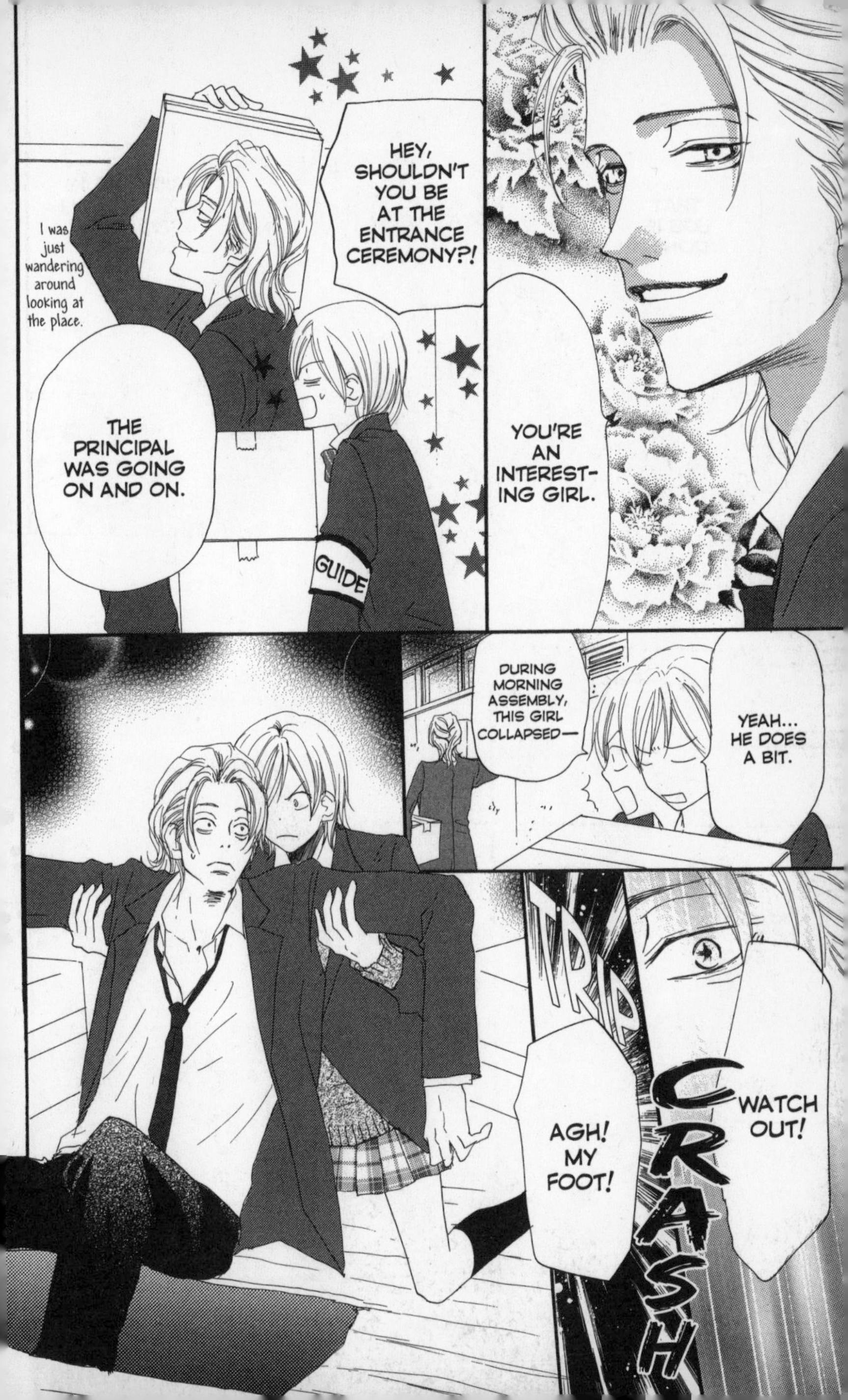
YOU'RE AN INTERESTING GIRL.
HEY, SHOULDN'T YOU BE AT THE ENTRANCE CEREMONY?!
I was just wandering around looking at the place.
THE PRINCIPAL WAS GOING ON AND ON.
YEAH... HE DOES A BIT.
DURING MORNING ASSEMBLY, THIS GIRL COLLAPSED—
GUIDE
WATCH OUT!
CRASH
TRIP
AGH! MY FOOT!

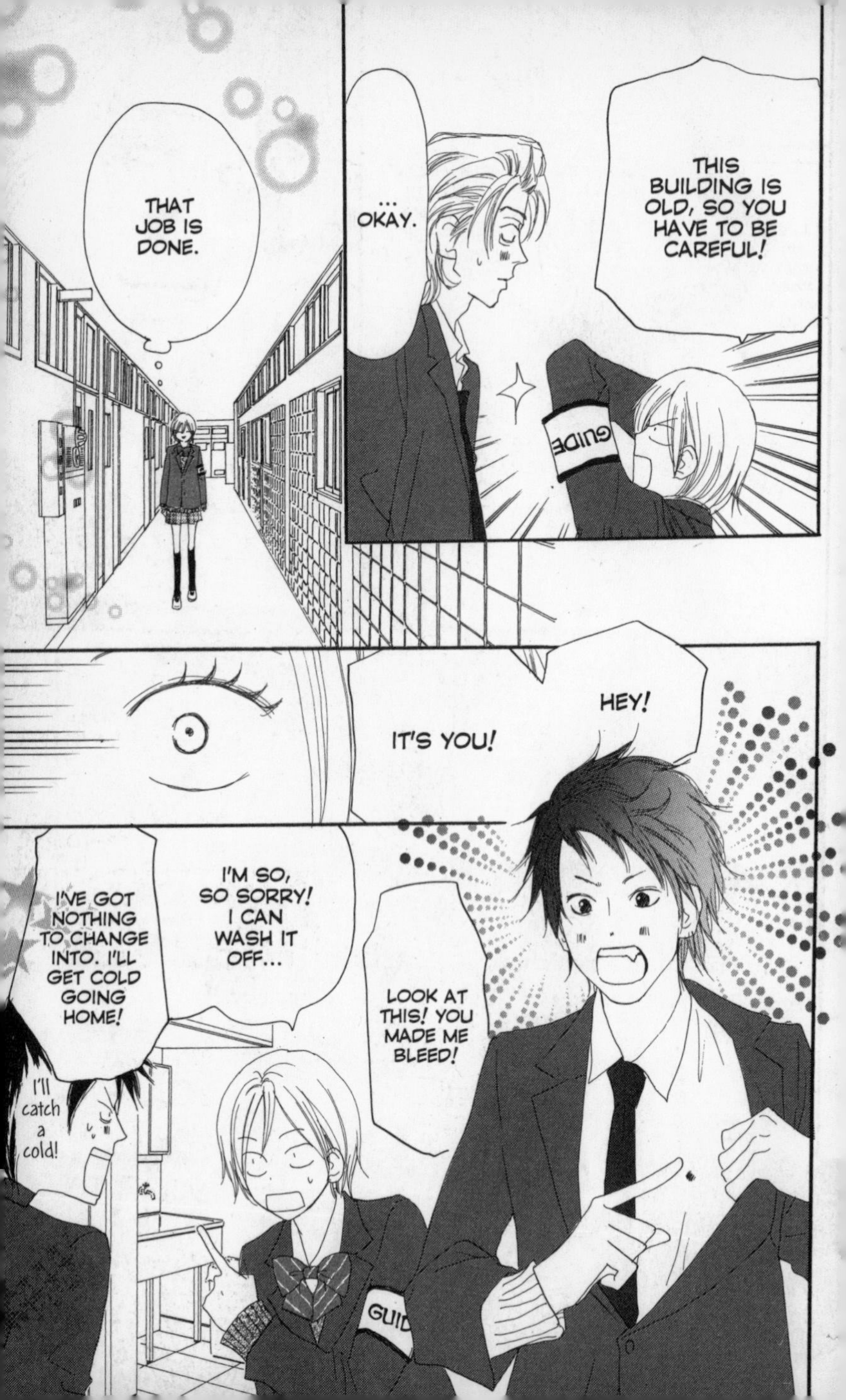
THIS BUILDING IS OLD, SO YOU HAVE TO BE CAREFUL!
... OKAY.
THAT JOB IS DONE.
HEY!
IT'S YOU!
LOOK AT THIS! YOU MADE ME BLEED!
I'M SO, SO SORRY! I CAN WASH IT OFF...
I'VE GOT NOTHING TO CHANGE INTO. I'LL GET COLD GOING HOME!
I'll catch a cold!

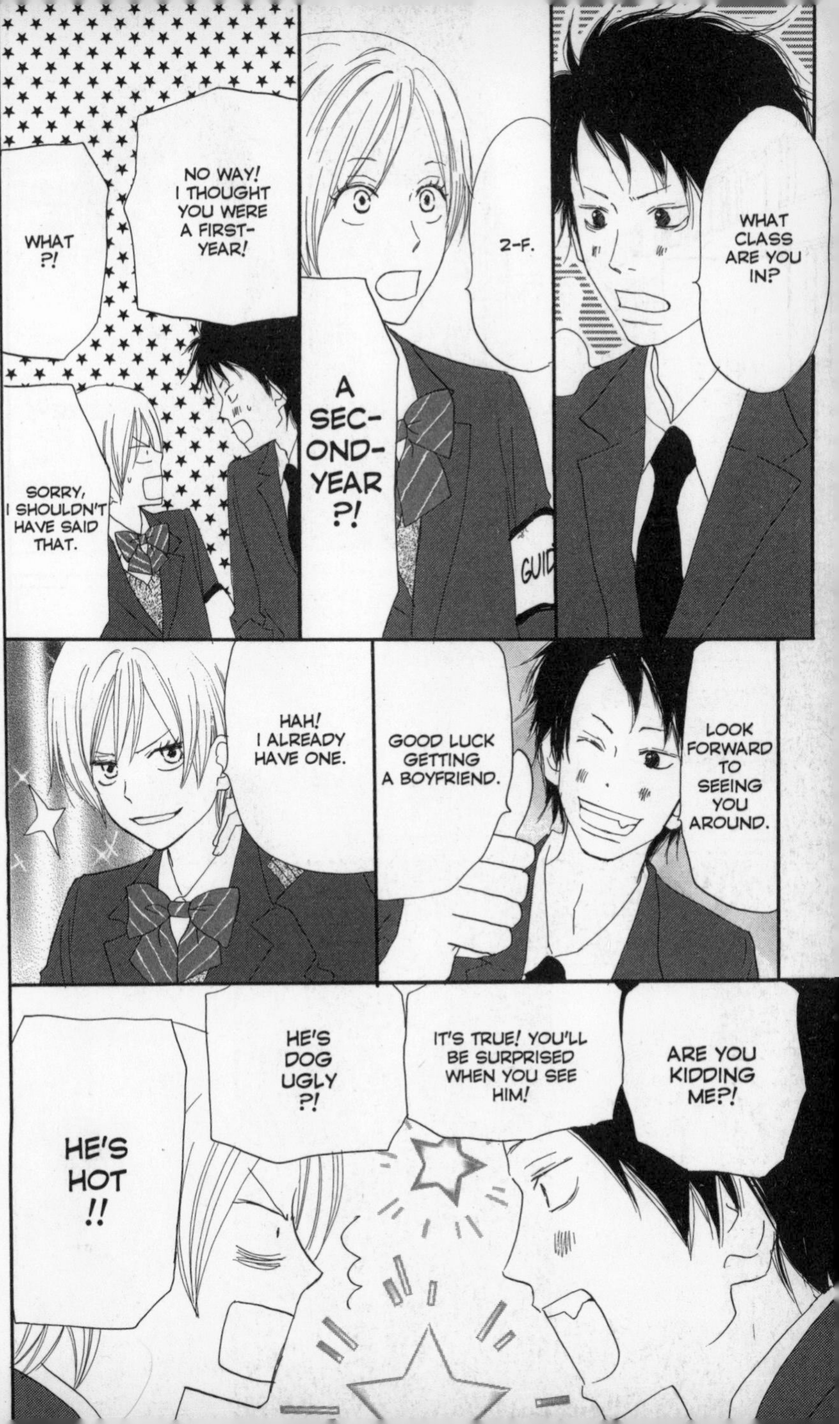
WHAT CLASS ARE YOU IN?
2-F.
A SEC-OND-YEAR?!
NO WAY! I THOUGHT YOU WERE A FIRST-YEAR!
WHAT?!
SORRY, I SHOULDN'T HAVE SAID THAT.
LOOK FORWARD TO SEEING YOU AROUND.
GOOD LUCK GETTING A BOYFRIEND.
HAH! I ALREADY HAVE ONE.
ARE YOU KIDDING ME?!
IT'S TRUE! YOU'LL BE SURPRISED WHEN YOU SEE HIM!
HE'S DOG UGLY?!
HE'S HOT!!

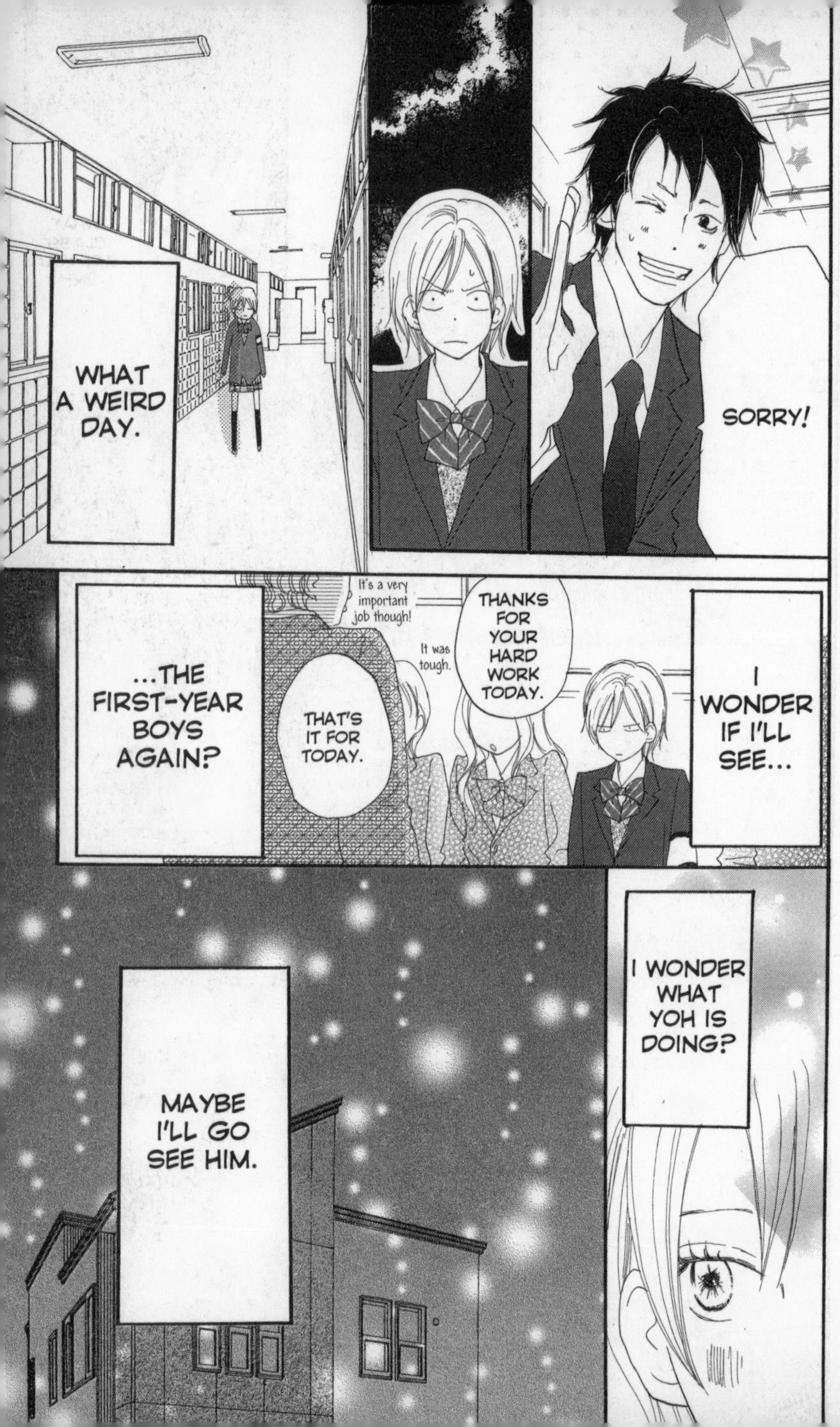
SORRY!
WHAT A WEIRD DAY.
I WONDER IF I'LL SEE...
THANKS FOR YOUR HARD WORK TODAY.
It's a very important job though!
It was tough.
THAT'S IT FOR TODAY.
...THE FIRST-YEAR BOYS AGAIN?
I WONDER WHAT YOH IS DOING?
MAYBE I'LL GO SEE HIM.

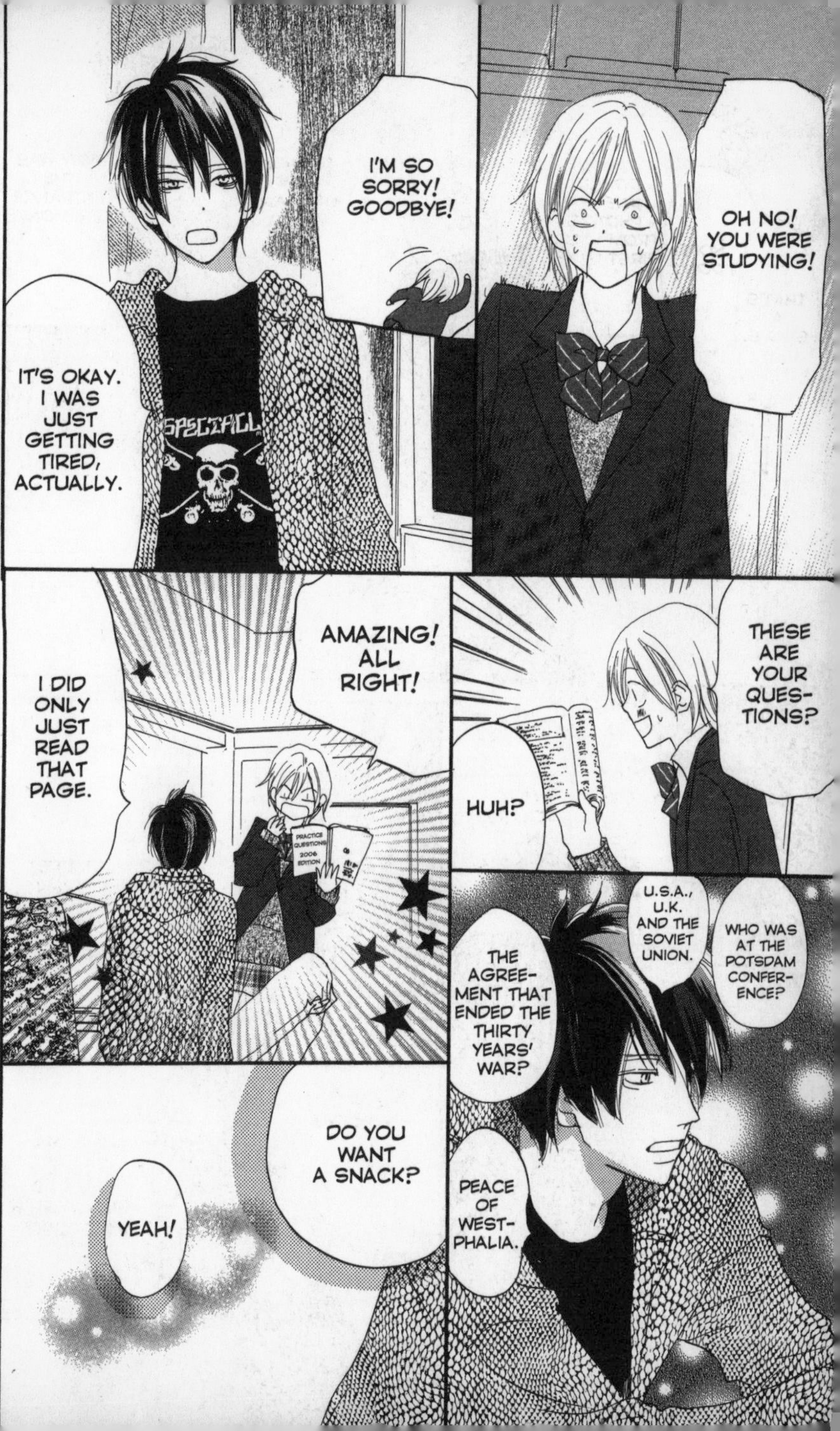
OH NO! YOU WERE STUDYING!
I'M SO SORRY! GOODBYE!
IT'S OKAY. I WAS JUST GETTING TIRED, ACTUALLY.
SPECIALL
THESE ARE YOUR QUES-TIONS?
HUH?
WHO WAS AT THE POTSDAM CONFER-ENCE?
U.S.A., U.K. AND THE SOVIET UNION.
THE AGREE-MENT THAT ENDED THE THIRTY YEARS' WAR?
PEACE OF WEST-PHALIA.
AMAZING! ALL RIGHT!
PRACTICE QUESTIONS 2006 EDITION
I DID ONLY JUST READ THAT PAGE.
DO YOU WANT A SNACK?
YEAH!

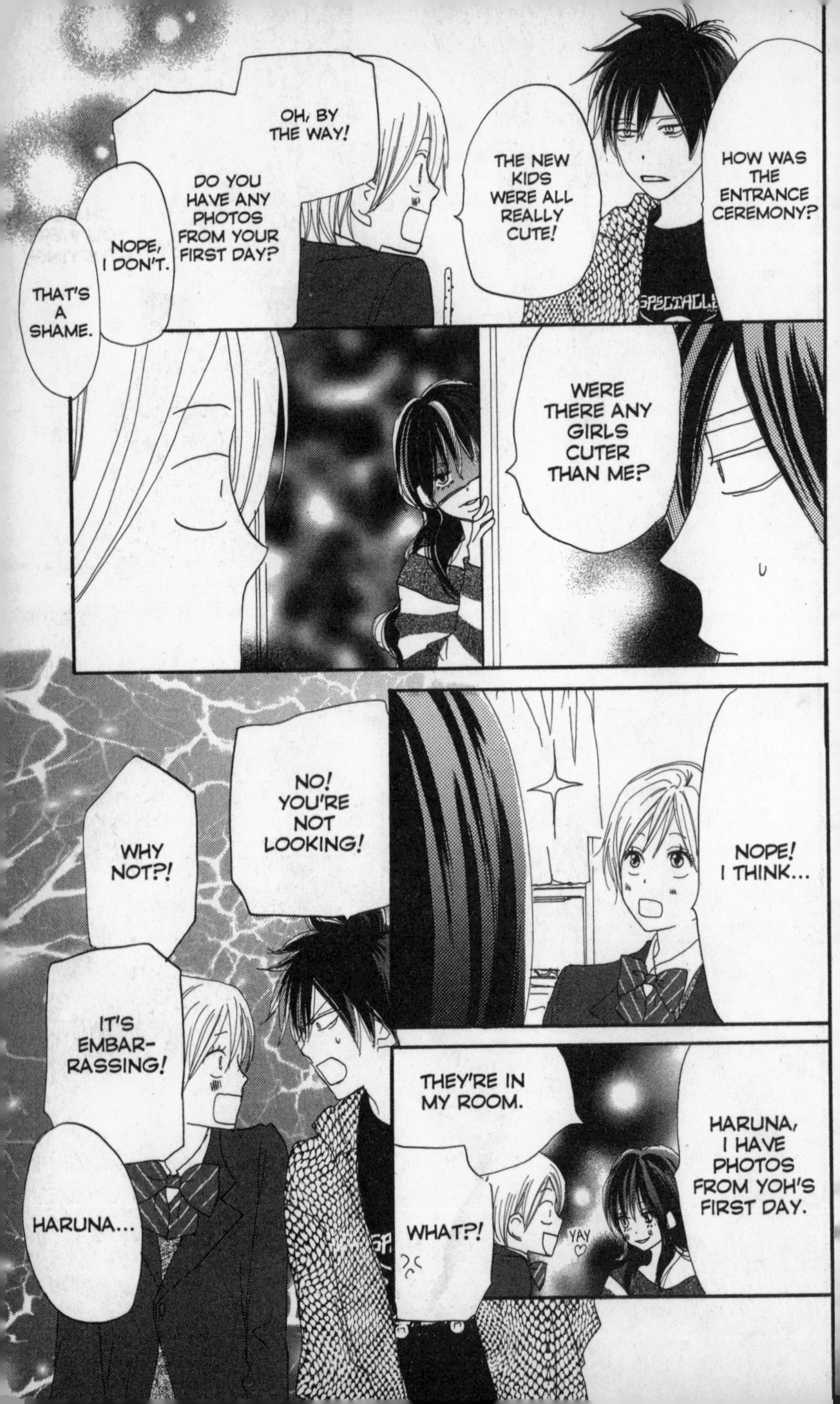
HOW WAS THE ENTRANCE CEREMONY?
THE NEW KIDS WERE ALL REALLY CUTE!
OH, BY THE WAY!
DO YOU HAVE ANY PHOTOS FROM YOUR FIRST DAY?
NOPE, I DON'T.
THAT'S A SHAME.
WERE THERE ANY GIRLS CUTER THAN ME?
NOPE! I THINK...
HARUNA, I HAVE PHOTOS FROM YOH'S FIRST DAY.
YAY
THEY'RE IN MY ROOM.
WHAT?!
NO! YOU'RE NOT LOOKING!
WHY NOT?!
IT'S EMBARRASSING!
HARUNA...

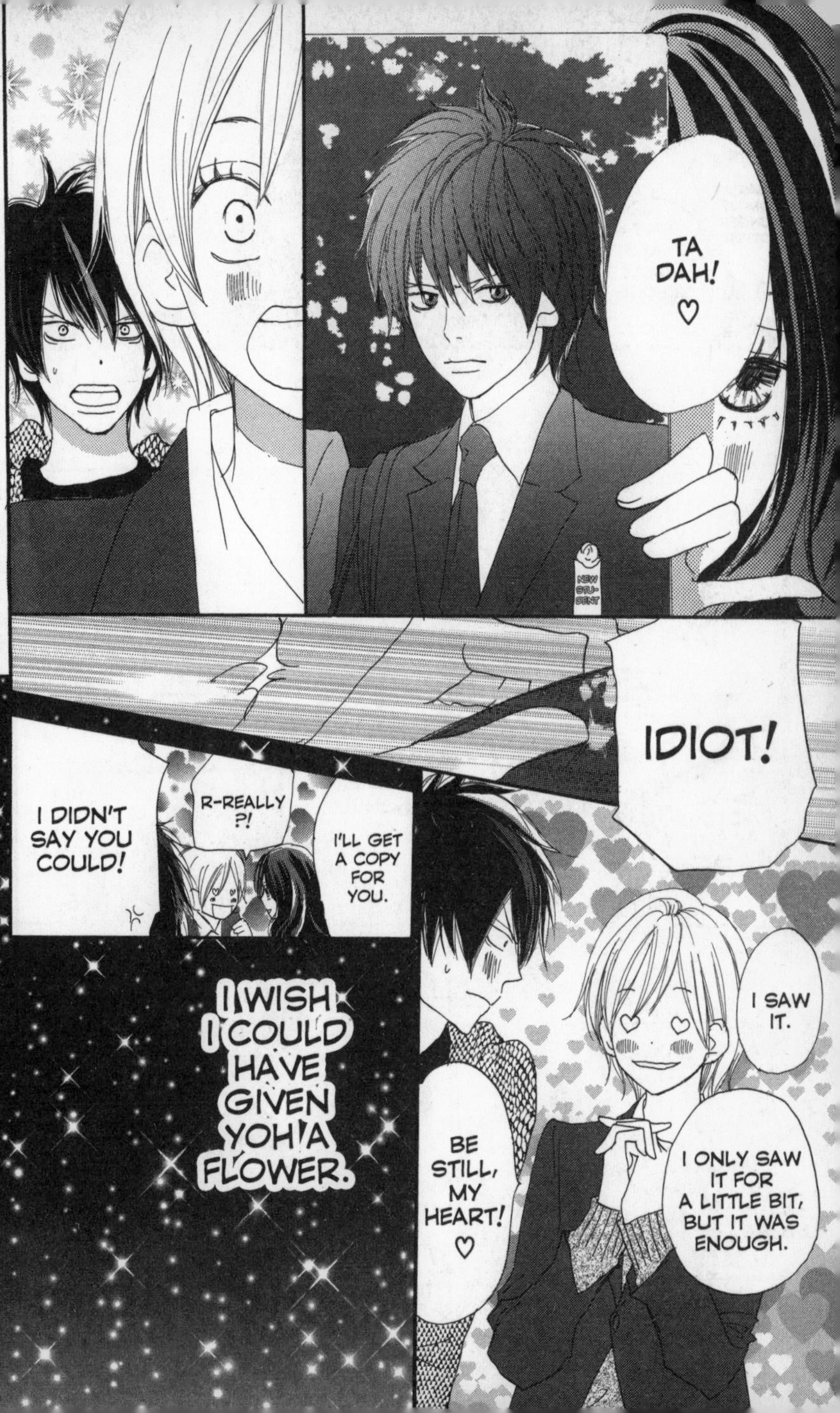
TA DAH! ♡
NEW STU-DENT
IDIOT!
I SAW IT.
I ONLY SAW IT FOR A LITTLE BIT, BUT IT WAS ENOUGH.
BE STILL, MY HEART! ♡
I'LL GET A COPY FOR YOU.
R-REALLY ?!
I DIDN'T SAY YOU COULD!
I WISH I COULD HAVE GIVEN YOH A FLOWER.

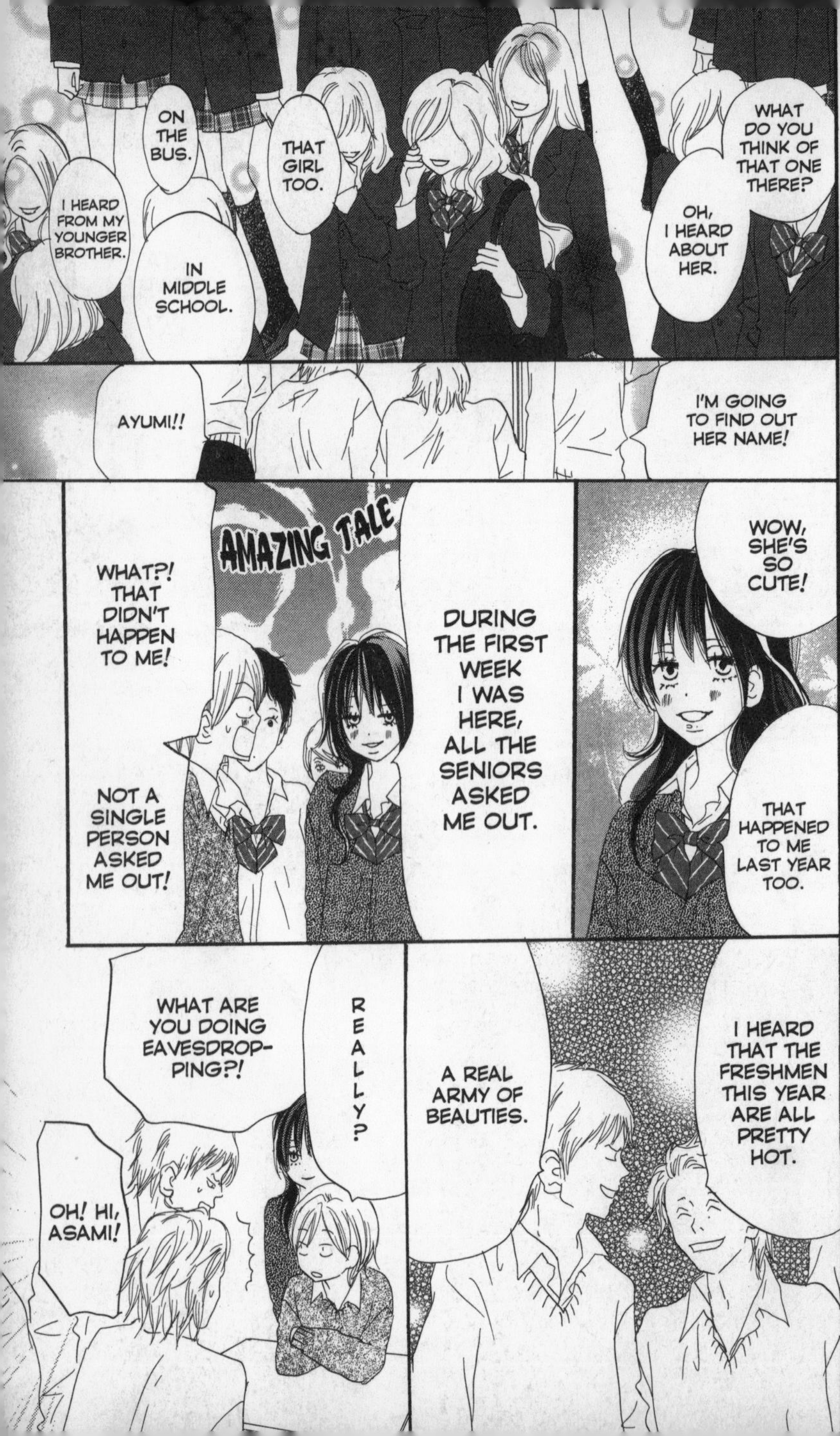
WHAT DO YOU THINK OF THAT ONE THERE?
OH, I HEARD ABOUT HER.
THAT GIRL TOO.
ON THE BUS.
I HEARD FROM MY YOUNGER BROTHER.
IN MIDDLE SCHOOL.
I'M GOING TO FIND OUT HER NAME!
AYUMI!!
WOW, SHE'S SO CUTE!
THAT HAPPENED TO ME LAST YEAR TOO.
DURING THE FIRST WEEK I WAS HERE, ALL THE SENIORS ASKED ME OUT.
AMAZING TALE
WHAT?! THAT DIDN'T HAPPEN TO ME!
NOT A SINGLE PERSON ASKED ME OUT!
I HEARD THAT THE FRESHMEN THIS YEAR ARE ALL PRETTY HOT.
A REAL ARMY OF BEAUTIES.
REALLY?
WHAT ARE YOU DOING EAVESDROPPING?!
OH! HI, ASAMI!

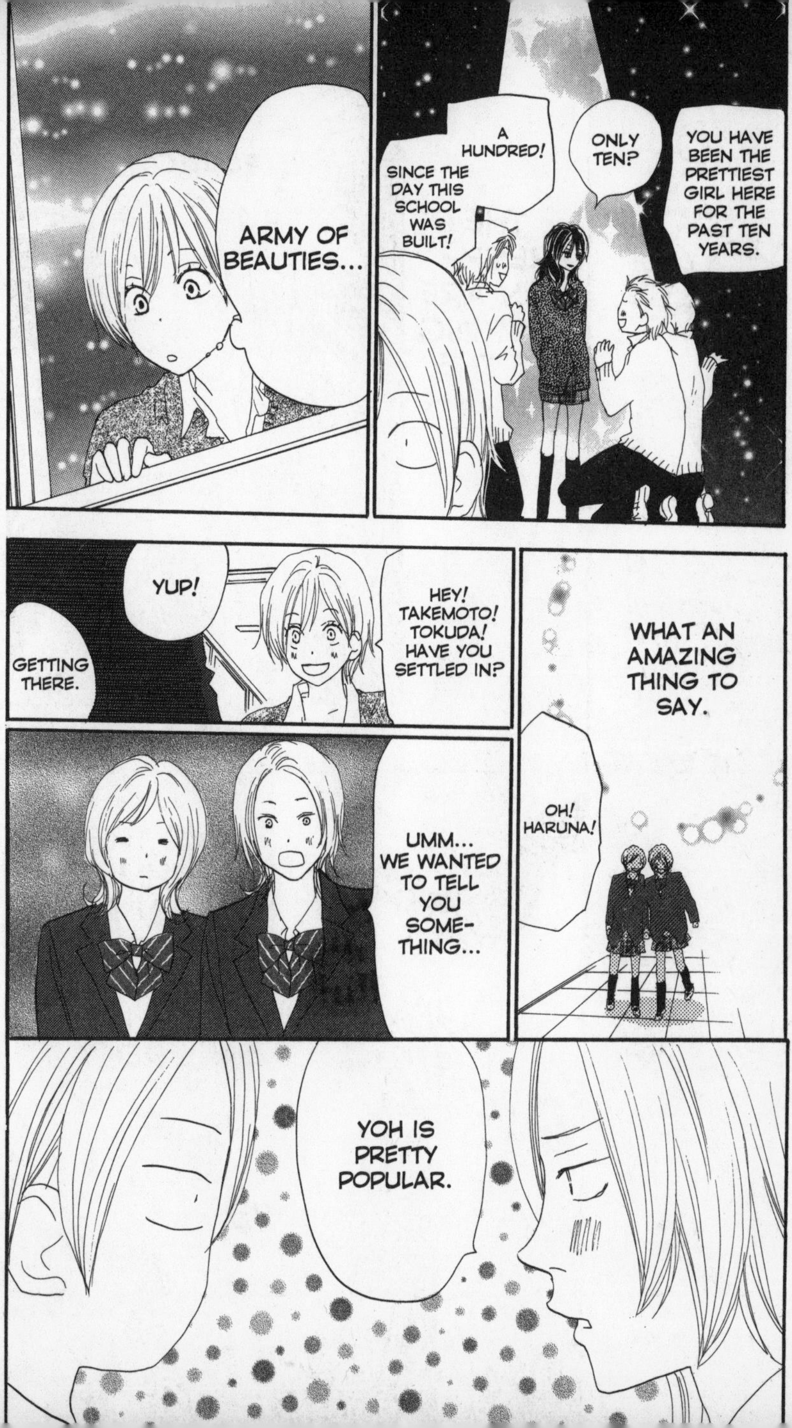
YOU HAVE BEEN THE PRETTIEST GIRL HERE FOR THE PAST TEN YEARS.
ONLY TEN?
A HUNDRED!
SINCE THE DAY THIS SCHOOL WAS BUILT!
ARMY OF BEAUTIES...
WHAT AN AMAZING THING TO SAY.
OH! HARUNA!
HEY! TAKEMOTO! TOKUDA! HAVE YOU SETTLED IN?
YUP!
GETTING THERE.
UMM... WE WANTED TO TELL YOU SOMETHING...
YOH IS PRETTY POPULAR.

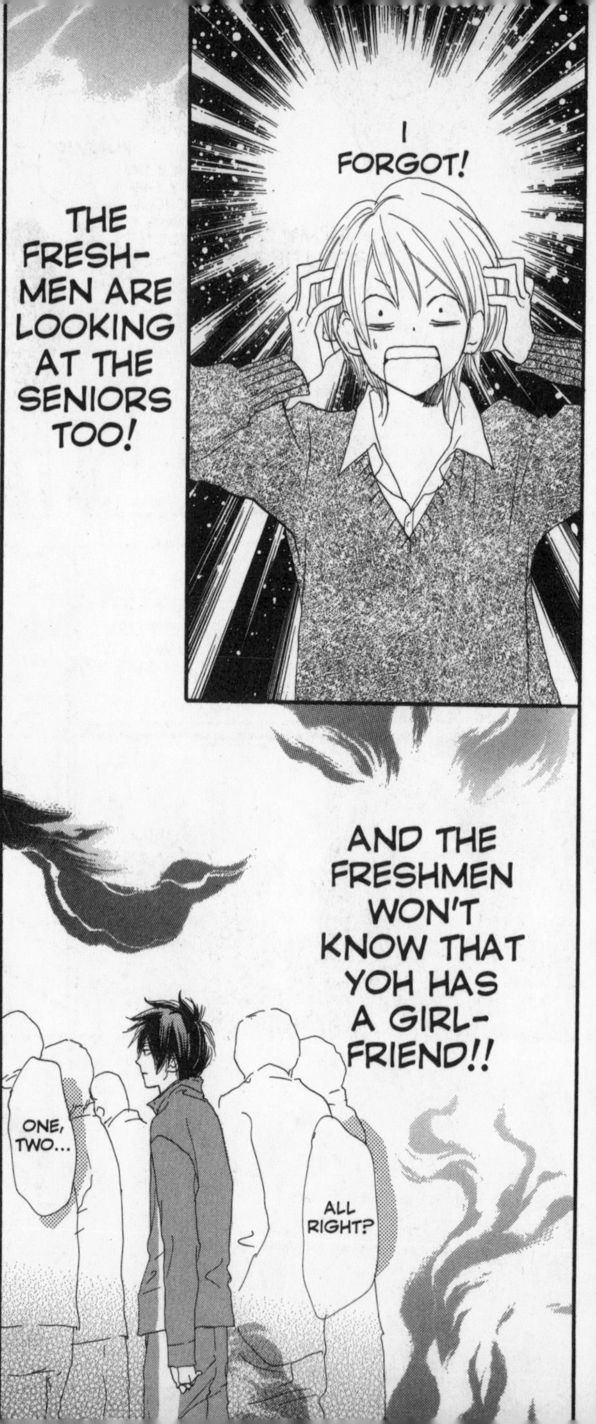
I FORGOT!
THE FRESHMEN ARE LOOKING AT THE SENIORS TOO!
AND THE FRESHMEN WON'T KNOW THAT YOH HAS A GIRLFRIEND!!
ONE, TWO...
ALL RIGHT?

3

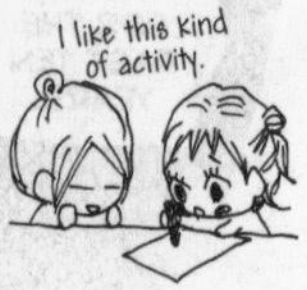
I like this kind of activity.

My niece is old enough now that she can do a lot more. I drew a picture for her and gave her some marker pens to trace with.

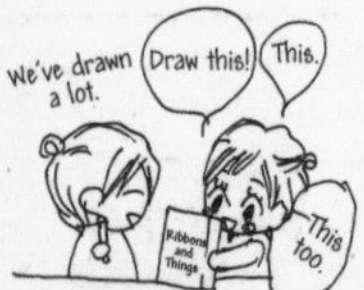
We've drawn a lot.
Draw this!
This.
This too.
Ribbons and Things

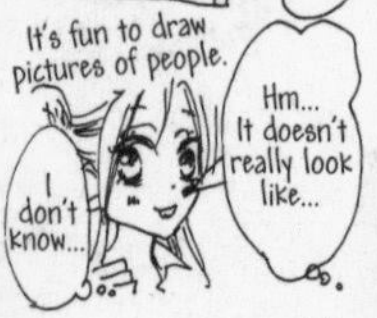
It's fun to draw pictures of people.
Hm... It doesn't really look like...
I don't know...

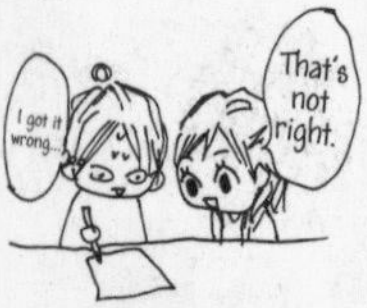
That's not right.
I got it wrong...

I felt good drawing it though, so I decided to send it in to the magazine.

But my niece took it to show her mom.

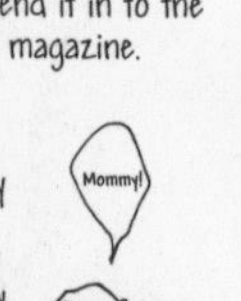
Mommy!

See you in the next volume.

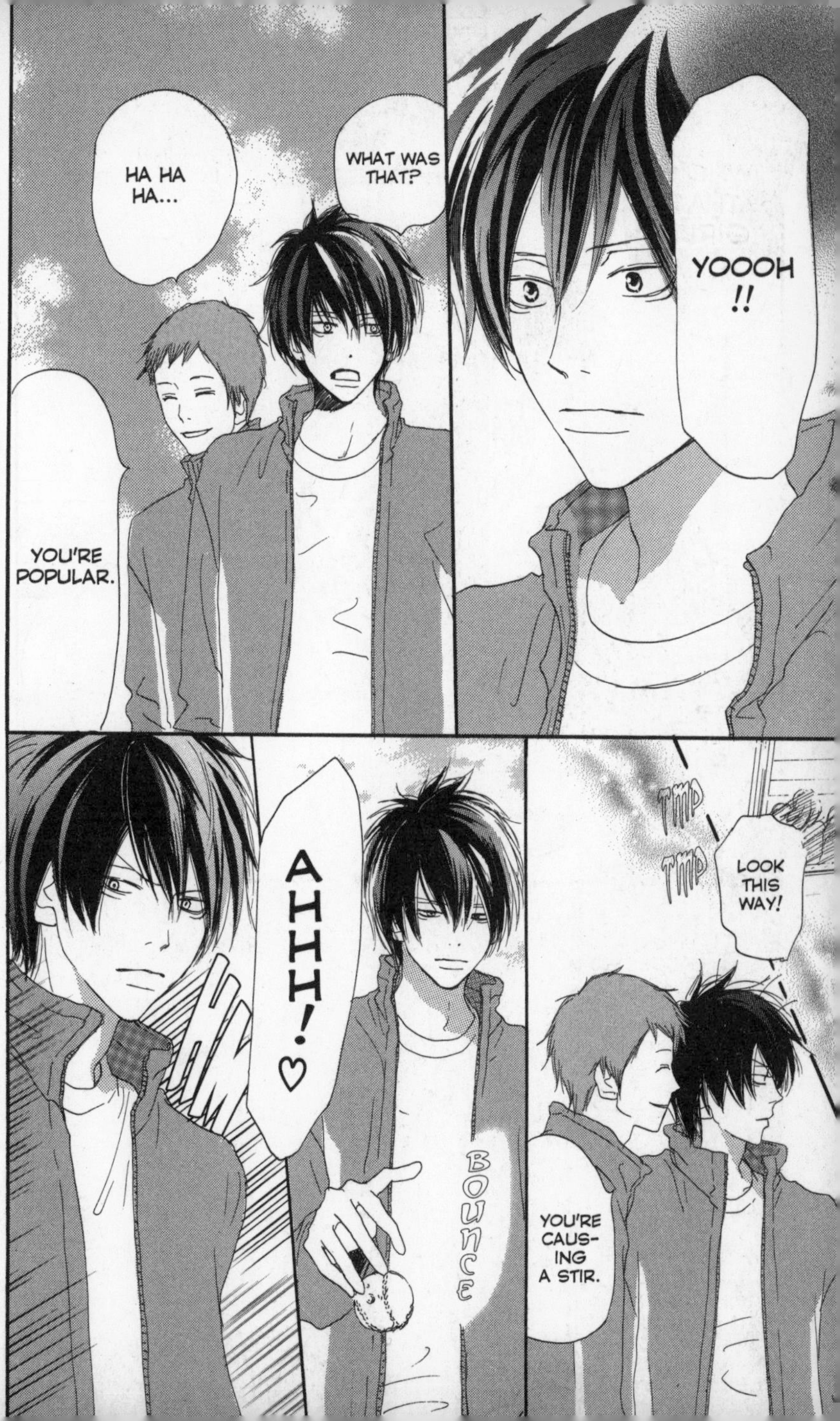
YOOOH !!
WHAT WAS THAT?
HA HA HA...
YOU'RE POPULAR.
TMP
TMP
LOOK THIS WAY!
YOU'RE CAUS-ING A STIR.
AHHH!♥
BOUNCE

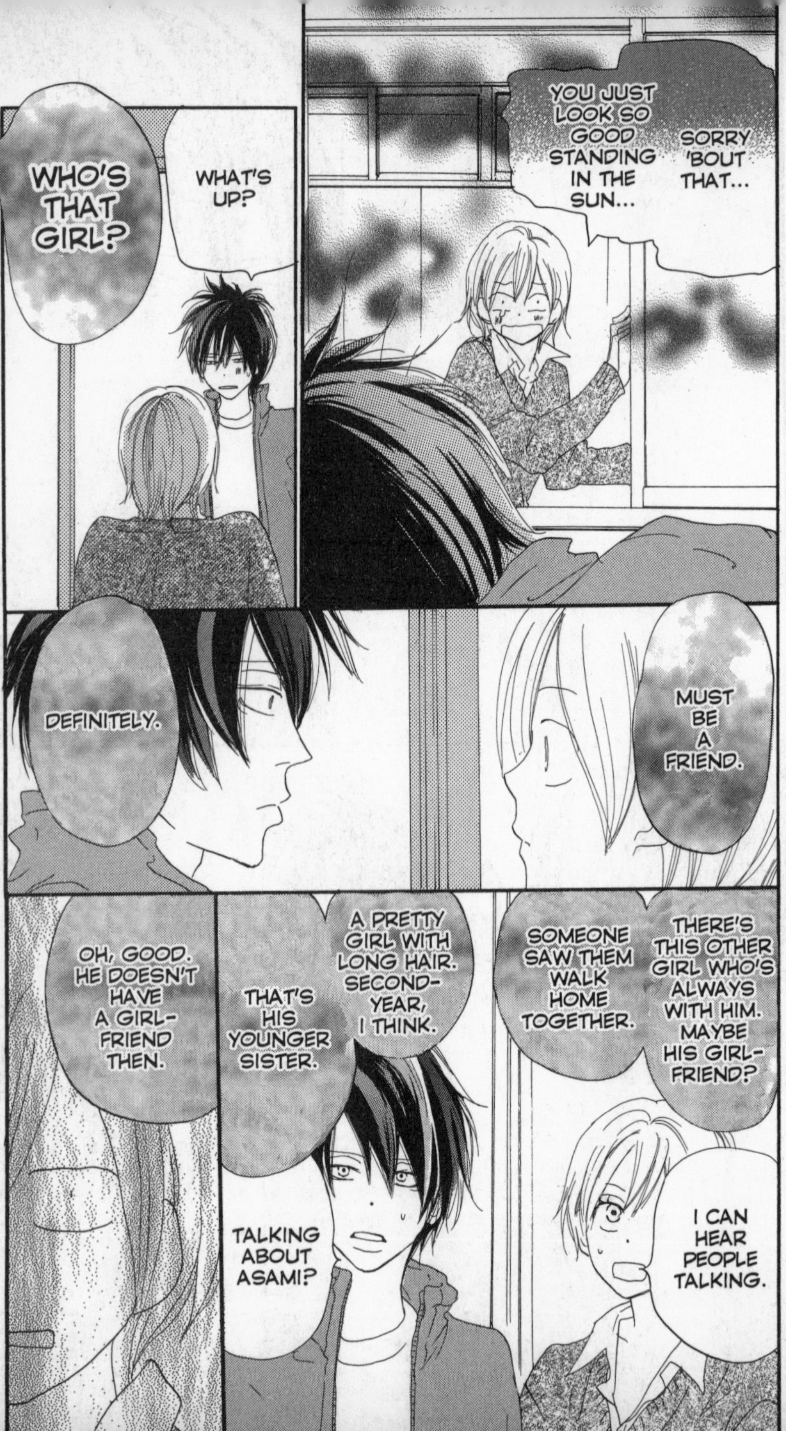
SORRY 'BOUT THAT...
YOU JUST LOOK SO GOOD STANDING IN THE SUN...
WHAT'S UP?
WHO'S THAT GIRL?
MUST BE A FRIEND.
DEFINITELY.
THERE'S THIS OTHER GIRL WHO'S ALWAYS WITH HIM. MAYBE HIS GIRLFRIEND?
SOMEONE SAW THEM WALK HOME TOGETHER.
I CAN HEAR PEOPLE TALKING.
A PRETTY GIRL WITH LONG HAIR. SECOND-YEAR, I THINK.
THAT'S HIS YOUNGER SISTER.
TALKING ABOUT ASAMI?
OH, GOOD. HE DOESN'T HAVE A GIRLFRIEND THEN.

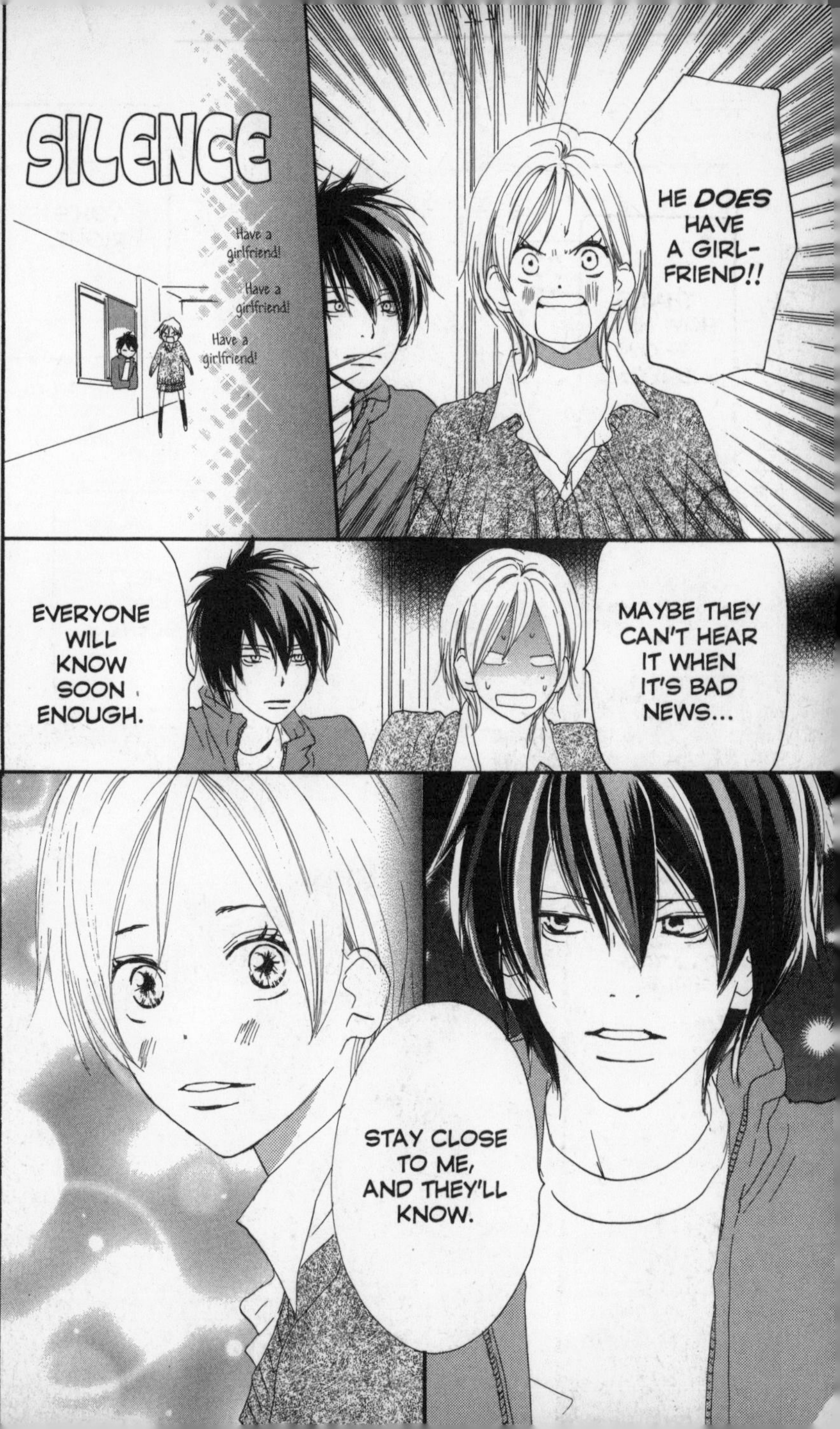
HE DOES HAVE A GIRL-FRIEND!!
SILENCE
Have a girlfriend!
Have a girlfriend!
Have a girlfriend!
MAYBE THEY CAN'T HEAR IT WHEN IT'S BAD NEWS...
EVERYONE WILL KNOW SOON ENOUGH.
STAY CLOSE TO ME, AND THEY'LL KNOW.

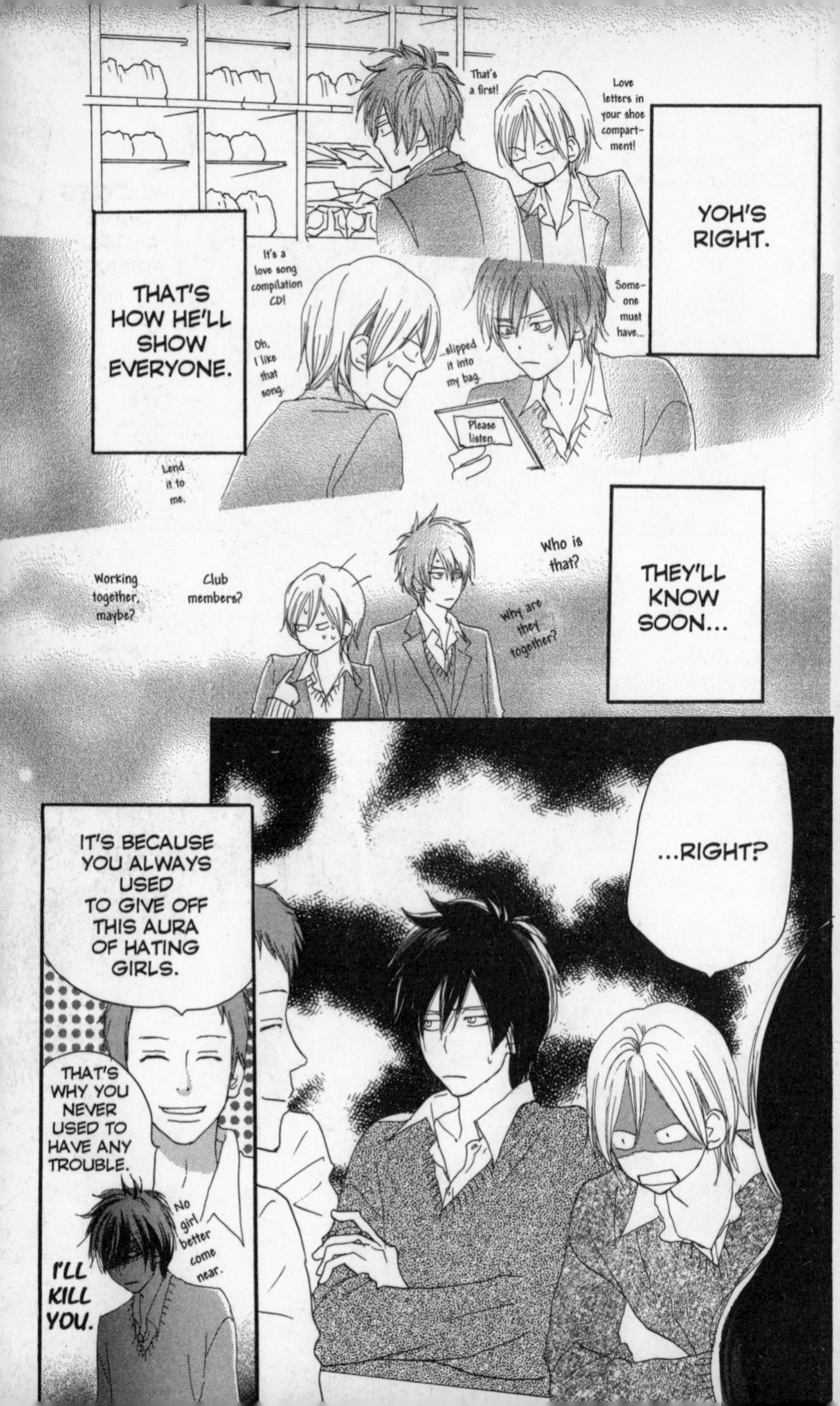
YOH'S RIGHT.
Love letters in your shoe compart-ment!
That's a first!
Some-one must have...
...slipped it into my bag.
Please listen.
It's a love song compilation CD!
Oh, I like that song.
Lend it to me.
THAT'S HOW HE'LL SHOW EVERYONE.
THEY'LL KNOW SOON...
Who is that?
Why are they together?
Club members?
Working together, maybe?
...RIGHT?
IT'S BECAUSE YOU ALWAYS USED TO GIVE OFF THIS AURA OF HATING GIRLS.
THAT'S WHY YOU NEVER USED TO HAVE ANY TROUBLE.
No girl better come near.
I'LL KILL YOU.

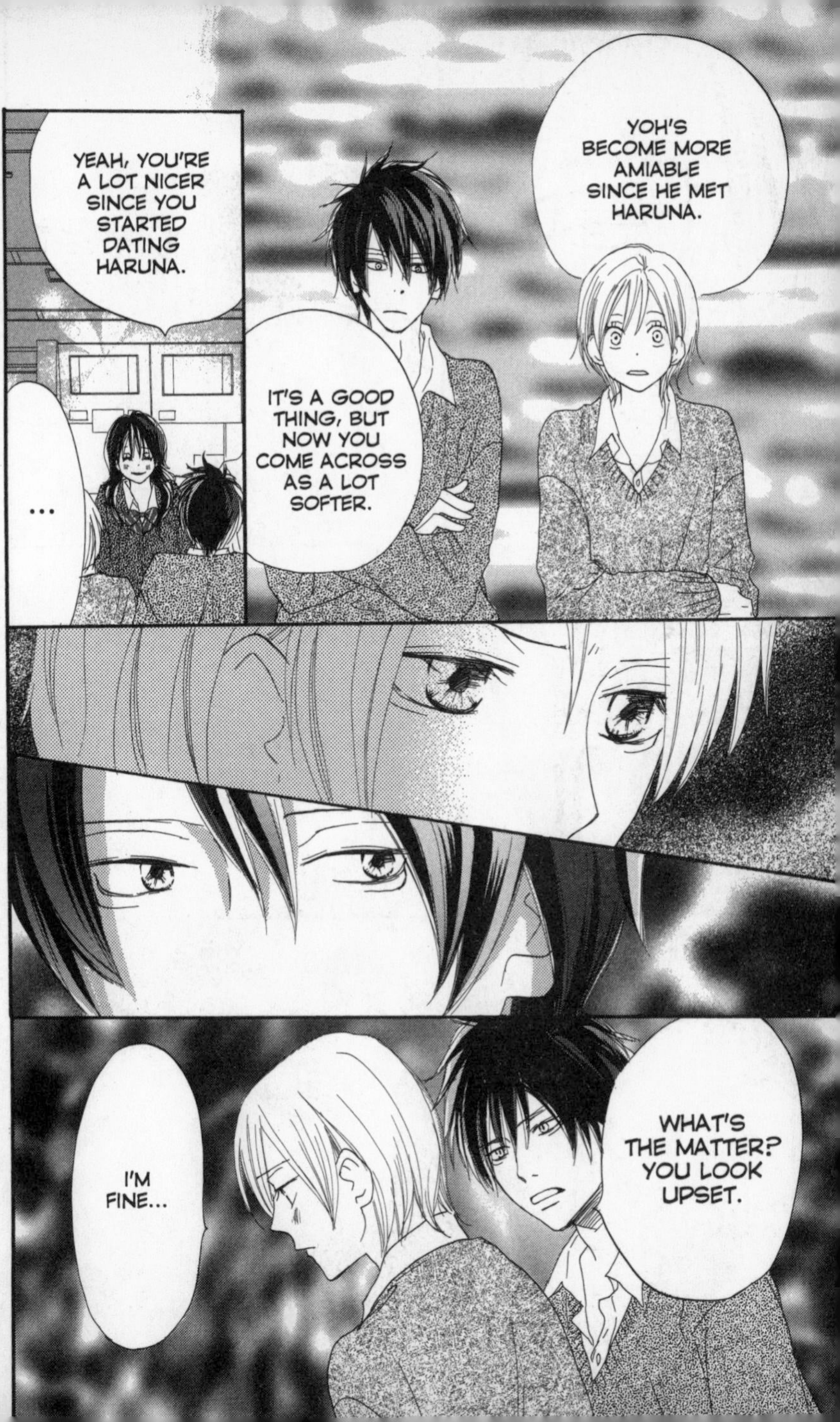
YOH'S BECOME MORE AMIABLE SINCE HE MET HARUNA.
IT'S A GOOD THING, BUT NOW YOU COME ACROSS AS A LOT SOFTER.
YEAH, YOU'RE A LOT NICER SINCE YOU STARTED DATING HARUNA.
...
WHAT'S THE MATTER? YOU LOOK UPSET.
I'M FINE...

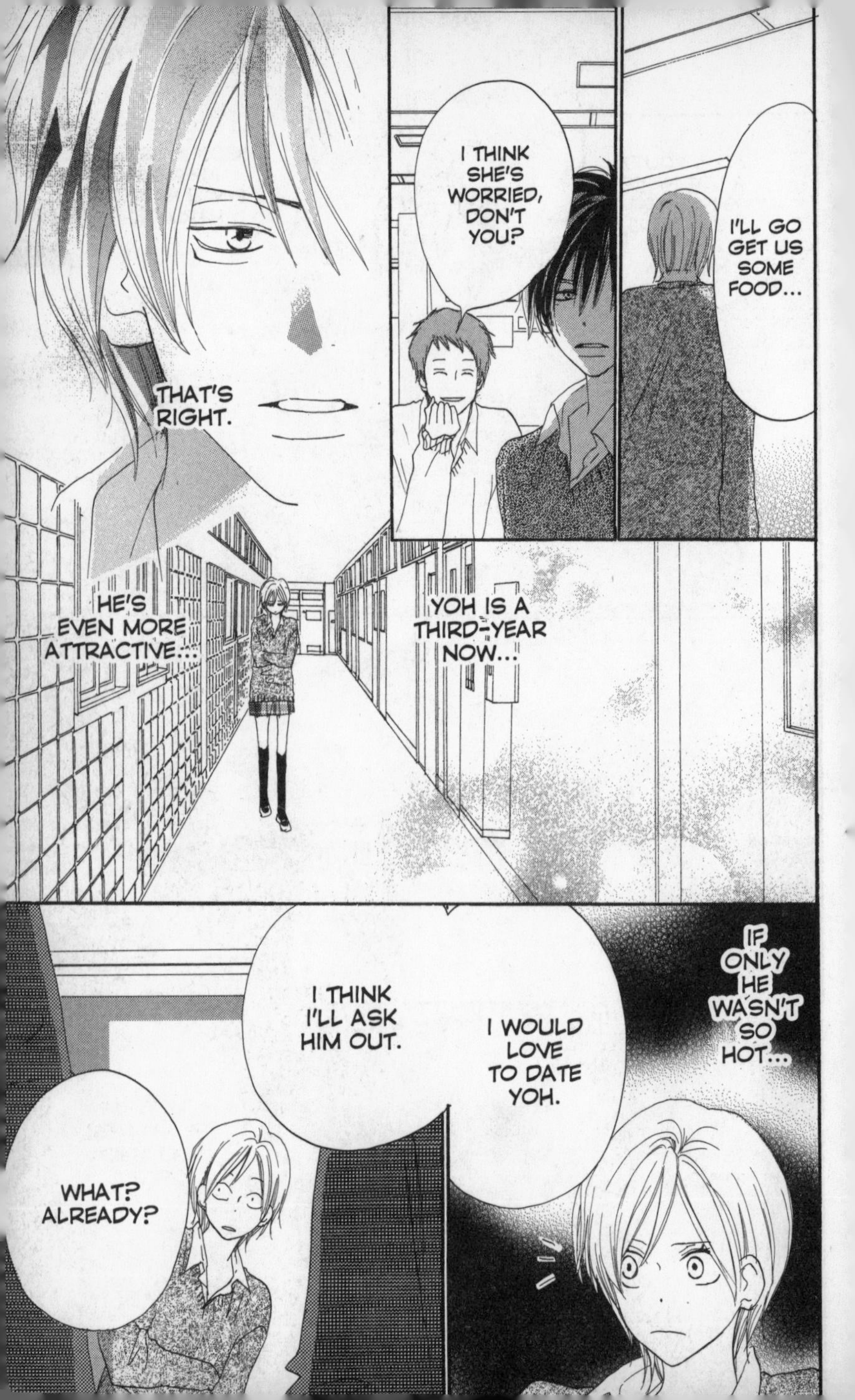
I'LL GO GET US SOME FOOD...
I THINK SHE'S WORRIED, DON'T YOU?
THAT'S RIGHT.
YOH IS A THIRD-YEAR NOW...
HE'S EVEN MORE ATTRACTIVE...
IF ONLY HE WASN'T SO HOT...
I WOULD LOVE TO DATE YOH.
I THINK I'LL ASK HIM OUT.
WHAT? ALREADY?

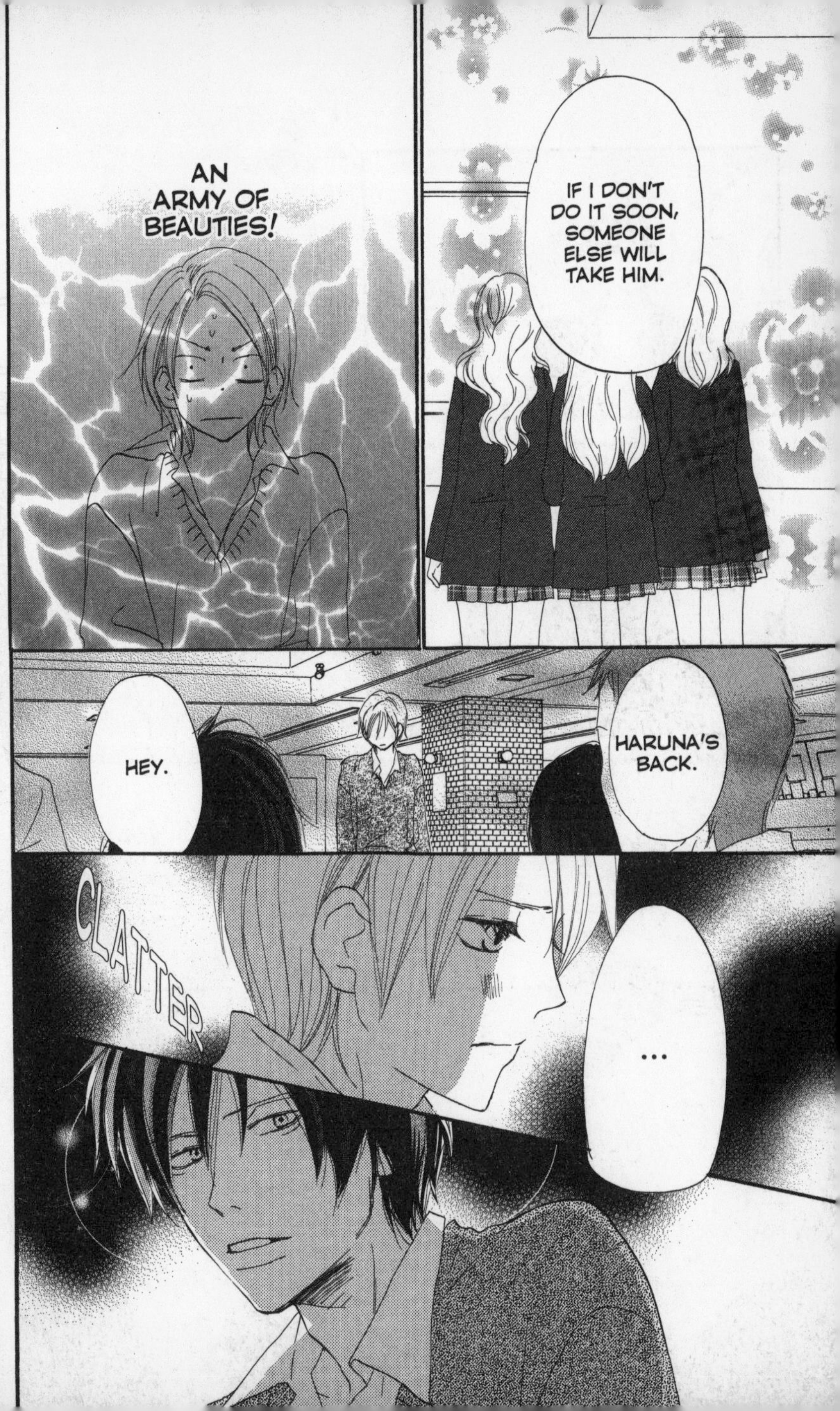
IF I DON'T DO IT SOON, SOMEONE ELSE WILL TAKE HIM.
AN ARMY OF BEAUTIES!
HARUNA'S BACK.
HEY.
...
CLATTER

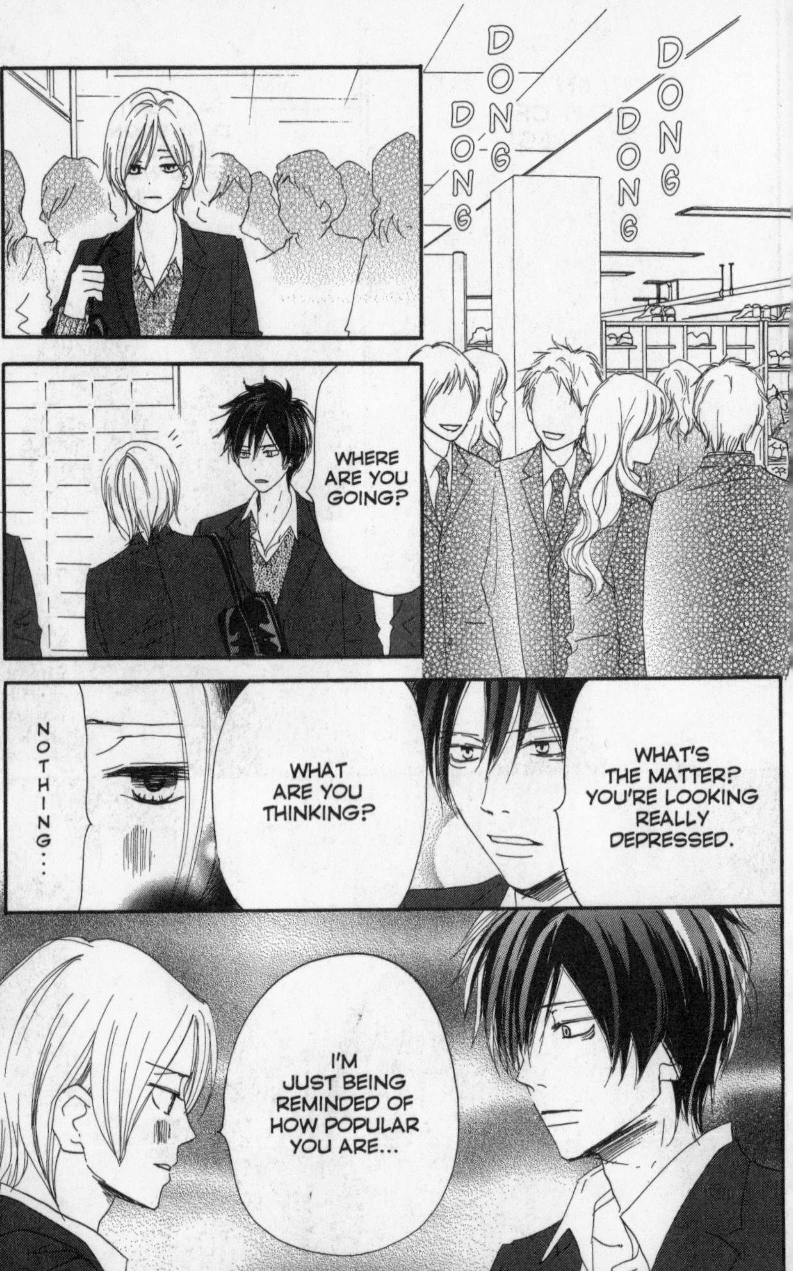
DONG
DONG
DONG
DONG
WHERE ARE YOU GOING?
WHAT'S THE MATTER? YOU'RE LOOKING REALLY DEPRESSED.
WHAT ARE YOU THINKING?
NOTHING...
I'M JUST BEING REMINDED OF HOW POPULAR YOU ARE...

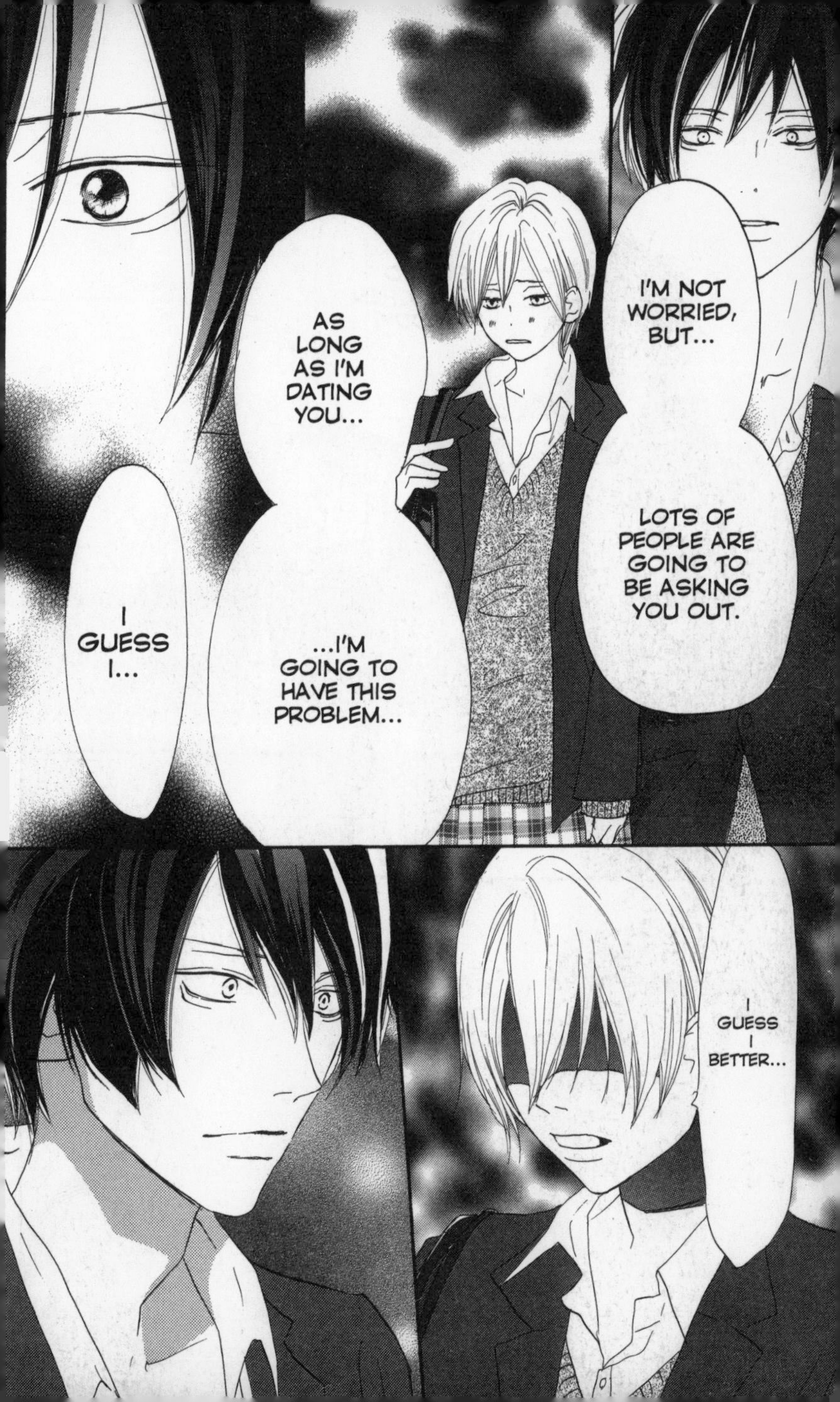

I'M NOT WORRIED, BUT...
LOTS OF PEOPLE ARE GOING TO BE ASKING YOU OUT.
AS LONG AS I'M DATING YOU...
...I'M GOING TO HAVE THIS PROBLEM...
I GUESS I...
I GUESS I BETTER...

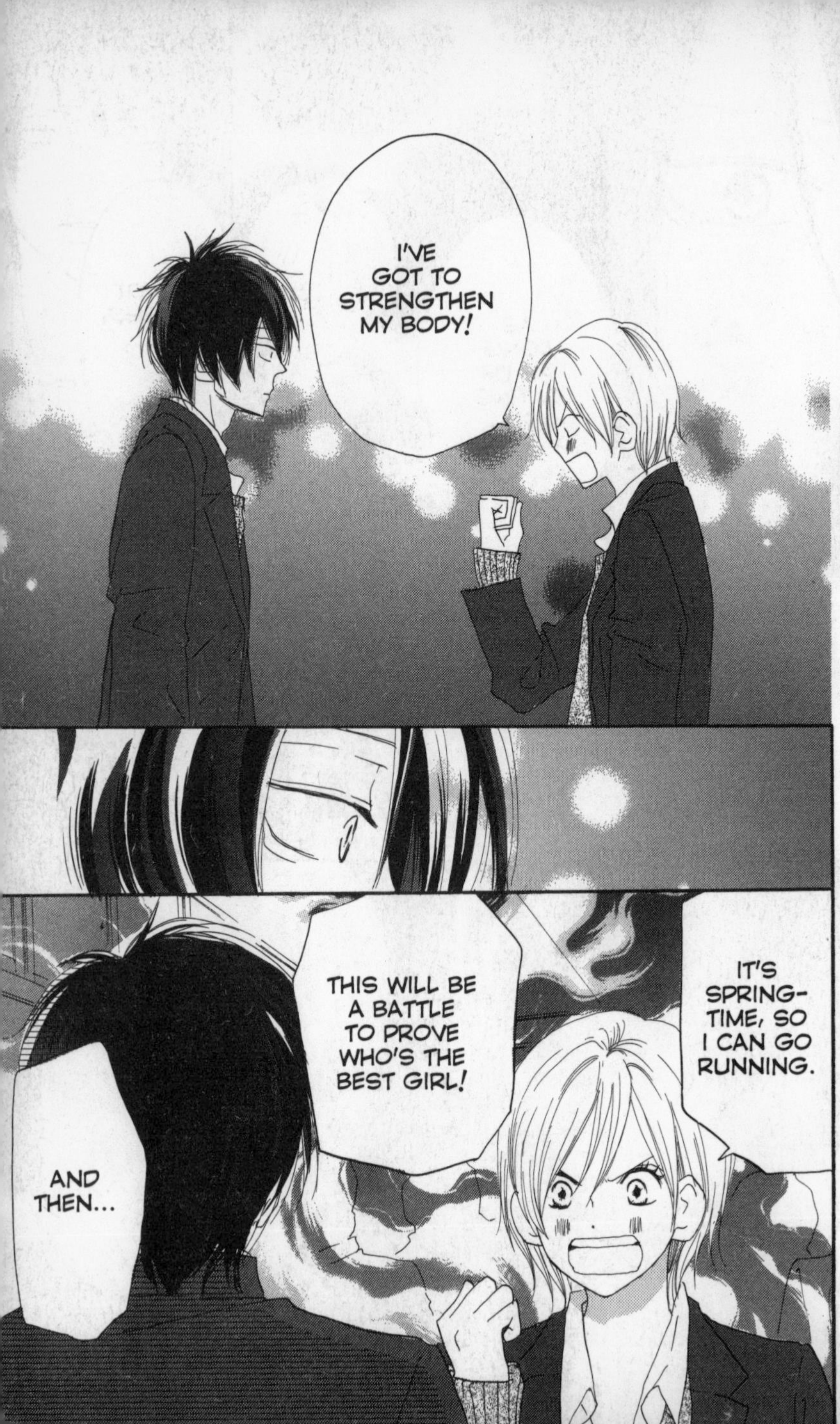
I'VE GOT TO STRENGTHEN MY BODY!
IT'S SPRING-TIME, SO I CAN GO RUNNING.
THIS WILL BE A BATTLE TO PROVE WHO'S THE BEST GIRL!
AND THEN...

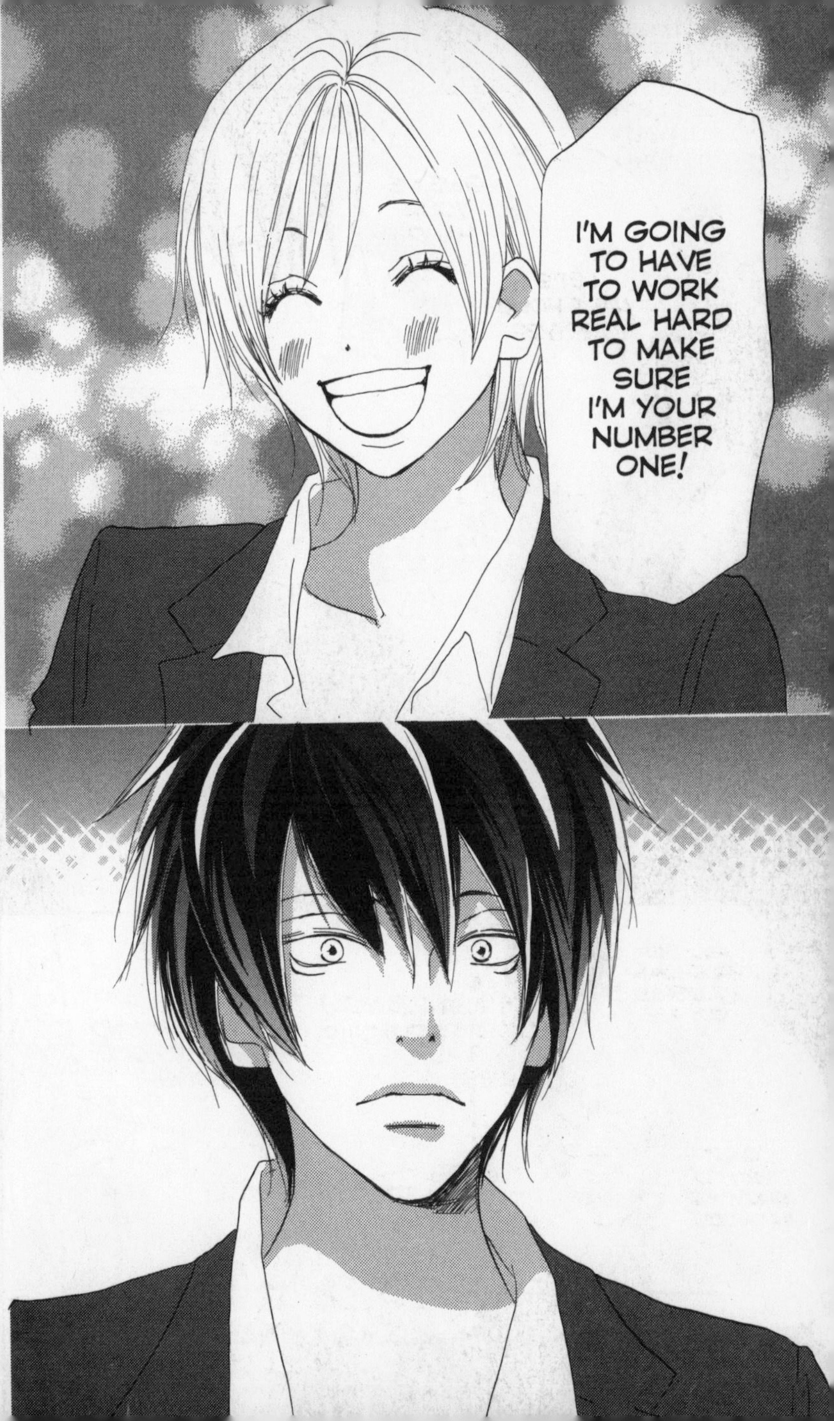
I'M GOING TO HAVE TO WORK REAL HARD TO MAKE SURE I'M YOUR NUMBER ONE!

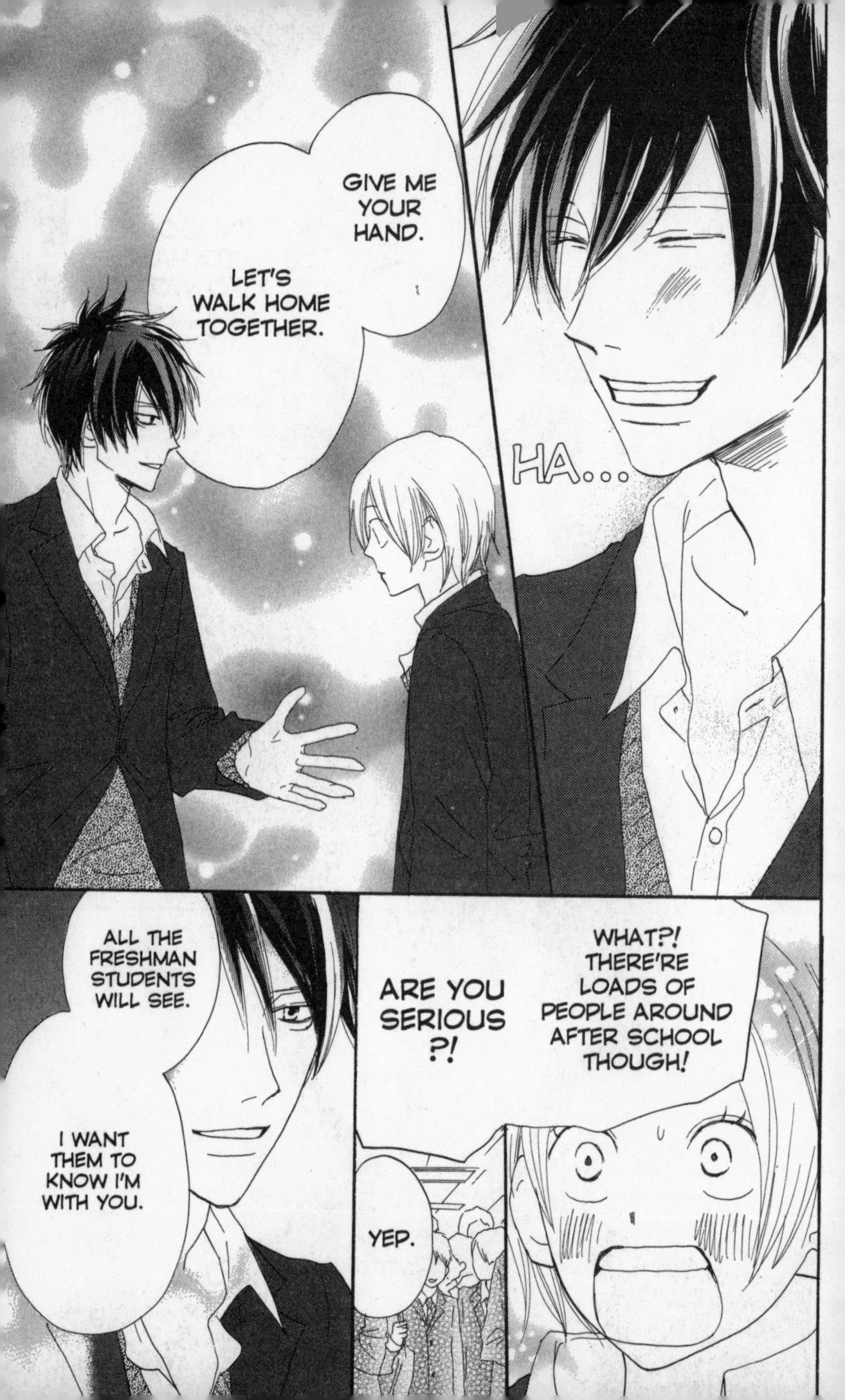
HA...
GIVE ME YOUR HAND.
LET'S WALK HOME TOGETHER.
WHAT?! THERE'RE LOADS OF PEOPLE AROUND AFTER SCHOOL THOUGH!
ARE YOU SERIOUS ?!
YEP.
ALL THE FRESHMAN STUDENTS WILL SEE.
I WANT THEM TO KNOW I'M WITH YOU.

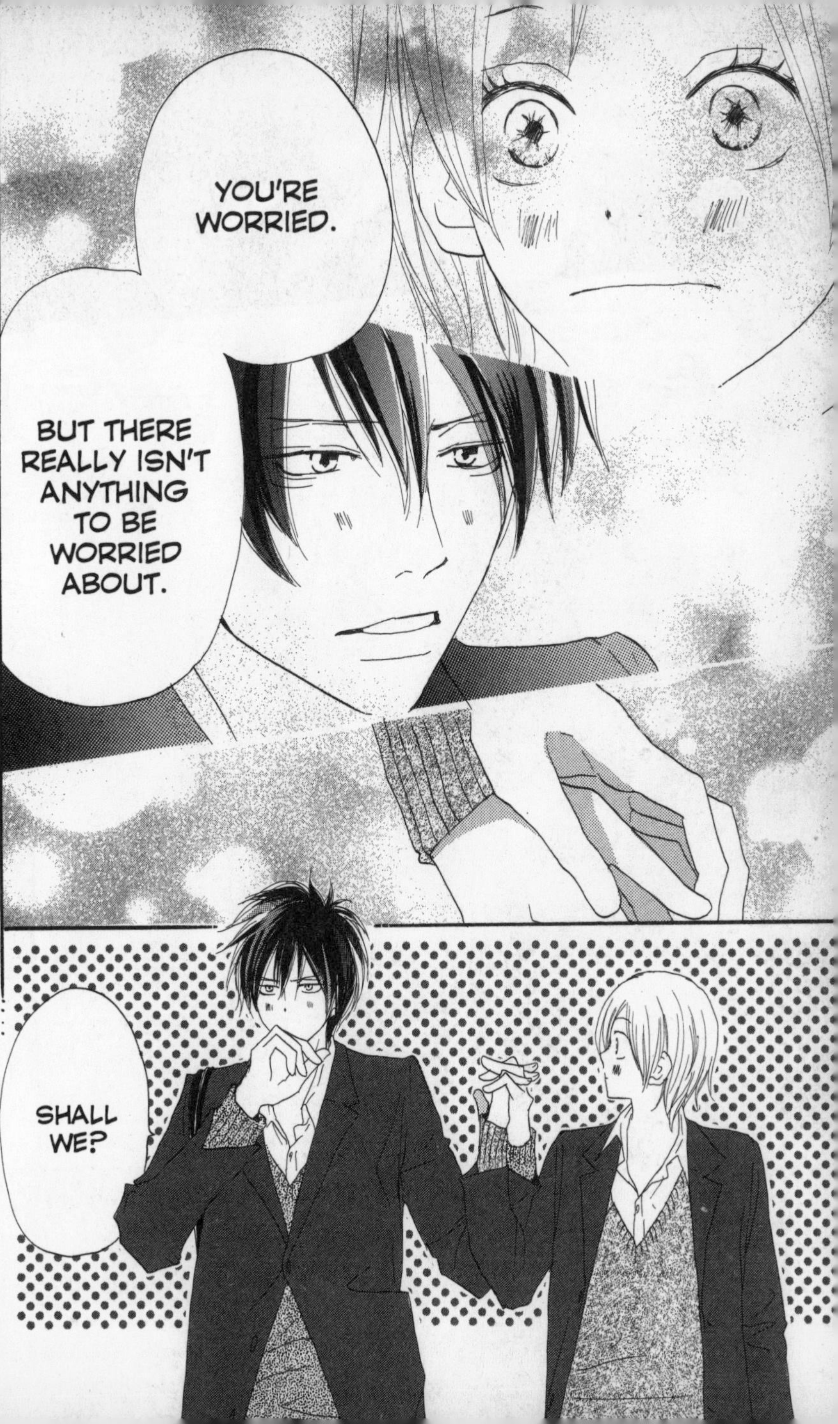
YOU'RE WORRIED.
BUT THERE REALLY ISN'T ANYTHING TO BE WORRIED ABOUT.
SHALL WE?

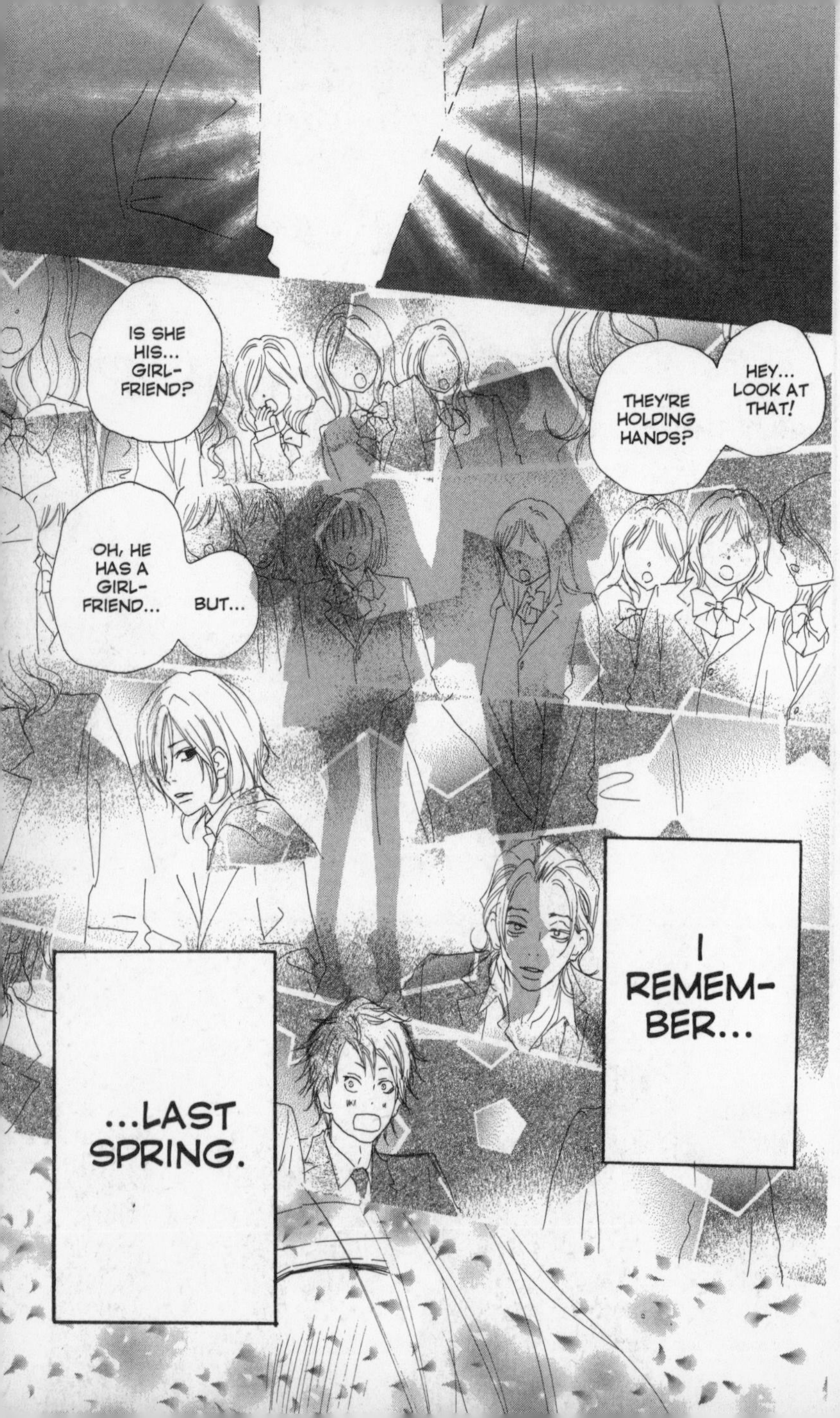
HEY... LOOK AT THAT!
THEY'RE HOLDING HANDS?
IS SHE HIS... GIRL-FRIEND?
OH, HE HAS A GIRL-FRIEND... BUT...
I REMEM-BER...
...LAST SPRING.

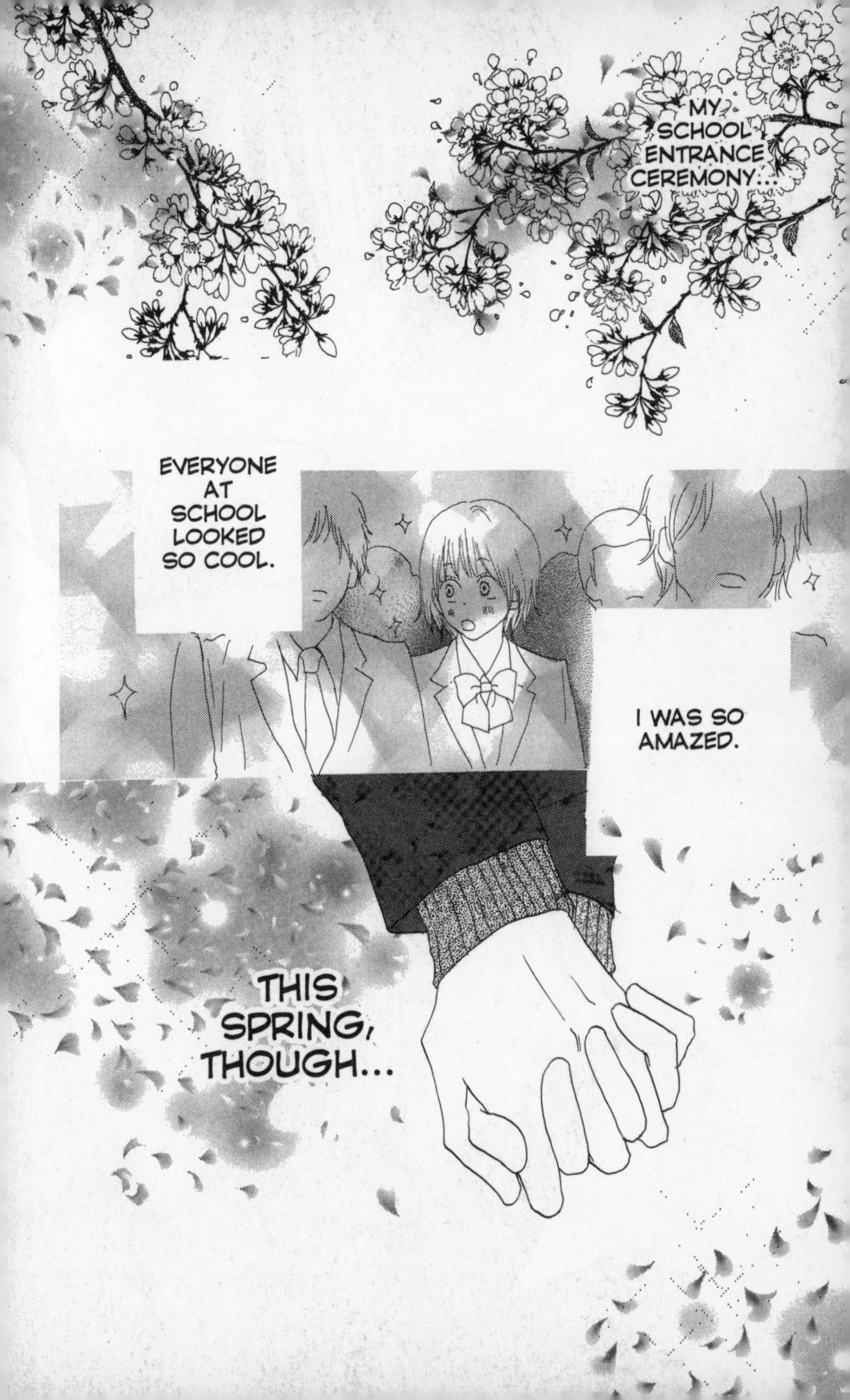
MY SCHOOL ENTRANCE CEREMONY...
EVERYONE AT SCHOOL LOOKED SO COOL.
I WAS SO AMAZED.
THIS SPRING, THOUGH...

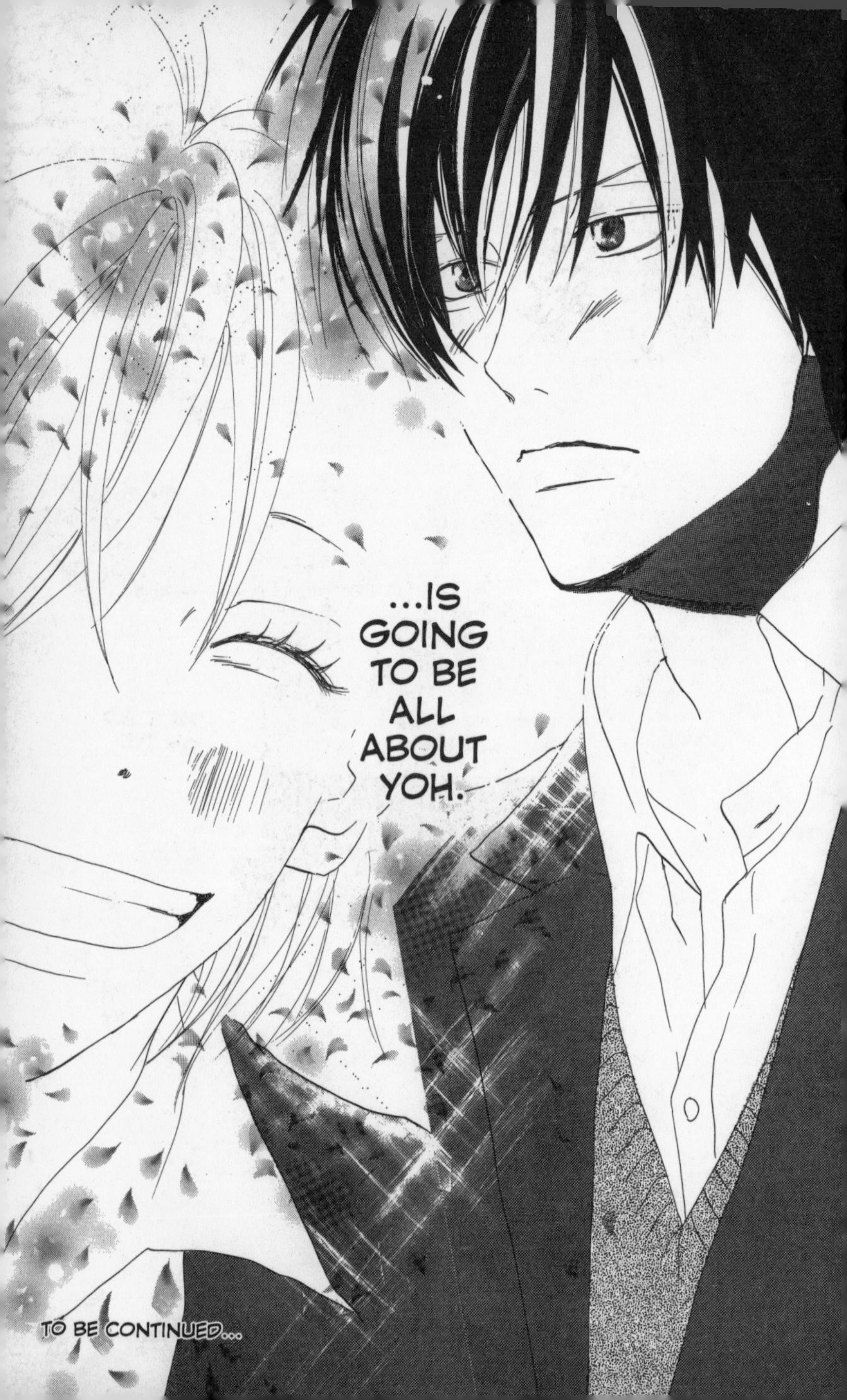
...IS GOING TO BE ALL ABOUT YOH.
TO BE CONTINUED...

I've been making lots of notes so that I don't forget to do important things. But then I lose them. I tried cleaning up my place to find them. Now I know where everything is! But it only stayed tidy for three days!

– Kazune Kawahara

Kazune Kawahara is from Hokkaido prefecture and was born on March 11th (a Pisces!). She made her manga debut at age 18 with *Kare no Ichiban Sukina Hito* (His Most Favorite Person). Her other works include *Sensei!*, serialized in *Bessatsu Margaret* magazine. Her hobby is interior redecorating.